Greed, Corruption, and the Modern State

Greed, Corruption, and the Modern State

Essays in Political Economy

Edited by

Susan Rose-Ackerman

Henry R. Luce Professor of Jurisprudence (Law and Political Science), Yale University, USA

Paul Lagunes

Assistant Professor, Columbia University, USA

 Edward Elgar
PUBLISHING

Cheltenham, UK • Northampton, MA, USA

Published by
Edward Elgar Publishing Limited
The Lypiatts
15 Lansdown Road
Cheltenham
Glos GL50 2JA
UK

Edward Elgar Publishing, Inc.
William Pratt House
9 Dewey Court
Northampton
Massachusetts 01060
USA

A catalogue record for this book
is available from the British Library

Library of Congress Control Number: 2015940716

This book is available electronically in the **Elgar**online
Law subject collection
DOI 10.4337/9781784714703

ISBN 978 1 78471 469 7 (cased)
ISBN 978 1 78471 470 3 (eBook)

Typeset by Servis Filmsetting Ltd, Stockport, Cheshire
Printed and bound in Great Britain by TJ International Ltd, Padstow

Contents

Contributors

CO-EDITORS

Susan Rose-Ackerman is the Henry R. Luce Professor of Jurisprudence (Law and Political Science) at Yale University, New Haven, CT, USA. She has written widely on corruption, administrative law, law and regulatory policy, the nonprofit sector, and federalism. Her recent books are *Due Process of Lawmaking: The United States, South Africa, Germany, and the European Union* (with Stefanie Egidy and James Fowkes, 2015); *Corruption and Government: Causes, Consequences and Reform* (1999), which has been translated into 17 languages (a second edition written with Bonnie Palifka is forthcoming), and *From Elections to Democracy: Building Accountable Government in Hungary and Poland* (2005) plus the edited volumes: *International Handbook on the Economics of Corruption*, vol. I (2006), vol. II (2011, with Tina Søreide); *Comparative Administrative Law* (2010, with Peter Lindseth); and *Anti-Corruption Policy: Can International Actors Play a Constructive Role?* (2013, with Paul Carrington). She holds a Ph.D. in Economics from Yale University and has held Guggenheim and Fulbright Fellowships. She was a fellow at the Wissenschaftskolleg zu Berlin in 2014–2015. Her current research focuses on comparative administrative law and public policymaking and the political economy of corruption.

Paul Lagunes is an Assistant Professor at Columbia University's School of International and Public Affairs. His research concentrates on the study of corruption, especially as it affects subnational governments in the Americas. Lagunes obtained his Ph.D. in Political Science from Yale University. Two basic questions motivate him. How does corruption actually work in practice? What tools are available for limiting corruption's harmful effects? By conducting randomized control trials that are supplemented by qualitative methodologies, Lagunes offers insights on corruption's regressive impact on society, the factors maintaining a corrupt status quo, and the conditions under which anti-corruption monitoring is most effective. He has published articles in *Latin American Research Review, Political Psychology, Harvard Journal of Hispanic Policy, Politics & Policy, Journal of Social Issues*, and other outlets.

CONTRIBUTORS

Peter Alldridge is Drapers' Professor of Law (since 2003) and was Head of the Department of Law (2008–2012) at Queen Mary University of London School of Law. He has published widely in the areas of criminal law, evidence, legal education, law and information technology, medical law, and law and disability. He is the author of *Relocating Criminal Law* (2000) and *Money Laundering Law* (2003) and editor (with C. Brants) of *Privacy, Autonomy and Criminal Law* (2003). He was specialist adviser to the joint Parliamentary Committees on the draft Corruption Bill (2003) and the draft Bribery Bill (2009) in the UK.

Dimitris Batzilis is a Ph.D. candidate at the Economics Department of the University of Chicago, specializing in the fields of political economics and public finance. His research focuses on the economics of corruption, and he has worked on topics such as bribery in international business transactions, and corruption in local government. Other recent work includes an empirical examination of various game theory models, using evidence from online rock-paper-scissors games. He graduated from Harvard University with a B.A. in economics in 2008, and before starting his graduate studies he worked as a Research Professional at the Becker Center on Chicago Price Theory.

Jennifer Bussell is the Gruber Assistant Professor in the Department of Political Science and the Goldman School of Public Policy at the University of California, Berkeley. Her research considers the effects of formal and informal institutions—such as corruption, coalition politics, and federalism—on policy outcomes. Her book *Corruption and Reform in India: Public Services in the Digital Age* (2012) examines the role of corrupt practices in shaping government adoption of information technology across sub-national regions. Her work has been published in *Comparative Political Studies, International Studies Quarterly* and *Economic and Political Weekly*.

Kevin E. Davis is Beller Family Professor at the NYU School of Law where he teaches courses on contracts, regulation of foreign corrupt practices, secured transactions, and law and development, as well as seminars on financing development and contract theory. His current research is focused on contract law, anti-corruption law, and the general relationship between law and economic development. Davis received his B.A. in economics from McGill University in 1990. After graduating with an LL.B. from the University of Toronto in 1993, he served as law clerk to Justice John Sopinka of the Supreme Court of Canada and later as an associate in the Toronto office of Torys, a Canadian law firm. After receiving an LL.M. from Columbia University in 1996, he was appointed an assistant professor at the University of Toronto and in 2001 was promoted to associate professor.

Alberto Diaz-Cayeros joined the Freeman Spogli Institute for International Studies (FSI) faculty at Stanford University in 2013 after serving for five years as the director of the Center for US-Mexico studies at the University of California, San Diego. He was an assistant professor of political science at Stanford from 2001–2008, before which he served as an assistant professor of political science at the University of California, Los Angeles. His work has primarily focused on federalism, poverty and economic reform in Latin America, and Mexico in particular. His book *Federalism, Fiscal Authority and Centralization in Latin America* was published by Cambridge University Press in 2007. His forthcoming book (with Federico Estevez and Beatriz Magaloni) is *Strategies of Vote Buying: Democracy, Clientelism and Poverty Relief in Mexico*.

Raymond Fisman is the Lambert Family Professor of Social Enterprise and co-director of the Social Enterprise Program at the Columbia Business School. His research—on topics ranging from corruption to the impact of corporate philanthropy—has been published in leading economics journals, including the *American Economic Review*, *Journal of Political Economy* and *Quarterly Journal of Economics*. His work has been covered widely in the popular press, from Maureen Dowd's column in the *New York Times* to al Jazeera to the *Shanghai Daily*. He also writes a monthly column for *Slate* magazine. He is the author of *Economic Gangsters: Corruption, Violence, and the Poverty of Nations* (2008, with Edward Miguel) and *The Org: The Underlying Logic of the Office* (2013, with Tim Sullivan).

Nancy Hite-Rubin joined the faculty of the Fletcher School at Tufts University after completing a Ph.D. in Political Science at Yale University. She teaches a course on global political economy and co-leads a Ph.D. field seminar on comparative politics and international relations. A scholar of comparative politics, Hite-Rubin is interested in the external factors that influence political engagement in developing countries, such as changing economic circumstances or changing institutions. Her work focuses on market informality, corruption and access to state institutions. She has studied a wide range of concrete issues from postal delivery theft in the Philippines to public opinion in Palestine. Hite-Rubin's research is unified by her use of experimental methods as well as her incorporation of mapping technologies.

Fu Hualing is a Law Professor at the University of Hong Kong. His research interests include constitutional law and human rights, with a special focus on criminal justice system and media law in China. His recent work includes *National Security and Fundamental Freedoms: Hong Kong's Article 23 Under Scrutiny* (2005, co-edited with Carole Petersen and Simon Young) and *The Struggle for Coherence: Constitutional Interpretation in Hong Kong* (2008, co-edited with Lison Harris and Simon Young). He teaches Corruption, Human Rights in China, and Legal Relations between Hong Kong and Mainland China.

Rongyao Huang received her Master's through the Quantitative Methods in the Social Sciences Program at Columbia University. She specializes in statistical modeling, text mining, and data visualization, and she is an advocate of open data in social science research. Her research interests include urban policy and social entrepreneurship. Born and raised in China, Rongyao obtained her B.A. at Zhejiang University with a major in Economics and a minor in English-Chinese Translation Studies.

Beatriz Magaloni is an Associate Professor in the Department of Political Science and a Senior Fellow at the Freeman Spogli Institute for International Studies (FSI) at Stanford University. Her first book, *Voting for Autocracy: Hegemonic Party Survival and its Demise in Mexico* (Cambridge University Press, 2006), won the Best Book Award from the Comparative Democratization Section of the American Political Science Association and the 2007 Leon Epstein Award for the Best Book. Her second book, *Strategies of Vote Buying: Democracy, Clientelism, and Poverty Relief in Mexico* (co-authored with Alberto Diaz Cayeros and Federico Estévez), studies the politics of poverty relief and clientelism as a prevalent form of electoral exchange. Her work has appeared in the *American Journal of Political Science*, *World Development*, *Comparative Political Studies*, *Annual Review of Political Science*, *Latin American Research Review*, *Journal of Theoretical Politics* and other journals.

Kalle Moene is Professor of Economics at the University of Oslo and the Director of ESOP—Centre for the Study of Equality, Social Organization and Performance. He is also affiliated with the International Peace Research Institute, Oslo. Among his main research interests are institutions, economic development and welfare states. He has published widely on these topics in journals such as *American Economic Review*, *Economic Journal* and *European Economic Review*.

Vidal Romero is a Professor of Political Science at the Instituto Tecnológico Autónomo de México (ITAM) after spending a year between 2012 and 2013 as a visiting associate professor at the Center on Democracy,

Development, and the Rule of Law (CDDRL). He holds a PhD in Political Science from Stanford University, and his research focuses on public opinion, the presidency, drug-related crime and violence. Romero's recent work has explored citizens' perceptions of crime and violence and how a climate of insecurity affects individuals' well-being, their support of crime fighting efforts and their assessment of authorities' performance. His work has also examined the determinants of violence and the type of relationship between the State, criminal organizations and citizens.

Sandra Sequeira is Assistant Professor in Development Economics at the London School of Economics and the lead academic for Mozambique at the International Growth Center. Her research applies both experimental and quasi-experimental methods to the study of infrastructure and growth, private sector development in developing countries and the economic costs of bureaucratic corruption. She holds a Ph.D. from Harvard University, an M.A. from the Fletcher School and a B.A. from Universidade Nova in Lisbon, Portugal.

Tina Søreide is Senior Researcher at Chr. Michelsen Institute (CMI) in Bergen, Norway, and a post-doctoral research fellow at the University of Bergen, Faculty of Law. She holds a Ph.D. in economics from the Norwegian School of Economics (NHH) and a Master's degree in economics from the University of Bergen. Her work concentrates on governance challenges with a particular focus on corruption and criminal law. She has conducted numerous assignments for policy purposes, including for the OECD, the EU, the World Bank and governments. She is the co-editor with Susan Rose-Ackerman of *International Handbook on the Economics of Corruption*, vol. II (2011).

Matthew C. Stephenson is Professor of Law at Harvard Law School where he teaches administrative law, legislation and regulation, anti-corruption law and political economy of public law. His research focuses on the application of positive political theory to public law, particularly in the areas of administrative procedure, anti-corruption, judicial institutions and separation of powers. Prior to joining the Harvard Law School faculty, Professor Stephenson clerked for Senior Judge Stephen Williams on the D.C. Circuit and for Justice Anthony Kennedy on the Supreme Court. He received his J.D. and Ph.D. (political science) from Harvard in 2003, and his B.A. from Harvard College in 1997.

Stéphane Straub is a Professor of Economics at the Toulouse School of Economics, and the head of its development lab, Arqade. His work revolves around issues of infrastructure, procurement and, more generally, institutional development in the context of developing countries, a subject on which he has published extensively. He has held academic positions in the US, the UK and France and is a consultant for international institutions such as the World Bank, the Inter-American Development Bank and the Asian Development Bank. He lived for ten years in Paraguay, where he worked as an entrepreneur, private consultant, government adviser and university professor, and he thus has a particular interest in that beautiful country in the heart of Latin America's Southern cone. He recalls this experience in the book *Frontières* (Amazon Digital Services, Inc.).

Federico Varese is a Professor of Criminology at the University of Oxford and a Senior Research Fellow at Nuffield College, Oxford. He is the author of two monographs—*The Russian Mafia* (OUP, 2001) and *Mafias on the Move* (PUP, 2011) and an edited collection titled *Organized Crime* (2010). His work has been translated into several languages. He writes mainly on organized crime, corruption, Soviet criminal history, and social network analysis. He has published papers in *Law and Society Review, Archives Européenes de Sociologie, Low Intensity Conflict and Law Enforcement, Political Studies, Cahiers du Monde Russe, Rationality & Society, European Sociological Review, British Journal of Criminology* and *Trends in Organized Crime*. In addition to publishing papers in academic journals and edited volumes, he contributes to *The Times Literary Supplement* and, in Italy, the daily *La Stampa*. His work has been featured in *The Economist, The BBC News & World Service, ABC, The Guardian, The New York Times, The Monkeycage Blog* and *Freakonomics* blog, among others.

Introduction

Susan Rose-Ackerman and Paul Lagunes

Across the world, private wealth seeks to influence public power. In the extreme, economic and political power unite to produce a kleptocratic system of exploitation. More often, the state and the private sector are distinct but overlapping; the wealthy pursue political influence through lobbying and policy arguments, but such behavior can easily shift toward illicit influence pedaling and outright bribery.

A few US examples can illustrate the overlap. In the state of Colorado the former owner of a major beer company helped fund Ronald Reagan's candidacy for the presidency. After the election, several of the brewery owner's close affiliates were appointed to the Environmental Protection Agency. Soon afterwards that Agency lifted restrictions that kept the brewery from dumping hazardous waste (Easterly 2002: 243). More recently, news reports claim that the private prison industry helped to draft the state of Arizona's harsh anti-immigrant law, a law that promised to boost demand for its immigrant detention centers (Sullivan 2010). Following a similar strategy, the Corrections Corporation of America offered to relieve the fiscal crises of 48 states by buying their prisons, but only provided the states agreed to keep the prisons 90 percent full for the next 20 years (Satz 2013: 1004). None of these cases involved illegal bribery; yet each illustrates the way private economic interests can influence policy decisions in violation of the public interest.

In light of these risks, state institutions must be willing and able to push back against excessive pressure from wealthy private actors and to safeguard the public interest. Bribery is only the most obvious manifestation of such pressure. As the US examples demonstrate, implicit quid pro quo deals are possible without the proverbial suitcases filled with cash. Nevertheless, it is useful to begin the analysis with straightforward cases of bribes paid to obtain public benefits. Some of the chapters in this volume concentrate on corruption in that sense, but others take a broader view and can help frame the debate on the links between private wealth and public power.

Fighting corruption, however, is not just about controlling the high-level malfeasance of so-called *big fish* as they interact with powerful private actors. Systemic corruption also occurs between low-paid and poorly monitored officials and ordinary citizens seeking to obtain benefits or avoid harms. Street-level bureaucrats—from local property tax assessors to police officers—are as much the public face of government as a president or cabinet member. Corruption at the base can undermine the legitimacy of the state in the eyes of ordinary citizens as surely as scandals at the apex of political power. Petty corruption can, moreover, complement and reinforce high-level corruption and undermine efforts to establish an honest and well-run state.

In the face of the corruption challenge, good governance has become a key item on the international agenda beginning in the 1970s and accelerating after the fall of the Berlin Wall in 1989. This global development had more than one point of origin, but it sometimes developed from grassroots movements seeking more responsible government. For instance, during the 1986 People Power Revolution in the Philippines nationwide demonstrations protested the high level of corruption in the military (Campbell 1984). The general outrage helped to drive President Ferdinand Marcos, who had embezzled some five to ten billion US dollars, from office (Clague 2003; Transparency International 2004). In Hong Kong in 1974, public protests over police corruption and the investigation that followed resulted in the creation of an Independent Commission Against Corruption or ICAC (Klitgaard 1988: 105–6; Manion 2004: 32–3; Cheng 2006: 34). The ICAC is widely recognized for transforming Hong Kong into a place where corrupt exchanges are the exception (Scott 2011).

A watershed moment for the United States occurred in the 1970s. Following the revelations of corruption underlying the Watergate scandal, Congress ordered an investigation into American business practices abroad. The ensuing report honed in on questionable payments to foreign officials by US corporations. More than 400 businesses admitted to making more than $300 million in illegal payments to obtain favorable actions from foreign government (Santangelo, Stein and Jacobs 2007). Given the troubling nature of these revelations, foreign officials in Japan, Italy and the Netherlands tendered their resignations. Congress responded by passing the Foreign Corrupt Practices Act (FCPA), which was signed by President Jimmy Carter on 20 December 1977 (Kaikati et al. 2000: 213).

The United States hoped that other countries would follow the US example and enact laws similar to the FCPA. However, many perceived the FCPA as an expression of American moralism (Brademas and Heimann 1998: 17–18). When the United States promoted a United Nations treaty to ban bribery worldwide, the effort ended in failure. At that time,

Germany, France, Denmark, Norway, Poland and the Netherlands even allowed businesses to deduct bribes as legitimate expenses (ibid.).

However, with the end of the Cold War came a new era. There was no longer a need to support corrupt regimes for national security reasons. In view of this fresh opportunity for anti-corruption reform, in 1993 Peter Eigen and nine associates founded Transparency International (TI), which is now considered the world's leading anti-corruption advocacy organization (*The Economist* 16 October 2014; Transparency International 2015).

Between 1995 and 1997, TI revived efforts to spur OECD members to reduce supply-side bribery worldwide (Eigen 2013). Then, in November of 1997, the OECD member nations signed the Convention on Combating Bribery of Foreign Public Officials in International Business Transactions (Baughn et al. 2010). The member countries agreed to make the bribery of foreign public officials illegal under domestic law. The OECD Convention came into force in 1999 and, as of this writing, has been ratified by 41 countries, some outside the OECD (Brademas and Heimann 1998: 17 and 19; Pacini, Swingen and Rogers 2002: 390; OECD 2015).

Although the level of enforcement of the Convention's provisions has varied across OECD member countries (Davids and Schubert 2011; Transparency International 2014), other notable efforts emerged to curb corruption worldwide. In the mid-1990s, after the then World Bank president James Wolfensohn referred to corruption as a cancer, the World Bank began to design anti-corruption strategies for particular countries and sectors and revised its procurement guidelines (Mallaby 2004: 176). Following the Bank's example, the International Monetary Fund, the United Nations Development Program, the World Trade Organization, and several regional development banks also redefined their position on corruption (Brademas and Heimann 1998: 20; FIDIC 2001). In 2002, more than a hundred Member States of the United Nations began negotiating an agreement on fighting corruption. Three years later, in 2005, the United Nations Convention against Corruption entered into force, signaling a global commitment, although the treaty itself has little enforcement capacity (UNODC 2015).

Unfortunately, in spite of the heightened global interest in the topic of corruption, we have no good evidence that its incidence has decreased. In fact, some argue that it has become more entrenched, at least in some sectors and countries. Part of the difficulty with assessing the extent and impact of corruption is definitional. What exactly is the subject of study? As Michael Johnston (2005) notes: 'Corruption is a deeply normative concern and can be a matter of considerable dispute.' At the most general level, corruption concerns the links between private wealth and public power. In some polities one cannot meaningfully distinguish between the obligations of public bodies and the private interests of elite political and economic actors. In such extreme cases of kleptocracy, the system is organized to benefit a select group. Technically, nothing has been 'corrupted' because there is no underlying commitment to honest and public-oriented government.

At the other extreme, in some polities corruption is the providence of a few 'bad apples' in positions of power, or it is the result of poorly designed public programs characterized by scarcity, too much discretion and too little oversight. In these cases, plausible policy responses are available— criminal law as a deterrent to the bad apples (see, for example: Becker and Stigler 1974) and program redesign to limit corrupt incentives in the day-to-day provision of public services, the regulation of economic and social life, and the collection of revenue (see, for example: Rose-Ackerman 1978; Klitgaard 1988). In this group of cases, the definition of corruption is narrow and clear. Public officials take advantage of their positions to demand or accept particularistic benefits, and citizens and firms pay to obtain what they should receive for free or make payoffs to induce officials to bend the rules in their favor.

The middle of the continuum is the most complicated. Consider several difficult cases. First, some countries appear to be success stories based on anti-corruption indices, but they are, in fact, controlled by a small elite. On the positive side, ordinary people pay few bribes and obtain adequate public services. However, real economic and political power is under the tight control of an oligarchy. Notable examples are Singapore (with a CPI 2014[1] score of 84), Qatar (CPI 2014: 69) and Rwanda (CPI 2013: 49).[2]

Second, cultural habits may entrench some kinds of personal payments and gifts. As a country develops, many of these interactions continue to be condoned as generous expressions of gratitude while others are viewed as corrupt efforts to undermine political and economic development. Drawing the line between one and the other may be difficult both legally and practically.

---

[1]   Transparency International publishes a yearly Corruption Perception Index (or CPI), which—not without controversy—ranks countries and territories based on their perceived level of public sector corruption. In 2014, the Index included 175 countries and territories. The average CPI score for these countries and territories was 43.19 and the highest-scoring country (in other words, Denmark) received a 92. For more information visit: http://www.transparency.org/cpi2014/ results (last accessed 6 May 2015).

[2]   On the authoritarian nature of the Singapore government see 'Rule of Law-Country Studies—Singapore' *Democracy Web*, http://www.democracyweb.org/ node/66 (last accessed 6 May 2015). The cases of Qatar and Rwanda are analyzed in Khatib (2014) and Bozzini (2014), respectively.

Third, in all modern societies the state signs contracts for large-scale procurement and infrastructure projects. These may be straightforward construction projects or complex public/private partnerships. All contain incentives for personal enrichment at the expense of the state and its citizens through inflated prices, projects with little social value, and padded costs. As a case in point, late in 2014 Mexico's presidency became mired by accusations of conflict of interest (*The Economist* 12 December 2014; Malkin 2014). Reporters discovered that the first lady and finance minister had each bought lavish homes from a firm that had received major government contracts, including one to build the country's largest infrastructure project in recent times (Montes 2014; Redacción AN 2014).

Fourth, the link between political and economic power may mean that campaign donors trade funds for favors from the state in the form of contracts or regulatory laxness. Revolving-door career paths may lead individuals to cycle between legislative staffs, lobbying firms or contractors and back to regulatory agencies and executive departments. In any of these cases, the machinery of government might function sufficiently well—and yet there are deep problems relating to the distribution of power and the role of gifts and donations in influencing the allocation of state contracts and other valuable public benefits. Ordinary citizens pay the price, but may not even realize the extent of their losses.

Given the diverse ways in which corruption can affect state functioning, it is no surprise that its control is difficult and contested. As a legal, economic, political and cultural or sociological phenomenon, its causes and consequences are varied and complex, even within a single polity. However, drawing on a number of different approaches, this volume suggests alternative routes to the control of corruption. One group of chapters explores the nature of corruption and the influence of private concentrations of wealth in democracies and autocracies, and critiques 'reforms' that are mere façades. Other contributions examine specific instances of corruption and self-dealing in infrastructure, tax collection, cross-border trade and military procurement. We then focus, in particular, on corruption involving international business—both licit and illicit. A particular focus is the domestic regulation of foreign bribery drawing on international experience with the US FCPA and the OECD Treaty.

The first section begins with an essay by Jennifer Bussell that sets the stage by arguing for a set of alternative typologies to assess corruption. If one is not sensitive to the different ways in which corruption arises, one may mistakenly conflate different types of phenomena. She demonstrates the diversity of approaches in the existing literature by reviewing a selection of influential works on corruption. Drawing on the literature on democracy, she suggests typologies that are relevant to the different empirical and theoretical contexts in which corruption arises.

Bussell suggests a conceptual framework that focuses on the kind of government resource—for example, mining licenses or welfare benefits— and that asks where corrupt incentives can arise. Different actors often control different kinds of state resources, so corruption can take many forms and involve a diverse set of actors. In the analysis of any particular sector, she urges researchers to distinguish between levels of government activity, for example, the legislative process, government contracting, public employment and public service provision. Studies would then seek direct and indirect corrupt incentives at various levels in the sector under study. Clarity about the location of these corrupt incentives would then facilitate comparisons across sectors and research efforts.

Bussell's focus is on corruption in an otherwise functioning state that has some degree of public legitimacy. She has not included outright kleptocracies in her framework although she reviews some studies from borderline cases such as Peru under President Fujimori. Nevertheless, the basic idea of clarifying the object of study and trying to place one's own research in a broader taxonomy of corrupt situations is an instructive way to begin our volume. It is not, however, the end of the inquiry. Getting the categories straight is only a first step toward realistic anti-corruption policies.

A next step would be to explore different strategies to see what works in fighting corruption. There are some known and tested anti-corruption tools that could be put in place by a regime that was serious about reducing bribery and self-dealing among its officials. They could be compared with suggested innovations to see which are most effective. Unfortunately, such a commitment to honest government cannot be presumed even when the needed reforms seem straightforward. As we have already pointed out, corrupt self-dealing can go to the very top of the government to include ministers, legislative leaders, top civil servants and even judges. Those at the top may exploit their offices for private gain and yet still want to appear to be reformers. Then, the stage is set for 'good governance facades' as outlined by Kalle Moene and Tina Søreide.

A country may be very dependent on foreign aid or on the good opinion of outside investors. Its leaders may thus put in place polices that are consistent with international 'best practice'. The result can be an impressive list of institutions that have little or no impact on state functioning. They are mere facades. Common examples are ombudsmen, anti-corruption commissions, freedom-of-information laws, or audit offices combined with a modern procurement law and civil service reforms. Of course, such reforms can play a positive role in some polities, but they can easily become empty shells if not supported by the political leadership. Worse, they can become tools for selective enforcement of anti-corruption programs that target regime opponents and suppress dissent. These problems are likely to arise if a narrow elite controls the state and can divert resources to itself—including foreign aid and investment. In such cases, although good governance reforms are touted as steps towards development, they may instead facilitate political rent extraction and corruption. Leaders may then actively seek to create such facades in order to attract more outside resources that they can steal. Hence, Moene and Søreide urge aid and lending agencies to be cautious about accepting procedural reforms at face value. Performance targets linked to service delivery and infrastructure construction must remain central to the evaluation of aid. Their model is consistent with the claim that democratization with comprehensive political competition is necessary to achieve real governance reforms. Their conclusion is linked to the types of corruption outlined above. Reforms of particular sectors that might be effective in an otherwise well-functioning state may simply be high-jacked by corrupt elites for their own purposes. Thus, Moene and Søreide provide a cautionary tale for anti-corruption reformers, especially those connected with aid and lending organizations.

The often-deep connections between political and bureaucratic corruption are the theme of the next three chapters in this section. The authors problematize the meaning of corruption by highlighting perfectly legal ways in which concentrated private wealth can influence the exercise of public power. The chapters by Ray Fisman and Matthew Stephenson are critical literature reviews of the links between political connections and democratic institutions. The section ends with Fu Hualing's overview of the recent crackdown on corruption in China showing how it both upholds the regime and undermines grassroots activism. It complements the more general analyses of Fisman and Stephenson with an in-depth look at a crackdown in an authoritarian regime.

Fisman considers the roll of political connections in both weak and established democracies—especially Indonesia, India and the United States. In one category are systems governed by stable autocracies (as in Indonesia's Suharto) or dynastic politics (for example, the Gandhi family in India), where direct personal ties are a steady and reliable way to maintain ties with those holding political power. In contrast, US national politics demonstrates a relatively high level of churn. Hence, those seeking political rents seek to adjust their political connections in response to changes in the political landscape. In the US, campaign finance and lobbying are complements: Financial support provides access, which may then be exploited through lobbying. Fisman summarizes one study showing that both personal connections and expertise matter to those seeking to lobby the US Senate. Much of the empirical work summarized in his chapter does not involve explicit bribe payments, but rather studies other quid pro quos that may be equally or more destructive of democratic accountability. Fisman's basic point is that personalistic systems are open to massive rent-seeking at the top, but more competitive, decentralized systems are also open to the influence of special interests even if the mechanisms are more open and less easy to characterize clearly.

Stephenson concentrates on the question of whether democratic elections help reduce corruption. As he notes, many reformers—both anticorruption advocates and democracy promoters—hope and believe the answer is yes. Stephenson concludes that, overall, the empirical evidence offers some support to the optimistic view that democracy may help reduce corruption, but it also demonstrates that the relationship between democracy and corruption control is not as straightforward, or as unambiguously positive, as is sometimes assumed. A better understanding of the particular corruption risks associated with democratic institutions may help reform-minded policymakers craft more appropriate and effective responses.

Stephenson lists a few ways that democracy might be an antidote for corruption. Voters can hold corrupt leaders accountable by withdrawing electoral support. Voters can also react to policies and outcomes that are affected by or associated with corruption even if the payoffs are not public. Finally, voters might judge leaders on how aggressively and effectively they combat corruption inside government. However, democracy also affects politicians' incentives to engage in political corruption intended to improve their odds of gaining or holding power, and it alters incumbent leaders' time horizons with an ambiguous impact on corruption. Hence, the average negative correlation between democracy and corruption across countries is not particularly illuminating; cross-country research ought to be evaluated cautiously.

Over and above the characterization of a polity as 'democratic', different types of democratic systems may be more or less prone to corruption. Is a parliamentary system less prone to corruption than a presidential system; does party organization matter; does federalism limit or enhance corrupt incentives? Once again the theories make contradictory predictions and the empirical results have not generated consistent findings. As a result of ambiguities in existing research, Stephenson concludes his extensive survey with a call for better theories of democracy itself and of its interaction with the self-seeking behavior of both politicians and private citizens and businesses.

Fisman and Stephenson concentrate on democracies, even if some of them are not fully institutionalized. A number of the studies that

Stephenson reviews, for example, include countries with democratic constitutional structures that have been so undermined by corrupt self-dealing that some would take them out of the democratic column entirely. Fisman also considers autocracies, such as Indonesia, but only to ask if the prosperity of some large firms was tied to their connections to the leader and his family. Fu Hualing, in contrast, digs deeply into China's recent anti-corruption campaign. Here, the president, rather than simply amassing a fortune for himself and his family, uses a crackdown on corruption as a tool of political control. Prosecutions are directed toward political enemies, and the state discourages and even prosecutes civil society activism and investigative reporting. The anti-corruption campaign is not a façade in the Moene and Søreide sense, but it is a political tool, not a route to overall state reform. As Fu writes:

> A defining characteristic of the on-going anti-corruption campaign is diminishing public participation in the control of corruption, in spite of immense public support . . . The new government suppresses civil society at the same time as it cracks down on corruption.

Fu also argues that the law is being used to support the Party's activities, but only up to a point. If laws start to impose checks on Party policy, they are ignored. According to Fu, the strongest critics of the recent campaign are the investigators in China's anti-corruption authority (ACA) who lack independence in initiating investigations. Fu predicts that the current campaign will turn out to be quite destructive and will not build any long-term anti-corruption capacity.

All together, the first section provides an overview of the complex links between government institutions, the political system, and the honesty of a country's leaders. We turn now to the sectoral studies in Part II, following the suggestions of Jennifer Bussell that one should isolate the loci of corrupt incentives in the structures of the state. The chapters discuss infrastructure spending, urban property tax collection, tariffs and military procurement. In practice, the cases show the difficulty of distinguishing between outright bribery and fraud, on the one hand, and waste, incompetence and political favoritism, on the other. Of course, these problems often go together. A poorly monitored infrastructure project is likely to hide both payoffs and waste. An over-budget procurement can include favoritism toward the politically powerful and bribes to those managing the purchase.

Stéphane Straub studies the cost overruns and corruption allegations for two massive dams in Paraguay, one of the poorest countries in South America. According to his analysis, corruption in Paraguay is the product of the systematic organization of political and economic relationships, not a set of simple isolated events. Moreover, it has become entrenched as a result of past public choices, such as large infrastructure investments. Hence, anti-corruption measures aimed at specific cases of wrongdoing have been ineffective, and corruption has had long-term adverse effects, even after a major political transition. Beyond the direct wrongdoing and abuse in the construction and operation of these dams, Straub illustrates how these projects shaped the rent-seeking nature of the economy over several decades, well into the twenty-first century.

The distortions introduced by these massive projects generated perverse incentives among the population and potential entrepreneurs. The free-flowing resources to the state budget from excess energy production meant that successive rulers did not need to foster the development of a healthy, private productive sector. Furthermore, the widespread diversion of resources left the country's physical infrastructure—in particular, the transport and energy networks—underdeveloped. The result was economic stagnation and low growth. According to Straub, the underlying problem was the construction of two large-scale hydroelectric infrastructure projects in a country characterized by little democratic oversight and weak institutions. One cannot tell ex post whether the top officials supported these projects *because* they were open to manipulation, or whether they were potentially good projects gone bad. Straub's study serves as a warning to those who support massive infrastructure investments as a route to economic growth in polities that lack strong independent and democratically accountable institutions.

Paul Lagunes and Rongyao Huang bring the analysis to the US with a study of corruption in the collection of property taxes in New York City. They explore what some have called the greatest case of municipal fraud in US history. In 2002, 18 current and former tax assessors were charged with taking bribes in exchange for undervaluing properties. For the duration of the scheme, over three decades, New York City may have lost up to one billion dollars in revenue. This revenue could have funded schools and other public services. Other localities—from Los Angeles (CA) to Cook County (IL)—have had a similar experience. The authors rely on multiple sources, including elite interviews, government reports, news articles and legal documents in the public domain, as a means to shed light on the mechanics of corruption in taxation. They conclude with a brief description of a study conducted in partnership with New York City's Department of Investigation.

Sandra Sequeira also focuses on revenue collection—in the ports of Maputo, Mozambique and Durban, South Africa. Corruption can increase firm-level trade costs if it acts as an additional tax to clear goods across borders, or it can decrease trade costs if it allows firms to circumvent cumbersome bureaucratic procedures or reduce clearing times. Her results are striking. For instance, products that experienced a tariff reduction recorded a 60 percent decline in the probability of paying a bribe at the border. Thus, there are clear policy complementarities between anti-corruption and trade facilitation policies. In her chapter Sequeira also deconstructs the incentives at work in these ports. She shows that corrupt port officials faced almost no risk of punishment, and she exposes the significant role that bribes play in complementing official salaries. Automation, bureaucratic discretion and officials' time horizons on the job are additional factors that influence the level and type of corruption observed. Therefore, as in many other corrupt settings, policy interventions can succeed only if they mitigate incentives for private agents to pay bribes and create fewer opportunities for public officials to extract payoffs.

Exploring a different, if equally troubling, facet of international trade, Nancy Hite-Rubin studies the relationship between FDI and military procurement, where corruption is reputedly common. Because of the large size and specialized nature of the contracts, bribes can be hidden in the selling price and passed on to the purchaser. Hite-Rubin, however, is not able to study corruption directly because of the secrecy that surrounds these deals and the lack of clear market price comparisons. Instead, she looks at the common practice of using 'offsets' to sweeten a contract. These are agreements by the seller to purchase certain products from the buyer's firms as part of the deal. These might be related to the equipment being purchased, for example, parts or service contracts. However, they also take the form of completely unrelated products abundant in the country or useful for its development, for example, an agricultural product, such as palm oil, or manufactured products, such as textiles or consumer electronics. Offsets may be inefficient and may be a way to curry favor, but they are not themselves illegal. However, they can be a way to hide illicit benefits. For example, a firm might agree to buy a product from a firm owned by the president's brother and to pay a price far above the market price. Such deals can be a way to siphon payoffs to powerful individuals in the buyer's country.

Completing this section, Alberto Diaz-Cayeros, Beatriz Magaloni and Vidal Romero describe a pathological situation in which drug trafficking organizations (DTOs) victimize citizens and firms with police complicity. Through the use of a list experiment the authors shed light on DTOs activities in Mexico. Their analysis reveals that criminal organizations and the police extort respondents at an equal and disturbingly high rate. Thus, it is no surprise that the public views municipal and state police as corrupt and untrustworthy—and that a climate of fear prevails. This chapter could not be timelier. As of this writing, 43 teacher-trainees from the state of Guerrero are missing, and there is evidence that a criminal gang and local authorities collaborated in their kidnapping and possible murder. The work by Diaz-Cayeros and coauthors helps us understand the dynamics that led to such an atrocity and serves as a warning of how deeply rooted the problem of police corruption is in Mexico.

Finally, Part III confronts the debate over corruption in international market transactions, both legal and illegal. The final four chapters discuss anti-corruption agreements, the enforcement of anti-bribery regulations, money laundering, and shadow banking. The issues are complex. They involve a diverse set of actors—from firms that practice bribery abroad to large criminal gangs—whose interests span multiple national jurisdictions. Reliable information about these actors' pursuits is difficult to come by; yet their activities have implications for trade, investment, capital flows, and even relations among nation-states.

Relying on cross-country analysis, Dimitris Batzilis studies the propensity of firms to bribe foreign public officials when they do business abroad. He uses survey data from Transparency International's Bribe Payers Index, which reflects business executives' expectations regarding the corporate conduct of foreign companies in their country. After controlling for economic, cultural and historical variables, Batzilis finds evidence that firms based in countries with high levels of corruption are more likely to bribe when conducting business abroad. As a concrete example, Russian firms are more prone than American ones to pay bribes when engaging in foreign trade or investment. He also shows that high rates of corruption in host countries increase the likelihood that foreign firms, regardless of where they are from, will practice bribery in their business dealings.

Batzilis also asks whether anti-corruption agreements, such as the OECD Anti-Corruption Convention, have an effect in restraining the behavior of signatory countries. Thus his study contributes to the general debate on whether international institutions constrain political, economic and social interactions that cross national boundaries. These institutions are rules that govern regional or global decision-making, but in spite of the high profile associated with some international institutions, a number of commentators argue that they are unimportant in and of themselves. Voices in this camp see the OECD Convention or the UN Convention against Corruption as inconsequential for all practical purposes. Batzilis avoids extreme conclusions, but contrary to what others have argued (for example, Baughn et al. 2010), he finds that laws against foreign bribery do not appear to have had a constraining effect. To be clear, companies from countries that have signed the OECD Convention on Combating Bribery of Foreign Public Officials in International Business Transactions do exhibit better corporate conduct overall, but his results indicate that this is not due to the Convention itself. As evidence, he shows that there is no difference in the probability that firms from signatory countries engage in corruption that is prohibited (for example, direct bribery of public officials) as opposed to corruption that is tolerated by the Convention (for example, facilitating payments). In the end, the author concludes that any anti-corruption effect associated with the international agreement must be explained by some unobserved variable, such as shared cultural norms.

However, even if there is little measurable difference between firms' propensity to engage in bribery prohibited by the Convention and to make facilitating payments, overall firm behavior could have been affected by the Convention. First of all, as a practical matter, firms may not be sure how their own law enforcement bodies will define the exempt category. They may err on the side of honesty. Second, although international institutions may be endogenous to culture or some other variable, they maintain the capacity to focus attention on otherwise hidden behavior and to limit impunity. Surely, major enforcement actions, such as those that led to massive fines levied against BAE and Siemens, helped to raise public consciousness worldwide.[3] These suppositions, at least, suggest that all would not stay the same if the Convention were to disappear. This brings us to the subject of enforcement—a defining factor in explaining whether an international convention is relevant as a disciplinary tool.

Unlike Batzilis, Kevin Davis does not question the impact of anti-corruption laws. Instead, his chapter is an invitation to reflect on alternative approaches to the enforcement of anti-corruption regulations. Enforcement, the author explains, can have several motivations, including self-interest, cosmopolitanism and altruism. It may also seek to achieve distinct objectives, such as retribution, prevention and compensation. Different combinations of motivations and objectives result in varying decisions about which cases to pursue and what sanctions to impose. Davis observes that the way the United States currently enforces FCPA is dominated by prosecutors (as opposed to private litigants and judges), the expectation of imposing liability on organizations, assertions of broad extraterritorial jurisdiction, and high-powered sanctions. The FCPA, thus, attracts criticism both because corporate liability is pursued even when direct responsibility lies with low-level employees, and also because of the opacity with which cases are usually resolved, the severity of the sanctions imposed on violating firms, and so on. Given that others are

---

[3] For more information about the charges levied against BAE Systems and Siemens AG see DOJ (2010) and O'Reilly and Matussek (2008), respectively.

treating the United States' anti-corruption enforcement strategy as a model, Davis argues for better understanding of its implications..

Peter Alldridge takes a recent trend in tax enforcement as his starting point. Tax offices have increasingly joined forces with authorities fighting to curb the financial reach of criminals and terrorists. Thus, tax avoidance, tax evasion, offshore centers and money laundering are progressively treated as complementary facets of the same problem. Yet, according to Alldridge, these are all distinct phenomena that should be dealt with separately—tax evasion, but not tax avoidance, should be dealt with through criminal law. He also argues that offshore financial centers, which provide secrecy and low tax rates, are not inherently objectionable. In his conclusion Alldridge joins other commentators in arguing that capital flight is a problem, but he insists that, although heightened transparency in the financial system would be welcome, respect for the rule of law demands more precision when crafting standards and recommending policy reform.

As a worthy conclusion to the volume, Federico Varese studies the overlap between underground banking and corruption. Underground banking—or Informal Value Transfer Systems (IVTS)—involves a web of anonymous agents who must trust each other in order to move money through unregulated channels and between distant locations. It is the means by which undocumented immigrants and people engaged in criminal activities channel funds—often illegally—across borders. Varese describes two cases of IVTS—in Italy and in China. In the latter, we follow the money trail from an underground mall in Zhuhai to VIP rooms in one of Macau's casinos. Those who use IVTS find it attractive, in part, because it appears to work beyond the reach of rent-seeking government officials. Thus, although the existing literature shows that other informal activities (from street vending to illegal gambling) rely on bribes in order to avoid the state's intervention, IVTS generally avoids corruption's grabbing hand. It does not need to use payoffs because it avoids contact with public officials, except for petty payoffs to low-level bank staff for changing small denomination bills to large ones. Nevertheless, it may, of course, be an attractive means for transferring corrupt benefits across national borders.

In conclusion, we wish to thank all of those who helped make possible both the May 2014 conference at Yale University and this subsequent publication. We are grateful to the Stephen and Ruth Hendel Fund for Africa, the John K. Castle Fund for Ethics and International Affairs, and Columbia University's School of International and Public Affairs for generous funding. We also thank the MacMillan Center, Joy Sherman, and Cathy Orcutt for logistical support. Lynn Hancock, a doctoral student in Political Science, was especially helpful in organizing the conference, including the website. The authors benefited immensely from the comments of the discussants: Natalia Bueno, Tumi Makgetla, Lucy Martin, Nicholas McLean, Gautam Nair, and Qiuqing Tai. We are also extremely pleased to have had the participation of leading figures in the anti-corruption movement including Nicola Bonucci, Director for Legal Affairs of the OECD; Fritz Heimann, a founder and long-time supporter of Transparency International; Alan P. Larson, board chair of TI-USA; and Mark Pieth, a Swiss lawyer who was a principal architect of the OECD Convention. Also present were Rose Gill Hearn, a Principal at Bloomberg Associates; Jamie Horsley, Executive Director of the Yale China Law Center; Macartan Humphreys, Political Science Professor at Columbia University; Etty Indriati, an Indonesian anti-corruption activist; Jennifer Rodgers, Executive Director of the Center for the Advancement of Public Integrity; and leading officials from Peru's anti-corruption agency. The conference was ably launched with an inspiring keynote address by Huguette Labelle, then the president of Transparency International. A few of the participants—James R. Hines, Melanie Manion and Michael Ross—decided not to include their papers in our volume, but we, nevertheless, want to thank them for their contributions and participation in the discussion.

REFERENCES

Baughn, Christopher, et al. 2010. 'Bribery in International Business Transactions', *Journal of Business Ethics* 95: 15–32.

Becker, Gary S., and George J. Stigler. 1974. 'Law Enforcement, Malfeasance, and Compensation of Enforcers', *The Journal of Legal Studies* 3(1): 1–18.

Bozzini, Alessandro. 2014. 'The Unlikely Achiever: Rwanda', in Alina Mungiu-Pippidi (ed.). *The Anticorruption Frontline*, vol. 2. Toronto, Canada: Barbara Budrich Publishers.

Brademas, John, and Fritz Heimann. 1998. 'Tackling International Corruption: No Longer Taboo', *Foreign Affairs* 77(5): 17–22.

Campbell, Colin. 1984. 'Looking Beyond Marcos', *New York Times* 8 January.

Cheng, Jinhua. 2006. 'Police Corruption Control in Hong Kong and New York City: A Dilemma of Checks and Balances in Combating Corruption', *Term Paper*. New Haven, CT: Yale University. 34 of *Law School*.

Clague, Christopher. 2003. 'The International Campaign against Corruption: An Institutionalist Perspective', *Collective Choice: Essays in Honor of Mancur Olson*. Jac C. Heckelman and Dennis Coates (eds). Germany: Springer.

Davids, Cindy, and Grant Schubert. 2011. 'The Global Architecture of Foreign Bribery Control: Applying the Oecd Bribery Convention', *Handbook of Global Research and Practice in Corruption*. Adam Graycar and Russell G. Smith (eds). Cheltenham, UK and Northampton, MA, USA: Edward Elgar, 319–39.

DOJ. 2015. 'Bae Systems Plc Pleads Guilty and Ordered to Pay $400 Million Criminal Fine'. 2010. *Justice News*. Department of Justice: Office of Public Affairs. 9 January. Online, http://www.justice.gov/opa/pr/bae-systems-plc-pleads-guilty-and-ordered-pay-400-million-criminal-fine (last accessed 6 May 2015).

Easterly, William. 2002. *The Elusive Quest for Growth*. Cambridge, MA: MIT Press.

Eigen, Peter. 2013. 'International Corruption: Organized Civil Society for Better Global Governance', *Social Research* 80(4): 1287–1308.

FIDIC. 2001. *Guidelines for Business Integrity Management in the Consulting Industry*. International Federation of Consulting Engineers (FIDIC).

Johnston, Michael. 2005. *Syndromes of Corruption: Wealth, Power, and Democracy*. Cambridge, UK and New York, USA: Cambridge University Press.

Kaikati, Jack G., et al. 2000. 'The Price of International Business Morality: Twenty Years under the Foreign Corrupt Practices Act', *International Business Ethics* 26(3): 213–22.

Khatib, Lina (ed.). 2014. *Doubts and Lessons Learned from Qatar's Progress Towards Good Governance*, vol. 2. Toronto, Canada: Barbara Budrich Publishers.

Klitgaard, Robert. 1988. *Controlling Corruption*. London, England: University of California Press.

Malkin, Elisabeth. 2014. 'Mexican Leader Offers Asset Disclosure', *The New York Times* 19 November, sec. Americas.

Mallaby, Sebastian. 2004. *The World's Banker: A Story of Failed States, Financial Crises, and the Wealth and Poverty of Nations*. Sydney, Australia: University of New South Wales Press Ltd.

Manion, Melanie. 2004. *Corruption by Design: Building Clean Government in Mainland China and Hong Kong*. Cambridge, MA: Harvard University Press.

Montes, Juan. 2014. 'Mexico Finance Minister Bought House from Government Contractor', *The Wall Street Journal* 11 December, sec. World News.

O'Reilly, Cary, and Karin Matussek. 2008. 'Siemens to Pay $1.6 Billion to Settle Briber Cases', *Bloomberg* 16 December, sec. News.

OECD. 2014. 'OECD Convention on Combating Bribery of Foreign Public Officials in International Business Transactions: Ratification Status as of 21 May 2014', available 6 May 2015 at http://www.oecd.org/daf/anti-bribery/WGBRatificationStatus.pdf.

Pacini, Carl, Judyth A. Swingen, and Hudson Rogers. 2002. 'The Role of the OECD and EU Conventions in Combating Bribery of Foreign Public Officials', *Journal of Business Ethics* 37: 385–405.

Redacción AN. 2014. 'La Casa Blanca de Enrique Peña Nieto (Investigación Especial)', *Aristegui Noticias* 9 November.

Rose-Ackerman, Susan. *Corruption: A Study in Political Economy*. NY: Academic Press, 1978.

Santangelo, Betty, Gary Stein, and Margaret Jacobs. 2007. 'The Foreign Corrupt Practices Act: Recent Cases and Enforcement Trends', *Journal of Investigative Compliance* 8(3): 31–55.

Satz, Debra. 2013. 'Markets, Privatization, and Corruption', *Social Research* 80(4): 993–1008.

Scott, Ian. 2011. 'The Hong Kong Icac's Approach to Corruption Control', in Adam Graycar and Russell G. Smith (eds), *Handbook of Global Research and*

Practice in Corruption. Cheltenham, UK and Northampton, MA, USA: Edward Elgar, 401–15.

Sullivan, Laura. 2010. 'Prison Economics Help Drive Ariz. Immigration Law', *NPR* 28 October.

The Economist. 'A More Combative Approach?' 16 October 2014.

The Economist. 'A Murky Mortgage', 12 December 2014.

Transparency International. 'World's Ten Most Corrupt Leaders'. 2004, available 6 May 2015 at http://www.infoplease.com/ipa/A0921295.html.

Transparency International. 'Exporting Corruption: Progress Report 2014: Assessing Enforcement of the OECD Convention on Combating Foreign Bribery', available 6 May 2015 at http://www.transparency.org/whatwedo/publication/exporting_corruption_progress_report_2014_assessing_enforcement_of_the_oecd.

Transparency International. 'Who We Are: Our History', available 6 May 2015 at http://www.transparency.org/whoweare/history.

UNODC. United Nations Convention against Corruption, available 6 May 2015 at http://www.unodc.org/unodc/en/treaties/CAC/index.html#UNCACfulltext.

PART I

Political connections, corruption and policy

1. Typologies of corruption: a pragmatic approach

Jennifer Bussell[1]

Studies of corruption provide much evidence on both the causes and consequences of corruption, and yet progress remains strikingly limited on the conditions under which these causes may be relevant and these consequences occur. If an anti-corruption reform successfully attenuates corruption in one context, should we expect the same to occur elsewhere? What information do we need about both the intervention and the nature of the corruption itself to answer this question?

The goals of this chapter are threefold: first, to highlight issues of conceptualization and measurement in the existing literature on corruption that limit our ability to cumulate knowledge about corruption's causes, effects, and the potential for reform. Second, to argue for a more explicit but pragmatic approach to typologies of corruption that should improve our ability to cumulate knowledge while not limiting the analytic endeavor. And, third, to present a new typology of corruption that is intended to facilitate analyses specifically aimed at identifying those individuals with a vested interest in existing forms of corruption.

I suggest that within a basic definition of corruption, there are many ways in which we can distinguish between different types of corrupt behavior. Each typology may be useful for a particular purpose. None may be useful for all purposes. Thus, it is essential to our analytical endeavors first, to acknowledge the diversity of ways in which we discuss and analyze corruption and, second, to be clear in each analysis about the form of corruption under investigation and why we are conceptualizing and measuring it in a particular manner. An important element of this is to recognize that we may work within a single typological tradition, such as that distinguishing between petty and grand corruption, while

[1] I would like to thank participants at the Conference on Grand and Petty Corruption in Developing States at Yale University for comments on an earlier draft.

only addressing a certain type of corruption in our analysis, such as petty corruption.

Using a range of examples from the rich literature on corruption, I highlight the lack of attention to these issues in most current research and the resulting difficulties related to cumulating knowledge on the nature of corruption. I then consider existing typologies of corruption and, drawing on the democratization literature, argue that a diversity of typologies, rather than one primary typology, may be most analytically useful. I subsequently present a new typology based on the nature of state resources and highlight how this framework offers leverage for distinguishing the types of actors involved in different forms of corruption.

1. FRAMEWORKS FOR CONCEPTUALIZING CORRUPTION

To a certain extent, 'corruption' is a case in which there is relatively little empirical debate about what corruption 'is'. While considerable work has deliberated on the concept of corruption itself (see, *inter alia*, Philp 2002, Heywood 1997, Gardiner 2002 (1993), Alatas 1990, and Friedrich 2002 (1972)), there is little substantive debate about the definition of corruption in practice. Corruption is taken to be *the abuse of public office for private gain* (see, *inter alia*, Olken 2007, Bardhan 2006, Jain 2001, and Rose-Ackerman 1975)—a definition that has become the most commonly utilized characterization. Rarely do analysts allocate substantial, or even minimal, discussion to the justification of this specific conceptualization.[2]

I want to suggest that there should be substantially more debate, or at the very least discussion, about the concept of corruption. I am especially concerned with conceptualizing various types of corruption. The phrase 'the abuse of public office for private gain' offers little insight into how to distinguish between different forms of abuse; yet analyzing the diverse forms is often at the heart of analyses of corruption. Thus, we need a more comprehensive consideration of variation within the concept of corruption.

A number of analysts have offered more specific typologies of corrupt behavior. One framework, posed by Kaushik Basu, differentiates between

---

[2] This is perhaps because this definition seems relatively straightforward and offers a concise starting point for categorizing various behaviors as corrupt or not. However, I set aside here a detailed analysis of why this particular conceptualization has taken root.

'harassment' bribes, those 'that people often have to give to get what they are legally entitled to', (Basu 2011: 3) and 'non-harassment' bribes, which are those 'that are believed to occur when government gives out big development contracts' (Basu 2011: 8). This is similar to Alatas' description of 'transactive' versus 'extortive' corruption, in which 'The former refers to a mutual arrangement between a donor and a recipient, actively pursued by, and to the mutual advantage of, both parties, whereas the latter entails some form of compulsion, usually to avoid some form of harm being inflicted on the donor or those close to him/her' (Heywood 1997: 425–6). The distinction is a powerful one, because it distinguishes between bribe givers who rightfully deserve whatever they receive as a result of the bribe and those who would not deserve the object/service/contract under question regardless of the bribe. Thus, the underlying incentives and legal rights of those involved in the two types of bribes may be quite different.

A more commonly utilized distinction, highlighted by Rose-Ackerman (1999), is between *petty* and *grand* corruption. The former refers to bribes citizens pay to lower-level officials either to speed the delivery of services or to bribe officials to 'bend the rules' (Rose-Ackerman 2002; Cisar 2003), while the latter 'involves large sums of money with multinational corporations frequently making the payoffs' and politicians using their power to shape policies in ways that benefit bribers (Rose-Ackerman 2002; Jain 2001; see also Bussell 2012). A related distinction is sometimes made between *retail* and *wholesale* corruption, with retail corruption described as 'millions of small transactions where people go to get a service and have to pay some . . . rent . . . for consummating that transaction' (Nilekani 2013), while 'wholesale corruption happens at a macro scale . . . in land, spectrum, or natural resources' (ibid.).

Heywood notes that, beyond these initial two, a multitude of typologies is possible:

> distinctions could be drawn between . . . the local and national level (the former being site of widespread corruption in regard, for instance, to municipal public works contracts); between personal and institutional corruption (that is, between corruption aimed at personal enrichment and that which seeks to benefit an institution such as a political party); between traditional and modern forms of corruption (for instance, nepotism and patronage versus money laundering through electronic means); and so forth (Heywood 1997: 426).

Thus, the literature and public discourse are rich with typologies, or potential typologies, of corruption, and yet there is little consideration of whether a particular typology should be used or when it should be used. I posit that this lack of deliberation is a problem. If we are serious about understanding the dynamics of corruption both theoretically and empirically, then a more meaningful conversation about the ways in which we operationalize the concept is necessary for pushing forward our knowledge.

Attention to typologies in work on corruption is particularly important due to limitations in the ways in which typologies are currently used, both generally and with regard to specific analytical tasks. First, the empirical literature, in practice, largely ignores variation in corruption, typically analyzing only one example of corrupt behavior without categorizing it as a particular form of corruption. This imprecise link between concept and measurement is highlighted in a review of classic and more recent works on corruption shown in Table 1.1. For each article or book, I note the definition of corruption used, if given, and the measurement technique of the analysis, as well as the associated independent or dependent variable(s). Although there is often a reasonably logical match between the measure of corruption and the independent or dependent variables under consideration, there is typically no definition of corruption provided, let alone a specification of the *type* of corruption that would allow us to compare results across individual analyses. Of the 26 pieces included in the review, only eleven (42 percent) explicitly state the definition of corruption with which they are working. Only three (11.5 percent) pieces, one of which is a review article and one of which is written by the author of this chapter, acknowledge the potential for different types of corruption and address these types in their discussion.

Hence, analyses of corruption are problematic for the purposes of cumulating knowledge on at least two levels. First, it is difficult to tell if analysts are using the same initial concept of corruption to inform their theoretical perspective. This makes it largely, if not entirely, impossible to determine whether the corruption considered in one analysis 'should' be the same or different from that evaluated elsewhere. Second, even in those cases where analysts specify their concept of corruption, the operationalization of that concept is likely to differ dramatically across empirical analyses. As Kramon and Posner note, 'some researchers measure [corruption] in terms of local bribe taking by civil servants; others in terms of the valuation of publicly traded companies with connections to top government officials; others in terms of tax evasion; and others in terms of leakage in public expenditure' (Kramon and Posner 2013: 469). These differences in measurement strategies may simply reflect the difficulty of collecting data on corruption, but this does not change the fact that any effort to compare across analyses will be stymied by differences in measurement. Such measurement issues may also result in a set of analyses with quite different findings regarding what factors encourage corrupt behavior and how corruption affects political and social outcomes.

Table 1.1 Studies analyzing corruption: variables, concepts, and measures

Article/Book	IVs and/or DVs[1]	Concept	Measurement Strategy
Ades, Alberto and Rafael Di Tella. 1999.	– IVs: 'Natural' rents, for example, from natural resources, and 'market' rents, for example, from lack of competition	– Undefined	– Business Intelligence corruption index, World Competitiveness Report scores for 'the extent to which improper practices (such as bribing or corruption) prevail in the public sphere' (World Competitiveness Report, as quoted in Ades and Di Tella, 986)
Alt, James E. and David Dreyer Lassen. 2014.	– IV: Prosecutorial resources	– The misuse of political and administrative power at the expense of citizens; the misuse of public office for private gain	– Corruption convictions in the United States, as reported by the Public Integrity Section of the US Department of Justice
Bertrand, Marianne, Simeon Djankov, Rema Hanna, and Sendhil Mullainathan. 2007.	– DV: Ability to obtain driver's license	– Undefined – Operationalized as extra payments to agents or bureaucrats to receive a government service (driver's license)	– Difference between proportion of subjects in the 'bonus for fast receipt of driver's license' treatment and those in the lesson and control conditions who receive their license, how quickly they receive it, whether they take the licensing exam, whether paid above official fees, whether tried to bribe, whether used an agent, etc.

Table 1.1 (continued)

Article/Book	IVs and/or DVs[1]	Concept	Measurement Strategy
Banerjee, Abhijit and Rohini Pande. No date.	– IV: Voter ethnicization (greater voter preference for the party representing her ethnic group)	– Undefined – Information not provided on details of corruption scale used and content of vignettes	Three measures: – Survey of journalists and politicians about politicians and candidates – Index of the economic gain by the politicians after entering politics, averaging: 'whether the politician used political office for personal gain, whether he or his family saw a significant improvement in their economic position, whether they started or expanded a business, and whether they started or expanded contracting activity' (19) – Whether the politician has a criminal record
Barr, Abagail and Danila Serra. 2010.	– IV: Country of origin	– Payment/receipt of a bribe for a 'corrupt' service (for example, reduction in tax, preferential treatment in court hearing, speedier admission to a hospital)	Individual corruption level – Whether subjects are willing to pay a bribe for a 'corrupt' service and how much – Whether willing to accept a bribe and how much Home country corruption level – Transparency International CPI

Bhavnani, Rikhil. 2010.	– IV: Holding political office	– Misuse of public office for private economic gain – Gains/benefits from public office	– Estimating changes in wealth among elected politicians versus those not elected who ran again in the next election
Bose, Niloy, Salvatore Capasso, and Antu Panini Murshid. 2008.	– DV: Quality of public infrastructure	– '[W]hen bureaucrats leverage their positions to further their own interests' (1174)	– Transparency International Corruption Perceptions Index
Bussell, Jennifer. 2012.	– DVs: Timing, comprehensiveness, and ownership and management model of government policies	– Corruption: the abuse of public office for private gain – Grand corruption: Corruption in procurement and government contracting – Petty corruption: Corruption in the delivery of public services	– Grand corruption: Index based on Government of India Report on the Member of Parliament Local Area Development Scheme – Petty corruption: Index based on Transparency International India and Centre for Media Studies Indian Corruption Study (survey of Indian citizens)
Chong, Alberto, Ana L. De La O, Dean Karlan, and Leonard Wantchekon. 2012.	– DV: Vote for candidates, turnout	– Undefined	– '[P]ercentage of resources mayors spent in a corrupt manner (in other words, spending where some form of irregularity was identified such as over-invoicing, fake receipts, diverting resources, fraud, etc.)' (3)

Table 1.1 (continued)

Article/Book	IVs and/or DVs[1]	Concept	Measurement Strategy
De Figueiredo, Miguel F. P., F. Daniel Hidalgo, and Yuri Kasahara. 2012.	– DV: Vote for candidates, turnout	– Undefined	– Convictions for impropriety while in government office
Ferraz, Claudio and Frederico Finan. 2008.	– DV: Election outcomes	– '[A]ny irregularity associated with fraud in procurements, diversion of public funds, or over-invoicing' (710)	– 'Each audit report contains the total amount of federal funds transferred to the current administration and the amount audited, as well as an itemized list describing each irregularity. Based on our readings of the reports, we codified the irregularities listed into those associated with corruption and those that simply represent poor administration' (709–710)
Fisman, Raymond and Edward Miguel. 2007.	– IVs: Cultural norms, legal enforcement	– 'The abuse of entrusted power for private gain.'	– Accumulation of unpaid parking violations by diplomats in Manhattan
Gerring, John and Strom C. Thacker. 2004.	– IVs: Territorial sovereignty (unitary or federal), composition of the executive (parliamentary or presidential)	– Corruption: 'An act that subverts the public good for private or particularistic gain' (300) – Political corruption: 'An act by a public official	– Kaufman, Kraay, and Zoido-Lobaton index; Transparency International Corruption Perceptions Index

Glaeser, Edward L. and Raven E. Saks. 2006.	– IVs: Education, income, income inequality, racial fractionalization – DV: Economic development	– 'Official corruption' – 'conflicts of interest, fraud, campaign-finance violations, and obstruction of justice' (1053) – 'Crimes by public officials for personal gain (Rose-Ackerman, 1975)' (1055)	(or with the acquiescence of a public official) that violates legal or social norms for private or particularistic gain' (ibid.) – The number of government officials convicted for corrupt practices through the Federal justice department/the number of Federal corruption convictions per capita by state – 'The usual problem with using conviction rates to measure corruption is that in corrupt places, the judicial system is itself corrupt and fewer people will be charged with corrupt practices. This problem is mitigated with focusing on Federal convictions, because the Federal judicial system is relatively isolated from local corruption and should treat people similarly across space' (1054)

Table 1.1 (continued)

Article/Book	IVs and/or DVs[1]	Concept	Measurement Strategy
Golden, Miriam A. and Lucio Picci. 2005.	– N/A	– Though not stated explicitly, the basic working definition of corruption here is the misuse of public finances	– 'The difference between the amounts of physically existing public infrastructure (roads, schools, hospitals, etc.) and the amounts of money cumulatively allocated by government to create these public works. Where the difference between the two is larger, more money is being lost to fraud, embezzlement, waste, and mismanagement; in other words, corruption is greater' (37)
Mauro, Paulo. 1995.	– DV: investment	– Undefined	– Business International Corruption measures, based on surveys of BI in-country correspondents responding to the statement: 'the degree to which business transactions involve corruption or questionable payments' (684)
McMillan, John and Pablo Zoido. 2004.	– IVs: opposition parties, the judiciary, the news media	– Undefined – Operationalized as bribes paid by the secret	– Secret police chief Vladimiro Montesinos Torres' records of bribes paid

Citation	Independent variables / method	Definition / operationalization	Measurement / data source
		police chief to judges, politicians, and the news media	
Montinola, Gabriella R. and Robert W. Jackman. 2002.	– IVs: Political competition, economic competition, inequality, public sector wages	– Undefined	– Business International corruption scores, Transparency International Corruption Perceptions Index
Olken, Benjamin A. 2007.	– IVs: Government audits, grassroots participation in monitoring	– Undefined – Operationalized as the misuse of public funds in building of roads	– The difference between official project cost (of building roads) and independent engineers' estimate of costs
Olken, Benjamin A. and Patrick Barron. 2009.	– IVs: Market structure, price discrimination	– Undefined – Operationalized as bribes paid by truckers to police, soldiers, and weigh station attendants	– Observation of payments made by truckers during trips to and from Ache, Indonesia
Reinikka, Ritva and Jakob Svensson. 2006.	– N/A (review article)	– 'Political and bureaucratic capture, leakage of funds, and problems in the deployment of human and in-kind resources, such as staff, textbooks, and drugs' (360)	– Public Expenditure Tracking Surveys – 'A public expenditure tracking survey (PETS) tracks the flow of resources through these strata [layers of government bureaucracy], on a sample survey basis, in order to determine how much of the originally allocated resources reach each level' (360)

Table 1.1 (continued)

Article/Book	IVs and/or DVs[1]	Concept	Measurement Strategy
		– Misuse of public office/ failure to perform required tasks while still taking salary – Payment/receipt of bribes for services	– Frontline Provider Surveys/ Quantitative service delivery survey – Unannounced visits to hospitals/schools to evaluate what fraction of professionals were at their posts – Firm/corporation surveys
Reinikka, Ritva and Jakob Svensson. 2004.	– IVs: Local community characteristics	– Undefined ('corruption' not used explicitly in the discussion, though it is referred to in footnotes and in further work by these authors citing this paper)	– The difference between money allocated to schools by the Ugandan government and money actually received
Shleifer, Andrei and Robert W. Vishny. 1993.	– IV: Market structure of the supply of government goods – DV: Economic efficiency	– Government corruption: '[T]he sale by government officials of government property for private gain' (599)	– Unmeasured

Treisman, Daniel. 2000.	– IVs: Religion, colonial history, economic development, import levels, federalism, democracy	– The misuse of public office for private gain	– Transparency International Corruption Perceptions Index, Business International index of perceived corruption
Van Rijckeghem, Caroline and Beatrice Weder. 2001.	– IV: Bureaucratic wages	– Undefined	– International Country Risk Group corruption scores
Wei, Shang-Jin. 2000.	– DV: Foreign direct investment	– Undefined – Operationalized, in the author's interpretation of the surveys used, as 'the administration of rules/laws pertinent to foreign firms . . . . weighted by efficiency level as perceived by those who were surveyed' (3)	– Business International index of perceived corruption, International Country Risk Group corruption measure, and Transparency International Corruption Perceptions Index

Note:
1. Unless otherwise noted, where an independent variable (IV) is listed, corruption is the dependent variable (DV) and vice versa.

A second limitation is that existing typologies are often insufficient for the range of potential analyses on this topic. Take, as an example, the common distinction between petty and grand corruption. Although this dichotomy can be quite useful in distinguishing between the type of corruption frequently faced by individual citizens in developing countries and the type of corruption engaged in by high-level officials around the world, it is insufficient for addressing, conceptually, certain other forms of corruption. For instance, in their analysis of municipal-level corruption in Brazil, Ferraz and Finan highlight that 'most corruption schemes used by local politicians to appropriate resources are based on a combination of fraud in procurements, the use of fake receipts or 'phantom' firms, and over-invoicing the value of products or services' (Ferraz and Finan 2008: 710). This corruption in contracting over government resources is quite common in developing countries but does not necessarily fit the characteristics of grand and petty corruption just discussed. Thus, if one is interested in analyzing contracting corruption engaged in by relatively low-level political and bureaucratic actors, the petty versus grand typology seems insufficient.

Similarly, consider the alternate distinction posed above between harassment and non-harassment bribes. Although this typology is arguably more comprehensive than the distinction between petty and grand corruption, it is too broad for certain types of analysis. For example, take two examples of non-harassment bribes. In one case, a traffic officer and a driver who has been speeding agree on a direct payment to the officer rather than a speeding ticket. In another case, a politician receives a kickback for shepherding particular industrial regulations through the political process. The actors in these two transactions are both engaging in non-harassment bribe-taking, yet they operate at different levels of government and under different authority structures.

Given the limitations of existing typologies, how should we think about appropriate strategies for typological alternatives and conditions under which one typology may or may not be appropriate? In the next section, I draw on debates in the literature on democracy to suggest a pragmatic model for analyzing corruption in its various forms.

2.   FROM GRADATIONS OF DEMOCRACY TO TYPES OF CORRUPTION

The literature on democracies and non-democratic regimes offers a useful example of a field in which, some argue, settling on a single definition and measurement strategy is less useful than allowing multiple approaches to thrive, depending on the analytic goal. In their discussion of debates on whether a dichotomous or graded measure of democracy is more appropriate, Collier and Adcock argue that 'This recurring and much debated question has important implications for how research is organized, for how data are collected and analyzed, and for inferences about the causes and consequences of democracy' (Collier and Adcock 1999: 537–8). In doing so, they highlight examples of analyses, such as those investigating the relationship between regime type and political stability (Elkins 1999), where different measurement strategies produce strikingly different findings (Collier and Adcock 1999: 538–9).

While scholars of democracy often express strong opinions about dichotomous versus graded measures, Collier and Adcock, instead of reflecting one side in this debate, argue that 'specific methodological choices are often best understood and justified in light of the theoretical framework, analytic goals, and context of research involved in any particular study' (Collier and Adcock 1999: 539). In other words, 'how scholars understand and operationalize a concept can and should depend in part on what they are going to do with it' (ibid.).

I suggest that this perspective is directly relevant to the literature on corruption. Where Collier and Adcock are responding to a debate over the appropriate measurement of democracy, be it graded or dichotomous, greater attention to the ways in which we distinguish between corrupt behaviors, or typologies of corruption, within a given general conceptualization, also offers important analytic opportunities. Concepts and typologies are useful for a great number of scholarly purposes, but they are particularly important for distinguishing what exactly is the topic under consideration and differentiating, within that topic, between different manifestations. Rather than attempting to fit one typological schema onto all efforts to analyze corruption, we are better served by explicitly identifying the character of corruption that is relevant to our analytic goals and then working within that conceptual definition and, if necessary, suitable typology.

What, then, is an appropriate strategy for thinking about what the most useful typology of corruption would be in a given analysis? Returning again to the literature on democracy, Collier and Adcock note that there may be multiple ways in which the theoretical and empirical goals of a particular piece of research can inform choices about concepts and measurement in general and the use of typologies in particular (Collier and Adcock 1999: 550). The choice of conceptual approach may be guided inductively by the empirical distribution of cases, it may be structured by a normative concern, or it may instead be informed by a theoretical hypothesis about the topic at hand (Collier and Adcock 1999). For example, one reason many analysts seem to use a dichotomous approach to democracy and non-democracy is the empirical context. Historically, country cases have tended to cluster in two groups, one with more democratic features and the other with more nondemocratic features (Collier and Adcock 1999: 554–5). Analysts saw this grouping itself as an important characteristic in the transition to democracy and so focused on a dichotomous measure (ibid.). Alternatively, O'Donnell and Schmitter (1986) adopted a normative standard for democracy, a 'procedural minimum' that would establish a target for transitional states and, in doing so, lead to a clear distinction between those states that do and do not meet these standards (Collier and Adcock 1999: 556–7). Finally, theoretical concerns may inform the use of a particular typological strategy, as was the case for O'Donnell's (1994) work on delegative democracies, which focused on a sub-type of democracy as an independent variable. In this case, he argued that a feature of specific democracies, 'regimes with strong presidencies in which the 'horizontal accountability' of the executive to the legislature is attenuated' (Collier and Adcock 1999: 553) had particular effects on political institutionalization.

Each of these perspectives may be relevant to analyses of corruption. Empirically, the distinction between petty and grand corruption, though limited in the ways I suggest above, seems to have been driven by a sorting of observed corrupt behaviors into those experienced by every-day citizens and those engaged in by high-level politicians and private companies 'behind the scenes'. Normatively, a simple dichotomous measure of corruption or its absence may be most relevant for distinguishing the effects of corruption on policy outcomes. For instance, do corrupt political leaders lead to lower growth rates? In order to answer this question, it might be most helpful to count the number of corrupt or honest politicians holding office, rather than to measure gradations of corruption among office holders. Theoretically, we might expect different kinds of corruption to be related to different types of policy outcomes. In my work on administrative reforms in India, I distinguish between petty and grand corruption because I hypothesized that petty corruption would have different effects on policy choices related to government technology adoption than would grand corruption (Bussell 2012). As a result, it was important both to differentiate between these forms of corruption conceptually and to measure them differently in the empirical analysis.

The implication of these different logics of conceptualization and measurement is that there is no one right strategy and, instead, there are different reasons for choosing different typological strategies. What is important is that one is explicit about one's strategy and, where possible, clear on the logic for choosing it for a particular analysis. In the next section, I provide an example of, and the logic for, a new typology that was developed specifically to address an analytic question where existing typologies seemed insufficient.

3. STATE RESOURCES AND TYPES OF CORRUPTION

Many corruption analyses seek to understand the underlying dynamics of corrupt transactions so as to facilitate anti-corruption reforms. In particular, we are often interested in the incentives of actors engaged in corrupt activities, so as to design anti-corruption interventions that target the underlying causes of these behaviors. Yet, these efforts tend only to consider the actors involved in a very general way—for example, civil servants or elected officials—which may be insufficiently specific for identifying the relevant incentives at play.

One strategy for distinguishing between individuals with different corrupt incentives is to focus on corruption as it relates to different types of state resources, such as welfare benefits, natural resources, and public contracts. Considering who has control over these resources can help to focus attention on the relevant sets of individuals. This approach is theoretically driven: if different individuals control different state resources, then identifying variations in corruption related to those resources should help us to understand how the incentives to engage in corruption differ across individuals. If one wants to understand who is benefitting from a particular form of corruption, such as bribes taken in the delivery of basic services, it is necessary to identify who has power over these resources.

The nature of control over state resources has previously been highlighted as an important factor shaping the nature of corruption. Shliefer and Vishny (1993) argue that two features of institutional structures, government centralization and bureaucratic competition, play primary roles in shaping opportunities to extract rents and so influence the prevalence and predictability of corruption in a given regime. Centralization makes corruption predictable because 'In such places it is always clear who needs to be bribed and by how much. The bribe is then divided between all the relevant government bureaucrats, who agree not to demand further bribes from the buyer of the package of government goods, such as permits' (Shleifer and Vishny 1993: 605). Competition between bureaucratic agents makes corruption less likely in general because individuals can go to an alternative provider if they are asked for a bribe (Rose-Ackerman 1978: 137–66).

Implicit in the discussion of centralization and competition is the understanding that these characteristics affect the incentives of agents who are responsible for distributing resources over which the state maintains control. These individuals can feasibly restrict access to state resources, such as welfare benefits or mining licenses, and so have the potential to extract bribes from individuals or organizations with an interest in the resources. Where power is centralized, agents of the state have little independence to determine their preferred level of rent extraction, and where there is competition, market forces exert downward pressures on rent-seeking.

Within these institutional constraints, however, the specific actor, or set of actors, with the potential to extract bribes will most likely depend on the type of state resource being distributed. Resources may be allocated either by elected officials or civil servants, with politicians, on one hand, typically overseeing resource allocation as they make policy, such as through pork barreling, or through direct spending in their region, as in constituency development funds. Bureaucrats, on the other hand, tend to allocate resources in the implementation of policy that is already in place, such as through negotiations over state contracts and the delivery of public services to particular individuals and firms. Within these two categories, there may be a wide range of individuals who have power over specific state resources, given their level of government and their positions within a particular department.

This spread of responsibility across actors is especially important in decentralized regimes, as noted by Shliefer and Vishny, because it increases the number of actors who may be able to act on their own to extract bribes from the public. More specifically, in a highly decentralized state there is likely to be substantially more variation in the power structures across government. This variation may affect patterns of corruption in at least two ways.

First, decentralization of authority implies that actors at different levels of government have control over different government resources. For example, a bureaucrat at the highest level of government may be in charge of implementing an auction to allocate licenses for land rights to build cross-country high-speed rail lines. A bureaucrat at a middle level of government may be charged with overseeing the building of health centers, while at the most local level, bureaucrats are likely to be responsible for delivery of resources such as welfare benefits and utility connections. Thus, we should observe differing actors benefiting from corrupt activities, depending on the type of resource and the level of government at which it is allocated.

Second, decentralization may also affect the range of actors who are able to benefit from the distribution of a single resource. For example, in the allocation of licenses to extract natural resources, a policy may be written by the central government legislature to structure licensing and then the license may be allocated to a large company by the central government, giving these bodies access to potential corrupt rents in these processes. At the sub-national level, however, the state or provincial government with control over the region in question may also play a role in giving approval to begin extraction in a specific location, and local governments may have the power to exert control over final access to the land. Thus, there may be multiple points at which different actors can extract rents related to a single resource.

The discussion to this point emphasizes only forms of formal control over the distribution of resources. However, there may be more informal ways in which actors who do not have direct control over a state resource can still extract rents from bribes paid for access to that resource. I characterize this kind of power over rent extraction as *indirect influence* and posit that it may arise from *direct control* over either individuals or over information. Where someone has power over another individual related to the latter's position within the state, the former individual may be able to leverage this power to extract rents from corruption in which the latter is engaged. Alternatively, if someone wants to engage in corruption but cannot do so without information provided by another individual, this latter individual may be able to use his or her power over information to collect some portion of any bribe payments.

I explore these dynamics in greater detail in the context of four types of state resources, which represent significant loci of corruption: policies (formal legislation and departmental regulations), public licenses and contracts, government jobs, and public goods and services. In each case, the specific individuals with direct control and indirect influence over a resource may differ across national contexts. I provide a generic discussion of one way in which these power dynamics could operate in a decentralized institutional environment.

With regard to policies, direct control typically sits with legislators, who shape the final content of legislation and with cabinet officials who issue departmental regulations. However, bureaucrats also often contribute to legislative content by participating in the drafting of bills and rules. External actors, such as lobbyists, may influence the content of policies through their relationships with politicians and top executive branch officials.

Public licenses and contracts, such as licenses allocating rights to natural resources and contracts to build public structures, may be shaped by legislation but determined in practice by procedures formally overseen by bureaucrats. At the same time, politicians may reassert their influence over these resources through indirect control over bureaucrats, such as with threats or promises related to transfers or promotions within government.

Control over the allocation of public sector jobs, however, is contingent on administrative guidelines related to merit-based procedures for hiring and promoting civil servants. Where merit-based procedures do not exist, patronage politics may instead determine the allocation of employment resources. These patronage relationships can then offer indirect influence over the distribution of resources, as previously noted.

Finally, civil servants also directly control the provision of goods and services to citizens. These individuals determine who receives benefits, among both the set of qualified individuals and those who do not meet eligibility criteria but still desire a specific good. Here, again, politicians who have influence over bureaucrats' jobs may be able informally to shape the allocation of these resources.

In any of these cases, middlemen may exert informal influence in the distribution of resources. This is most likely in situations where there is an opportunity to provide information and coordinate corruption because politicians or bureaucrats require private information, which can be accessed by the middleman, on which individuals are willing to pay an additional 'fee' to secure the resource.

This discussion highlights the ways in which paying attention to the particular resource can help to illuminate the specific actors with potentially entrenched interests in corruption. In each of these cases, the individuals with direct control and indirect influence over the allocation of the resource are those most likely to benefit from corruption. As a result, they are the individuals who are the most relevant for consideration in any effort to reduce corruption. Table 1.2 summarizes this discussion and provides a typological framework distinguishing between legislative, contracting, employment, and services corruption, using the type of government resource as a starting point for analyzing the actors involved in corrupt activities.[3]

CONCLUSION

Analysis of corruption is an inherently difficult task, due to its illicit nature. As a result, the accumulation of knowledge about corruption is a

---

[3]   As noted in the earlier discussion, the specific actors with power over a given resource may change across institutional settings and so must be revisited in the context of any given analysis.

Table 1.2 *Corruption and types of government resources*

Corruption Type	Type of Government Resource	Examples of Corruption	Holder(s) of Direct Control	Holder(s) of Indirect Influence
Legislative	– Government policies and regulations	– Payments for favorable legislation	– Presidents/ Ministers/ Legislators – Top department bureaucrats	– Bureaucrats with control over implementation
Contracting	– Allocation of licenses/ contracts (natural resources, schools, roads, etc.)	– Kickbacks on licenses/contracts	– Bureaucrats at level of contract/project	– Politicians with power over bureaucrats – Middlemen
Employment	– Government jobs	– Bribes or favors for jobs	– Politicians and bureaucrats with hiring and transferring authority	– Middlemen
Services	– Provision of individual benefits (for example, IDs, welfare) or sanctions (for example, traffic violations)	– Bribes for 'speedy' services	– 'Street-level' bureaucrats	– Politicians with power over bureaucrats – Local politicians – Middlemen

significant but problematic goal. In addition, our understanding of corruption has been stymied by inattention to the ways in which we conceptualize and measure the forms of corruption. I posit that this is a substantial, but surmountable, barrier to progress both in research on corruption and attempts to implement anti-corruption reforms.

In this chapter, I have highlighted how existing research conceptualizes or does not conceptualize corruption in practice with an emphasis on the limited and insufficient use of typologies to clarify the practice(s) being evaluated. Not only do analysts often not specify what they mean by 'corruption', they are even less likely to specify the type of corruption they study.

Rather than arguing for one single shared typology for use across all analyses, a strategy that would, in theory, promote more consistent, comparable analyses, I have argued for a more pragmatic, problem-driven approach. Given the complex nature of corruption, it is highly unlikely that a single typology will be sufficient for all research questions. Instead, we should strive to be transparent and clear about the model being used and the logic behind its adoption. In doing so, we can encourage the adoption of specific typologies for appropriate research programs, to be shared across analysts with interests in related questions, and thereby facilitate the building of knowledge within these specific domains.

In order to illustrate how this might be done, I first highlighted limitations in existing typologies. I then presented a new typology that I claim is useful for analyses where the researcher seeks to identify specific individuals who may be involved in corrupt activities. By disaggregating the types of state resources over which corruption may occur, I highlight different sets of actors who may have vested interests in corrupt practices. While the specific actors with power over a given type of resource will vary across institutional contexts, the general framework should provide useful guidelines for thinking about which actors are relevant to different forms of corruption. Alternative typologies, including existing distinctions between harassment and non-harassment bribes or petty and grand corruption, may be more relevant for other analytic tasks. What is most important is that we, as analysts, are clear about the strategy that we adopt, with the goal of increasing our ability to know what we have learned and what its policy implications might be.

REFERENCES

Ades, Alberto and Rafael Di Tella. 1999. 'Rents, Competition, and Corruption', *The American Economic Review* 89(4): 982–93.

Alatas, Syed Hussein. 1990. *Corruption: Its Nature, Causes and Functions.* Aldershot, UK: Avebury.

Alt, James E. and David Dreyer Lassen. 2014. 'Enforcement and Public Corruption: Evidence from the American States', *Journal of Law, Economics, and Organization* 30(2): 306–38.

Banerjee, Abhijit and Rohini Pande. No date. 'Parochial Politics: Ethnic Preferences and Politician Corruption', working paper.

Bardhan, Pranab. 2006. 'The Economist's Approach to the Problem of Corruption', *World Development* 34(2): 341–48.

Barr, Abagail and Danila Serra. 2010. 'Corruption and Culture: An Experimental Analysis', *Journal of Public Economics* 94(11–12): 862–9.

Basu, Kaushik. 2011. 'Why, for a Class of Bribes, the Act of Giving a Bribe should be Treated as Legal', Ministry of Finance, Government of India Working Paper No. 1/2011-DEA (March 2011).

Bertrand, Marianne, Simeon Djankov, Rema Hanna, and Sendhil Mullainathan. 2007. 'Obtaining a Driver's License in India: An Experimental Approach to Studying Corruption', *Quarterly Journal of Economics* November: 1639–76.

Bhavnani, Rikhil. 2009. 'Corruption Among India's Politicians: Insights from Unusual Data', working paper.

Bose, Niloy, Salvatore Capasso, and Antu Panini Murshid. 2008. 'Threshold Effects of Corruption: Theory and Evidence', *World Development* 36(7): 1173–91.

Bussell, Jennifer. 2012. *Corruption and Reform in India: Public Services in the Digital Age.* New York and New Delhi: Cambridge University Press.

Chong, Alberto, Ana L. De La O, Dean Karlan, and Leonard Wantchekon. 2012. 'Looking Beyond the Incumbent: The Effects of Exposing Corruption on Electoral Outcomes', Economics Department Working Paper No. 94, Economic Growth Center Discussion Paper No. 1005, Yale University.

Cisar, Ondrej. 2003. 'Strategies for Using Information Technologies for Curbing Public Sector Corruption. The Case of the Czech Republic', Research Report for the Open Society Institute, Budapest.

Collier, David and Robert Adcock. 1999. 'Democracy and Dichotomies: A Pragmatic Approach to Choices and Concepts', *Annual Review of Political Science* 2: 537–65.

De Figueiredo, Miguel, D. Daniel Hidalgo, and Yuri Kasahara. 2012. 'When Do Voters Punish Corrupt Politicians? Experimental Evidence from Brazil', working paper.

Elkins, Zachary. 1999. 'Gradations of Democracy: Empirical Tests of Alternative Conceptualizations', paper presented at Seminar on Democratization, Stanford Institute on International Studies, Stanford University, 21 January, Stanford, CA.

Ferraz, Claudio and Frederico Finan. 2008. 'Exposing Corrupt Politicians: The Effects of Brazil's Publicly Released Audits on Electoral Outcomes', *The Quarterly Journal of Economics* May: 703–45.

Fisman, Raymond and Edward Miguel. 2007. 'Corruption, Norms, and Legal Enforcement: Evidence from Diplomatic Parking Tickets', *Journal of Political Economy* 115(6): 1020–48.

Friedrich, Carl J. 2002 (1972). 'Corruption Concepts in Historical Perspective', in Arnold J. Heidenheimer and Michael Johnston (eds), *Political Corruption: Concepts & Contexts.* 3rd edn, New Brunswick, NJ: Transaction Publishers, 15–24.

Gardiner, John A. 2002 (1993). 'Defining Corruption', in Arnold J. Heidenheimer and Michael Johnston (eds), *Political Corruption: Concepts & Contexts*. 3rd edn, New Brunswick, NJ: Transaction Publishers, 25–40.

Gerring, John and Strom C. Thacker. 2004. 'Political Institutions and Corruption: The Role of Unitarism and Parliamentarism', *British Journal of Political Science* 34: 295–330.

Glaeser, Edward L. and Raven Saks. 2006. 'Corruption in America', *Journal of Public Economics* 90: 1053–72.

Golden, Miriam A. and Lucio Picci. 2005. 'Proposal for a New Measure of Corruption, Illustrated with Italian Data', *Economics and Politics* 17(1): 37–75.

Heywood, Paul. 1997. 'Political Corruption: Problems and Perspectives', *Political Studies* XLV: 417–35.

Jain, Arvind. 2001. 'Corruption: A Review', *Journal of Economic Surveys*, 15(1): 71–119.

Kramon, Eric and Daniel N. Posner. 2013. 'Who Benefits from Distributive Politics? How the Outcome One Studies Affects the Answer One Gets', *Perspectives on Politics* 11(2): 461–74.

Mauro, Paulo. 1995. 'Corruption and Growth', *The Quarterly Journal of Economics* 110(3): 681–712.

McMillan, John and Pablos Zoido. 2004. 'How to Subvert Democracy: Montesinos in Peru', CDDRL working paper No. 3, Stanford Institute on International Studies, Stanford University.

Montinola, Gabriella R. and Robert W. Jackman. 2002. 'Sources of Corruption: A Cross-Country Study', *British Journal of Political Science* 32: 147–70.

Nilekani, Nandan. 2013. 'There is a Difference between Wholesale, Retail Corruption', *Economic Times*, 5 September. Accessed 6 May 2015 at http://economictimes.indiatimes.com/et-now/daily/there-is-a-difference-between-wholesale-retail-corruption/videoshow/22345610.cms.

O'Donnell, Guillermo. 1994. 'Delegative Democracy', *Journal of Democracy* 5(1): 55–69.

O'Donnell, Guillermo and Phillipe C Schmitter. 1986. *Transitions from Authoritarian Rule: Tentative Conclusions about Uncertain Transitions*. Baltimore, MD: Johns Hopkins University Press.

Olken, Benjamin. 2007. 'Monitoring Corruption: Evidence from a Field Experiment in Indonesia', *Journal of Political Economy* 115(2): 200–249.

Olken, Benjamin A. and Patrick Barron. 2009. 'The Simple Economics of Extortion: Evidence from Trucking in Aceh', *Journal of Political Economy* 117(3): 417–52.

Philp, Mark. 2002. 'Conceptualizing Political Corruption', in Arnold J. Heidenheimer and Michael Johnston (eds), *Political Corruption: Concepts & Contexts*. 3rd edn, New Brunswick, NJ: Transaction Publishers, 41–58.

Reinikka, Ritva and Jakob Svensson. 2004. 'Local Capture: Evidence from a Central Government Transfer Program in Uganda', *The Quarterly Journal of Economics* 119(2): 679–705.

Reinikka, Ritva and Jakob Svensson. 2006. 'Using Micro-Surveys to Measure and Explain Corruption', *World Development* 34(2): 359–70.

Rose-Ackerman, Susan. 1975. 'The Economics of Corruption', *Journal of Public Economics* 4(2): 187–203.

Rose-Ackerman, Susan. 1978. *Corruption: A Study in Political Economy*. New York: Academic Press, Inc.

Rose-Ackerman, Susan. 1999. *Corruption and Government: Causes, Consequences, and Reforms*. Cambridge: Cambridge University Press.

Rose-Ackerman, Susan. 2002. 'When is Corruption Harmful?' in Arnold J. Heidenheimer and Michael Johnston (eds), *Political Corruption: Concepts & Contexts*. 3rd edn, New Brunswick, NJ: Transaction Publishers, 353–72.

Shleifer, Andrei and Robert W. Vishny. 1993. 'Corruption', *Quarterly Journal of Economics* 108(3): 599–617.

Treisman, Daniel. 2000. 'The Causes of Corruption: A Cross-National Study', *Journal of Public Economics* 76: 399–457.

Van Rijckeghem, Caroline and Beatrice Weder. 2001. 'Bureaucratic Corruption and the Rate of Temptation: Do Wages in the Civil Service Affect Corruption, and by How Much?' *Journal of Development Economics* 65: 307–31.

Wei, Shang-Jin. 2000. 'How Taxing is Corruption on International Investors?' *The Review of Economics and Statistics* 82(1): 1–11.

2. Good governance facades

Kalle Moene and Tina Søreide[1]

1. INTRODUCTION

Fashions come and go in the development community. When a policy idea becomes popular, some governments implement a cosmetic variant of the policy. What looks like development, are institutional facades; pretty from the outside, ugly from the inside. A good governance facade can be introduced deliberately to mislead observers and stakeholders to cover political theft. An example from the past is development planning, introduced with good intentions but sometimes exploited as a cover for corruption. In the 1960s donors rewarded developing countries that introduced five-year plans by offering more aid.[2] Recipient governments were therefore tempted to come up with cosmetic plans to satisfy foreign donors rather than the needs of their citizens. With recipient governments appearing to follow the suggestions from development experts, the donors raised few questions about their actual performance. Accordingly, it became possible for recipients to appropriate aid money for personal enrichment without facing reactions from the donor community.

Another example is the donor community's demand for privatization in the 1980s and 1990s. In some cases cosmetic privatization led to unhealthy reductions in the provision of public goods rather than to healthy market orientation. Both the downsizing of government and the sale of underpriced assets to friends and allies, made it possible for the elite in some countries to grab more rents. This is why many privatization programmes

[1] We wish to thank Michael Kramer, Khusraw Parwez and Natalia Volosin for useful details and examples, and we are grateful for comments from Ivar Kolstad, Itumeleng Makgetla and participants at the Castle conference at Yale May 2014. Special thanks to Susan Rose-Ackerman and Paul Lagunes for all advice and support.
[2] The development planning processes, also referred to as neoliberal governmental restructuring (among other terms), have been described by many authors. For a recent critical perspective, see Roberts (2010).

in retrospect are seen as failures, despite the benefits associated with well-functioning markets.[3]

Among more recent examples is the fashion for budget support, which for recipient governments implies huge transfers combined with wide discretion. This lending modality has been promoted as efficient because it allows recipient countries to 'take ownership' of the funds so that spending can depend on the country's most important needs. The use of these unsupervised grants has been difficult to trace or evaluate, however, and in some countries, budget support has opened the door to theft and government contracting in ways that are neither fair nor efficient. Similarly, many anti-corruption agencies, charged with powers to prosecute civil servants and politicians, have not served their expected role in promoting government accountability. Too often these agencies are paralyzed at the very moment when members of the government are investigated. As a result, political theft continues behind an anti-corruption facade.

Legal and institutional reforms are difficult to carry out in a developing country. To some extent, honest reformers must expect some disappointing results. Despite the risk of failure, it may still be worth trying reforms. The reform initiatives that we have in mind, however, are different. In their purest form, facades are used for the personal enrichment of government representatives who may face few consequences when development goals fail. Those involved can insist that all the rules and development targets are implemented, but in reality, state resources are directed to the elite itself.

We argue in this chapter that rents can be extracted under the cover of executing good policies; that nominally beneficial policies permit corrupt decision-makers to hide in plain sight. Hidden behind facades, the real social and economic policies can vary almost inversely with what is needed to serve the population. Popular reforms frequently reduce the opportunity costs of political theft. The reforms cover, or in other ways facilitate, incumbents' efforts to divert resources away from the general public and to their own group. When this is the case, a higher international demand for integrity may lead to more fake supplies of good governance. We are afraid that placing institutional and legal reform at the center of development advice implies a higher risk of such facade institutions, especially in countries where better governance is needed the most.

The view, that the introduction of institutions and laws in some settings can reduce the risk of being held responsible for crime, reflects a declining

---

[3] For review of cases and explanation, see Manzetti (1999), Black et al. (2000) and Bjorvatn and Søreide (2005) – among others.

confidence in laws as a tool for development. Kevin Davies (2004) describes 'the rise and fall of the law and development movement'—the academic interest in promoting development through better laws which came to expression primarily in the US from the 1960s to the early 1970s. After various disappointments and political incidents, 'the principal participants in the exercise became disillusioned and lost their faith in the ability of law, much less legal scholarship, to contribute to development' and '. . . from mid-1970s to mid-1990s the American legal academy turned its back on development studies' (p. 141).

The next wave of optimism about law as a tool for promoting development, he explains, was brought forward by economists and political scientists—who believed that the development would come with the right legal backbone. Yet laws as remedies for poverty often lack solid empirical support, he claims. New cross-country governance data tempted researchers to study the impacts of policy recommendations without actually visiting countries and understanding the context of development. Enticed by the quick and convincing results, investigators often ignored the methodological difficulties in impact assessments of legal reform. Despite the use of large data sets and sophisticated statistics, their claims of causality were often based on thin inferences.

The policy initiatives directed at law enforcement and redistributive tax reforms had the clearest results (Davies and Trebilcock 2001). The evidence in other areas, such as property law, contract law and property rights, was less convincing. The intended legal mechanisms may well have a positive impact on development, but the data collected to assess the impact of laws have been weak. As summarized by Davies and Trebilcock (2001: 33): 'legal institutions do not play a wholly autonomous role in development; their effectiveness is contingent upon the effectiveness of a number of other institutions'.[4]

Our approach is based on the premise that legal institutions are indeed important, but that they must be understood as part of a political and economic equilibrium. Partial reforms are very different from comprehensive reforms: 'Governance reform is unlikely to be successful unless we understand the political forces that generate bad governance in the first place. In lieu of such an understanding, policy reforms to improve governance are often ineffective. To be effective, we suggest, reforms have to change the

---

[4]   The claim is supported by Tamanaha (2011), pointing at how 'factors that influence law extend far beyond law itself' (p. 214). As one example of naive confidence in legal reform, he refers to a speech by President Obama where he claims that new laws and institutions in Afghanistan will 'make it possible to accountably bring troops home'.

political equilibrium of a society. Though it is possible that small changes may do this, it is more likely that reform has to take place simultaneously in many dimensions.' (Baland, Moene and Robinson 2010).

2. THE LOGIC OF FACADE INVESTMENT AND DIVERSION

To clarify the mechanisms at play we begin with an overly simplified representation of the basic trade-offs between political fraud and good governance. Although good governance makes the cake bigger for the incumbent, political fraud makes it smaller but gives bigger slices to those in power. First, we present the relevant trade-offs from the perspective both of a totally benevolent incumbent and an opportunistic incumbent without scruples. Next, we relax some of the narrow assumptions, and discuss the theory's relevance and implications.

2.1 Theory

We start at an abstract level and consider a well-informed incumbent with complete control. He represents the group in power. The group is a small privileged minority, consisting of a share n of the population.[5] The incumbent determines the institutional governance structure and may divert some of the gains to the members of his group. In doing so, the incumbent is obviously affected by the rules and institutions in the country, including the ones that he himself implements. For now, we disregard this constraint. We do maintain, however, that the choice both of governance institutions and how much money to divert, affect the flow of state revenues. So, by consciously exaggerating the incumbent's ability to coordinate corruption, we ask the following question: *which level of good governance would benefit his group in power?*

To answer that question, we need some notation. The flow of revenues may stem from natural resource extraction, foreign aid, foreign investment, or a combination of these. We denote this flow of income by M. As stated, this flow is affected by governance, good and bad. It is affected by laws and institutions, represented by an indicator of good governance v, such that 'more is always better' for the flow of income. An improvement of good governance is costly, though, and these costs need to be covered by the incumbent. The flow of income is also affected by political fraud as

---

[5]   This implies no assumption about ethnicity.

measured by an indicator s, such that 'more is always worse' for the flow of income. The level of political fraud indicates rent diversion to the group in power.

De facto governance is determined by indicators of good governance v (institutions and laws) and bad governance s (political fraud or theft). Accordingly, the flow of income can be written as $M = M(v, s)$. Better institutions and laws lead to a higher flow of income as they improve efficiency (a partial increase in v raises the flow of income; the partial derivative is indicated by $M_v > 0$). More political fraud reduces the flow of income because the incumbent must accept a bad reputation and may have to create distortions to divert money, (hence, a higher s lowers the flow of income; the partial derivative is indicated by $M_s < 0$). The fraction of income that is *not* stolen $(1 - s)$ indicates political honesty.

The flow of income increases with good governance and political honesty with a constant elasticity for both. In other words, the flow of income is a Cobb-Douglas function of good governance and honesty. A one percentage increase in political honesty raises the flow of income by a constant $\alpha < 1$ percent. Similarly, a one percentage improvement in good governance increases the flow of income by the constant $\beta < 1$. The revenue gain of a certain increase in the good governance indicator becomes smaller the higher the institutional quality (that is, the more improvements that are already in place). Likewise the expected impact of an increase in political fraud on the flow of income, is smaller the more income is already being diverted.

What is a facade investment? We can define a successful facade as the level of good governance v that can sustain the initial flow of income with a higher level of diversion sM, or, in other words; that may allow a higher level of diversion without reducing the flow of income. Since diversion of income reduces future flows of income, a facade that sustains the initial flow with more diversion must involve a higher amount of institutional investments.

Now, consider an incumbent who diverts a share s of the flow of income to his group consisting of a fraction n of the population. He puts a weight μ on the income going to his own group and a weight $1 - \mu$ on the average income of the remaining population who all in all receives $(1 - s)M$. The weights reflect the way the incumbent values different groups in the population, their influence on political decisions. A higher weight on own group relative to its share of the population means that the incumbent becomes tempted to divert income to that group. If he, by contrast, is benevolent and attaches the same weight per member independently of which group they belong to, he is, as we shall see, less tempted to divert income.

Formally, the pay-off to the ruler is:

$$R = \gamma M(v,s) - c(v) \text{ with } \gamma = \mu \frac{s}{n} + (1 - \mu) \frac{1 - s}{1 - n} \equiv \gamma(s,\mu)$$

In this expression $c(v)$ is the (convex) costs of facade improvements. We also assume that the costs of good governance has a constant elasticity $\rho > 1$. In this expression $\gamma(s,\mu)$ is the incumbent's personal evaluation of each unit of income. It is greater the more he values members of his own group relative to others, and the higher the share of income that he diverts to his own group.

We recognize the basic trade-off between political fraud and good governance and how it depends on the incumbent's concern for the rest of the population outside his core group of supporters. The essence is that a higher level of v makes the flow of state income bigger, while a higher s makes it smaller, though with a higher share to those in power. Notice also that we have a simple representation of possible reasons for having 'bad governance' in the first place, namely a high value of μ – the power of the ruling elite. Such a position could be the result of insufficient political competition where too much political and economic inequality has diminished the power of the great majority.

We can think of the level of political fraud as the outcome of short-run opportunism, and the indicator of good governance as the outcome of a more long-run investment decision. Before we turn to analytic results, however, it should be noted that the institutional costs of good governance as a share of the flow of income, expressed as $g = c/M$, is increasing in both v and s. It increases in v since there is decreasing returns to investment in good governance, and it decreases in political theft s since the flow of income for a given level of good governance v declines in the level of theft, in the following referred to as $g(v, s)$.

Our simple framework can now be used to illustrate some general points. The first establishes a benchmark:

(i) A benevolent ruler diverts nothing and chooses the social optimum of good governance

Being benevolent means that the ruler cares equally much about all citizens whether they are in his group or not, implying that the weights he applies to each group equals the group's share of the population, $\mu = n$. Such a ruler would not divert any income to his own group. Diversion would have opportunity costs as the flow of income declines. Therefore to make the value of R as high as possible the incumbent must choose $s = 0$ and invest in good governance v, till $M_v = c'$. We call this the social optimum of good governance.

Using the constant elasticity both in the flow of incomes ($\beta < 1$) and in the cost of good governance ($\rho > 1$), we can, after some algebraic manipulation, write the first order condition as:

$$\beta = \rho g(v^*,0)$$

v^* is the social optimum of the good governance indicator. Since the cost share g is increasing in the level of good governance, there is a unique equilibrium level v^*. As stated, a benevolent incumbent cares equally much about the population as about his own group. Therefore he would not divert any income. Rather, he would invest in real governance reforms in a manner that benefits the entire population. We now contrast this benchmark to the case of political opportunism and favoritism.

(ii)   An opportunistic ruler uses good governance facades to divert income
A less angel-like ruler favors himself and his own group more than the rest of the population. In other words, he attaches a weight to his own group that is larger than its share of the population, $\mu > n$. He would then benefit from diversion till the marginal gain of diverting more money to his own group equals the opportunity cost of the corresponding higher theft. The marginal gain of a higher s is $[(\mu/n) - (1 - \mu/1 - n)]M$. The opportunity costs is the ruler's reduction in income, $-\gamma Ms$. Solving the first order condition, using the constant elasticity (and some patience), we obtain:

$$s = \frac{1}{1+\alpha} - \frac{\alpha}{1+\alpha}\frac{n(1-\mu)}{\mu - n}$$

This expression shows that the incumbent diverts more (i) the more he cares about his own group as expressed by a higher μ, and (ii) the less sensitive the flow of income is to diversion as measured by the elasticity α.

(iii)   A corrupt ruler may have more nominal good governance than a benevolent ruler
Opportunism implies corruption in our set-up. To show whether a corrupt ruler who diverts some of the income to his own group, invests more or less in good governance than a benevolent ruler, consider the first order condition for optimal investments in v. Using straightforward algebra, marginal gain equals the marginal cost can be expressed as:

$$\gamma(s,\mu)\beta = \rho g(v,s)$$

This expression states that the value of the relative increase in the flow of income of a one percent increase in *good* governance should equal the relative increase in its costs, modified by the cost share of governance g. While a benevolent ruler has $\gamma = 1$ and $s = 0$, an opportunistic ruler has $\gamma > 1$ and $s > 0$.

The introduction of opportunism has two opposing effects: The first captures how the value of g goes up as political fraud increases. Thus facade improvements become more costly as a share of the flow of income. The other effect captures how the incumbent's personal evaluation of income increases. The gain of more institutional window dressing increases as γ goes up for a given value of political theft.

The first effect of higher costs draws in the direction of lower investments in good institutions. The second effect of a higher value of income draws in the direction of more institutional investments. In general we cannot tell which one of the two opposing effects is strongest. The case where the second effect dominates, that is, the case where μ is sufficiently high and the share of the population n that belongs to the ruling elite is low, we have the interesting case where investment in a good governance facade is higher when the ruler is corrupt than when he is benevolent.

It is unequal power that yields both high political fraud and a high level of investments in facade institutions. If political theft was not possible, the fact that μ is high and n low would not have had the same positive effect on investments in v. In that sense the high investment in good governance is corruption-induced in this scenario.

(iv) Citizens under corrupt leaders may be exposed to 'double punishment'

Do the facades investments benefit the great majority? In other words, will the income obtained by the majority $(1 - s)M$ increase with the social forces that lead to higher investments in v? Political theft and good governance are both results of inequality in the distribution of power, reflected in $\mu > n$. Does more political bias (a higher μ) benefit the great majority as well when we account for a higher income – despite the higher level of fraud that it also induces?

A benevolent ruler choose the level of good governance that maximizes $M - c$, while for instance a corrupt ruler who puts all the weight on his own group $\mu = 1$, chooses the level of good governance that maximizes $(s/n)M - c$. The corrupt ruler would divert $s = 1/(1 + \alpha)$, while the benevolent ruler would divert nothing $s = 0$. In this case the investment in good governance would be highest with a benevolent ruler, and obviously, the level of diversion is highest with the corrupt ruler. Political fraud implies a 'double punishment' of the great majority of citizens—who get a smaller share of a smaller pie.

So far, the main insight from our exercise is that the *de jure* good governance and political theft sM may be complements. An incumbent who favors his own group may have both a high diversion and a high investment in facade institutions (introduced to hide the high level of diversion)—and, it is the same political biases that lead to a high level of diversion that also stimulate a high level of facade investments. In most instances the great majority of the population is the clear loser as *de jure* institutional change may go hand in hand with *de facto* abuse of power.

2.2 The Theory's Assumptions

This theory is based on overly simplified assumptions of how good and bad governance determines the flow of income—as if stakeholders believe in every governance improvement. The dependence of M on good governance v and bad governance s, however, does not require that stakeholders are naive. When governments invest more in a facade, stakeholders do not necessarily take the investment by its face value. Rather, changes in good governance indicators may just make them less convinced that governance was as bad as they thought. Facade investments may modify negative beliefs without changing them completely, and this is sufficient for the results to hold.

The incumbent's ability to coordinate all political theft is exaggerated in this theory. If we instead let political theft be more decentralized and uncoordinated, but otherwise continue to assume that (i) the ruling elite basically benefits from diversion, and that (ii) political power is unequal as above ($\mu > n$), the same conclusions hold. The more the elite is able to divert at the local level, the more willing the elite is to invest in good governance institutions to attract a higher flow of income to grab from.

Moreover, the theory is based on three further exaggerations. Firstly, we exaggerate the inability of the good governance reforms to constrain the level of political fraud. If good governance actually puts constraints on political theft, and all else were the same, the incumbent would under-invest in such arrangements. He would, however, search for less restrictive reforms that might have a similar flavor for outsiders and that might attract almost the same flow of income.

Secondly, we exaggerate the level of autocracy in the simple model. A more realistic approach would posit imperfect competition between potential autocrats. This could be captured by a less unequal division of power, narrowing $\mu - n$.

Thirdly, we exaggerate the simple trade-off. Even if the model is crude, it sheds light on basic mechanisms, relevant for development support more generally. For instance, should the development community punish political fraud or reward good governance reforms? What will most efficiently promote development? If the elasticities α and β capture the concern about political fraud relative to good governance reform, we may wonder which one of them should be raised to promote development? A high level of α means that the international income flows may decline dramatically once the fraud is made known. A high level of β, by contrast, would raise the international flow of income once good governance reforms are initiated—whether the benefits of institutional reforms are stolen by the political leaders or not.

In the simplest version of our exercise only α has a direct effect on the share of political theft; a high level of α reduces the share accruing the ruling elite. A high level of β would, all else being the same, lead to a higher level of good governance reforms. The share $s\beta$ goes to the ruling elite for every one percent increase in the good governance indicator. If the goal of the international community is to raise the share of income to the great majority $(1 - s)M$, it seems that assuring a high α is more appropriate than seeking a high β. If this is true, it seems more important to crack down on political fraud rather than rewarding good governance. More generally, this implies that development partners should rather put more weight on performance targets than on procedures that control government spending.

Finally, the model is consistent with the claim that democratization with comprehensive political competition is required to achieve real governance reforms. In our analytic framework, such comprehensive reforms would be reflected in a smaller difference between influence weights μ and population shares n, thus bringing political decisions closer to what would be the social optimum of good governance.

3. POLICY AREAS EXPOSED

The fraud-facade trade-off for a government is a concern in countries all over the globe. A study on Kenya refers to the mechanism as *straddling*. According to Bigsten and Moene (1996), the government had a financial need to meet donors' demand for democracy and good governance, while at the same time, it sought to broaden its political support by rewarding followers with jobs, licenses, and contracts—regardless of their qualifications. In a setting with limited political competition, members of the government could 'use their political positions as a base for private economic activities'. Political and bureaucratic insiders profited personally from their authority when they invested (as individuals) in the private sector (Bigsten and Moene 1996: 182 and 191). This Kenya case study describes why *straddling*—in terms of hiding rent extraction behind an institutional facade that promised growth and development—was considered necessary for the government to keep its political authority and to sustain the country's inflow of aid money.

It is generally difficult, however, to determine whether corruption behind a facade is intended at the planning stage of a law or institution, or an unintended result of opportunities that arise because of weak control systems. The effect of laws and institutions in terms of distracting awareness of corruption, as spelled out in the theory above, is nonetheless the same.

We now point at some areas where facade institutions may be particularly pronounced. The risk of political corruption is higher in sectors with large investments, wide discretion, and where there is a justified need for significant government intervention—for example to secure essential public services at low cost. As the listed examples illustrate, facade institutions introduced to reduce the suspicion of corruption may include a range of integrity mechanisms and explicit anti-corruption initiatives.

3.1   Infrastructure Provision

Infrastructure services are usually subject to more government intervention than other sectors because they are essential services, typically dependent on state investment and subsidies, while their natural monopoly features imply government regulation of service delivery. Estache (2008) summarizes development partners' support of utility sectors over several decades and finds infrastructure performance in developing countries to be generally far below the performance expected by the development partners.

Estimates of the impact of reforms may have been optimistic. Nevertheless, it is a huge gap between the actual achievements and the feasible achievements with many years of loans, aids and development advice. The gap is difficult to explain without reference to some governance failure.[6] Being aware of this risk, donors have asked for a number of institutional reforms, including independent utility regulation, privatization, the use of independent procurement agents and more detailed audits. The initiatives make it easier to transfer funds to governments, but none of the steps offer any guarantee against corruption.

Argentina is a case in point. According to Natalia Volosin, a corruption expert on the Latin American region, the Argentine government allocated

---

[6] Benitez, Estache, Søreide (2012) explain why governance failure in this sector is the result not only of corruption, but also populism, patronage and protectionist priorities, and suggest indicators that may help distinguish between these different dysfunctions.

'an unimaginably huge amount of subsidies to privatized utilities for the past 11 years with the purpose of supporting internal demand and maintaining jobs. These subsidies include the energy sector, gas, and others, whose rates were frozen in 2002. The worst sector in this context was transport, where subsidies were given to companies (trains, buses, etc.) with absolutely no control under the leadership of former Ministries of Transport Ricardo Jaime and his successor Juan Pablo Schiavi, who both are under several investigations, not only for corruption.'[7]

The corruption in these cases grew up behind the political aim of industrial support and job creation. Despite the potentially corrupt ministers' high position, they needed an institutional cover for their corrupt transfers. External controls were not targeted on performance that deteriorated as the result of the fraud. As a facade strategy in Latin American infrastructure sectors, Natalia Volosin also points at privatization. It is constantly defended as a development strategy, while its effects depend on implementation. In Argentina, privatization was first defended by President Menem to benefit the poor, while those involved in the process drew huge benefits. After the change of incumbent (from Menem to Kirchner), several entities were re-nationalized, now with 'allies or even partners to government officials and high-rank politicians' securing profitable positions.

Corruption-driven infrastructure provision is not only a developing country problem.[8] Spain, for example, has a political inclination to over-invest in transport infrastructure, according to Bel et al. (2014). Like other OECD members, the Spanish government applies strict procurement rules and public investments have to be defended with references to society's needs, demands and opportunity costs. Nonetheless, Spain has spent far more revenues on infrastructure than most European countries. At first glance their transport networks look impressive, but digging deeper behind the figures, the networks rank worse when it comes to cost-efficiency, quality and the match between users' needs and service delivery. Ghost projects like huge airports that are built, but never put into use, are other examples. Subsidy rates to the sector are among the highest in Europe. Despite the general perception that political parties are among the most corrupt institutions in Spain, the rules and procedures for infrastructure regulation and investment make it difficult to hold government representatives legally responsible. Some incidents of obvious corruption

---

[7] Personal interview, July 2014. Natalia Volosin is Senior Researcher at Centro de Investigaciones sobre Desarrollo Econmico de America del Sur at the Universidad Nacional de San Martin, Argentina.

[8] Estache (2011) provides a collection of chapters explaining challenges in utility regulation and investment across Europe.

have been revealed, but according to Bel et al. (2014) most of the corruption takes subtle forms hidden in various legitimate reasons for a close relationship between owners of infrastructure construction companies and Spain's political elite. The combination of formal procedures and discretion enables the political elite to benefit personally from decisions they make as politicians with sector oversight responsibility.

3.2 Development Programs

Social development programs are sometimes used as a facade for corruption. Politicians gain popular support for their noble ambitions while, in reality, few transfers are made to benefit the poor in these cases. Our Argentinean contact, Natalia Volosin, illustrates the point with the scandal of Sueños Compartidos, a program destined to construct social houses for the poor, which, through the engagement of an intermediary with high moral credentials—the organization called Mothers of Plaza de Mayo—avoided the usual procurement controls. It ended up with houses of poor quality, while several staff members from the Fundación were indicted. The housing benefits to the poor were offered 'at glacier speed' according to one media source. President Kirchner secured large public transfers into this housing program, and has in return, benefited from the organization's pronounced support in various political combats.

Another example is reported by the media in Zambia. The Citizens Economic Empowerment Fund Commission was supposed to provide investment support for innovative business projects proposed by citizens in need of start-up capital. In reality it appeared to be a scam to benefit politicians at the expense of the eligible citizens. It gave government officials an opportunity to benefit personally from public funds and make transfers to their patrons. All decisions passed through evaluation formalities and appeared legitimate.[9] Zambia is one of the most aid-dependent countries in Sub-Saharan Africa, and the government operates in close dialogue with development partners. Apparently, without institutional facades it would not be possible to allocate parts of loans and aid transfers to clients of the ruler.

A similar but more sophisticated example is reported in the pharmacy sector in Colombia, as described by Hussmann and Rivillas (2014). A public health insurance fund was set up as an independently managed fiduciary under the Ministry of Health with the purpose of subsidizing

---

[9] The Director was arrested in February 2013. The case is covered by Zambian media sources; see among others the *Times of Zambia* on 23 January 2013.

medicines for the poor. The whole scheme would be subject to scientific as well as financial scrutiny. At first sight, the system's targets and formal procedures appeared corruption-proof.

In practice, however, the fund was subject to grand corruption. Ministry representatives executed the fraud in terms of reimbursement at prices far above the market prices of medicines. They also allowed collusion between health companies and made transfers to health care institutions that did not exist. Hussmann and Rivillas (2014) list a number of warning signals which were not acted on by the investigators. In the end the fraud was simply too excessive to be ignored. The scandal was eventually revealed, apparently because the ministry representatives had too much appetite for illegal rents—leading to suspiciously high drug prices and too low benefits to the poor. The corruption could not have gone that far without the facade which kept investigators at a distance, while attention was directed towards procedures while ideas where emphasized. A sharper focus on results from day one would have limited the opportunity to hide the corruption behind the facade of a development program.

3.3 Anti-corruption Agencies

The most obvious integrity facade for covering up political corruption is perhaps the anti-corruption agencies (ACAs). Recanatini (2011) presents a comprehensive study of how anti-corruption agencies worldwide perform, and what constitutional aspects secure their independence. They are often politically celebrated when established, but curtailed once they use their authority against members of the incumbent's political party. She also finds that 'the legislative set-up for the agencies is critical but cannot alone guarantee independence since ACAs cannot be fully insulated from political interference'.

A study of anti-corruption agencies in Central Europe confirms this impression: 'the impetus for setting up ACAs has strong implications for how viable these organizations will be'—and 'the desire to please an external actor (international organization) or to flaunt anticorruption credentials to voters could well result in nothing more than a symbolic action' (Batory 2012: 649).

Challenges of this sort were confirmed in interviews for this book chapter. Khusraw Parwez, a Governance Advisor at the German Cooperation Organization in Afghanistan, explains how the government decided to curtail the High Officer of Oversight and Anti-corruption when it reacted against the Attorney General's Office for its tolerance of grand corruption. As a result, the parliament suspended (with only four votes against) the High Officer of Oversight and Anti-Corruption by claiming that this institution was 'not efficient given the budget it spends every year'.

In order to keep an integrity facade, it seems, the government submitted a new law to the parliament for its approval; the Anti-Money Laundering and Terrorism Financing Law. Interpreting the proceedings, Parwez comments that the parliament of Afghanistan consists of many warlords, gunmen and mafia leaders. Through suspending the High Officer of Oversight and Anti-corruption and at the same time approving the anti-money laundering law, the strongmen managed to divert anti-corruption efforts and limit the ability of prosecutors to track their own illicit funds.[10]

Over the last decade billions of US dollars have been transferred to Afghanistan from the allied forces, especially the United States. This collaboration has been challenged in many ways—including by a USD 920 million fraud case involving government representatives and the Kabul Bank.[11] Continued financial support is now subject to more scrutiny than before. If corrupt intentions are constant among the Afghan political elite, more institutional facades are needed if they seek to maintain prior levels of illegal revenues.

In Zambia the government in 2009 curtailed the anti-corruption commission's work by removing 'the abuse of office clause', a section of a law that empowered the commission to investigate any government official with wealth disproportionate to their official emoluments.[12] The government found the clause unconstitutional and a drawback to personal development of public officers as the law presumed whoever amassed some wealth guilty of abuse of office.[13] Despite the public outcry, the government (then led by a vice president who was at the same time minister of justice), went on and removed the mentioned section of the law. The government claimed that another regulation compensated for the amendment.[14] Nonetheless, this legal modification permitted top government officials to engage in corruption at a lower risk. After a change of government, the abuse of office clause was reinstated to produce the Anti-Corruption Act no.3 of 2012. The former regime's corruption has been investigated and the then president, Rupiah Banda, is being prosecuted for abuse of office.[15]

---

[10] Personal dialogue July, 2014.
[11] The case is summarized by Strand (2014).
[12] Section 37 of Anti-Corruption Commission Act no.42 of 1996.
[13] http://www.lusakatimes.com/2010/11/09/section-37-unconstitutional-insists-mvunga/ (last accessed 5 May 2015).
[14] Specifically, a section in the Zambia Police Penal Code Act.
[15] These details are all debated in Zambian online media sources; see for instance articles by Zambian newspapers *The Post* and *Lusaka Times*.

The examples in this section refer to cases where the corruption was eventually revealed. We do not know how often legal reform is initiated or institutions established with the purpose of covering up corruption and projecting an image of public accountability. What we know is that there are many cases where such schemes have made it possible for officials to secure more illegal revenues than would have been possible to grab without the pro-development facade.

4. THREE CASE COUNTRIES

Our facade argument applies not only to particular areas of governance such as infrastructure, development aid and anti-corruption agencies. It is also relevant for understanding the governance of countries more generally. The facade-theory does not explain all their development challenges, but does help to explain why some reforms have failed. The more gullible the stakeholders, the more likely are reforms to fail because of corruption. To illustrate our point, we consider the cases of Indonesia, Colombia and Angola. Government corruption is serious in each of them, but their facades differ.

4.1 Indonesia

Can we expect the World Bank-denoted *priority reforms* to improve financial stability in Indonesia, or will it offer opportunities for facade strategies? More than ten years of reform effort have not produced the needed results. Instead there are numerous examples of fraud in the state administration, demonstrating that behind the country's image of prosperous development and financial modernization, public fraud goes on at high political levels. The reforms and the many institutions and laws to improve governance, seem ineffective at best. Indonesia has severe weaknesses in politics, finance, public procurement, courts and security hidden behind its image of a modern democratic state. The country is still dependent on development aid and lending. The civil society and the press are aware of the country's deep-seated governance challenges, and therefore, those who seek corrupt revenues need to hide their illegal transactions behind some kind of facade, typically a cosmetic reform that is too good to be true.

Nevertheless the World Bank country website insists that Indonesia is 'one of Asia Pacific's most vibrant democracies that has maintained political stability and emerged as a confident middle-income country'. The country has developed a formal modern state with a system of educated civil servants without extravagant salaries, and a well-organized administration on the best principles of procurement legislation—it is claimed.

Accordingly the World Bank has granted Indonesia a USD 500 million loan for the promotion of financial reforms.[16] Loans for similar purposes have been granted several times since 2004, including one for USD 300 million in 2012. According to business analysts, there is now more financial stability in Indonesia, but progress on important reforms in the sector has been slow. *Strategic Review* emphasizes how 'weaknesses exist that have the potential to destabilize the sector and damage the real economy. Specifically, diversification of the financial sector is low. The financial sector is still highly concentrated, with the banking sector dominating. Within the banking system, the top three state-owned commercial banks account for one-third of all banking sector assets and deposits, while the top 15 banks account for about 70 percent.' Apparently, these distortions and their associated ownership concentration have not been dealt with—despite a decade of collaboration on financial sector reform. The reason seems related to the finding that 'the Indonesian banking sector may be one of the most profitable in the Asian region'[17] for those who control this industry and the grants for reforms. Most likely, a genuine financial reform would threaten their interests.

The financial problems must be understood in light of the 31-year-long rule of Suharto (Aspinall and Van Klinken 2010). President Suharto offered low wages to state officials while allowing them access to extra funds by an informal 'franchise system' of allocating power, a system which secured him authority while it damaged state administrative integrity. The corruption implied *de facto* informal taxes on individuals and firms, making public sector careers 'far more attractive than what formal remuneration levels would suggest' (McLeod 2010: 45).

The resulting demand for lucrative civil servant positions generated an auction system for such jobs and extra authority for local and central leaders, while the low formal wage at the same time served to 'discourage the entry of highly principled individuals' (McLeod 2010: 47). At the end of the Suharto era in 1998, public officials and the ordinary citizenry alike saw nothing wrong in making extra illegal payments for public

---

[16]   http://www.worldbank.org/en/news/press-release/2014/07/01/indonesia-recei ves-500-million-world-bank-support-financial-sector-reform-policies (last accessed 5 May 2015).

[17]   *Strategic Review* on 14 March 2013, article written by P.S. Srinivas, a World Bank economist. Made available by *Stratfor*: http://www.stratfor.com/the-hub/ind onesia%E2%80%99s-financial-sector-half-full-glass#axzz3C2wHkgSa (last accessed 5 May 2015).

services. Corruption is still a cross-cutting challenge—'wherever one goes in Indonesia, state officials are especially likely to be involved in criminal activities that involve a high degree of organization, such as extortion and protection rackets, smuggling, illegal logging and the narcotics trade, while law enforcement officers enjoy murky relations' (Aspinall and Van Klinken 2010: 3–4). The problem is especially difficult to combat since one of the sectors most exposed to corruption is law enforcement and the courts (Butt and Lindsay 2010).[18]

Moreover, what Dick and Mulholland (2010) call 'slush funds in current Indonesian politics' are essential for understanding the challenges. The slush funds are 'off-budget, non-accountable and discretionary revenues' for the political elite, extracted from public procurement contracts, the allocation of permits and licenses, funds siphoned informally from budgetary and project revenues, and gift loans from state banks (non-or part-repayable loans). In addition, they describe how political positions are still 'allocated by internal auction, moderated by patronage and influence' (Dick and Mulholland 2010: 76). The funds are financially supported by business firms including state enterprises pressured for payments in return for political favors. Access to illegal rents has created public sector surplus labor and has permitted Indonesia to sustain a government apparatus that is much larger than that which could be supported out of legitimate forms of revenue (Cribb 2010: 43).

The existence and purpose of slush funds suggest that corruption after the Suharto reign is as pervasive as it was under his regime. One difference today, however, is the 'need for concealment' and how that can be achieved via 'a series of intermediate transactions between the principals' (Dick and Mulholland 2010). Considering the case of Indonesia, we find several examples of how promises to development partners of new reforms and institutions may have fostered corruption instead of corruption control.[19]

---

[18]   Corruption in courts has been a problem at all levels of the judiciary. In June 2014 the Chief Justice of Indonesia's Constitutional Court, Akil Mochtar, was found guilty in accepting bribes in exchange for favorable rulings in regional election disputes.

[19]   In this respect, the mentioned case of the World Bank USD 500 million loan, for example, would be 'safer' if the benefits were to some extent contingent on the owners of the country's profitable banks giving up their shares—which seems to be a critical aspect of true reform.

4.2 Colombia

Recently Colombia has developed behind a policy of *democratic security*.[20] Whether this policy is a facade or not is perhaps a question for debate. The strategy has helped in launching peace negotiations between the government and the FARC guerillas, and in that sense, it has real content. Nonetheless, thus far the strategy has been more successful in attracting foreign investments to certain areas of the country than to improve the life of the entire population.

It started when Alvaro Uribe was elected president in 2002, introducing a democratic security tax, followed by a military offensive that removed the Revolutionary Armed Forces of Colombia (FARC) from half of the municipalities where it was present. The policy might have impressed outsiders. Columbia is no longer considered a failed state; foreign investments have risen from $1.5 billion to $13 billion; investment has grown from 17 to 27 percent of GDP. All this is 'a response to enhanced security and greater optimism about the future', according to Robinson (2013).

Besides, Colombia has experienced steady economic growth over the last decade. Its government institutions, constitution and legal system are commended for their qualities, and the country is ranked well on several indices, such as the Open Budget Index and the Index of Economic Freedom. The government appears receptive to international collaboration on several forms of cross-border crime, and when it comes to anti-corruption and money laundering its legislation is among the most advanced in the world.

Yet, behind the facade serious problems continue as before. The country is still among the most violent in the world and also the main supplier of cocaine to US markets. Colombia has now experienced 'half a century of intense armed conflict with insurgent and paramilitary groups perpetuated by their involvement in widespread illegal drug production and trafficking, along with criminal and narcotics trafficking organizations' (the US Department of State website). The financial support from the United States, totaling USD 1.600 million in the period 2010–2015, includes, primarily, support to counter-narcotics programs and to support the military.

However, the trade in narcotics and the operations of paramilitary groups also fuel political corruption, and any financial support to counter

---

[20] The term refers to a specific Colombian security policy presented by President Uribe, launched in 2003 (see for instance BBC, 30 June 2003: 'Colombia unveils security plan'), available 5 May 2015 at http://news.bbc.co.uk/1/hi/world/americas/3030768.stm.

the illegal activities bears the risk of being misused and stolen. Political corruption is not only a decentralized problem, but extends to levels high up in the government and the military system. At the same time, civil servants, soldiers and politicians seem protected from prosecution and sanctions, almost regardless of what offences they have committed.

The widespread corruption is often 'excused' by the difficulty of controlling the guerilla and the paramilitary groups profiting from the narcotics trade. The high degree of informality implies that many citizens pay bribes without even being aware of their own involvement in corruption (Mehling and Boehm 2014). US AID explains: 'In reality, there are two Colombias: a dynamic and sophisticated Colombia in a half-dozen urban centers, such as Bogota and Medellin, which coexists with a poor, conflictive and neglected rural Colombia.'[21] The level of informality and corruption is so high that there is no need to launder criminal revenues abroad. Despite the country's superb anti-money laundering legislation, there is 'no reason to take illegal capital abroad to protect it' (Thoumi and Anzola 2012: 165).

The military insecurity seems to create financial security for illegal revenues: 'the power of the paramilitary, guerrillas, and drug trafficking organizations' and 'culturally accepted informal laws' have 'shaped an extralegal economy that is immune to traditional mechanisms for combating illegal economic activities' (Thoumi and Anzola 2012: 147). Citizens often prefer to reinvest illegal revenues locally so that they can secure not only an economic return, but also political influence.

One may suspect that 'the dynamic and sophisticated Colombia' draws advantages from the existence of 'a poor, conflictive and neglected rural Colombia'. The inequality is huge. The rich rural elites are inclined to condone human rights violations, corruption and poverty—or as Robinson (2013: 45) suggests, the 'conflicts in rural areas guarantee that the periphery is not able to cooperate against the center ... the center foments chaos in the periphery in order to divide and rule'—an economic and political situation in constant need of a nicer facade.

4.3 Angola

Being one of Sub-Sahara's largest and fastest growing economies, Angola attempts to build the facade of a *successful petroleum exporter*. The incumbent MPLA government brags about its democratic rule that has

---

[21] Citation from the US Aid website on Colombia: http://www.usaid.gov/colombia/our-work (last accessed 5 May 2015).

secured political stability for more than a decade; its development friendly priorities, poverty reduction programs, and an impressive reconstruction program that started in 2002 after 27 years of civil war. Through efficient petroleum sector regulation, the government has secured stable state revenues. A public procurement reform, planned construction of houses for the poor, and more transparency into state finances are among its recent good governance goals.

Are they signs of real progress or a cosmetic facade that enables members of government to continue its fraud? Regardless of the organization of elections, political power in Angola is concentrated primarily in the president himself. He is Head of State, Commander of all armed forces, the Main Adviser on all aspects of governance, and he holds the power to dismiss the Prime Minister, the cabinet and provincial governors. Besides, all government expenses above a rather limited amount must be approved by the President himself. His power is bolstered by a patronage system consisting of threats and corrupt benefits for politicians and high-ranking civil servants. The government controls most information circulating throughout the country, according to Roque (2009: 137). And, when it comes to elections, she explains how they have 'served as a vehicle for the MPLA to transform Angola into a de facto one-party state while at the same time, gaining long-elusive national and international legitimacy'.

The President not only controls state institutions, expenses and political recruitment; his family owns and controls large parts of the private sector and benefits grossly from (often inflated) government contracts. The international press reports on the unbelievable wealth of the President's family—his daughter being one of the world's richest individuals, it is said. All this is consistent with Global Financial Integrity pointing at huge transfers out of the country to tax havens abroad, while Transparency International points at systemic corruption in the country.

The higher growth has not reduced the country's severe development problems. Angola is one of the countries with the highest levels of inequality in the world. Life expectancy is among the lowest. The child mortality rate is among the highest, and so is the illiteracy rate. Modernization is slow. Only 40 percent of the population has access to electricity. With the help of its security and intelligence services, the government has neutralized most forms of serious opposition. Independent civil society and the press are strictly restrained, while the often-lauded democracy is a complete scam.

With absolute control, one may wonder why the government needs a facade. Petroleum is exported and sold however the country is governed, and given the revenues from its sale, the government does not need tax revenues from the citizens. So, why give anything in return? Why conceal the fraud?

Apparently, even a corrupt dictator with solid revenues from extractive industries may benefit from the image of a well-functioning society. A facade of good institutions reduces the risk of riots, a concern during the North Africa uprisings in 2011. There are limits to how far the loyalty of civil servants can be secured by threats and fear. The facade can improve domestic relations as well as international relations. The image of the government as 'not so bad after all' facilitates international collaboration more generally. The development community, including the IMF, the World Bank, the United Nations, and powerful governments, is concerned about government legitimacy and the supply of essential services to the citizens. Even if development experts understand the realities on the ground, these organizations have a political interest in maintaining a good dialogue and collaboration with the Angolan government—by offering development loans and aid.

In addition there is an efficiency argument for facades. As Coolidge and Rose-Ackerman (1997) explain, a corrupt regime may well seek productive efficiency except where inefficiency creates extra rents. Institutional reform may therefore be intentional in some areas, while decentralized corruption is generally facilitated with an excessive amount of state intervention in other markets. Moreover, the clearest reason why powerful incumbents conceal their fraud is perhaps the need for foreign direct investment. For firms concerned about corporate social responsibility, often constrained at home by anti-bribery legislation, the facade makes their presence in Angola much easier to bear and defend, and that again strengthens their business opportunities.

In short, a facade of good institutions and governance is useful to be able to claim that the government does what it can to promote development, while the personal wealth of its members and military leaders accumulates.

5. CONCLUSION

It is a current development paradigm that good institutions can help to cure bad governance performance. Poor countries are poor because they have bad institutions, and countries that grow, or are rich, are those that have improved their institutional quality. It is 'the combination of transparent and accountable institutions, strong skills and competence, and a fundamental willingness to do the right thing', said former President Wolfowitz of the World Bank, emphasizing how such good institutions can 'balance the power of governments, and hold them accountable for delivering better services, creating jobs, and improving living standards'.

He did not, however, pay attention to the other possibility where a claim to a 'fundamental willingness to do the right thing' blinds observers—and makes them ignore how supposed institutional improvements help the rich to benefit at the cost of the poor. Too much attention directed at institutions and policies, rather than on outcomes and performance, has made it possible for governments to be treated as legitimate despite their failures in securing development for society at large.

As long as governments act as if there is a certain degree of law and order (regardless of whether court decisions are steered by those in power), hold elections (regardless of how much the result is manipulated), and hold speeches about the ambition of providing essential services to a poor population (regardless of what services are indeed provided), they can govern without much risk of actually being held accountable for their fraud—and in fact, attract higher revenues regardless of how they actually perform.

Politicians with a grabbing hand favor reforms that are evaluated by procedures not by its results. The emphasis on fashionable procedures may increase the flow of income to grab; the lack of control of end results makes it politically sustainable.

REFERENCES

Aspinall, E. and G. van Klinken (eds). 2010. *The State and Illegality in Indonesia*. Leiden: KITLV Press.

Baland, J. M., K.O. Moene and J.A. Robinson. 2010. 'Governance and Development', *Handbook of Development Economics*, 5, 4597–656.

Batory, A. 2012. 'Political Cycles and Organizational Life Cycles: Delegation to Anticorruption Agencies in Central Europe', *Governance: An International Journal of Policy Administration and Institutions*, 25(4): 639–60.

Bel, G., A. Estache and R. Foucart. 2014. 'Transport Infrastructure Failures in Spain: Mismanagement and Incompetence, or Political Capture?' in T. Søreide and A. Williams (eds), *Corruption, Grabbing and Development: Real World Challenges*. Cheltenham, UK, and Northampton, MA, USA: Edward Elgar.

Benitez, D., A. Estache, and T. Søreide. 2012. 'Infrastructure Policy and Governance Failures', CMI Working Paper. Bergen: Chr. Michelsen Institute (CMI).

Bigsten, A. and K.O. Moene. 1996. 'Growth and Rent Dissipation: The Case of Kenya', *Journal of African Economies*, 5(2): 177–98.

Bjorvatn, K., and T. Søreide. 2005. 'Corruption and Privatization'. *European Journal of Political Economy*, 21: 903–14.

Black, B., R. Kraakman, and A. Tarassova. 2000. 'Russian Privatization and Corporate Governance: What Went Wrong?' *Stanford Law Review*, 52: 1731–808.

Butt, S. and T. Lindsey. 2010. 'Judicial Mafia: The Courts and State Illegality in Indonesia', in E. Aspinall and G. van Klinken (eds). *The State and Illegality in Indonesia*. Leiden: KITLV Press.

Coolidge, J. and S. Rose-Ackerman. 1997. 'High-level Rent-seeking and Corruption in African Regimes: Theory and Cases', World Bank Policy Research Paper No. 1780. Washington DC: The World Bank.

Cribb, R. 2010. 'A System of Exemptions: Historicising State Illegality in Indonesia', in E. Aspinall and G. van Klinken (eds). *The State and Illegality in Indonesia*. Leiden: KITLV Press.

Davies, K. 2004. 'What Can the Rule of Law Variable Tell Us about Rule of Law Reforms?' *Michigan Journal of International Law*, 26: 141–61.

Davies, K. and M.J. Trebilcock. 2001. 'Legal Reforms and Development', *Third World Quarterly*, 22(1): 21–36.

Dick, H. and J. Mulholland. 2010. 'The State as a Marketplace: Slush Funds and Intra-elite Rivalry', in E. Aspinall and G. van Klinken (eds). *The State and Illegality in Indonesia*. Leiden: KITLV Press.

Estache, A. 2008. 'Infrastructure and Development: A Survey of Recent and Upcoming Issues', *Rethinking Infrastructure for Development*, 2(47).

Estache, A. (ed.). 2011. *Emerging Issues in Competition, Collusion and Regulation of Network Industries*. London: Centre for Economic Policy Research (CEPR).

Hussman, J. C., and K. Rivillas. 2014. 'Financial Blood-letting in the Colombian Health System: Analysis of the Systemic Rent-seeking in the Use of a Health Insurance Fund', in T. Søreide and A. Williams (eds), *Corruption, Grabbing and Development: Real World Challenges*. Cheltenham, UK, and Northampton, MA, USA: Edward Elgar.

Manzetti, L. 1999. *Privatization South American Style*. New York: Oxford University Press.

McLeod, R. 2010. 'Institutionalized Public Sector Corruption: A Legacy of the Suharto Franchise', in E. Aspinall and G. van Klinken (eds), *The State and Illegality in Indonesia*. Leiden: KITLV Press.

Mehling, M.L. and F. Boehm. 2014. 'Corruption and Informality: Complements or Substitutes? Qualitative Evidence from Barranquilla, Colombia', Working Paper 54817. Munich Personal RePec Archive.

Recanatini, F. 2011. 'Anticorruption Authorities: An Effective Tool to Curb Corruption?' in S. Rose-Ackerman and T. Søreide (eds), *International Handbook on the Economics of Corruption*, vol. 2. Cheltenham, UK, and Northampton, MA, USA: Edward Elgar.

Roberts, A.S. 2010. *The Logic of Discipline. Global Capitalism and the Architecture of Government*. Oxford: Oxford University Press.

Robinson, J.A. 2013. 'Colombia: Another 100 Years of Solitude', *Current History*, 112(751): 43–8.

Roque, P.C. 2009. 'Angola's Facade Democracy', *Journal of Democracy*, 20(4): 137–50.

Strand, A. 2014. 'Elite Capture of Kabul Bank', in T. Søreide and A. Williams (eds), *Corruption, Grabbing and Development: Real World Challenges*. Cheltenham, UK, and Northampton, MA, USA: Edward Elgar.

Tamanaha, B.Z. 2011. 'The Primacy of Society and the Failures of Law and Development', *Cornell International Law Journal*, 44: 209–47.

Thoumi, F.E., and M. Anzola. 2012. 'Illicit Capital Flows and Money Laundering in Colombia', in P. Reuter (ed.), *Draining Development: Controlling Flows of Illicit Funds from Developing Countries*. Washington DC: The World Bank. 145–70.

3. Political connections and commerce—a global perspective

Raymond Fisman

What are connections worth? Conventional wisdom, amply backed by shocking anecdotes in just about any country one might consider, is that businesses profit from all manner of political ties. There are, of course, numerous means of influence that companies have at their disposal: they lobby politicians, make campaign contributions, appoint former (or current) politicians to their boards or executive teams, place former executives in influential government posts, and pay bribes to have things their way.

How much is this conventional wisdom backed up by evidence, and to what extent does it reflect misconceptions borne of high-profile examples rather than broader realities? Indeed, the very existence of public enforcement actions that create the perception of corruption could indicate a judicial system that is generally in good health: In Israel, for example, at the time of writing a former prime minister and former president were serving prison sentences for accepting bribes. Does that mean the Israeli economy is corrupt, or is it a case of a system that is effective at catching and punishing the few renegades in politics? Global comparisons are further complicated by the fact that many channels of influence are perfectly legal, and the latitude in exercising them differs vastly across countries. A common response to the notion that corruption is a 'Third World problem' is that developed economies have merely legalized the channels of influence through campaign finance and lobbying. To what extent are there substantive differences in the role of political ties in business across countries, and to what degree are similar mechanisms simply given different names and legal status?

In this chapter, I will discuss some of the evidence on the role that political ties play in commerce. By examining how the value of connections varies across countries, levels of government, and type of industry, I aim to provide some insights on the different roles that political ties play around the world. In the latter part of my discussion, I will consider the social consequences of businesses exploiting their connections to government officials and ask what steps may be useful in limiting such influence.

I wish to be clear upfront on the modest scope and goals of this chapter. It is not meant to be a comprehensive survey of the vast body of work on the role of political connections in the global economy. Nor will I aim to provide a thorough discussion of questions such as how to define connections—that task has been taken up elsewhere. Rather, I will selectively survey the empirical contributions to this literature to give the reader with a sense of what research can tell us about the role of political connections in global commerce. I will also highlight areas where I believe that future research would be particularly helpful or productive. Finally, this survey will also be shamelessly self-referential in places, using my own work as illustrative evidence.

I first describe the methodological challenges confronting researchers in providing rigorous evidence relating political ties to firm-level (and social) outcomes. Most of this chapter then describes the benefits that private firms derive from political ties and how these benefits vary across circumstance. I then summarize the evidence from complementary avenues of research: First, how have politicians on the receiving end of business-politics ties benefited? And second, what are the wider social consequences of allowing firms to exploit political ties for private benefits?

1. MEASURING THE VALUE OF POLITICAL CONNECTIONS

A naïve approach to assessing the value of political ties would examine whether firms with connections—somehow defined—outperform unconnected firms financially. There are, however, obvious biases in either direction, depending on one's beliefs about the unobserved attributes that are correlated with political ties. The 'efficient nepotism' perspective, for example, would suggest that the raw correlation between political connections and profitability overestimates the value from connections: Under this view, a president's progeny, for example, would have the abilities—whether derived from genetic endowment or human capital development—to run a business effectively.

The difficulty in making an assessment of this bias is challenging even on a case-by-case basis. The son of Indonesia's President Suharto, for example, led a playboy's life, and his business decisions seemed more driven by personal taste than any concern for income. He purchased a controlling stake in Lamborghini in 1994 and soon chased away top executives, accompanied by complaints of his controlling and incompetent management style. His stake was, nonetheless, sold at a handsome profit only a few years later, even amidst the distressed conditions of the Asian financial crisis.

For these reasons, researchers have generally focused on shocks to the political environment, which leave a company's management team intact and ownership unchanged—hence holding constant the competence of the company's leadership—while altering the strength of their political linkages. The most common economic approach to estimating the value of connections has been to look at stock market reactions to unexpected political news. Presuming that the news differentially affects (previously) well-connected firms relative to less-connected ones, this analysis provides a market-based estimate of how investors value connections.

To illustrate the merits and complications associated with this approach, consider the following pair of examples. In one early event study, Fisman (2001) looks at how fears and rumors about the health of Indonesia's long-time dictator, President Suharto affected companies traded on the Jakarta Stock Exchange. The triggering event was news that he would travel to Germany for a health check-up. As a measure of connections, this paper utilizes a 'Suharto Dependency Index' developed for investors by a local consulting company, the Castle Group. Bimantara Citra, a company where Suharto's son Bambang held a sizable equity stake, received a rating of 5 (most dependent), while listed companies controlled by the Bakrie Brothers, who were better known for their management acumen and engineering expertise, received a rating of 1 (least connected). The basic analysis relating connections to profitability takes the following form:

$$R_c = \alpha + \beta * Suharto\_Index_c + \varepsilon_c \qquad (1)$$

where c indexes listed companies, Rc are cumulative returns of company c over the three-day trading window from Thursday, 4 July, the date when Suharto's Germany trip was announced, to 9 July, the day before he received a clean bill of health, and $Suharto\_Index_c$ is a 1–5 rating of the dependence of company c on its ties to the Suharto regime. The coefficient on $Suharto\_Index_c$ reflects the change in the valuation of companies with strong versus weak dependence on government ties, and provides a straightforwardly interpretable estimate of the value—in terms of expected stream of profits—of political connections in Indonesia.

Underlying this approach is the assumption that there would be no strong backlash against Suharto-favored companies in a post-Suharto era. If such a backlash did occur, β will overestimate the value of political ties; if investors expected continuity in leadership, then β will be an underestimate, since connections will remain valuable in the event of Suharto's demise. It is also worth emphasizing that in all analyses of this type, the value of connections is assessed relative to a benchmark set of firms. In highly politicized economies, such as Indonesia, it was likely impossible to operate in an entirely apolitical fashion, so that in practice β provides a measure of the value of highly connected versus minimally connected firms.

Consider now the approach of Jayachandran (2006), who looks at the effect of the political shifts that resulted from Senator Jim Jeffords' defection from the Republican Party in May 2001, thus tipping control of the US Senate in favor of the Democrats. Jayachandran's specification closely parallels (1) above, though her measure of connections is based on political campaign contributions by publicly traded companies, taking the following form:

$$R_c = \alpha + \beta_1 * Republican_c + \beta_2 * Democrat_c + \varepsilon_c \qquad (2)$$

Once again, Rc reflects (abnormal) stock returns for company c on the date of Jeffords' defection, while *Republican* and *Democrat* reflect connections to the two main political parties. Reflecting the distinct channels of influence between Indonesia and the United States, the right-hand side variables in Jayachandran embody a very different measure of connections relative to Fisman (2001). Note also the complications involved in interpreting the β coefficients as causal estimates of ties to a political party. Campaign contributions may reflect the compatibility of business interests with political ideologies of the two parties. Consider, for example, two energy companies, one that engages in domestic oil drilling, and the other that builds wind turbines. The former will donate to the Republicans in the hopes of electing a party with a platform of increased extraction as a solution to America's energy needs; the latter will donate to the Democrats in the hopes of securing continued subsidies for alternative energy. This will generate a negative coefficient on β_1 and a positive coefficient on β_2, but the interpretation has causation running in the opposite direction: donations follow favorable political platforms, rather than donations causing platforms to be favorable.[1]

As this pair of examples indicates, interpretation of event study results should be made with some caution and with an eye on local circumstances

---

[1]   Knight (2006) studies how firm valuations co-move with expected election outcomes based on election prediction markets for the 2000 presidential election. He finds support for the view that companies in industries favored the Republicans (Democrats) are positively correlated with probability of Bush's (Gore's) election, thus providing evidence that would suggest a concern of reverse causation in looking at the 'Jeffords effect'.

and institutions. This goes beyond the standard proviso accompanying any event study: that the results reflect investor beliefs which may depart, particularly in the short run, from underlying realities.

Although an event study provides in many cases the crispest link between political affiliations and firm-level outcomes, in the sections that follow we will consider studies that are based on a wider range of outcome variables. In some cases, these different approaches allow researchers to trace the mechanisms through which political connections generate value by, for example, looking at infrastructure procurement. Looking beyond market valuations also allows for analyses in countries with less-developed capital markets, and a consideration of a much broader set of companies. This limitation is important in, for example, thinking about the role of connections at lower levels of government since, almost by definition, publicly traded firms are at the very high end of the size distribution.

2.   THE VALUE OF CONNECTIONS

2.1   The Value of Connections among Publicly Traded Firms Worldwide

Fisman (2001) was perhaps the first to attempt to tie firm valuation to 'pure' political ties, as distinct from a coincidence of interests among legislators and their business constituencies.[2] The paper's main finding is best-illustrated through a figure comparing the change in the Jakarta Composite Index – an indication of the market-wide response – to the change in value of Bambang Suharto's company, Bimantara Citra, in response to news of Suharto's health check-up in Germany. This graph, from Fisman and Miguel (2008), is reproduced in Figure 3.1. Most obviously, Bimantara falls precipitously on the initial announcement date of 4 July. The overall market dips only modestly, presumably due to the destabilizing effect of the political vacuum that Suharto would have left

---

[2]   Roberts (1990) is the clear precedent in this political event study literature. This paper examines the impact of the sudden middle-of-the-night death of Senator Henry 'Scoop' Jackson, who was then ranking minority member of the Senate Arms Services Committee. Roberts analyzes the impact on share valuations of firms in Jackson's home state of Washington (such as Boeing) to the impact on valuations in firms headquartered in Georgia, the home state of Jackson's successor, Sam Nunn. The study also examines the impact of firms with significant campaign donations to the two senators. Roberts' main purpose is in trying to infer the value of seniority on the committee by comparing the change in Jackson-connected companies to the change in valuations of Nunn-connected companies.

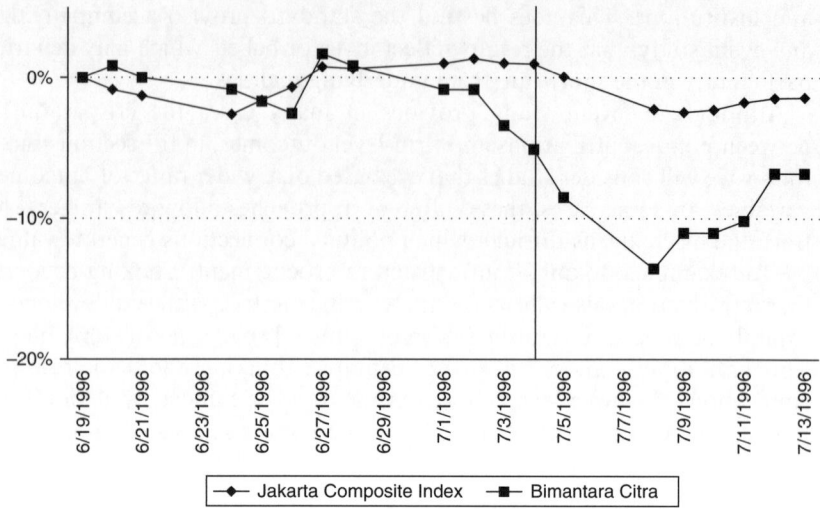

Figure 3.1   *Change in the value of Jakarta shares during Suharto's 1996 trip to Germany*

behind, combined with the fact that most publicly traded companies had relatively strong connections to the regime. It is also noteworthy that Bimantara Citra begins its decline ahead of the official announcement, likely a result of rumors of health concerns leaking out beforehand. (This is another shortcoming of event studies—it is possible, even likely, that Fisman underestimates the full value of political connections by using relatively narrow event windows that miss out on value lost prior to the event start date.) Finally, after Suharto's clean bill of health issued by (presumably objective) German physicians on 10 July, Bimantara's value reverts somewhat, but remains well below its pre-checkup level.

Fisman demonstrates that well-connected companies in general suffered large losses in value on the several occasions when markets were concerned about Suharto's health due to rumors or other adverse events. A back-of-the-envelope calculation estimates that as much as a quarter of the valuation of Suharto-dependent companies relative to less dependent ones could be attributed to their connections.

Of course, at the time, Indonesia was ranked as amongst the most corrupt countries on the planet. So in some ways it would have been surprising and indeed have strained credibility if the study's finding had been otherwise. But it *has* provided a relatively straightforward methodology that can be applied across a range of political and economic circumstance: All that is required is a reasonably well-functioning capital market where equity prices plausibly capture companies' expected future profits, a measure of political connectedness, and an external shock that affects the value of these connections.

Fisman, Fisman, Galef, Khurana, and Wang (2012) use this approach to examine the value of connections to Vice-President Richard Cheney. As with Suharto, there were concerns about Cheney's health during his eight years in office. In Cheney's case, these worries were far more extreme. The Vice-President had heart problems prior to his election, and he suffered several heart attacks while in office, allowing for much the same type of health-based event study. Further, immediately preceding his joining the Bush ticket in 2000, Cheney had served as CEO of Halliburton, a publicly traded oil services company, and was also on the boards of several other (publicly traded) firms. This allowed for the construction of a measure of political connections derived from linkages among corporate boards: For example, Cheney sat on the board of EDS during this time (and an EDS board member, in turn, was on Halliburton's board), thereby classifying EDS as a Cheney-connected company.

Before proceeding to the results of this study, it should be noted that Cheney had already been convicted of favoring Halliburton in the court of public opinion. Jane Mayer of *The New Yorker*, for example, wrote that, '[Cheney] has been both an architect and a beneficiary of the increasingly close relationship between the Department of Defense and an élite group of private military contractors—a relationship that has allowed companies such as Halliburton to profit enormously.' However, when one looks at how the stock price of Halliburton responded to what were, according to cardiologists, major threats to Cheney's life, one observes nothing. In this case, the data belie accusations of corruption.[3]

These polar examples fit with the more general patterns uncovered by Faccio (2006) in her examination of the value of political connections worldwide. As motivating examples, Faccio illustrates her main findings using the market reactions to the appointments of two auto executives to political positions: when Rolls-Royce chairman Sir John Moore was

---

[3]   Acemoglu et al. (2014) take a similar event study approach to looking at the value of personal connections to Timothy Geithner by examining share price responses to his appointment as Treasury Secretary in 2008, at the height of the financial crisis. They report very high returns to connections, and reconcile their findings with those of Fisman et al. by observing that connections may have greater value in times of crisis, when government dollars are spent with relatively little oversight. A similar argument is made by Snyder and Querubin (2011) in explaining why US legislators accumulated wealth more rapidly during the Civil War.

appointed to the House of Lords in low-corruption Britain, there was no detectable effect on Rolls-Royce's stock price. In Faccio's native Italy—a country that is consistently ranked as among Western Europe's most corrupt—the Senate appointment of Fiat boss Giovanni Agnelli boosted his companies' stock prices by 3.4 percent, translating into billions of dollars in additional value. More generally, Faccio finds that events like these move markets in high corruption countries, but have almost no effect on share prices in countries that rank well in global corruption rankings.[4]

2.2　The Value of Lobbying

The non-responsiveness of markets to news of Cheney's heart attacks or the appointment of a Rolls Royce exec to the House of Lords does not necessarily vindicate the United States, Great Britain, and other relatively low corruption countries. As I noted at the outset, there are many channels that may link businesses to government agents. If, for example, the means by which businesses influence government are tethered less to individual politicians in the United States, then our analysis to the present could be focused on the wrong type of connections.

Based on research to date, there is reason to believe there is at least some merit to this view. Two recently published studies, in particular, point to evidence from the lobbying industry which suggests that firms may use the lobbying channel to ensure continued influence in government, regardless of who is in the White House or which party holds sway on Capitol Hill.

Blanes I Vidal et al. (2012) examine the revenues of US lobbying firms as a function of their ties to individual legislators. They focus on congressional staffers turned lobbyists, and document how the revenues of these lobbyists are affected by their ties to Senators or Members of Congress that employed them. Their results are well-captured by a figure from their paper, reproduced as Figure 3.2 below. This graph documents the authors' 'event study' analysis of the impact of a Senators' retirements on revenues at the lobbying firms that employ their former staff members. $T = 0$ denotes the date that the legislator who previously employed the lobbyist exited from the Senate.

There is a very clear post-departure fall in lobbying revenues, consistent with personal connections, via lobbyists, playing a central role in facilitating business-government connections in the United States. There are surely many reasons for the different mechanisms for political influence

---

[4]　In addition to looking at surprise political appointments, Faccio also analyzes the impact of surprise election outcomes to identify the value of connections.

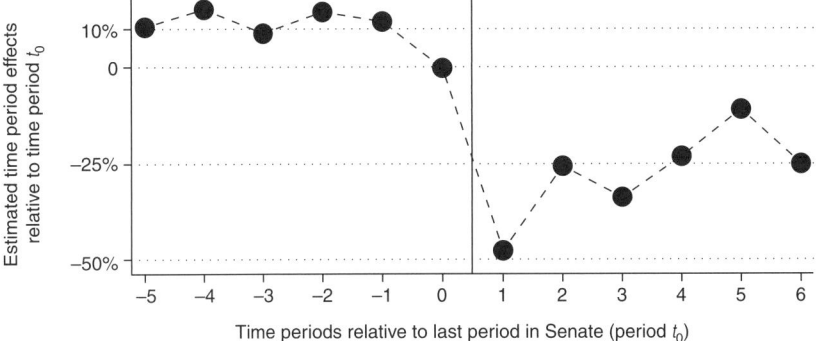

Source: Blanes i Vidal, Jordi, Mirko Draca, and Christian Fons-Rosen. 2012. *American Economic Review*, 102(7): 3731–48.

Figure 3.2   Revolving door lobbyists

across countries.[5] However, the relatively high level of churn in US federal politics at least has an affinity for an approach to rent-seeking where there is a market for political connections that can be adjusted in response to the political landscape. By contrast, if one considers systems governed by stable autocracies (as in Indonesia's Suharto) or dynastic politics (for example, the Gandhis in India), direct personal ties may be a steadier and more reliable form of maintaining ties.

I am not aware of any study that compellingly calculates the financial returns from lobbying for firms in the US or other low-corruption countries—most efforts are subject to various endogeneity concerns, such as the challenge of separating the value of lobbying from coincidence of interests described above.[6] It is, however, possible to adduce some evidence on the extent to which lobbyists profit from their ties. First, Blanes I Vidal et al. estimate that '[l]obbyists with experience in the office of a US Senator suffer a 24% drop in generated revenues when that Senator leaves office'.

A second piece of evidence on the role of personal ties in US lobbying comes from Bertrand, Bombardini, and Trebbi (2012), who take

---

[5]   This survey will not delve too deeply into theoretical models on such questions, though there is a handful of interesting theories.

[6]   For some helpful studies that link lobbying expenditures to policy outcomes see, for example, de Figueiredo and Silverman (2006) for lobbying by universities for academic earmarks; Mian, Sufi, and Trebbi (2010) for post-crisis lobbying by financial firms, and Ansolabehere, Snyder, and Tripathi (2002) for a study linking campaign finance to lobbying.

a different approach to studying the returns to lobbying but generate broadly consistent results. The study develops an independent measure of lobbyist-politician connection based on campaign finance contributions rather than prior employment relationships. The measure has some basis in prior research (and an endless list of anecdotes) by Ansolabehere et al (2002), which argues that campaign finance and lobbying are complements: financial support provides access, which may then be exploited through lobbying.

Bertrand et al. present several pieces of evidence on the primary role of individuals in maintaining business-government ties. Their first main finding is that a lobbyist who focuses on, say, health care, is much more likely to nurture a connection to a Senator that works on health-related legislation. Much more interestingly, if the Senator is reassigned to doing defense-related work in the next Congress, lobbyists connected to him are likely to switch to working on defense as well.

Bertrand et al. also provide evidence that expertise and the provision of information—the stated rationale for the lobbying industry—*does* play some role in lobbying activities. Specifically, they document that lobbyists with technical expertise (as indicated by the fact that they lobby only on a single issue) are more likely to lobby across party lines—at least consistent with information trumping partisan considerations in some cases.

In comparing the relative importance of personal connections versus expertise in the US Senate, Bertrand et al. utilize lobbyist revenue data to examine whether either of these attributes is associated with higher earnings per unit of lobbying. They show that both attributes add to lobbyists' earnings, though personal connections are 'more consistently associated with a positive revenue premium'. Overall, the study concludes that, 'the lobbying process is a complex activity where both the personal connections and issue expertise of the lobbyists play a role. However, the evidence on returns points to connections being the scarcer [and hence more valuable] resource.'

This section and the one that precedes it report findings from a small but growing body of evidence on the importance of personal ties in business-government relations. As Bertrand et al. note, lobbying is itself a complex and nuanced phenomenon. This picture vastly complicates efforts to answer the question, already mentioned above, of how companies choose among the many mechanisms they have at their disposal, and how these may fit with institutional (or individual firm-level) circumstance. This is clearly one area for further research.

We may nonetheless make some general distinctions between the way that businesses connect to government in the United States—primarily via lobbying and campaign finance—versus countries such as Indonesia and Italy. Although stopping far short of suggesting that the US system is optimal, it is noteworthy that Blanes I Vidal et al. and Bertrand et al—along with many others—have been able to develop detailed information on financial flows and relationships among lawmakers and the private sector that are not available elsewhere. This is due to the relatively high level of transparency and disclosure that characterizes US federal politics. (See, for example, Djankov et al. (2009) for a comparison of the extent of and adherence to disclosure laws across countries.) An active media can then make use of this information—Opensecrets.org publishes campaign finance data online, and investigative journalists provide scrutiny that can put pressure on legislators to serve the public interest.

2.3   Channels of Benefit

There are numerous mechanisms through which businesses may benefit from their ties to government. Well-connected firms may have a leg up in securing government contracts—a company run by Suharto's daughter, to take just one example, was awarded a lucrative concession to build toll roads in Jakarta. Connected companies may also be given government-sanctioned licenses (one of Suharto's sons, for example, had the sole distribution rights for clove cigarettes). They may be given tax breaks and preferential access to capital, and be less harassed by regulators. These various mechanisms, one imagines, contribute to the value premiums documented in Section 2.1.

But evidence on the precise channels of benefit is limited. I will briefly describe one illustrative example, but I primarily want to note this as one area that would benefit most from more intensive investigation. Without a clear sense of how companies benefit from political ties, it is hard to think about optimal regulatory or civil society responses.

The most compelling study to date relating political connections to a particular form of business benefit comes from Khwaja and Mian (2005), who examine connected lending in Pakistan. They combine data on all corporate lending obtained from the State Bank of Pakistan with information on elected politicians at all levels of government. By matching names and addresses of company directors to names and addresses of politicians, Khwaja and Mian classify firms as politically connected based on whether they have a politician on their board. They are then able to examine how lending to firms is affected as their political fortunes wax and wane due, for example, to new appointments to their boards, or shifts in which party is in power at the national level.

Khwaja and Mian find that politically connected firms have much readier access to credit—they estimate that a political connection increases borrowing by 50 percent. And this is not because it improves the company's credit risk (for example, because they are more likely to get government contracts)—default rates increase by nearly 50 percent as well. This indicates both the benefit that the company derives from its political ties, but also hints at the social cost due to capital misallocation. I take up the concern of the social costs of political connections in greater detail in Section 4.

2.4 Rent-Seeking in the Least Corrupt Country on Earth

The studies discussed to this point have focused exclusively on rent-seeking at the national level. A recent analysis by Amore and Bennedsen (2013) on the profitability of Danish firms looks instead at municipal politics where, arguably, there is less oversight and greater scope for rent extraction through political ties. This study has the further novel attribute that its setting, Denmark, is plausibly the least corrupt country on the planet: Since 2007, Denmark has received the top (that is, least corrupt) ranking in Transparency International's Corruption Perceptions Index.

Amore and Bennedsen take advantage of the detailed and linkable information from various Danish ministries on firm profits, the identities of their managers, and these firms' family connections in local politics. They further exploit a one-time change in municipal boundaries that effectively expanded the populations under the leadership of some local politicians, while leaving the constituency sizes of other politicians unchanged, allowing them to generate a difference-in-differences estimate on the value of connections. Consistent with political ties serving the interests of connected firms, the authors document 'a unitary elasticity of connected firms' performance to political power (as measured by population per elected politician)'. In other words, a one percent increase in population in a politician's municipality increased firm performance, measured as operating returns, by one percent. The authors go on to show that the impact is notably greater in industries that rely on public sector demand, further reinforcing the interpretation of their diff-in-diff estimate as the impact of increased political power on connected firm profits.

The results of Amore and Bennedsen are striking, and suggest that the literature on political connections may be suffering from the streetlight effect: we search for corruption only where it is easiest to do so.[7] Given the ease

---

[7] The parable of the streetlight is told by Freedman (2010) in the following form: 'A policeman sees a drunk man searching for something under a streetlight and asks what the drunk has lost. He says he lost his keys and they both look under the streetlight together. After a few minutes the policeman asks if he is sure he lost

of access to data on connections in Washington DC, and other national capitals, we are ignoring local politics where political ties and rent seeking may loom larger.[8] This bias is exacerbated by the tendency of researchers to focus on publicly traded firms, again owing to data availability.

3. THE VALUE TO POLITICIANS FROM CONNECTIONS

My emphasis to this point has been on the benefits extracted by only one side in the (implicit) exchange of favors between firms and politicians. This is in part another illustration of the streetlight effect, given that it is easier to measure company profits than individual politicians' earnings. But an emerging literature also provides insights on the nature of business-government ties by examining rents extracted by politicians.

This literature has largely focused on the financial returns to holding office, usually by comparing the declared wealth of politicians at the time of their election to their wealth after several years in office. This immediately raises a number of concerns. These studies most often utilize public disclosures, and it is plausible that in many cases rents extracted by office-holders will go unreported. Second, even with credible wealth data, there is the question of what the relevant benchmark for wealth accumulation should be. This latter concern is comparable to the unobserved heterogeneity issue raised in the previous section: high-ability individuals may be selected for by the electorate, and these abilities may also serve them well in commerce or as investors.

The primary approach that researchers have taken to dealing with the selection problem is to use the outcomes of close elections: if one candidate barely ekes out a victory over his opponent, they are assumed to be randomly assigned to winner and runner-up status, and hence of comparable ability. It is only the winner, however, who obtains the privilege of serving in higher office, along with any associated rents. (Note that any measured rents represent the full set of financial benefits of holding office. For example, politicians may skim funds from public works programs in ways that do not implicate private sector partners.)

Using this regression discontinuity design, Fisman, Schulz, and Vig

---

them here, and the drunk replies, no, that he lost them in the park. The policeman asks why he is searching here, and the drunk replies, "this is where the light is"'.

[8]   A notable exception is among economic historians, who have studied the reform of American cities extensively. See, in particular, Menes (2003, 2006).

(2014) examine the rents extracted through holding public office by state-level legislators in India. In this paper, we exploit the passage of disclosure laws that require political candidates at all levels of government to disclose their assets prior to an election. At the time of the paper's publication, two elections had taken place in most states since the passage of the law, allowing for a calculation of asset growth during a politician's time in office. Since all *candidates* were required to file disclosures, even if they did not win, for politicians that lost but chose nonetheless to run in a subsequent election it is thus possible to calculate a 'counterfactual' asset growth rate for non-winners. While, as noted above, there are legitimate concerns over under-reporting of assets, we argue that under plausible assumptions our comparison of winner versus runner-up wealth accumulation provides a credible measure of the returns to public office.

Our main findings are as follows. First, for rank-and-file members of state legislative assemblies, the returns to public office are decidedly modest—election winners generate only a 3.4 percent per year premium in the rate of asset growth relative to runners-up. More interestingly, the asset growth premium increases as one ascends through the political hierarchy—first-time politicians earn even more modest (or even negative) premiums, while incumbents generate asset growth premiums of 8 percent per year. The assets of those holding cabinet posts, where there exist the greatest scope for rent extraction, grow 12.3 percent faster than those they defeat at the polls. These patterns, as well as a visual exposition of the regression discontinuity approach, are provided in Figures 3.3a–3.3d. In each case, the horizontal axis is the election margin—negative for runners-up and positive for winners—aggregated into 0.5 percent bins. The vertical axes in the graphs show the average rate of asset accumulation for politicians in each bin. In each case, the relationship between electoral margin and asset growth is estimated using a third order polynomial, allowing for a break point at the win-loss margin of zero.[9] For the full sample of politicians, there is a small—albeit statistically significant—jump in asset growth at the win-loss margin; however, this margin is much wider when we limit the sample to elections contested in high corruption states (Figure 3.3b)—this serves as a basic reality check that our winner-loser asset growth gap is likely capturing rent-seeking.[10] In Figures 3.3c

---

[9] I will not address here the various methodological concerns about applying regression discontinuity methods to close elections. See Snyder, Folke and Hirano (2013) for a discussion.

[10] We define Bihar, Madhya Pradesh, Rajasthan, and Uttar Pradesh—the so-called BIMARU states as being high-corruption. We get similar results if we use Transparency International's state corruption ranking.

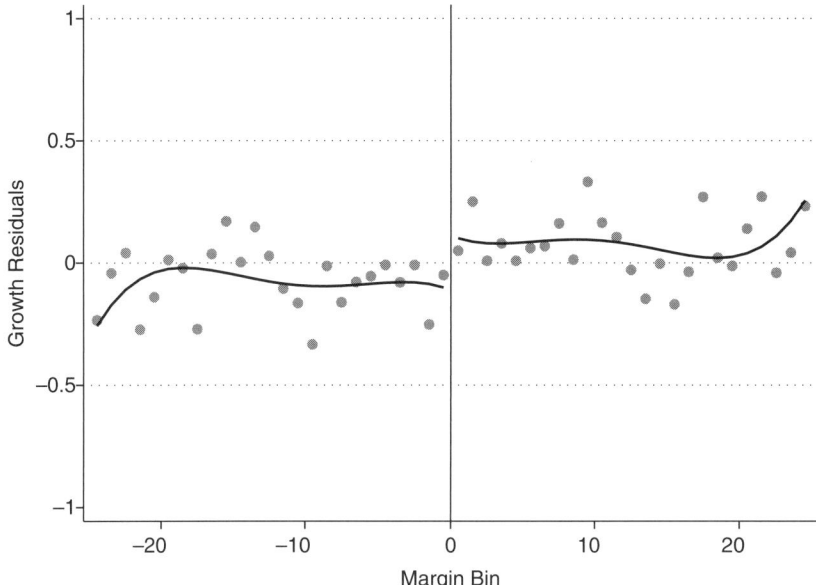

Figure 3.3a   Full sample of winners

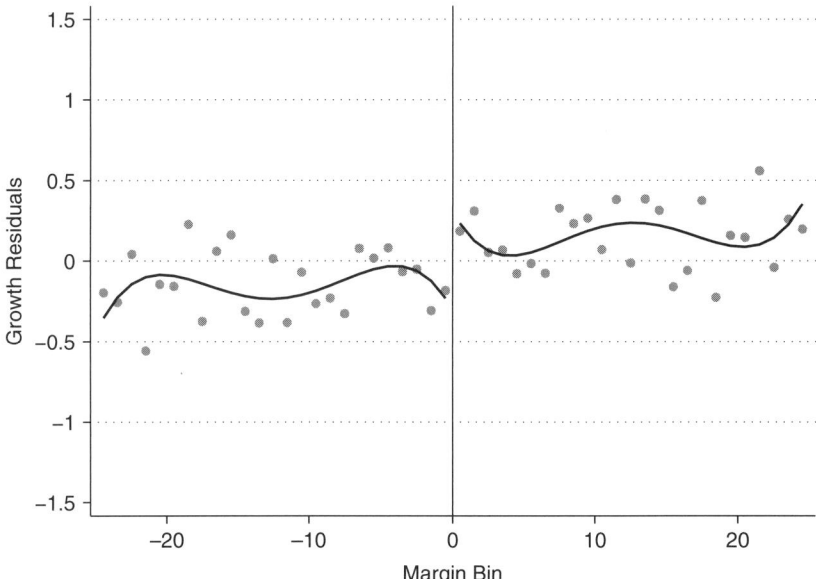

Figure 3.3b   BIMARU (high-corruption) states

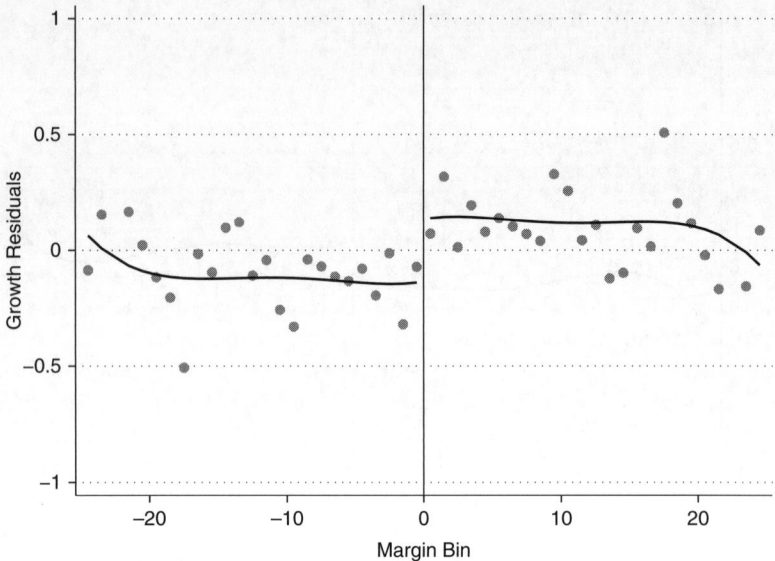

Figure 3.3c   Constituencies with incumbents standing for re-election

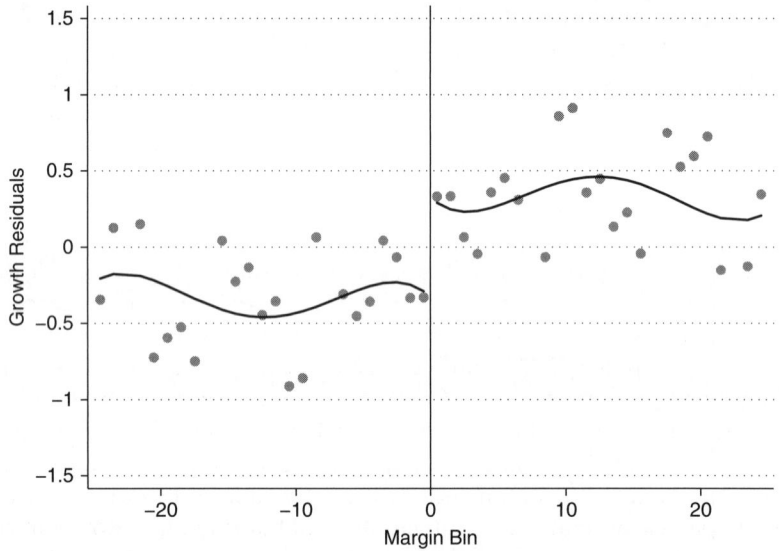

Figure 3.3d   Winners that went on to become cabinet members

Source: Fisman, Raymond, Florian Schulz, and Vikrant Vig. 2014. 'The Private Returns to Public Office', *Journal of Political Economy*, 122(4), 806.

Figure 3.3   Regression discontinuity estimates of the returns to holding state office in India

and 3.3d we show the discontinuity for elections where an incumbent stood for re-election and for elections where the winner went on to hold a cabinet position. These figures show the widening gap between winner and runner-up in asset growth as politicians progress through the political hierarchy.

These results represent a contrast to earlier research focused on lower corruption economies. In particular, Eggers and Heinmeuller (2009) examine the lifetime wealth accumulation of British Members of Parliament by using data on assets at time of death. Using a similar election-based regression discontinuity design, they find that British Conservative party MPs benefit financially from public office while Labour MPs do not. But the mechanism they describe is instructive: the primary source of financial benefit for Conservative MPs appears to be legitimate post-office employment as company directors. While this sort of revolving door may have a cost (through the all-too-common quid pro quo of favor-for-employment exchange), its legality allows at least for exposure and public scrutiny. (Further, the cost must be weighed against the consequences of banning post-office board appointments, which may affect the quality of candidates standing for office.)

As I noted in the prior section, one institutional feature that has allowed researchers to study the lobbying industry in such detail is the strength of disclosure laws in countries like the United States. Given the recent increase in transparency in India and other countries,[11] one interesting avenue for future work may be to try to understand the consequences that increased disclosures have on the nature of ties between businesses and politicians. Will disclosure laws cause ministers to leave public life after a term in office to avoid embarrassing or legally problematic revelations? Will it shift the composition of candidates in a way that affects the scope for rent-seeking? Answers to such questions will not only inform our understanding on the nature of rent-seeking, but also serve as useful guidance to policymakers in the design of disclosure mechanisms.

---

[11]　Issues of data quality may preclude comparable analyses in other countries. We have looked at asset disclosure data from Pakistan and concluded that they fail to pass a basic reality check. One would imagine, basic on formal disclosures, that the Bhutto family are deeply impoverished, for example.

4.   THE SOCIAL COSTS OF POLITICAL CONNECTIONS

In this penultimate section, it is natural to ask what the social costs are of a system built on the sort of favor exchange documented in earlier parts of this chapter. Societal effects may be positive—the 'efficient corruption' view of bribery—or negative. The answer hinges on whether political connections allow companies to circumvent frivolous regulations, or whether connections lead companies to flout social welfare improving constraints.

There is a decades-old debate on these questions going back at least to Leff's (1964) seminal contribution on the topic. My intention here is *not* to take up the thorny matter of how business-politics relationships affect social welfare overall. I would instead assert that more case study analysis, as described below, is needed to marshal greater evidence on this question.

One view is that the purchase of favors by firms has distributional consequences—likely regressive—as some firms end up extracting rents and politicians enrich themselves through bribes, but has minimal efficiency consequences. This argument implicitly invokes the Coase Theorem—the most efficient, lowest-cost provider should value a contract the most, and hence 'bid' (make) the highest bribe offer. If an inferior firm wins the contract owing to favorable political connections, the problem of social inefficiency should be solvable through a subcontracting relationship or sale of the concession. Of course, bargaining frictions exist in reality, and could plausibly be more prevalent in illicit transactions. As a result, allocation of resources through political connections may result in allocative inefficiencies. (Separately, since this favored exchange channels funds to politicians' bank accounts rather than public coffers, it may result in suboptimal public good provision.)

One intriguing effort to analyze this set of issues empirically comes from Sukhtankar (2012), which analyzes the 2008 allocation of 2G wireless spectrum by the Indian government. The study documents a fascinating set of rule manipulations that were designed to deliver contracts to companies favored by then Telecom Minister Andimuthu Raja. The subsequent scandal brought to light the fact that Mr. Raja received as much as US\$1 billion in bribes from favored firms. Despite the epic corruption that occurred in the allocation of spectrum licenses, Sukhtankar finds no effect on the quality of telecom service in the wake of contracts where corruption was implicated, arguing effectively that in this case the Coase Theorem prevailed: either efficient providers obtained licenses initially and were forced to provide high service to survive in a competitive telecom market, or initial winners simply flipped their licenses to other more competent providers.

In work with Yongxiang Wang, I reach a different conclusion in examining the social consequences of firms exploiting their political connections (Fisman and Wang, 2015). In this study, we look at the death rates of workers at publicly traded Chinese firms and examine whether the political ties of a company's executive team affected these rates. We find that firms where a 'C-Suite' executive had previously held a high-level government post (specifically, mayor or vice-mayor of the firm's municipality) had worker death rates that were as much as *five times* those of firms without high-level government ties. We argue that this is because political ties allow firms to shirk on safety expenditures, which can be very significant for firms in the safety-regulated industries that are the focus of our analysis.

I conclude this section on a positive note: responding to public pressures, the Chinese government imposed province-level 'death ceilings' in 2004: if local bureaucrats were unable to meet their worker safety targets, it would greatly diminish their career prospects (the program's name is roughly translated as, 'No safety, no promotion'). A subset of provinces, in turn, provided municipalities with worker safety quotas and incentives. In a set of preliminary analyses, we find that the gap in workplace death rates between connected and unconnected firms is greatly diminished in provinces that provide safety incentives to local governments. One explanation could be that, because workplace safety is administered at the municipal level, these are the provinces that have best aligned regulators' career incentives with providing stringent oversight. These findings hold out some promise that policy may be effective in diminishing some of the negative effects of political connections.

CONCLUSION AND AGENDA FOR THE FUTURE

Arguably, the general conclusions that may be drawn from this survey are neither shocking nor surprising: both firms and their counterparts in government benefit financially from their relationships; these benefits are greater in higher-corruption environments; in many cases, other groups suffer as a result. Although the existing literature has thus helped to confirm some aspects of conventional wisdom—an important function of research—other commonly held views have been refuted or diminished (the relatively modest effect of firms' high-level connections in government in low-corruption environments, for example).

The evidence to date has also helped to fill in some intriguing details on the nature of rent-seeking in specific places or situations. For example, the finding by Fisman, Schultz, and Vig (2014) suggests that rent-seeking in government may resemble a tournament model where increasing returns are extracted through illicit gains as one progresses through the political hierarchy. Such findings may be useful in informing future research, or future policies aimed at reducing rent-seeking in government.

But the main conclusion is that the area is ripe for further research. I have tried to highlight these possibilities throughout. Additional work will help to provide some subtlety, depth, and specificity to our understanding of rent-seeking relationships globally and, one hopes, contribute to our ability to respond.

There already exists a deep and rich institutional literature that analyzes the preconditions for anti-corruption reforms to succeed: It may involve the opening to external trade or influence, as in Acemoglu, Johnson, and Robinson (2005). Or it may require the alignment of business interests with those of reformers to push for change when the efficiency costs of poor public services outweigh the private benefits of favor-seeking (Rose-Ackerman, 1999). Hopefully, by bringing more contemporary and data-driven evidence to bear on these questions, we can equip policymakers with the tools they require to bridge the gap between theory and action.

REFERENCES

Acemoglu, Daron, Simon Johnson, and James Robinson. 2005. 'The Rise of Europe: Atlantic Trade, Institutional Change, and Economic Growth', *American Economic Review* 95(3): 546–79.

Acemoglu, Daron, Simon Johnson, Amir Kermani, James Kwak and Todd Mitton. 2014. 'The Value of Connections in Turbulent Times: Evidence from the United States', NBER Working Paper 19701.

Amore, Mario and Morten Bennedsen. 2013. 'The Value of Local Political Connections in a Low-Corruption Environment', *Journal of Financial Economics* 110(2): 387–402.

Ansolabehere Stephen, James M. Snyder and Micky Tripathi. 2002. 'Are PAC Contributions and Lobbying Linked? New Evidence from the 1995 Lobby Disclosure Act', *Business and Politics* 4(2): 1–26.

Bertrand, Marianne, Matilde Bombardini and Francesco Trebbi. 2012. 'Is It Whom You Know or What You Know? An Empirical Assessment of the Lobbying Process', NBER Working Paper 16765.

Blanes i Vidal, Jordi, Mirko Draca, and Christian Fons-Rosen. 2012. 'Revolving Door Lobbyists', *American Economic Review* 102(7): 3731–48.

de Figueiredo, John and Brian S. Silverman. 2006. 'Academic Earmarks and the Returns to Lobbying', *Journal of Law and Economics* 49(2): 597–625.

Djankov, Simeon, Rafael La Porta, Florencio Lopez-de-Silanes and Andrei Shleifer. 2009. 'Disclosure by Politicians', NBER Working Paper 14703.

Eggers, Andrew, and Jens Hainmueller. (2009). 'MPs for Sale? Returns to Office in Postwar British Politics', *American Political Science Review* 103: 513–33.

Faccio, Mara. 2006. 'Politically Connected Firms', *American Economic Review* 96(1): 369–86.

Fisman, Raymond. 2001. 'Estimating the Value of Political Connections', *American Economic Review* 91(4): 1095–1102.

Fisman, Raymond and Edward Miguel. 2008. *Economic Gangsters: Corruption, Violence and the Poverty of Nations*, New Haven: Princeton.

Fisman, Raymond, David Fisman, Julia Galef, Rakesh Khurana and Yongxiang Wang. 2012. 'Estimating the Value of Connections to Vice-President Cheney', *The B.E. Journal of Economic Analysis & Policy* 13(3): 1–20.

Fisman, Raymond, Florian Schulz and Vikrant Vig. 2014. 'The Private Returns to Public Office', *Journal of Political Economy* 122(4): 806–62.

Fisman, Raymond, and Yongxiang Wang. 2015. 'The Mortality Cost of Political Connections', forthcoming, *Review of Economic Studies*.

Freedman, David H. 2010. *Wrong: Why Experts* Keep Failing Us – and How to Know when not to Trust Them (*Scientists, finance wizards, doctors, relationship gurus, celebrity CEOs, high-powered consultants, health officials and more)*. New York: Little, Brown & Co.

Jayachandran, Seema. 2006. 'The Jeffords Effect', *Journal of Law and Economics* 49(2): 397–425.

Khwaja, Asim Ijaz and Atif Mian. 2005. 'Do Lenders Favor Politically Connected Firms? Rent Provision in an Emerging Financial Market', *Quarterly Journal of Economics* 1371–411.

Knight, Brian. 2006. 'Are Policy Platforms Capitalized into Equity Prices? Evidence from the Bush/Gore 2000 Presidential Election', *Journal of Public Economics* 90(4–5): 751–73.

Leff, Nathaniel H. 1964. 'Economic Development through Bureaucratic Corruption', *American Behavioral Scientist* 8(3): 8–14.

Mayer, Jane. 2004. 'Contract Sport: What did the Vice-President do for Halliburton?' *The New Yorker*, 16–23 February 2004.

Menes, Rebecca. 2003. 'Corruption in Cities: Graft and Politics in American Cities at the Turn of the Twentieth Century', NBER Working Paper 9990.

Menes, Rebecca. 2006. 'Limiting the Reach of the Grabbing Hand. Graft and Growth in American Cities, 1880 to 1930', in Edward L. Glaeser and Claudia Godlin (eds), *Corruption and Reform: Lessons from America's Economic History*. Chicago: University of Chicago Press, 63–94.

Mian, Atif, Amir Sufi and Francesco Trebbi. 2010. 'The Political Economy of the US Mortgage Default Crisis', *American Economic Review* 100(5): 1967–98.

Querubin, Pablo, and James M. Snyder Jr. 2011. The Control of Politicians in Normal Times and Times of Crisis: Wealth Accumulation by US Congressmen, 1850–1880. NBER Working Paper 17634.

Roberts, Brian, 1990. 'A Dead Senator Tells No Lies: Seniority and the Distribution of Federal Benefits', *American Journal of Political Science* 34(1): 31–58.

Rose-Ackerman, Susan. 1999. *Corruption and Government: Causes, Consequences, and Reform*. Cambridge, UK: Cambridge University Press.

Snyder, James M., Olle Folke and Shigeo Hirano. 2013. 'A Simple Explanation for Bias at the 50–50 Threshold in RDD Studies Based on Close Elections'. Cambridge, MA: Harvard University Press. Mimeo.

Sukhtankar, Sandip. 2012. 'Much Ado about Nothing? Corruption in the Allocation of Wireless Spectrum in India'. Dartmouth College. Mimeo.

4. Corruption and democratic institutions: a review and synthesis

Matthew C. Stephenson

Do democratic elections help reduce corruption? Many reformers—both anti-corruption advocates and democracy promoters—hope and believe the answer is yes. Does the evidence support that view? Social scientists have been investigating this and associated questions for at least a quarter-century, and—as is often the case—the answers they have found are not straightforward. Nonetheless, this research has added significantly to our understanding of the relationship between democracy and corruption. This chapter will summarize and synthesize some of that research, offer some tentative conclusions about the democracy-corruption relationship, and identify some of the most important open questions that could and should be addressed in future research.[1]

The chapter is organized as follows. Section I considers how democracies and non-democracies might differ with respect to the extent or type of corruption. This section first reviews the various mechanisms by which democracy might affect corruption, and then provides a brief summary of the existing empirical evidence. Section II turns to how differences in

---

[1] A quick note about definitions: One of the challenges in researching, or presenting research about, the corruption-democracy relationship is the fact that both 'corruption' and 'democracy' are imprecise and contested concepts. This chapter does not attempt to provide a fully specified definition for either term; such an exercise would likely prove futile. The working definition of 'corruption' for purposes of this chapter will be 'the abuse of entrusted power for private gain', and would include bribery, embezzlement, and similar acts. This chapter's working definition of corruption will not include lawful campaign contributions or lobbying activities. As for 'democracy', this chapter adopts a 'thin' procedural conception of democracy, characterized by the selection of leaders through regular competitive elections in which most adult citizens are eligible to vote, along with guaranteed political participation rights. An important caveat to this definitional clarification, however, is that a great deal of the empirical literature surveyed in this chapter relies on index scores for both corruption and democracy—often based on perception or subjective evaluations—and it is not always clear what implicit definitions of the underlying concepts these scores are actually measuring.

electoral institutions—within and across democratic countries—might affect the nature and extent of corruption. This section will focus mainly on three dimensions of institutional variation: (1) whether legislators are elected under plurality rule or through some form of proportional representation, as well the extent to which party leaders control ballot access, (2) the ratio of legislators to legislative districts, and (3) whether the chief executive is directly elected or selected by the legislature.[2]

Although this evidence, taken together, does offer some support to the optimistic view that democracy may help reduce corruption, it also suggests that the relationship between democracy and corruption control is not as straightforward, or as unambiguously positive, as is sometimes assumed. The evidence also suggests that democracy, and variation in the form of democratic institutions, may not only affect the overall *amount* of corruption, but may also influence the *types* of corruption that are most likely. This may be a more important insight, as better understanding the particular corruption risks that are most likely to be associated with different political institutions may help reform-minded policymakers craft more appropriate and effective responses.

I. DEMOCRATIC ELECTIONS AND CORRUPTION

This section will consider the relationship between democracy (or democratization) and corruption generally, asking how democratic elections might affect the nature and extent of corruption within a polity. The section proceeds in two parts. The first part surveys the various mechanisms by which democracy may affect corruption. The second part turns to the existing empirical research on the democracy-corruption relationship.

A. How Might Democracy Affect Corruption? A Survey of Mechanisms

The existing literature has identified five mechanisms through which democracy might affect the extent or type of corruption, relative to non-democracy. The first three all have to do with the fact that democratic elections enable citizens to hold public officials accountable. In particular,

---

[2] There are a number of other institutional features of the political system that might influence corruption, including other aspects of the separation of powers (including both 'horizontal' separation of powers mechanisms like bicameralism and 'vertical' separation of powers mechanisms, such as federalism or other forms of political decentralization), as well as regulation of campaigns and lobbying. These topics will not be covered here due to space constraints.

voters can hold elected officials accountable for (1) the officials' own (perceived) corruption, (2) other policies and outcomes that may be affected by or associated with corruption, and (3) government decisions regarding how, and how aggressively, to combat corruption. The two additional mechanisms derive from the fact that democracy affects—and generally increases—the competitiveness of the political system, which (4) affects politicians' incentives to engage in forms of instrumental political corruption intended to improve their odds of gaining or holding power, and (5) alters incumbents' time horizons. Let us consider each of these mechanisms in turn, before assessing the available evidence on the net impact of democracy on corruption.

1. Holding politicians accountable for corrupt acts

The most intuitive channel through which democracy might affect corruption arises from the fact that elections enable voters to remove corrupt leaders from power. This is a specific application of the more general idea that democratic elections allow the citizenry both to 'select good [representatives]' and to 'sanction poor performance' (Fearon 1999; see also Besley and Burgess 2002). In the corruption context, sanctioning poor (corrupt) performance is likely to be more significant than selecting good (uncorrupt) public officials, because it is more difficult to observe ahead of time whether a politician or party is corrupt than it is to evaluate whether that politician or party has behaved corruptly when in office. It is likely that this mechanism—voting corrupt politicians out of office—is what most commentators have in mind when they suggest that democratization may substantially reduce corruption (Harsch 1993; Mohtadi and Roe 2003; Wilson and Damania 2005; Schumacher 2013).

Is the optimism about the potential for democratic elections to constrain corruption justified? On the one hand, despite occasional suggestions that voters do not mind or do not care much about corruption, there is considerable evidence that voters in fact dislike corruption and are less likely, all else equal, to support an incumbent perceived to be corrupt. The most convincing such evidence comes from studies of voter attitudes or behavior within individual countries (Dimock and Jacobson 1995; Fackler and Lin 1995; Eggers 2014; Ferraz and Finan 2008; Pereira et al. 2009; Winters and Weitz-Shapiro 2013; De Figueiredo et al. 2011; Chong et al. 2013; Klasnja et al. 2012). There is also some suggestive cross-country evidence that tends to corroborate the claim that the perceived extent of the incumbent government's corruption is negatively correlated not only with citizens' reported satisfaction with government performance (Manzetti and Wilson 2007), but also with the incumbent's electoral success (Bagenholm 2009; Choi and Woo 2010; Krause and Mendez 2009).

On the other hand, there are numerous examples of countries where democracy does not seem to have reduced corruption (Olowu 1993; Colazingari and Rose-Ackerman 1998; Werlin 2013), and several cases in which democratization appears to have been associated with *increased* corruption (Harriss-White and White 1996; Mungiu-Pippidi 2006; Geddes and Neto 1992; Lindberg 2003; Fritz 2007). Moreover, although opposition parties do sometimes make corruption a campaign issue, they do not do so nearly as much as one might expect—even when there is credible evidence of government corruption that the opposition could exploit (Bagenholm 2009). Why is this? Why are the corruption-reducing effects of democratic elections not as strong as one might expect, given the widespread voter disapproval of corrupt behavior? The literature has identified four factors that might limit or undermine the effectiveness of electoral accountability in disciplining corrupt politicians:

The first factor is *lack of information*: Even if voters would be less inclined to support a politician implicated in corrupt practices, many voters may not be sufficiently aware of the existence or extent of corruption. This problem is likely to be especially acute where levels of voter education and awareness are low, and where the media is underdeveloped or not fully free. Indeed, there is convincing evidence that variation in voter information—in terms of both baseline education levels and media coverage—is correlated with the degree to which corruption adversely affects politicians' and parties' electoral fortunes (Geddes and Neto 1992; Chang et al. 2010; Klasnja 2011). And there is likewise both historical and contemporary evidence that media access and penetration is a key factor in promoting accountability for corrupt behavior by public officials (Gentzkow et al. 2006; Reinikka and Svensson 2005, 2011). Insofar as this is true, one would expect democratic elections to have a greater corruption-reducing effect in polities where overall education levels are higher, where government is more transparent, where citizens are more interested and engaged in politics, and where a vigorous free media is active and widely accessible.

One must be cautious, however, about concluding that more information about corruption will always enhance the efficacy of democratic elections in deterring corruption. A potential countervailing factor—and a second reason why democracy may sometimes be a less effective anti-corruption device than many hope—concerns the so-called *demoralization effect*. Disgust with corruption may cause some citizens to drop out of the political process altogether; perversely, these may be the voters who would be least inclined to support the (corrupt) incumbent. There is some anecdotal evidence that the demoralization effect has indeed attenuated the anti-corruption impact of democracy (Fritz 2007; Sun and Johnston 2009), and more systematic quantitative evidence—principally from research in Latin America—tends to corroborate the existence of this demoralization effect, and its attendant dilution of the impact of perceived corruption on election outcomes (McCann and Dominguez 1998; Davis et al. 2004; Chong et al. 2013). Of course, the *net* effect of perceived corruption on voter turnout and incumbent support rates is an empirical question, and it is quite possible that more information about government corruption tends to reduce overall support for the incumbent relative to the opposition.[3] But even then, the demoralization effect may mean that perceived corruption reduces an incumbent's electoral success less than one would expect.

A third factor that might limit the extent to which voters punish corrupt politicians is the *importance of other issues.* Put simply, even if voters dislike corruption and would be inclined—all else equal—to withdraw support from a corrupt politician, all else is rarely equal. A party perceived as corrupt might be able to maintain support because enough voters have a sufficiently strong preference for that party on other grounds, such as (perceived) competence, ideology, or ethnic affinity. The evidence on how much competing considerations attenuate the significance of corruption is mixed. Survey experiments tend to find that most voters say they would be willing to withdraw support from a (hypothetical) corrupt politician, even if that politician has succeeded in providing public goods or has a partisan or ethnic affiliation that matches the respondent's (Winters and Weitz-Shapiro 2013; Banerjee et al. 2014). However, behavioral evidence from actual elections suggests that voters often allow other factors—such as ideology, performance, and ethnic affinity—to take precedence over their distaste for corruption (Banerjee and Pande 2009; Eggers 2014). Also, surveys that ask respondents not about their *own* preferences, but rather ask them to predict how *other* voters would behave, have found that most respondents assume other voters would care more about things like economic conditions than corruption (Klasnja et al. 2012). This evidence tends to support the claim that, even if voters dislike corruption, other factors may attenuate the significance of corruption in voters'

---

[3]   Although most studies do not attempt to work out the net effects, a notable exception is Kostadinova (2009), which examines the impact of perceived corruption on voter turnout in eight post-communist Eastern European countries in the 2001–2005 period. This study finds that although corruption indeed has cross-cutting effects on voter turnout (a direct mobilization effect and an indirect demoralization effect), the net effect of corruption on voter turnout is mildly positive—though it is not clear whether that result is statistically significant.

decisions—with the consequence that democratic elections are less effective in deterring incumbents from engaging in corrupt activities (Myerson 1993; Feichtinger and Wirl 1994; Choi and Woo 2010).[4] This suggests that democratic elections will be less effective in reducing corruption in the presence of intense disagreement—and vigorous political competition—along other dimensions.

Of course, the relative importance of other issues is not by itself a completely satisfying explanation for why corruption may not always play a significant role in voting decisions. After all, if a corrupt incumbent's support was based on other factors (ideology, ethnicity, and so on), one might think that incumbent would be vulnerable to challenge by an entrant who was similar on those other dimensions but who was perceived as less corrupt. This leads directly to a fourth explanation as to why democratic elections may not be as successful as many hope in deterring incumbent corruption: *lack of viable alternatives*. Consistent with this hypothesis, there is some evidence that the extent to which corruption allegations influence voters' decisions depends on whether voters perceive an alternative, less corrupt candidate or party to be sufficiently appealing on other dimensions, such as ideology (Renno 2011; Klasnja et al. 2012). Voters may perceive a lack of viable alternatives for a number of reasons. Cynical voters might perceive corruption as so widespread that they believe all viable political competitors are equally corrupt, but the electoral institutions may also play a role. For example, electoral institutions might restrict the number of political competitors (often with good reason). Furthermore, even when an anti-corruption candidate is among the available alternatives, voters may have difficulty coordinating their support for that candidate, and this coordination problem might be exacerbated or ameliorated by the electoral rules (Myerson 1993). The broader implication here is that democracy may be more effective in countering corruption when electoral rules—as well as other social, economic, and political factors—allow for the entry (or credible threat of entry) by new challengers; this will be particularly important in more polarized polities, and in polities where voter loyalties on other dimensions are stronger and less fluid.

---

[4]   Moreover, the perceived significance of other issues may interact with the (apparent) lack of information about corruption through subtle cognitive channels: There is some suggestive evidence that voters may suffer from cognitive biases, such that voters are less aware of corruption allegations against politicians they are inclined to support for other reasons (Dimock and Jacobson 1995).

2.   Holding politicians accountable for the consequences of corruption

The usual arguments for democracy as a corruption-reducing mechanism focus on the ability of voters to hold elected officials accountable for corruption itself. But democratic elections also enable voters to hold officials accountable for policy outcomes more generally, like the performance of the economy and the provision of public goods, welfare, and social services. If these outcomes are adversely affected by corruption—if corruption, for example, worsens economic outcomes, renders governments less effective, and undermines education, public health, and other government programs—then voters are more likely to vote out corrupt politicians even if the voters are not specifically aware that the government's bad performance is due to corruption.

But that optimistic story is more complicated, and not only because several of the problems noted earlier (such as lack of information and lack of viable alternatives) might also apply here. More troubling is the fact that politicians' accountability for delivering particular policies or outcomes—before the next election—may sometimes *encourage* politicians to engage in certain forms of corruption. For example, democracies may be more likely to adopt extensive systems of government redistribution, and these systems—however well-intentioned and however well-justified on other grounds—may be particularly susceptible to corruption, for the simple reason that they involve giving government agents (including lower-level administrators subject to imperfect supervision) control over substantial resources. Of course, democratic incentives may encourage more senior leaders to squeeze as much corruption out of the system as they can, but it is unlikely they will ever be wholly successful, and the net effect might still be an increase in certain types of bureaucratic corruption. Moreover, elected officials do not always have an incentive to squeeze corruption out of these redistributive systems: they may instead participate in the corruption, perhaps targeting resources to favored constituencies in explicit or tacit exchange for political support. A related concern is that even if democratic competition reduces 'grand' corruption, such that legislatures and high-level executive officers adopt policies favored by a majority of voters (rather than allowing policy to be 'bought' by powerful interest groups), this may have the collateral consequence of increasing corruption at the bureaucratic level, as those same interest groups have a stronger incentive to use bribery and other corrupt methods to thwart the effective implementation of those unfavorable policies (Wilson and Damania 2005).

More generally, sometimes corruption may actually help politicians produce short-term results that voters like, even at the expense of longer-term adverse effects on voters' well-being and overall satisfaction with

government (Charron and Lapuente 2010). Another, perhaps more chari-
table but nonetheless troubling possibility, is that in some polities, with
relatively under-developed institutions, certain types of 'corruption'—
particularly the use of patronage networks to distribute (perhaps unlaw-
fully) valuable resources, including government jobs—is the only way,
or at least the most effective way, for electoral competitors to credibly
commit to provide benefits to constituents (Keefer 2007; Keefer and
Vlaicu 2008; Robinson and Verdier 2013). For these and other reasons,
incumbent politicians' accountability for policy and performance more
generally may not always produce significant reductions in corruption,
even if corruption may prove detrimental to voter welfare in the long term.

3.   Democratic accountability for anti-corruption enforcement efforts

Democratic elections not only provide a means by which voters can hold
elected officials accountable for the officials' own corruption (or that of
the incumbent administration); elections also provide a means by which
voters can hold representatives accountable for their efforts to prevent
and punish corruption by other actors, such as bureaucrats, police, and
bribe-paying private parties. Admittedly, the line between an elected government's own corruption and its efforts to police corruption by others is
often blurry—as when the government appears to turn a blind eye to malfeasance by cronies and supporters, or when bureaucratic corruption is
closely integrated with, and protected by, systems of political corruption.
Nonetheless, it may be helpful to view these issues as at least potentially
distinct. How does democracy affect a government's incentives regarding
anti-corruption policy?

Again, the answer is complicated. Most straightforwardly, mechanisms
of democratic accountability may put pressure on elected officials to act
more decisively against corruption by others for all the same reasons that
democratic accountability might deter elected officials from engaging in
corruption themselves: If voters dislike corruption, then they may be more
inclined to retain or reward politicians who fight it effectively and less
likely to retain or reward those who do not. That said, all the factors noted
above that may attenuate the anti-corruption effects of democracy could
apply here as well. Moreover, several other factors may influence how,
and how aggressively, democratically elected governments take action
against corruption, relative to non-democratic governments. At least five
considerations may be worth noting here.

First, non-democratic governments may rely on a narrower base of
support (including, for example, the military, key business elites, and
powerful local or ethnic leaders), and may consequently be more reluctant
to act aggressively against corrupt activities by those groups—but more

willing to take aggressive action against corruption by less politically salient groups. Thus, the political bias in anti-corruption enforcement—which is always a problem—may be less pronounced in democracies than in authoritarian states.

Second, even if most voters dislike corruption, they might be uncomfortable with—or downright opposed to—some of the more aggressive or draconian methods that a government might employ to fight corruption. Consider the fact that some of the modern anti-corruption success stories—Hong Kong, Singapore, and more recently the Republic of Georgia—have employed measures that would be unacceptable in many liberal democracies, at least those where the citizens and the courts care sufficiently about civil liberties and restraints on executive power (Skidmore 1996; Quah 2009; Di Puppo 2014).[5]

The third consideration is something of a hybrid of the first two: Anti-corruption enforcement efforts may impose very high costs on certain groups—not only corrupt or potentially corrupt officials, but also those in the populations singled out for scrutiny, or those who are burdened by new rules. Even if anti-corruption enforcement is broadly popular, the benefits from lower corruption are often broad and diffuse. And, consistent with standard political economy models (for example, Olson 1965), if anti-corruption policies create concentrated costs (easily observable by those who bear those costs) and diffuse benefits (not always directly observed or appreciated by the beneficiaries), the result may be strong political opposition to those policies. Such opposition may make it politically difficult—particularly in a democracy—to implement aggressive anti-corruption policies even if a majority of voters would tend to support them.

Fourth, effective anti-corruption policies often require not only changes in legal or bureaucratic institutions, but also increases in the allocation of resources to anti-corruption efforts (including law enforcement, audits, and longer-term investments in education and institutional improvements). As noted earlier, voters generally care about other issues in

---

[5]   The statement in the text is admittedly controversial, as many observers might attribute the success of anti-corruption efforts in these and other countries to other factors, such as the independence of the anti-corruption agencies and the 'political will' of the leadership. Yet it is hard to ignore the fact that these anti-corruption efforts employed law enforcement techniques that would make civil libertarians uncomfortable, as well as the fact that the 'independence' and 'political will' in these cases appears to result at least in part from a powerful chief executive, subject to relatively few political checks, who threw support behind the anti-corruption enforcement efforts.

addition to (and perhaps more than) corruption, which may lead politically accountable leaders, at least in some countries, to invest fewer resources in fighting corruption and improving governance, so as to dedicate those resources to popular programs that produce short-term benefits (Charron and Lapuente 2010).[6]

A fifth consideration, closely related to the preceding point, is that the diffusion of power that often accompanies democratic reform may make it difficult to implement aggressive anti-corruption programs. Indeed, some case studies have suggested that in newly-democratizing states, intense partisan competition, coupled with bureaucratic fragmentation, impedes the government from adopting and implementing reforms that would improve governance and reduce corruption (Davis 2006). The broader hypothesis is that, at least for young democracies, the transition from autocracy to democracy can erode administrative capacity, including the capacity to keep corruption under control (Back and Hadenius 2008).[7]

The net effects of democratization on anti-corruption enforcement efforts are therefore uncertain. On the one hand, authoritarian countries may be able to undertake more aggressive anti-corruption efforts than democracies (though key supporters may remain insulated from these efforts). It is easier for a country like China or Singapore to initiate and sustain a thoroughgoing anti-corruption crackdown than it would be for, say, India or the Philippines to do something similar. But on the other hand, authoritarian countries may not be under as much pressure as

---

[6]   Charron and Lapuente (2010) further suggest that voters in poor countries are more likely to be 'myopic', demanding higher levels of investment in short-term economic benefits (for example, redistribution) rather than longer-term investments in improving the quality of governance, and Charron and Lapuente report supportive evidence that one composite measure of 'quality of governance' tends to be positively correlated with democracy in wealthy countries but negatively correlated with democracy in poor countries.

[7]   Back and Hadenius (2008) investigate this possibility in a cross-country panel study, examining the correlation between a composite democracy index and an index of 'administrative capacity' (which incorporates corruption control as one component). The results show strong evidence of a 'J-shaped' relationship between democracy and administrative capacity: moving from a lower to a higher score on the democracy index is associated first with a worsening and then with an improvement in the administrative capacity score. Back and Hadenius interpret this as evidence that administrative capacity requires control 'from above' and 'from below': authoritarian countries typically have good top-down controls but weak bottom-up control; democratization initially weakens the top-down controls, but bottom-up controls are not fully developed. Over time, as democratization proceeds, bottom-up controls develop and complement top-down controls, for more effective administrative capacity.

democracies to fight corruption aggressively. Autocracies may be especially reluctant (even more than democratic states) to take action against certain kinds of grand corruption at very high levels—particularly since corrupt, oligarchic relationships may be the glue that holds an authoritarian state together. Because the relationship between democracy and anti-corruption enforcement policy is complex, the relationship between democracy and overall corruption levels may be similarly complex—and might be so even if democracy provided straightforward incentives for elected officials to avoid personally engaging in corrupt activities.

4. Corruption to achieve or maintain power

The three factors discussed above all concern how democratic accountability may influence elected officials' incentives to engage in corruption or to take action against corruption. But in addition to increasing the accountability of politicians to the people, democracy also tends to increase the competitiveness of the political system, and this may have additional implications for corruption. In principle, democratic political competition is supposed to take place within a system of rules, but the strong incentives created by more robust political competition can intensify incentives to bend or break those rules. Indeed, although optimists stress how democracy can hold politicians accountable for corruption (or for failing to take effective action against corruption), pessimists argue that the pressures of democratic competition can increase politicians' incentives to engage in various kinds of political corruption in order to secure an unfair edge in the electoral arena (Olowu 1993; Mungiu-Pippidi 2006; Rose-Ackerman 1999). These forms of instrumental political corruption might include electoral fraud (Nyblade and Reed 2008; Ziblatt 2009), vote buying (Stokes 2005; Khemani 2013), political interference with the operation of social welfare programs in order to reward political supporters (Weitz-Shapiro 2012), diversion of resources from public programs to partisan political activities (Reinikka and Svensson 2004), and other corrupt activities designed to raise money to fund election campaigns (Weyland 1998; Lim and Stern 2002; Roper 2002; Lindberg 2003).[8]

---

[8] Some critical commentators have gone further, suggesting that campaign finance and lobbying practices that are currently *legal* in many democracies (particularly the United States) should nonetheless be considered 'corrupt' (Lessig 2011, Teachout 2014). However, as noted above (see *supra* note 1), this chapter uses a narrower definition of corruption, focusing on illegal activities like bribery or embezzlement. Thus, the argument that money has a 'corrupting influence' on politics in a broader sense, while important, is not the main focus of the discussion here.

Indeed, a great deal of the (perceived) corruption in democratic states may take the form of instrumental political corruption.[9] This is not to say that authoritarian governments do not also have strong incentives to engage in corrupt activities to stay in power. But democratization does create pressures for certain kinds of corruption that might not be as pronounced in non-democratic systems, and this can create at least the appearance, and perhaps the reality, of an increase in certain forms of corruption following a democratic transition.[10]

Moving from the level of the polity to the level of the individual candidate, there is indeed evidence that the level of genuine political competition faced by an incumbent candidate may affect, and may sometimes increase, the odds that this candidate will engage in corrupt acts to try to retain his or her office. The best available evidence suggests a non-monotonic relationship between political competitiveness and corruption at the candidate level: within democratic states, legislators who are very secure or very insecure are the most likely to be implicated in corrupt acts—the former because they are less worried that a corruption scandal would be damaging enough to cost them their seats, the latter because they have the strongest incentives to 'cheat' to try to gain an extra advantage in the election (Chang 2005; Nyblade and Reed 2008).[11]

5.   Democracy, corruption, and political time horizons

Another important factor that may influence a political actor's willingness to engage in corrupt activity is the actor's 'time horizon'—how long he, she, or it expects to be in power (and in a position to potentially abuse that power for personal gain). Importantly, both very long and very short political time horizons tend to produce higher levels of corruption, but the *type* of corruption may be quite different in these two cases. Officials

---

[9]   One piece of suggestive evidence consistent with that assertion is that, within the subset of democratic countries, a country's perceived corruption level has a strong statistically significant correlation with estimates of illegal campaign donations in that country (Tavits and Potter 2012).

[10]   For example, in the post-communist transition in Eastern Europe, corruption in the context of rigid central planning was replaced by other forms of corruption to deal with—or take advantage of—weak or dysfunctional political, economic, and regulatory institutions.

[11]   These cross-cutting effects, and the non-monotonicity they produce, may also partially explain the conflicting results of Ferraz and Finan (2011) and Pereira ct al. (2009), both of whom examine the effect of re-election incentives on corruption by Brazilian mayors. Ferraz and Finan (2011) find more competitive elections were associated with lower levels of corruption, while Pereira et al. (2009), using a larger sample and a different set of controls, reach the opposite result.

facing very short time horizons—those who do not expect that they will be in power for very long, and who anticipate that once they lose power they are unlikely ever to hold it again—have an incentive to engage in unilateral theft, and perhaps also to extort or solicit bribes in exchange for immediate favors. The fact that such corruption may do serious economic damage to the country—and will likely reduce the public resources available in the future for both legitimate use and illegitimate diversion—is less salient for incumbents focusing only on the near-term (Campante et al. 2009; Roberts 2008). However, public officials with short time horizons are less likely to enter into long-term corrupt deals with private interest groups—not because the officials wouldn't want to, but because potential private counterparts are less confident that the incumbent officials will be around to honor their part of the deal (Fredrikson and Svensson 2003; Campante et al. 2009; Milanovic et al. 2010). Why pay a corrupt leader massive bribes for, say, a mining concession when, a few years down the road, a new leader may take over and either demand more bribes or transfer the concession to some other party? By contrast, incumbent officials who expect to be in power for a long time have less of an incentive to engage in destructive short-term looting, primarily because it reduces their expected stream of (misappropriated) resources over the long term (Olson 1993; Clague et al. 1996). At the same time, private actors would view such incumbents are extremely desirable partners for long-term corrupt exchanges, making such exchanges much more likely (Fredrikson and Svensson 2003; Campante et al. 2009; Milanovic et al. 2010; Morris 1991).

The above hypotheses imply that there is likely to be a U-shaped relationship between political time horizons and corruption. And indeed, the available evidence, though not conclusive, is generally consistent with that hypothesis: countries with very low or very high levels of political stability—usually measured with various proxies, such as the frequency of leadership turnover—seem to have higher (perceived) corruption than do countries at an intermediate level of stability (Campante et al. 2009; Schleiter and Voznya 2014).[12] There is also some within-country evidence, noted above, that elected politicians who are very secure or very insecure are more likely to engage in corrupt activities (Chang 2005; Nyblade and Reed 2008). Moreover, and perhaps more interestingly, the above analysis suggests that changes in political time horizons may alter the *form* of cor-

---

[12]   Other studies, which only test for linear effects, reach conflicting results, with some finding that political turnover is correlated with lower perceived corruption (Pellegata 2009, Milanovic et al. 2010), others finding that political turnover is correlated with higher perceived corruption (Serra 2006, Tavits 2007, Pellegrini and Gerlagh 2008), and still others finding null results (Treisman 2000).

ruption, not just the extent. On this point there is less empirical evidence at the cross-country level, given that the existing country-level corruption indexes do not disaggregate corruption by type, though some within-country evidence (both qualitative and quantitative) does seem consistent with that hypothesis (Campante et al. 2009; Nyblade and Reed 2008).

However, even if we have a sense of how changes in political time horizons may affect the type and extent of corruption, the implications of this relationship for the effects of democracy on corruption are not immediate, because the impact of democratization on political time horizons is not straightforward. Some authoritarian leaders (or leadership organizations, such as the dominant party, clique, or family) have very long time horizons; their grip on power is secure, and so they can take the long view. Democratization, in that context, is likely to shorten leaders' time horizons. Other authoritarian states, by contrast, are highly unstable, with frequent, and often violent, leadership turnover; leaders in such states likely have quite short time horizons. And just as there is huge variation among non-democracies with respect to leaders' time horizons, the same is true of democracies. Here, perhaps the key difference across systems is the extent to which there are a few stable political parties with long expected lifespans, which cycle in and out of power. If there are, then it is likely that these parties will be able to act as entities with long time horizons. By contrast, if parties tend to be organized around individual politicians and for that reason tend to appear and dissolve quickly, and where a party or leader that has lost power in an election is unlikely to make a comeback, incumbent officials are more likely to have fairly short time horizons.

Putting this together, one might conjecture that a transition from a stable authoritarian political dynasty to a fractious democracy without institutionalized parties will shorten political time horizons—perhaps increasing incentives for short-term grabbing while reducing opportunities for long-term collusive corruption. By contrast, compared to an unstable authoritarian regime with lots of turmoil and turnover, a stable democratic system with institutionalized parties will foster longer political time horizons. Moreover, a democratic system with long-lived parties that cycle in and out of power may be the best of both worlds: the parties' long-term horizons discourage short-term looting, but at the same time, private interests may still find corrupt collusion unattractive because there is no guarantee that the bribed party or official will be in power when the time comes to follow through on the government's side of the deal. (One can always bribe multiple parties, of course, but that is more expensive, and so would likely happen less often.)

B.   The Aggregate Impact of Democracy on Corruption

Given all of the cross-cutting effects discussed above, the net impact of democracy on corruption is far from obvious. Indeed, this relationship is so nuanced that it is not clear whether the average correlation between democracy and corruption, across countries, is particularly illuminating. That said, there has been a great deal of cross-country research on this topic, and it is worth briefly summarizing the main findings here—and then also discussing some of the reasons to be extremely cautious in drawing any firm conclusions from these findings.

1.   Democracy and corruption: the cross-country empirical research
The cross-country research on this question typically examines the correlation between 'democracy' (usually measured with one or more of the existing democracy indexes, such as those provided by Polity, Freedom House, or the World Bank's Database of Political Institutions, and sometimes with more direct proxies like turnout rates and competition measures) and perceived corruption (usually measured with the Transparency International Corruption Perceptions Index, the World Bank Institute's 'control of corruption' index, or the International Country Risk Guide's 'graft' score). The results of this research, taken as a whole, are mixed and somewhat inconclusive. Some studies find that higher democracy index scores are correlated with lower perceived corruption index scores, perhaps suggesting that democracy on net does indeed reduce corruption (Sandholtz and Koetzle 2000; Adsera et al. 2003; Bohara et al. 2004; Lederman et al. 2005; Gurger and Shah 2005; Halim 2006; Pellegata 2009; Billger and Goel 2009; Kolstad and Wiig 2011). Other cross-country studies, however, have failed to find a robust negative correlation between various democracy measures and corruption index scores (Treisman 2000; Morris 2004; Xin and Rudel 2004; Chowdhury 2004; Blake and Martin 2006; Serra 2006; Pellegrini and Gerlagh 2008; Brown et al. 2011). And yet other studies find that, at least when certain control variables are included (particularly those that measure various aspects of 'economic freedom'), some democracy measures seem to have a *positive* correlation with perceived corruption (Saha and Su 2012).

These conflicting, inconclusive results have led scholars to consider refinements to the research question. Work in this vein has produced a number of studies offering more qualified hypotheses about the democracy-corruption relationship, as well as some intriguing evidence in support of those hypotheses. First, there is evidence that the *duration* of democracy may matter more than the current *level* of democracy (Treisman 2000; Gerring and Thacker 2004; Bohara et al. 2004; Chang and Golden 2006;

Blake and Martin 2006; Serra 2006; Keefer 2007; Tavits 2007; Pellegrini and Gerlagh 2008; Pellegata 2013; Schleiter and Voznaya 2014).[13] This is consistent with the observation that most of the modern democracies that currently enjoy a relatively low level of corruption experienced a fairly long period with high corruption, which only declined over time—the United States being a prime example.[14] Second, there is fairly convincing evidence of a pronounced non-linear relationship between democracy and corruption: Countries that score very high on the various democracy indexes tend to have significantly lower perceived corruption, but for levels of democracy below the very top end of the scale, a negative correlation between democracy and perceived corruption is much less evident (Montinola and Jackman 2002; Sung 2004; Back and Hadenius 2008; Dong and Torgler 2011; Pellegata 2013). Moreover, there is evidence suggesting that the relationship between the duration of democracy and the level of perceived corruption is also non-linear: rather than each year of continuous democracy being associated with a roughly equivalent decrease in the perceived corruption score, several studies find substantial 'threshold effects', with the level of perceived corruption significantly lower in countries that have been continuously democratic for somewhere between 20 and 40 years (Treisman 2000; Blake and Martin 2006). Taken together, this evidence suggests that long-established, fully-institutionalized democracies have lower levels of perceived corruption than other countries, but new democracies and partial democracies do *not* seem to have lower perceived corruption than do non-democracies. Indeed, some studies even find that new or partial democracies have (slightly) *higher* perceived corruption than do non-democracies, even though the perceived corruption levels in long-standing, fully institutionalized democracies are (much) lower (Sung 2004; Pellegata 2013; Rock 2009; Milanovic et al. 2010).[15]

---

[13]   It may be worth noting that the age of democracies may be correlated with other features of democratic institutions, which are not always controlled for in these studies. For instance, Keefer (2007) reports that younger democracies are more likely to be presidential rather than parliamentary, and more likely to use plurality voting as opposed to proportional representation, than are older democracies.

[14]   Part of the explanation for this might be that democracy does not reduce corruption until the country becomes a *liberal* democracy, with institutions such as a free press, checks and balances, and a robust civil society, as well as a sufficiently educated and informed citizenry.

[15]   Sung (2004) reports a *cubic* relationship between democracy and perceived corruption, with improvements on the democracy score associated first with lower, then higher, then (much) lower perceived corruption. However, the first of these effects is relatively small in magnitude, and subsequent work by Pellegata (2013)

2. Interpreting the results: reasons for caution

Even though the correlations discussed above—particularly the non-linear negative association between democracy and corruption—are suggestive, one must be extremely cautious about using these correlations to make inferences about causation. There are at least four reasons why correlations between democracy levels and corruption levels might not necessarily imply that the former are responsible for the latter.

First, the measures of both democracy and corruption—which are usually perception indexes—may be 'contaminated' by the evaluators' knowledge of (and implicit assumptions about) the influence of the other variable. To be more concrete: Some measures of 'democracy' may incorporate—deliberately or inadvertently—perceptions of corruption. For example, the Freedom House Political Rights Index, often used as a measure of democracy, explicitly incorporates questions about the whether the government 'is free from pervasive corruption'. In the reverse direction, critics of the various perception-based corruption or governance indicators have raised concerns about 'halo effects'—the subconscious presumption that certain countries that perform well on other dimensions (perhaps including democracy) probably have lower corruption (Sequeira 2012).

Second, and also related to the fact that most cross-country research relies on perception indexes to measure corruption, democracies and autocracies may vary systematically in the amount of information available about how the government operates, which can influence perceptions of corruption independent of the actual level of corruption. This could cut both ways: On the one hand, democratization may increase perceived corruption (at least in the short term) not so much because corruption has actually increased, but rather because other dimensions of political liberalization have led to more widespread exposure and discussion of corruption. On the other hand, the very secrecy associated with most autocracies may cause observers to assume the worst, substantially overstating the amount of actual corruption that takes place in those systems. Closely related to this is the fact that, as the earlier theoretical discussion suggested, democracy may affect not only the amount but also the type of corruption, and some types of corruption may be more likely than others to get picked up in perception-based indexes. Thus reliance on perception index scores may cause a change in the *form* of corruption to be misinterpreted as a change in the *level* of corruption.

---

could not replicate the finding of a cubic, as opposed to quadratic, relationship between democracy and perceived corruption.

Third, although most cross-country empirical studies attempt to rule out alternative explanations by including a range of control variables (such as GDP per capita, education, colonial heritage, population size, and so on), it is probably impossible to incorporate every factor that might simultaneously affect both democracy and corruption. Consider two alternative explanations of the finding that, although partial or new democracies do not have significantly lower perceived corruption than other states, well-established democracies (those that have been democracies for several decades and score near the top of the various democracy indexes) do have much lower corruption scores. The usual interpretation is that it takes time for democratic institutions to take root and to effect a more general political transformation. But there are at least two complicating factors. First, almost all of those well-established democracies with low corruption levels are both very rich and geographically concentrated. (They are, with only a handful of exceptions, wealthy countries in Northwestern Europe, along with the former European settler colonies in North America and Oceania.) Although most studies try to control for wealth (usually using per capita GDP), some researchers have suggested that the apparent nonlinearity in the democracy-corruption relationship is due more to the fact that democracy is associated with lower corruption levels only in sufficiently rich countries (Charron and Lapuente 2010). Additionally, the research suggesting that the duration of democracy makes a difference—and that democracy only has a corruption-reducing effect after a sufficient number of years of continuous democracy—typically neglects to distinguish *duration effects* from *cohort effects*—despite the fact that the literature on age and corruption attitudes at the individual level is careful in drawing this distinction (Torgler and Valev 2006). To elaborate: Because most existing studies use outcome data from the 1990s and 2000s, the finding that only those countries that have been democratic for at least 20–40 years have lower perceived corruption levels implies that those low-corruption democracies are those that were democratic prior to the 'third wave' of democratization that ran from roughly the late 1970s through the end of the 1990s (Huntington 1991). If there are systematic differences between third-wave democracies and those countries that became democracies earlier—differences that affect corruption levels and are not fully captured with the usual control variables—then the finding that longstanding democracies have lower corruption levels may be due to a cohort effect rather than the duration effect that most of the literature typically assumes.

Fourth, although the usual assumption is that democracy levels may affect corruption, it is also possible that corruption may affect democracy. If the causal arrow could run both ways (if, to use the standard jargon, democracy is 'endogenous' to corruption rather than purely exogenous), then correlations can be highly misleading. There are several reasons why corruption could, at least in theory, influence the degree or duration of democracy. First, although transitions from non-democracy to democracy, and from democracy to non-democracy, are not exactly frequent, they are not as rare as one might think, and it is quite plausible that corruption may influence the likelihood of such transitions. Widespread corruption in authoritarian regimes may spark or intensify democratization movements (think of the Arab Spring); it is also possible that more corrupt democracies are at greater risk of reversion to non-democracy (think of the recent coup in Thailand). These possibilities cut in opposite directions, and it is hard to say which is more significant (or whether either is), but it is at least possible that these relationships could influence the strength and direction of the correlation between democracy and corruption. Suppose, for example, that among the set of authoritarian countries, the ones with higher (perceived) corruption are, on average, more likely to become democratic over a given time period. If that were so, then the pool of democratic countries—especially young democracies—would be more corrupt, on average, even if democracy does tend to reduce corruption. There is also a more general and indirect endogeneity concern: Corruption may affect many aspects of a country's economy, politics, and society, which could in turn affect democracy—and even though researchers can try to control for these variables, perfect control is likely impossible. Therefore, correlations between democracy and corruption, even when they seem robust, may not (only) reflect democracy's effect on corruption, but (also) corruption's direct or indirect effect on democracy.[16]

---

[16] Some of the literature on the corruption-democracy relationship exhibits keen awareness of the potential endogeneity problem and attempts to address it by finding an instrumental variable—a variable that has a causal effect on democracy, but that also satisfies the 'exclusion restriction', which requires that the instrument cannot be correlated with the outcome variable (corruption) except through its effect on the explanatory variable (democracy). Unfortunately, none of the instruments that have been proposed would seem to satisfy the exclusion restriction, as most of them—for example, fraction of the population that speaks a European language (Chowdhury 2004), percentage of population that is Protestant (Rock 2009), education (Musila 2013), and latitude (Chowdhury 2004, Rock 2009, Keefer 2007)—seem like they could clearly affect corruption through other channels. (One other proposed instrument—whether the country has ever fought a war with a democracy (Kolstad and Wiig 2011)—is invalid for a different reason: the proposed instrument is causally posterior to the explanatory variable, meaning that it is really just another imperfect proxy for whether the country is a democracy, and cannot be used as an instrument to assess whether democracy affects corruption.)

One final note about the empirical research on the democracy-corruption relationship: Although most of the quantitative empirical research on the correlations between democracy and corruption has relied on cross-country comparisons, some studies have examined variation within single countries, particularly federal countries with substantial variation in democratic institutions at the sub-national level. The advantages of this approach are twofold: First, looking within a single country may effectively control for differences in political culture and traditions as well as other potentially omitted variables. Second, the key variables—both the extent of democracy and the level of corruption—can be measured using more objective indicators, rather than relying on perception indexes. For example, comparing turnout rates may be a more plausible way to compare levels of democracy across sub-national units than it would be to measure differences in democracy levels across countries. And in systems where the central government prosecutes sub-national corruption, law enforcement statistics may provide more reliable comparative information about actual corruption rates than would be possible when comparing national law enforcement data across countries. However, existing within-country research is still relatively sparse. There is some evidence that US states with higher political participation rates have fewer federal corruption convictions per capita, but the correlation does not appear especially strong (Adsera et al. 2003; Hill 2003). Likewise, Italian regions with higher electoral participation rates appear to have lower rates of reported public corruption offenses (Del Monte and Papagni 2007). These results are consistent with more general findings, for example from studies of Indian states, that political competition and turnout rates seem to make local governments more responsive to the public (Besley and Burgess 2002), and are broadly supportive of the notion that democratic accountability may limit some forms of corruption. This evidence is not, however, inconsistent with the broader results from the cross-country research, which suggest that the relationship between democracy and corruption is complicated, contingent, and likely non-linear.

II.   VARIATION IN DEMOCRATIC INSTITUTIONS

Perhaps asking whether 'democracy' reduces 'corruption' asks the wrong question—or at least asks the question too generally. As we have already seen, democracy may have different effects on different sorts of corruption—tending to decrease some and increase others—making aggregate-level data potentially misleading. Likewise, 'democracy' encompasses a range of institutions, and even though it may be worthwhile to consider democracy as a single category, it is also worthwhile to disaggregate democracy along a number of dimensions in order to get a better sense of how variation in the institutions of democracy, and not just the presence or absence of regular elections, may affect different sorts of corruption. This section will therefore consider three dimensions of institutional variation within democratic polities: (1) the voting rule (how the vote totals are used to allocate legislative seats), (2) district magnitude (the number of legislators selected in each district, or in the average district), and (3) whether the system is presidential or parliamentary (whether the chief executive is directly elected by the voters or selected by the legislature). These are, of course, only three of a much larger set of institutional dimensions along which democracies may vary, but they are three of the most significant and frequently studied, particularly in the context of corruption research. For this reason, and for reasons of space, this chapter will focus on these three institutional variables, leaving consideration of other factors (for example, whether the legislature is bicameral or unicameral, and whether there is substantial political decentralization to sub-national units) to other work.

A.   The Voting Rule

One of the most basic forms of institutional variation across democratic systems is the electoral rule—that is, the system for translating votes into seats. (For a useful overview and classification, see Cary and Shugart 1995.) Of the many possible rules, three of the most common are plurality rule, open-list proportional representation (PR), and closed-list PR. In a plurality system, two or more candidates compete for a single open seat, and whichever candidate receives the most votes wins.[17] In PR systems, multiple parties compete for multiple seats in the same election, and the number of seats allocated to each party is proportional to the number of votes cast for that party (with some minimum number of votes required before a party is entitled to any seats). In a *closed-list* PR system, voters cast their ballots only for parties, not for individual candidates; the number of seats allocated to each party depends on its vote share, and the individual candidates who fill those seats are determined by each party's list, which is set by party leaders. (If, for example, the party's vote share entitles it to five legislative seats from the district, the top five names on

---

[17]   Some systems require the winning candidate to receive a majority of votes; such systems may use run-off elections, or some form of ordered preference voting (for example, a 'transferrable vote'), when no one candidate wins an outright majority on the first ballot. For simplicity, this discussion focuses on simple plurality voting.

the party list get those seats.) In an *open-list* PR system, voters generally also vote for a party, but they can express their preference for individual candidates from that party. (In some open-list PR systems, voters vote for candidates rather than parties, but the total number of candidates elected from each party depends on the party's overall vote share.)[18]

Different electoral rules may have implications for a range of important political and policy outcomes, including the type and extent of corruption. The choice among these three voting rules may affect corruption through two main channels: (1) the degree to which the electoral system encourages candidate-centric or party-centric elections; and (2) the degree of political fragmentation (the number of viable parties running in the election and securing seats in the legislature). Let us consider each in turn, before evaluating the existing empirical evidence on the overall impact of the voting rule on corruption levels.

1.   Candidate-centered vs. party-centered electoral competition

Electoral systems vary in the degree to which they encourage competition between *parties* or between individual *candidates*. These are not, of course, mutually exclusive, and indeed most voters are likely influenced both by their partisan preferences and by their views of the individual candidates representing the different parties. Nonetheless, the electoral rule affects the relative significance of parties, party leaders, and candidates. Of the three electoral rules under consideration, open-list PR tends to produce the most candidate-centric elections, with a great deal of *intra*-party competition in addition to (or in some extreme cases instead of) *inter*-party competition. This leads individual candidates to try to cultivate a 'personal vote', rather than (or in addition to) a vote for the party. At the other end of the spectrum, closed-list PR tends to produce the most party-centric elections, with most electoral competition taking place between parties; in these systems, party leadership tends to be centralized, and party discipline strong. Plurality systems tend to fall somewhere in between open-list and closed-list PR on this dimension (Carey and Shugart 1995; Mitchell 2000).[19]

---

[18]   Some PR systems use a hybrid of open-list and closed-list voting rules. Again for simplicity, and in keeping with most of the existing empirical research in the anti-corruption area, this chapter will focus on open-list PR and closed-list PR, along with plurality voting, as ideal types.

[19]   Other, less widely-used systems might generate even stronger incentives to cultivate a personal vote—for example, a single non-transferrable vote with open endorsement (Carey and Shugart 1995). For simplicity, though, the text will focus on the three most common types of electoral system.

The implications of these differences in incentives for corruption is not, however, straightforward. In understanding the potentially complex and cross-cutting effects, it is perhaps helpful to draw three distinctions with respect to types of corruption. The first distinction, which will be familiar from the more general discussion of the impact of democracy on corruption from Section I, is the distinction between instrumental political corruption and venal personal corruption. The second distinction is between corruption at the candidate level and (organized) corruption at the party level. The third distinction, again familiar from the discussion in Section I, is the distinction between engaging in corruption, on the one hand, and failing to take action against corruption, on the other. All three of these distinctions are admittedly over-simplified, and are better thought of as continuous rather than dichotomous. Nonetheless, these simple categorizations may be useful in understanding how variation in the electoral system can affect the amount, type, and locus of corrupt behavior. With these simple distinctions in mind, let us consider the incentives that different electoral rules create for individual politicians to engage in different types of corrupt activities.

Assuming voters dislike corruption—and therefore are less likely, all else equal, to support a corrupt candidate—then politicians in a candidate-centric system have a disincentive to engage in both venal corruption and instrumental corruption. After all, being implicated in a corruption scandal may be bad for the candidate's electoral prospects, especially if voters have a number of ideologically-similar candidates from which to choose. In party-centric systems, by contrast, an individual candidate's electoral prospects depend more on the party's overall electoral success in the district, and also the individual candidate's position on the party list. In such a situation, although a candidate's implication in a corruption scandal would still be damaging, the impact on the candidate's electoral prospects would be less severe.

At first blush the above considerations might seem to imply that candidate-centric systems, like open-list PR, will tend to have less corruption (at least at the candidate level) than will party-centric systems like closed-list PR. But there are three important countervailing factors. First, even if candidate-centric elections discourage individual politicians from engaging in corruption, such systems may also reduce incumbents' incentives to take (collective) action to fight corruption elsewhere in the system, because the political benefits associated with such efforts are more likely to be associated with the government or the party, rather than an individual legislator. Second, each individual candidate's incentive to cultivate a personal vote can create strong incentives to engage in instrumental political corruption if doing so gives the candidate a leg up in the competition for personal support. Therefore, if the probability of getting caught is sufficiently low, a candidate-centric electoral system may end up producing more instrumental political corruption than a party-centric system, even if venal personal corruption is lower in the former (Geddes and Neto 1992; Golden and Chang 2001; Golden 2003).[20] Third, because party discipline tends to be stronger in party-centric systems like closed-list PR, and because individual corruption scandals may damage the party's 'brand', party leaders may have a stronger incentive and ability to monitor and discipline candidates in party-centric systems. If that internal monitoring is more important to deterring corruption than the risk of exposure in a public scandal, then strong party discipline—internal accountability to the party leaders—may be more effective in reducing corruption than direct external accountability to the voters.

Once we shift the focus from individual candidates to the party organization overall, things are more complicated still: What if the party leaders are themselves corrupt, and willing to orchestrate systematic instrumental political corruption to benefit the party? Of course, it may be that party leaders conclude that the electoral advantages associated with political corruption are not worth the expected costs. But suppose the party leaders reach the opposite conclusion—suppose they determine that the expected benefits for the party of using corrupt means to pursue political advantage outweigh the risks associated with the occasional scandal. Or suppose that party leaders are simply interested in enriching themselves, but they need the collaboration, or at least the acquiescence, of the party apparatus in order to succeed. Under these circumstances, the ability of the party to reward supporters (say, with a favorable list position, or an

---

[20]   Kselman (2011) provides an unintentional illustration of the ambiguous implications of these incentive effects for corruption. Kselman develops a formal game-theoretic model of the impact of electoral systems on legislators' allocation of a fixed effort budget as between 'constituency service' (delivering particularistic benefits to constituents) and 'personal consumption', and finds that constituency service is higher under open-list PR than closed-list PR or plurality rule. The implications of this finding for corruption, however, are unclear. Kselman interprets 'personal consumption' as corruption and 'constituency service' as uncorrupt activity, but that interpretation is not inevitable. 'Constituency service' could be re-labeled corrupt provision of particularistic benefits (for example, Della Porta 2004), and 'personal consumption' could be re-defined as (uncorrupt) pursuit of policy or ideological goals (collective goods that do not much improve the incumbent's probability of winning, particularly when in competition with co-partisans). The model and results would be identical, but the implications for corruption would be reversed, with this alternative and equally plausible interpretation of the key variables.

endorsement in a primary) and to punish dissenters (by withholding those or other benefits) may facilitate party-directed corruption (Kunicova and Rose-Ackerman 2005; Gingerich 2009).

It is difficult to synthesize so many cross-cutting effects, but here is a stab at a quick synopsis. Electoral systems that encourage the cultivation of a personal vote and reduce the significance of parties are likely to have the following effects, relative to systems that promote party-centric competition: (1) Individual rank-and-file candidates are less likely to engage in personal venal corruption. (2) Individual rank-and-file candidates may engage in more or less instrumental political corruption, depending on whether the risk of external exposure and/or internal discipline outweighs the expected political benefits. When monitoring is effective, candidate-centric systems do a better job discouraging instrumental political corruption, but when monitoring is weak, they are worse on this dimension than party-centric systems. (3) At the party/government level, there is less likely to be aggressive anti-corruption policy reform, just as there is likely to be less provision of collective legislative goods generally. (4) Party leaders may engage in more or less corruption (both venal and instrumental), depending on whether they benefit more from protecting the reputation of the party or from engaging in corrupt activities. (In a polity where party leaders are very responsive to demands for integrity in government, party-centric electoral systems are likely to reduce corruption, relative to candidate-centric systems, by strengthening internal party discipline and encouraging aggressive anti-corruption action more generally—even though there may still be some venal corruption by individual legislators. By contrast, in a polity where party leaders view corruption as personally or politically advantageous, an electoral rule that encourages candidate-centric elections may lead to less corruption overall, or will at least shift corruption from the organized, systemic level to the individual candidate level.)

2.   The electoral rule and partisan fragmentation

A second important difference among these three ideal-type electoral systems, which also has implications for corruption incentives, concerns the degree of political fragmentation these systems produce. In general, the number of viable parties tends to be positively correlated with the number of open seats in each election (Cox 1997; Benoit 2006). As a result, PR systems, particularly those with many legislators selected in each district, tend to produce a larger number of parties, while single-member districts operating pursuant to a plurality rule tend to produce two-party competition—if not at the national level, then at least at the district level. The number of parties is also influenced by other institutional factors that determine how easy it is for new parties to enter. And it may be easier for identifiable factions within each party to emerge and compete (electorally) with one another in an open-list system than in a closed-list system. (While there is plenty of factional competition in closed-list systems, it typically takes place outside of the electoral arena.) Do systems that are more conducive to a larger number of viable parties tend to produce more or less corruption than systems that tend to limit competition to two or three major parties? Again, a decisive answer is not possible, due to several cross-cutting factors.

On the one hand, systems that facilitate participation by a larger number of parties or factions make it more likely that perceptions of corruption (or failure to act aggressively against corruption) may be decisive in how voters cast their ballots. Recall that one of the factors that may undermine the efficacy of democratic elections in checking corruption is the relevance of other considerations—ideology, perceived competence, ethnic or religious affiliation, and so on—that take precedence over corruption for many voters, even if those voters dislike corruption. When it is easier for new parties or factions to compete, it is easier for candidates to emerge who are sufficiently similar to the incumbents on these other dimensions, but who are perceived as less corrupt. Moreover, systems in which it is generally easier for new parties to secure legislative representation facilitate the entrance specifically of 'anti-corruption parties', which may help raise the profile of corruption issues and push for attention to those issues (Bagenholm 2013). This is especially so when the anti-corruption parties secure enough seats in the legislature to make them attractive coalition partners. Closely related to the above observations is the fact that some systems, like PR, make shifting votes to an ideologically congenial party viewed as less corrupt than the established parties—or to an anti-corruption party—more attractive, because voters do not need to worry as much about 'wasting' their votes and thereby risking a worse overall outcome (Myerson 1993).

On the other hand, there are at least two reasons why corruption levels might actually be higher in systems with a larger number of effective parties, compared to systems with a lower number of effective parties. To appreciate the first reason, it is helpful to recall from Section I that although one factor that might limit the extent to which democratic elections curtail corruption is the predominance of other issues, another such factor is the absence of sufficient information about corrupt activity. Although increasing the number of effective parties may help alleviate the first problem, it may exacerbate the second. After all, in democratic systems it is often the political competitors who play a leading role in unearthing and publicizing information about their opponents' corruption—but because this information is a collective good, the incentive to provide it may be weaker in systems that produce a large number of viable competing parties (Kunicova and Rose-Ackerman 2005). To see this, consider what happens when an opposition candidate publicizes credible evidence that the incumbent legislator (or the government with which that legislator is affiliated) has engaged in corrupt acts. Although this revelation may well decrease support for the incumbent, there is no guarantee this will translate to an equivalent increase in support for the candidate who made the charges. Rather, *all* opposition parties may benefit from the incumbent's loss of support. Moreover, the party or candidate that made the disclosures may be singled out for retaliation by the tarnished incumbent, or might simply suffer from association with 'mudslinging'. This implies that the incentive to monitor and disclose government corruption will be stronger, all else equal, when there is a single opposition party that stands to benefit from the incumbent's loss of support (Charron 2011). That incentive is likely to be all the stronger when the competing parties are strongly ideologically opposed (Brown et al. 2011).

The second reason why multiparty systems might have higher corruption levels is the fact that a large number of parties at the legislative level—and the frequent emergence of fractious coalition governments—can exacerbate corruption. There are several reasons for this. First, when there are many parties in the legislature, the government may need to cut lots of particularistic deals to get anything done, which may lead to more corruption (Geddes and Neto 1992; Della Porta 2004). Second, and related to the earlier point about monitoring incentives, when there are many small parties and constantly shifting governing coalitions, parties may be reluctant to criticize one another for corruption, lest they alienate potential future coalition partners (Kunicova and Rose-Ackerman 2005). Third, a large number of effective parties in the legislature may make it more difficult to implement aggressive new anticorruption policies, just as it is often more difficult for coalition governments to move ahead with potentially controversial action in other policy arenas, because of the need for agreement among multiple parties. Finally, and closely related to that last point, a large number of legislative or government parties may produce a so-called 'clarity of responsibility' problem in which voters are not sure whom to fault for the failure of the government to take appropriate action to address corruption, and likewise any credit for effective action would be shared across parties (Tavits 2007).

3.   The net effect of the voting rule on corruption

The preceding discussion implies that although we might be able to make some tentative generalizations as to the impact of the voting rule on corruption—at least the types of corruption risks that are most significant under each rule—it is not possible to make confident predictions as to the net effect of the voting rule on perceived corruption levels. In light of that theoretical indeterminacy, and the crudeness of the existing measures of corruption, it is perhaps unsurprising that the raft of cross-country quantitative empirical research on this issue has not generated consistent findings. Nonetheless, a brief survey of the existing literature is in order.

A number of studies have compared systems that use plurality rule to systems that use some form of PR. Several of these studies find that PR is associated with higher perceived corruption (Persson et al. 2003; Kunicova and Rose-Ackerman 2005; Testa 2010; Schleiter and Voznaya 2014), but other studies—using somewhat different samples or measures, and different combinations of control variables—find either that PR is associated with lower perceived corruption (Verardi 2004), or that there is no statistically significant difference between the perceived corruption levels of plurality systems and PR systems (Adsera et al. 2003; Serra 2006; Keefer 2007).

These results, however, might be misleading insofar as they conflate open-list PR and closed-list PR, which, as we have seen, might have very different effects. Yet those studies that do distinguish open-list and closed-list PR also reach inconsistent conclusions. Some find that closed-list PR systems are associated with higher perceived corruption than open-list PR systems (Chang and Golden 2006; Persson et al. 2003; Tavits 2007; Kselman 2011), while other research has found that closed-list PR systems have lower perceived corruption than open-list systems (Brown et al. 2011; Testa 2010; Tavits and Potter 2012), and many studies fail to find evidence of a statistically significant difference in the perceived corruption levels associated with open- and closed-list PR (Kunicova and Rose-Ackerman 2005; Serra 2006; Pellegata 2009; Schleiter and Voznaya 2014).

Other researchers have looked specifically at the number of parties and/or the degree of ideological polarization across parties, but again the results—though intriguing—are not terribly robust. For example, although one influential study found that systems with a higher number of effective legislative parties have higher perceived corruption (Chang and Golden 2006), other studies have failed to replicate these results, finding instead either that there is no statistically significant correlation between the effective number of legislative parties and the level of perceived corruption when appropriate control variables are included (Tavits and Potter 2012; Pellegata 2009), or that a larger number of effective legislative parties is correlated with *lower* perceived corruption (Tavits 2007). Again, these conflicting results are not very surprising, given the indeterminacy of the theoretical predictions and the fact that all these studies, though broadly similar in research design, use different samples, measures, and control variables.

Given that the theory predicts cross-cutting effects, perhaps the most intriguing recent empirical findings are those that suggest a non-monotonic relationship between the number of effective parties and perceived corruption levels. This sort of relationship—with perceived corruption higher when the number of effective parties is either very small or very large, but lower for intermediate levels of partisan fragmentation—has been found in both cross-country data (Schleiter and Voznaya 2014) and within-country data (Del Monte and Papagni 2007, studying Italy).[21] These findings, though hardly dispositive, are consistent with the conjecture that when the electoral system produces very few viable parties, voters' ability to hold politicians accountable for corruption is hampered by the paucity of alternatives, while when the electoral system produces a multitude of parties, voters' ability to hold politicians accountable is hampered by some combination of information costs and coordination problems.

There is likewise some suggestive evidence of a non-monotonic relationship between the degree to which the electoral system encourages candidates to seek a personal vote and the level of corruption. At the cross-country level, Panizza (2001) reports evidence of a U-shaped relationship between the degree to which an electoral system is more 'candidate-centered' (rather than 'party-centered') and the level of perceived corruption. This finding is consistent with the notion that corruption is more likely when incentives to cultivate a personal vote are either very strong (because this leads to a temptation to 'cheat') or very weak (because in such cases legislators are insufficiently accountable). There is persuasive

---

[21] In a similar vein, Charron (2011) finds that multiparty plurality systems had higher perceived corruption levels than either PR systems (regardless of the number of parties) or two-party plurality systems. (Although, as noted in the earlier theoretical discussion, plurality voting rules tend to produce two-party systems, this is not invariably true, and Charron's data include several multiparty plurality systems.) Charron's explanation for this result, broadly consistent with the earlier theoretical discussion, is as follows: In two-party plurality systems, parties have strong incentives to monitor one another and reveal corruption. In multiparty plurality systems, this incentive is weakened because of the collective action problem discussed earlier. In multiparty PR systems, the collective action problem is less acute, because even if the political benefits of disclosing the incumbent's corruption flow to multiple opposition parties, the disclosing party does stand to gain something in terms of higher vote share. PR also has the benefit of allowing easier entry, so voters can vote for a non-corrupt party with a similar ideology, without worrying about contributing to the election of an ideologically less-preferred party.

within-country evidence as well, most notably Nyblade and Reed (2008), who study legislative malfeasance in Japan. Consistent with the theoretical discussion above, this study distinguishes between instrumental political corruption ('cheating') and venal personal corruption ('looting') and finds that the former is more likely for politicians who have very strong incentives to cultivate a personal vote (due to electoral competition), while the latter is more likely for politicians who are very secure. Thus, the overall relationship between personal vote incentives and corruption appears to be non-monotonic, with those legislators facing an intermediate level of political competition least likely to be implicated in any form of scandal.

B. District Magnitude

A second important dimension of variation across democratic electoral systems, at least within PR systems, is the number of legislators elected per district in each election. This legislator-to-district ratio is conventionally referred to as 'district magnitude', though the nomenclature can be somewhat confusing because 'magnitude' here refers to the number of legislators elected in each district, not to the population or geographic size of the district.

District magnitude may affect corruption by intensifying or muting the tendencies of open-list and closed-list PR systems, respectively, to produce candidate-centric or party-centric elections. In open-list PR systems, a larger number of legislators per district generally implies more intra-party competition for preference votes, and so open-list PR coupled with high district magnitude tends to produce especially candidate-centric elections. By contrast, when district magnitude is small, the tendency of an open-list PR system to generate intra-party competition is more attenuated, and inter-party competition becomes relatively more significant. The effects of district magnitude are quite different in closed-list PR systems. In those systems, smaller district magnitude increases rather than decreases individual candidates' incentive to cultivate a personal vote: When very few legislators are selected in each district, whichever legislators are at the top of the party list have strong incentives to build a personal reputation with voters, because in practice a vote for the party is really a vote for those individuals. By contrast, when district magnitude is large in a closed-list PR system, voters are more likely to vote by party than by candidate—the top candidates from the major parties are almost guaranteed a seat, it is less clear which individual candidates are on the margin, and therefore voting decisions are more likely to be based on party preference than on attachment to particular candidates farther down on the list. (Carey and Shugart 1995).

Given that the previous section established that the relative propensity of candidate-centric systems and party-centric systems to produce corruption is indeterminate theoretically and unclear empirically, it probably comes as no surprise that cross-country quantitative studies of the impact of district magnitude on perceived corruption produce mixed—and mostly null—results. Some studies find that larger district magnitude—more legislators per district—is associated with lower perceived corruption (Verardi 2004), while others find that larger district magnitude is associated with higher perceived corruption (Testa 2010). But most cross-country studies either find no statistically significant relationship between district magnitude and perceived corruption (Panizza 2001; Persson et al. 2003; Tavits 2007; Campante 2009), or find a relationship that is not very robust, losing statistical significance in plausible alternative specifications (Persson et al. 2003; Serra 2006).[22]

Of course, given the fact that theoretical analysis predicts that the impact of district magnitude depends on whether the system uses open or closed lists, it may not make much sense to look for simple correlations between district magnitude and perceived corruption. A handful of studies have taken this into account, but again the results are unclear. At least one influential study found that (1) in open-list systems, higher district magnitude (more legislators per district) is associated with higher levels of perceived corruption, but that (2) this relationship does not hold in closed-list systems—with the result that open-list systems tend to have higher levels of perceived corruption when district magnitude is relatively small (fewer than approximately 15 legislators per district), but open-list systems have higher levels of perceived corruption than closed-list systems when district magnitude is large (Chang and Golden 2006). The proposed explanation is that when districts are very large, the intra-party competition for

---

[22]   Although most research on the impact of district magnitude on corruption relies on cross-country comparisons, using perception indexes as the proxy for corruption, some researchers have attempted to exploit within-country variation in district magnitude, using more objective measures of corruption. The leading study in this vein is Chang and Golden (2006), which examines variation in district magnitude in Italy prior to 1994 (during which time Italy used an open-list electoral system). Rather than relying on corruption perceptions, the study estimates corruption by taking the ratio of government spending on public capital to actually existing amounts of public infrastructure, on the assumption that a high ratio implies losses due to corruption. This study finds that larger-magnitude districts had worse spending-infrastructure ratios. However, this result appears not to be robust to the inclusion of a dummy variable for 'southern Italy', which has historically been viewed as more corrupt, and this calls into question the robustness and generalizability of the finding.

personal votes induced by an open-list system produces higher levels of electoral corruption, and because of the large number of candidates and seats, monitoring will be less effective and candidates will be less likely to be caught and held accountable for corruption. However, this intriguing finding appears not to be terribly robust: an attempted replication, using more recent data and a larger sample, was unable to reproduce the results (Tavits and Potter 2012). Thus, there still seems to be relatively little strong evidence on whether district magnitude has a substantively meaningful impact on corruption.

C. Presidentialism vs. Parliamentarism

A third salient institutional difference across democratic systems concerns the method for selecting the chief executive. There are two main models (though there are also many variants and hybrids as well): parliamentary systems, in which the chief executive—usually called the Prime Minister—is selected by the legislature, and presidential systems, in which the chief executive—usually called the President—is directly elected by the citizens. Does this fundamental institutional distinction within democratic systems have significant effects on the amount or type of corruption within those systems? Yet again, the theoretical predictions are not straightforward, and the empirical evidence at the aggregate level is not dispositive.

First, the theory: At least in principle, a presidential system is supposed to create a greater division of power, as both the legislature and the executive—which, by virtue of their separate elections and possible partisan divisions, are more likely to have different interests and objectives—participate in the policymaking process. This is not invariably true: some presidential systems concentrate most important powers in the president, with the legislature relegated to a subordinate role. But let us assume for the moment that presidential systems do have a greater separation of powers—and consequently more checks and balances—in the lawmaking process than do parliamentary systems. The implications of this institutional difference for corruption are not clear. On the one hand, it might be harder for private actors to cut corrupt deals with the government in a presidential system, because they might need to bribe both a sufficient number of legislators *and* the president in order to secure certain policy favors. On the other hand, for precisely the same reason, it would be easier for corrupt private actors to *prevent* policy changes—including changes that would crack down on their corrupt activities—if they only need to buy off the president *or* the legislature. Furthermore, as was true in the earlier discussion about the effective number of parties, there is a trade-off here between different effects on voter information: Inter-branch competition may increase the amount of information voters have about corruption, as the legislative and executive branches—institutional (and perhaps partisan) rivals—have an incentive to monitor one another. But this division may also create or exacerbate a 'clarity of responsibility' problem, as voters may not know whom to credit or blame for the government's failure to effectively control corruption.

Of course, as noted above, some presidential systems do not actually feature more checks and balances than parliamentary systems, because in practice they concentrate most important powers in the president, who may also have a number of institutional advantages over the legislature. When that is the case, the analysis differs in important respects, but the bottom-line predictions remain complicated, and perhaps indeterminate: Concentration of power in the president, and the marginalization of the legislature, may reduce the clarity of responsibility problem and enable the president to act more decisively (if he or she chooses to do so) against corruption. At the same time, the concentration of power in the president may make it much more difficult for the legislature to monitor and check the president, enabling the latter a freer hand to engage in various forms of corruption, should the electoral mechanism prove an inadequate constraint.

Perhaps unsurprisingly, given the uncertainty suggested by the theoretical discussion, the empirical evidence concerning the net impact of presidentialism on corruption is thin, and the results are decidedly mixed. Most of the existing evidence comes from cross-country studies that include an index variable for presidentialism among a set of potential explanatory variables, with one or more of the standard corruption perception indexes as the outcome measure. A few studies in this vein find suggestive evidence that presidential systems are associated with lower perceived corruption (Testa 2010; Brown et al. 2011), but other studies find that presidential systems have higher levels of perceived corruption than do parliamentary systems (Panizza 2001; Verardi 2004; Gerring and Thacker 2004; Lederman et al. 2005; Halim 2006). And perhaps the most common finding in studies on this topic is the absence of any statistically significant correlation between the 'presidentialism/parliamentarism' index variable and perceived corruption, at least when a plausible set of control variables is included (Adsera et al. 2003; Chang and Golden 2006; Keefer 2007; Pellegata 2009; Tavits and Potter 2012; Schleiter and Vonayza 2014).

Another complication for this sort of empirical inquiry is the fact that, as with district magnitude, the impact of presidentialism on corruption levels may depend on the legislative voting rule. One notable study found that the combination of presidentialism with closed-list PR appeared to be particularly associated with very high perceived corruption levels

(Kunicova and Rose-Ackerman 2005), though there are some questions about the degree to which these results are actually driven by the hypothesized variation in electoral institutions.[23] Another study looking at similar interactive effects reached somewhat different conclusions, finding suggestive evidence that the combination of a parliamentary system with PR had the lowest perceived corruption, while countries that used plurality electoral systems (whether presidential or parliamentary) had the highest perceived corruption, and those that combined PR with presidentialism fell somewhere in the middle (Halim 2008).[24]

CONCLUSION

This chapter opened with a question: Do democratic elections help reduce corruption? After over two decades of sustained research, the answer is, alas, unclear. But, while the relationship between democracy and

---

[23]   There are two concerns about this study that may be worth highlighting. First, and more generally, the Kunicova and Rose-Ackerman (2005) study counts countries as 'democracies' if they hold periodic elections and exceed a cutoff in the Freedom House score, even if the same party always wins the election. This leads them to classify a number of one-party-dominant states (including, for example, Singapore and Zimbabwe) as democracies, even though many of those countries are classed as 'autocracies' in other data sources, such as Polity IV. It is not clear how these countries should be classified for purposes of this research question. Including autocracies (with formal but not genuine elections) might bias the results if, for example, these countries are more likely to adopt certain formal electoral rules, but excluding one-party-dominant countries on the grounds they are not 'true democracies' might introduce a different kind of bias, because the electoral system might be one determinant of whether a single party can maintain perpetual control. Second, on the joint effect of presidentialism and closed-list PR specifically, it is worth noting that 13 of the 23 countries in the Kunicova and Rose-Ackerman (2005) dataset that feature this combination are in Latin America (and only six Latin American countries in the dataset do not feature this combination), and the regression specifications that look at the joint effect of presidentialism and closed-list PR do not include region dummies. In the specifications that include the regional dummies but not the interaction terms, the Latin American regional dummy is associated with higher perceived corruption. It is thus difficult to tell whether Latin America has higher-than-expected corruption because so many Latin American countries feature the undesirable combination of presidentialism and closed-list PR, or whether the apparent adverse effect of that combination is actually a spurious result driven by some other features specific to Latin America.

[24]   Halim (2008) emphasizes, however, that these findings are only suggestive and should be interpreted with caution. Moreover, in contrast to Kunicova and Rose-Ackerman (2005), Halim (2008) does not distinguish open-list from closed-list PR.

corruption remains uncertain, we nonetheless have a much better sense of the complexity and nuance of this relationship than we did when that research began in earnest. An appreciation of that complexity makes the inconclusive and at times contradictory results of the cross-country empirical research easier to understand, even as the lack of a clear empirical resolution to the core questions remains frustrating.

That is not to say we have learned nothing from the cross-country empirical work. We do seem to have rather robust evidence of a non-linear relationship between democracy (or duration of democracy) and perceived corruption, with only long-standing, well-established democracies exhibiting notably lower levels of perceived corruption than other polities (though we must be cautious about the inferences we draw from that correlation). There is also some suggestive evidence of a non-monotonic relationship between some potential explanatory variables—such as the degree of political competition, the length of incumbent time horizons, and the degree to which the electoral system promotes cultivation of a 'personal vote'—and corruption. But on the whole, the cross-country evidence has not produced many consistent, robust findings.

This is the point where one is sometimes tempted to say: 'More research on this issue is needed.' But while that may be true, an alternative reasonable conclusion might be that 'more (cross-country) research on this issue is not likely to prove productive', because the institutional dynamics are so complex and contingent, and the available cross-country evidence is so inherently limited, that it is not clear running ever-more regressions on the same datasets is likely to produce sufficiently robust results to move the discussion forward. Yet this is not a counsel of despair. The research to date has suggested a couple of avenues that appear to be worth further exploration.

First, one of the more interesting findings to emerge from the existing research is that democracy—or particular variations in democratic institutions—may have more consistent and predictable effects on the *type* of corruption than on the *level* of corruption. We might not be able to consistently predict, for example, whether open-list PR or closed-list PR systems will have more corruption, but we might be able to predict with more confidence that open-list PR systems will tend to have more candidate-centered, instrumental political corruption, while closed-list PR systems will likely have more venal personal corruption and party-directed corruption. We might not be able to say whether the transition from a stable autocracy to a fractious democracy will increase or decrease corruption, but we might still be able to predict a transition from long-term collusive corruption to more short-term embezzlement and extortion. The research is still not quite far enough along to develop a full schema for the primary corruption risks associated with different political systems, but such a schema seems potentially within our grasp, and work in this direction may prove more useful than trying to figure out whether, on average, democracy or a particular feature of democracy is associated with higher or lower corruption. Better understanding of how corruption risks vary across political systems has a practical as well as intellectual payoff, in that one may be able to design more appropriate anti-corruption measures when one has a clearer sense of the most salient corruption risks in different contexts.

Second, greater attention to the various causal mechanisms through which democratic institutions might affect corruption might help us to produce more research that focuses specifically on those mechanisms (and intermediate outcomes associated with those mechanisms), rather than trying to answer the high-level question about average effects on corruption. We could focus more attention, for example, on how anti-corruption enforcement policy varies across countries with different institutions, or on the factors that influence the entry of anti-corruption parties into politics, or on how different electoral systems affect the production and dissemination of information about corrupt activities. This sort of research might not directly address the questions about average effects of democratic institutions on corruption, but might prove more helpful in understanding the relative significance of different potential causal mechanisms, which in turn might prove more useful in crafting appropriate policy interventions.

REFERENCES

Adsera, Alicia, Carles Boix and Mark Payne. 2003. 'Are You Being Served? Political Accountability and Quality of Government', *Journal of Law, Economics & Organization* 19(2): 445–90.

Back, Hanna and Axel Hadenius. 2008. 'Democracy and State Capacity: Exploring a J-Shaped Relationship', *Governance* 21(1): 1–24.

Bagenholm, Andreas. 2009. 'Politicizing Corruption: The Electoral Impact of Anti-Corruption Discourse in Europe, 1983–2007', QoG Working Paper 2009: 10. University of Gothenburg: Quality of Government Institute.

Bagenholm, Andreas. 2013. 'The Electoral Fate and Policy Impact of "Anti-Corruption Parties" in Central and Eastern Europe', *Human Affairs* 23: 174–95.

Banerjee, Abhijit V. and Rohini Pande. 2009. 'Parochial Politics: Ethnic Preferences and Politician Corruption', Working Paper.

Banerjee, Abhijit, Donald P. Green, Jeffrey McManus and Rohini Pande. 2014. 'Are Poor Voters Indifferent to Whether Elected Leaders are Criminal or Corrupt? A Vignette Experiment in Rural India', *Political Communication* 31(3): 391–407.

Benoit, Kenneth. 2006. 'Duverger's Law and the Study of Electoral Systems', *French Politics* 4(1): 69–83.

Besley, Timothy and Robin Burgess. 2002. 'The Political Economy of Government Responsiveness: Theory and Evidence from India', *Quarterly Journal of Economics* 117(4): 1415–51.

Billger, Sherrilyn M. and Rajeev K. Goel. 2009. 'Do Existing Corruption Levels Matter in Controlling Corruption?: Cross-Country Quantile Regression Estimates', *Journal of Development Economics* 90(2): 299–305.

Blake, Charles H. and Christopher G. Martin. 2006. 'The Dynamics of Political Corruption: Re-Examining the Influence of Democracy', *Democratization* 13(1): 1–14.

Bohara, Alok K., Neil J. Mitchell and Carl F. Mittendorff. 2004. 'Compound Democracy and the Control of Corruption: A Cross-Country Investigation', *Policy Studies Journal* 32(4): 481–99.

Brown, David S., Michael Touchton and Andrew Whitford. 2011. 'Political Polarization as a Constraint on Corruption: A Cross-National Comparison', *World Development* 39(9): 1516–29.

Campante, Filipe R., Davin Chor and Quoc-Anh Do. 2009. 'Instability and the Incentives for Corruption', *Economics & Politics* 21(1): 42–92.

Carey, John M. and Matthew Soberg Shugart. 1995. 'Incentives to Cultivate a Personal Vote: A Rank Ordering of Electoral Formulas', *Electoral Studies* 14(4): 417–39.

Chang, Eric C.C. 2005. 'Electoral Incentives for Political Corruption under Open-List Proportional Representation', *Journal of Politics* 67(3): 716–30.

Chang, Eric C.C. and Miriam A. Golden. 2006. 'Electoral Systems, District Magnitude and Corruption', *British Journal of Political Science* 37(1): 115–37.

Chang, Eric C.C., Miriam A. Golden and Seth J. Hill. 2010. 'Legislative Malfeasance and Political Accountability', *World Politics* 62(2): 177–220.

Charron, Nicholas. 2011. 'Party System, Electoral Systems and Constraints on Corruption', *Electoral Studies* 30(4): 595–606.

Charron, Nicholas and Victor Lapuente. 2010. 'Does Democracy Produce Quality of Government?', *European Journal of Political Research* 49(4): 443–70.

Choi, Eunjung and Jongseok Woo. 2010. 'Political Corruption, Economic Performance, and Electoral Outcomes: A Cross-National Analysis', *Contemporary Politics* 16(3): 249–62.

Chong, Alberto et al. 2013. 'Looking Beyond the Incumbent: Exposing Corruption and the Effect on Electoral Outcomes', Working Paper.

Chowdhury, Shyamal K. 2004. 'The Effect of Democracy and Press Freedom on Corruption: An Empirical Test', *Economics Letters* 85(1): 93–101.

Clague, Christopher, Philip Keefer, Stephen Knack and Mancur Olson. 1996. 'Property and Contract Rights in Autocracies and Democracies', *Journal of Economic Growth* 1(2): 243–76.

Colazingari, Silvia and Susan Rose-Ackerman. 1998. 'Corruption in a Paternalistic Democracy: Lessons from Latin American Countries', *Political Science Quarterly* 113(3): 447–70.

Cox, Gary. 1997. *Making Votes Count*. Cambridge: Cambridge University Press.

Davis, Charles L., Roderic Ai Camp and Kenneth M. Coleman. 2004. 'The Influence of Party Systems on Citizens' Perceptions of Corruption and Electoral Response in Latin America', *Comparative Political Studies* 37(6): 677–703.

Davis, Diane E. 2006. 'Undermining the Rule of Law: Democratization and the

Dark Side of Police Reform in Mexico', *Latin American Politics & Society*, 48(1): 55–86.

De Figueiredo, Miguel F.P., F. Daniel Hidalgo and Yuri Kasahara. 2011. 'When Do Voters Punish Corrupt Politicians? Experimental Evidence from Brazil', Working Paper.

Del Monte, Alfredo and Erasmo Papagni. 2007. 'The Determinants of Corruption in Italy: Regional Panel Data Analysis', *European Journal of Political Economy* 23(2): 379–96.

Della Porta, Donatella. 2004. 'Political Parties and Corruption: Ten Hypotheses on Five Vicious Circles', *Crime, Law & Social Change* 42(1): 35–60.

Di Puppo, Lili. 2014. 'The Construction of Success in Anti-Corruption Activity in Georgia', *East European Politics* 30(1): 105–22.

Dimock, Michael A. and Gary C. Jacobson. 1995. 'Checks and Choices: The House Bank Scandal's Impact on Voters in 1992', *Journal of Politics* 57(4): 1143–59.

Dong, Bin and Benno Torgler. 2011. 'Democracy, Property Rights, Income Equality, and Corruption', Working Paper.

Eggers, Andrew. 2014. 'Partisanship and Electoral Accountability: Evidence from the UK Expenses Scandal', *Quarterly Journal of Political Science* 9(4): 441–72.

Fackler, Tim and Tse-min Lin. 1995. 'Political Corruption and Presidential Elections, 1929–1992', *Journal of Politics* 57(4): 971–93.

Fearon, James D. 1999. 'Electoral Accountability and the Control of Politicians: Selecting Good Types Versus Sanctioning Poor Performance', in Adam Przeworski et al. (eds) *Democracy, Accountability, and Representation*. Cambridge: Cambridge University Press.

Feichtinger, Gustav and Franz Wirl. 1994. 'On the Stability and Potential Cyclicity of Corruption in Governments Subject to Popularity Constraints', *Mathematical Social Sciences* 28: 113–31.

Ferraz, Claudio and Frederico Finan. 2008. 'Exposing Corrupt Politicians: The Effects of Brazil's Publicly Released Audits on Electoral Outcomes', *Quarterly Journal of Economics* 123: 703–45.

Ferraz, Claudio and Frederico Finan. 2011. 'Electoral Accountability and Corruption: Evidence from the Audits of Local Governments', *American Economic Review* 101(4): 1274–311.

Fredriksson, Per G. and Jakob Svensson. 2003. 'Political Instability, Corruption and Policy Formation: The Case of Environmental Policy', *Journal of Public Economics* 87: 1383–405.

Fritz, Verena. 2007. 'Democratization and Corruption in Mongolia', *Public Administration & Development* 27(3): 191–203.

Geddes, Barbara and Artur Ribeiro Neto. 1992. 'Institutional Sources of Corruption in Brazil', *Third World Quarterly* 13(4): 641–61.

Gentzkow, Matthew, Edward L. Glaeser and Claudia Goldin. 2006. 'The Rise of the Fourth Estate: How Newspapers Became Informative and Why It Mattered', in Edward L. Glaeser and Claudia Goldin (eds), *Corruption and Reform: Lessons from America's Economic History*. Chicago: University of Chicago Press, pp. 187–206.

Gerring, John and Strom C. Thacker. 2004. 'Political Institutions and Corruption: The Role of Unitarism and Parliamentarism', *British Journal of Political Science* 34: 295–330.

Gingerich, Daniel W. 2009. 'Ballot Structure, Political Corruption, and the

Performance of Proportional Representation', *Journal of Theoretical Politics* 21(4): 1–33.

Golden, Miriam A. 2003. 'Electoral Connections: The Effects of the Personal Vote on Political Patronage, Bureaucracy and Legislation in Postwar Italy', *British Journal of Political Science* 33: 189–212.

Golden, Miriam and Eric C.C. Chang. 2001. 'Competitive Corruption: Factional Conflict and Political Malfeasance in Postwar Italian Christian Democracy', *World Politics* 53(4): 588–622.

Gurgur, Tugrul and Anwar Shah. 2005. 'Localization and Corruption: Panacea or Pandora's Box?', World Bank Policy Research Working Paper 3486.

Halim, Nafisa. 2008. 'Testing Alternative Theories of Bureaucratic Corruption in Less Developed Countries', *Social Science Quarterly* 89(1): 236–57.

Harriss-White, Barbara and Gordon White. 1996. 'Corruption, Liberalization, and Democracy', *IDS Bulletin* 27(2): 1–5.

Harsch, Ernest. 1993. 'Accumulators and Democrats: Challenging State Corruption in Africa', *Journal of Modern African Studies* 31(1): 31–48.

Hill, Kim Quaile. 2003. 'Democratization and Corruption: Systematic Evidence from the American States', *American Political Research* 31(6): 613–31.

Huntington, Samuel P. 1991. *The Third Wave: Democratization in the Late Twentieth Century*. Norman, OK: University of Oklahoma Press.

Keefer, Philip. 2007. 'Clientalism, Credibility and the Policy Choices of Young Democracies', *American Journal of Political Science* 51(4): 804–21.

Keefer, Philip and Razvan Vlaicu. 2008. 'Democracy, Credibility, and Clientalism', *Journal of Law, Economics & Organization* 24(2): 371–406.

Khemani, Stuti. 2013. 'Buying Votes vs. Supplying Public Services: Political Incentives to Under-Invest in Pro-Poor Policies', World Bank Policy Research Working Paper WPS 6339.

Klasnja, Marko. 2011. 'Why Do Malfeasant Politicians Maintain Public Support? Testing the "Uninformed Voter" Argument', Working Paper.

Klasnja, Marko, Joshua Tucker and Kevin Deegan-Krause. 2012. 'Pocketbook v. Sociotropic Corruption Voting', Working Paper.

Kolstad, Ivar and Arne Wiig. 2011. 'Does Democracy Reduce Corruption?' CMI Working Paper 4.

Kostadinova, Tatiana. 2009. 'Abstain or Rebel: Corruption Perceptions and Voting in East European Elections', *Politics & Policy* 37(4): 691–714.

Krause, Stefen and Fabio Mendez. 2009. 'Corruption and Elections: An Empirical Study for a Cross-Section of Countries', *Economics & Politics* 21(2): 179–200.

Kselman, Daniel. 2011. 'Electoral Institutions and Political Corruption: Ballot Structure, Electoral Formula, and Graft', in Norman Schofield (ed.), *Political Economy of Institutions, Democracy, and Voting*. London: Springer, pp. 327–71.

Kunicová, Jana and Susan Rose-Ackerman. 2005. 'Electoral Rules and Constitutional Structures as Constraints on Corruption', *British Journal of Political Science* 35: 573–606.

Lederman, Daniel, Norman Loayza and Rodrigo Soares. 2005. 'Accountability and Corruption: Political Institutions Matter', *Economics & Politics* 17(1): 1–35.

Lessig, Lawrence. 2011. *Republic Lost: How Money Corrupts Congress—and a Plan to Stop It*. New York: Twelve.

Lim, Linda Y.C. and Aaron Stern. 2002. 'State Power and Private Profit: The Political Economy of Corruption in Southeast Asia', *Asian-Pacific Economic Literature* 16(2): 18–52.

Lindberg, Staffan I. 2003. 'It's Our Time to "Chop": Do Elections Feed Neo-Patrimonialism Rather than Counteract It?' *Democratization* 10(2): 121–40.

Manzetti, Luigi and Carole J. Wilson. 2007. 'Why Do Corrupt Governments Maintain Public Support?' *Comparative Political Studies* 40(8): 949–70.

McCann, James A. and Jorge I. Dominguez. 1998. 'Mexicans React to Electoral Fraud and Political Corruption: An Assessment of Public Opinion and Voting Behavior', *Electoral Studies* 17(4): 483–504.

Milanovic, Branko, Karla Hoff and Shale Horowitz. 2010. 'Turnover in Power as a Restraint on Investing in Influence: Evidence from the Postcommunist Transition', *Economics & Politics* 22(3): 329–61.

Mitchell, Paul. 2000. 'Voters and Their Representatives: Electoral Institutions and Delegation in Parliamentary Democracies', *European Journal of Policy Research* 37: 335–51.

Mohtadi, Hamid and Terry L. Roe. 2003. 'Democracy, Rent Seeking, Public Spending, and Growth', *Journal of Public Economics* 87(3): 445–66.

Montinola, Gabriella R. and Robert W. Jackman. 2002. 'Sources of Corruption: A Cross-Country Study', *British Journal of Political Science* 32(1): 147–70.

Morris, Stephen D. 1991. *Corruption and Politics in Contemporary Mexico.* Tuscaloosa, AL: University of Alabama Press.

Morris, Stephen D. 2004. 'Corruption in Latin America: An Empirical Overview', *SECOLAS Annals* 36: 74–92.

Mungiu-Pippidi, Alina. 2006. 'Corruption: Diagnosis and Treatment', *Journal of Democracy* 17(3): 86–99.

Musila, Jacob W. 2013. 'Does Democracy Have a Different Impact on Corruption in Africa?' *Journal of African Business* 14(3): 162–70.

Myerson, Roger B. 1993. 'Effectiveness of Electoral Systems for Reducing Government Corruption: A Game-Theoretic Analysis', *Games & Economic Behavior* 5: 118–32.

Nyblade, Benjamin and Steven Reed. 2008. 'Who Cheats? Who Loots? Political Competition and Corruption in Japan, 1947–1993', *American Journal of Political Science* 52(4): 926–41.

Olowu, Dele. 1993. 'Roots and Remedies of Governmental Corruption in Africa', *Corruption & Reform* 7(3): 227–36.

Olson, Mancur. 1965. *The Logic of Collective Action.* Cambridge, MA: Harvard University Press.

Olson, Mancur. 1993. 'Dictatorship, Democracy, and Development', *American Political Science Review* 87(3): 567–76.

Panizza, Ugo. 2001. 'Electoral Rules, Political Systems, and Institutional Quality', *Economics & Politics* 13(3): 311–42.

Pellegata, Alessandro. 2009. 'Democracy, Government Alternation and Political Corruption', GSSEPS Working Paper Series, 6/2009.

Pellegata, Alessandro. 2013. 'Constraining Political Corruption: An Empirical Analysis of the Impact of Democracy', *Democratization* 20(7): 1195–218.

Pellegrini, Lorenzo and Reyer Gerlagh. 2008. 'Causes of Corruption: A Survey of Cross-Country Analyses and Extended Results', *Economics of Governance* 9: 245–63.

Pereira, Carlos, Marcus Andre Melo and Carlos Mauricio Figueiredo. 2009. 'The Corruption-Enhancing Role of Re-Election Incentives? Counterintuitive Evidence from Brazil's Audit Reports', *Political Research Quarterly* 62: 731–44.

Persson, Torsten, Guido Tabellini and Francesco Trebbi. 2003. 'Electoral Rules and Corruption', *Journal of the European Economic Association* 1(4): 958–89.

Quah, Jon S.T. 2009. 'Curbing Corruption in a One-Party Dominant System: Learning from Singapore's Experience', in Gong, T. and S.K. Ma (eds), *Preventing Corruption in Asia: Institutional Design and Policy Capacity*. London: Routledge.

Reinikka, Ritva and Jacob Svensson. 2004. 'Local Capture: Evidence from a Central Government Transfer Program in Uganda', *Quarterly Journal of Economics* 119: 679–705.

Reinikka, Ritva and Jacob Svensson. 2005. 'Fighting Corruption to Improve Schooling: Evidence from a Newspaper Campaign in Uganda', *Journal of the European Economics Association* 3: 259–67.

Reinikka, Ritva and Jacob Svensson. 2011. 'The Power of Information in Public Services: Evidence from Education in Uganda', *Journal of Public Economics* 95: 956–66.

Renno, Lucio R. 2011. 'Corruption and Voting', in Timothy Power and Matthew Taylor (eds), *Corruption and Democracy in Brazil: The Struggle for Accountability* (Notre Dame, IN: University of Notre Dame Press), pp. 56–78.

Roberts, Andrew. 2008. 'Hyperaccountability: Economic Voting in Central and Eastern Europe', *Electoral Studies* 27(3): 533–46.

Robinson, James A. and Thierry Verdier. 2013. 'The Political Economy of Clientalism', *Scandinavian Journal of Economics* 115(2): 260–91.

Rock, Michael T. 2009. 'Corruption and Democracy', *Journal of Development Studies* 45(1): 55–75.

Roper, Steven D. 2002. 'The Influence of Romanian Campaign Finance Laws on Party System Development and Corruption', *Party Politics* 8(2): 175–92.

Rose-Ackerman, Susan. 1999. *Corruption and Government: Causes, Consequences, and Reform*. New York: Cambridge University Press.

Saha, Shrabani and Jen-Je Su. 2012. 'Investigating the Interaction Effect of Democracy and Economic Freedom on Corruption: A Cross-Country Quantile Regression Analysis', *Economic Analysis & Policy* 42(3): 389–96.

Sandholtz, Wayne and William Koetzle. 2000. 'Accounting for Corruption: Economic Structure, Democracy, and Trade', *International Studies Quarterly* 44: 31–50.

Schleiter, Petra and Alisa M. Voznaya. 2014. 'Party System Competitiveness and Corruption', *Party Politics* 20(5): 675–86.

Schumacher, Ingmar. 2013. 'Political Stability, Corruption and Trust in Politicians', *Economic Modelling* 31: 359–69.

Sequeira, Sandra. 2012. 'Advances in Measuring Corruption', in Danila Serra and Leonard Wantchekon (eds), *New Advances in Experimental Research on Corruption*. Bingley, UK: Emerald Publishing.

Serra, Danila. 2006. 'Empirical Determinants of Corruption: A Sensitivity Analysis', *Public Choice* 126(1/2): 225–56.

Skidmore, Max J. 1996. 'Promise and Peril in Combating Corruption: Hong Kong's ICAC', *Annals of the American Academy of Political and Social Science* 547: 118–30.

Stokes, Susan C. 2005. 'Perverse Accountability: A Formal Model of Machine Politics with Evidence from Argentina', *American Political Science Review* 99(3): 315–25.

Sun, Yan and Michael Johnston. 2009. 'Does Democracy Check Corruption? Insights from China and India', *Comparative Politics* 42(1): 1–19.

Sung, Hung-En. 2004. 'Democracy and Political Corruption: A Cross-National Comparison', *Crime, Law & Social Change* 41: 179–94.

Tavits, Margit. 2007. 'Clarity of Responsibility and Corruption', *American Journal of Political Science*. 51(1): 218–29.

Tavits, Margit and Joshua D. Potter. 2012. 'Electoral Institutions and Corruption in Campaign Finance', Working Paper.

Teachout, Zephyr. 2014. *Corruption in America*. Cambridge, MA: Harvard University Press.

Testa, Cecilia. 2010. 'Bicameralism and Corruption', *European Economic Review* 54(2): 181–98.

Torgler, Benno and Neven T. Valev. 2006. 'Corruption and Age', *Journal of Bioeconomics* 8: 133–45.

Treisman, Daniel. 2000. 'The Causes of Corruption: A Cross National Study', *Journal of Public Economics* 76(3): 399–457.

Verardi, Vincenzo. 2004. 'Electoral Systems and Corruption', *Revista Latonoamericana de Desarrollo Economico* 3: 117–50.

Weitz-Shapiro, Rebecca. 2012. 'What Wins Votes: Why Some Politicians Opt Out of Clientalism', *American Journal of Political Science* 56(3): 568–83.

Werlin, Herbert. 2013. 'Understanding International Corruption and What to Do About It', *Challenge* 56(3): 53–73.

Weyland, Kurt. 1998. 'The Politics of Corruption in Contemporary Latin America', *Journal of Democracy* 9(2): 108–21.

Wilson, John K. and Richard Damania. 2005. 'Corruption, Political Competition, and Environmental Policy', *Journal of Environmental Economics & Management* 49(3): 516–35.

Winters, Matthew S. and Rebecca Weitz-Shapiro. 2013. 'Lacking Information or Condoning Corruption? When Will Voters Support Corrupt Politicians?', *Comparative Politics* 45(4): 418–36.

Xin, Xiaohui and Thomas K. Rudel. 2004. 'The Context for Political Corruption: A Cross-National Analysis', *Social Science Quarterly* 85(2): 294–309.

Ziblatt, Daniel. 2009. 'Shaping Democratic Practice and the Causes of Electoral Fraud: Theory and Evidence from Pre-1914 Germany', *American Political Science Review* 103(1): 1–21.

5. Wielding the sword: President Xi's new anti-corruption campaign

Fu Hualing

A state achieves legitimacy through multiple sources, one of which is the effectiveness of its governance. Generations of scholars since Hobbes have identified the maintenance of peace and order as core functions of a legitimate state. In the modern world, economic prosperity, social stability and effective control of corruption often provide adequate compensation for a deficit of democracy. Corruption closely correlates with legitimacy. While a perceived pervasive, endemic corruption undermines the legitimacy of a regime, a successful anti-corruption campaign can allow a regime to recover from a crisis of legitimacy (Gilley 2009; Seligson and Booth 2009).

This is the rationale behind the periodical campaigns against corruption that have been conducted by the Chinese Communist Party ('Party' or 'CCP') (Manion 2004; Wedeman 2012). Political leaders in China have found it expedient to use anti-corruption campaigns to remove their political foes, to rein in the bureaucracy and to restore public confidence in their ability to rule. Through anti-corruption campaigns, emerging political leaders consolidate their political power, secure loyalty from political factions and regional political forces, and enhance their legitimacy in the eyes of the general public.

In an authoritarian state that experiences a high level of corruption, an anti-corruption campaign is a delicate political battle that addresses two significant concerns. The first concern is to orchestrate the campaign so that it is regime-reinforcing instead of regime-undermining. To remain credible, the regime must demonstrate its willingness and capacity to punish corrupt officials at the highest levels. Beyond rhetoric, there must be real, visible and convincing action that actually punishes some 'tigers'—senior political officials. But at the same time, because corruption is deeply entrenched, wide-spread and an integral part of the governing system, overly rigorous anti-corruption law enforcement would necessarily target core supporters of the regime and, if allowed to be carried out to its full extent, may ultimately cause a significant defection of a substantial part of the supporters, which would undermine the regime.

A not unrelated dilemma relates to the transparency and publicity associated with credible anti-corruption law enforcement. Enforcement must be carried out in the public domain, and the public whose support is sought must be aware of it in order for a campaign to be credible. The authoritarian regime may not have a choice in the information age with more equality of access to information; moreover, it is no longer feasible for an authoritarian regime to govern by controlling the flow of information. There is, however, an inherent tension between the imperative of disclosure and the imperative of secrecy. A meaningful disclosure of the degree of corruption within the Party may make the campaign credible, however, it risks outraging instead of placating the general public. Full disclosure of the extent to which the Party is embroiled in corruption may invite further cynicism, supporting the contention that the Party is irredeemably rotten to its core. An anti-corruption campaign, if not well-managed, may not only cause significant defection among core supporters of the regime but also generate public anger and hostility toward the regime when the minutiae of corruption scandals are fully laid bare in the public domain.

A campaign that is not credible is unlikely to enhance the legitimacy of the regime; conversely, a credible campaign could ultimately threaten the regime's survival. Therefore, a regime-reinforcing campaign has to be highly selective and well-managed so that it will punish certain corrupt officials while not undermining the regime. In President Xi's case, the anti-corruption campaign is deeply instrumental and designed to serve the larger goal of his political and economic reforms.

The second political concern relates to the methods used in anti-corruption campaigns, including the responsible institutions and actors and the procedures that the authoritarian state uses. Because an anti-corruption campaign has to be regime-affirming, unsurprisingly, an authoritarian state tends to distrust institutions, actors and procedures with a strong democratizing potential that may pose a challenge to the regime in the long run. Although authoritarian regimes like China's could develop the political will and capacity to combat corruption, such regimes fight corruption in ways that are congruent with the political system and that rely on the concentration of political power and *ad hoc* political mobilization outside existing legal institutions. However, in general, successful, anti-corruption enforcement have relied on effective external checks on political power together with the institutionalization and normalization of law enforcement based on a transparent rule of law. If these are indeed necessary conditions, then the Chinese approach seems misguided. It risks undermining the very institutions and designs upon which successful anti-corruption enforcement depends. However, perhaps there are other ways to carry out a successful anti-corruption campaign. In that context, I ask whether China is developing a sui generis model for anti-corruption enforcement that relies on a different control model.

This chapter broadly outlines the political nature of the Party's anti-corruption campaign and the way in which corruption and anti-corruption are used as tools for the concentration of political power. It is divided into five parts. Following the introduction in Part 1, Part 2 touches on four potential objectives of the ongoing campaign that may benefit the Xi government. Part 3 discusses the process by which power has been centralized in the anti-corruption campaign in terms of three relationships, namely centralization of the central-local relationship; centralization of the state-society relationship; and centralization of the relationship between political and legal institutions. Part 4 critiques the current Chinese anti-corruption enforcement model—outlining its achievements but pointing to its serious limitations, especially in the long run, arguing that the shock therapy used by Xi is achieving some short-term results in controlling the further spread of corruption, but the tough medicine he prescribes may produce future uncertainties in the political system, Part 5 concludes.

1.   THE POLITICS OF ANTI-CORRUPTION ENFORCEMENT

The Chinese Communist Party under Xi Jinping and Wang Qishan has launched an unprecedented anti-corruption campaign beginning in 2013 (CCP Central Committee 2013). This is a sustained national campaign that targets both 'tigers' (senior officials) and 'flies' (low ranking bureaucrats) in the government and State-owned Enterprises (SOEs). The CCP designed and led the campaign, and implemented it through the CCP's disciplinary arm, especially the Central Committee of Disciplinary Inspection (CCDI) under Wang's leadership, targeting principally Party officials. Xi's campaign resembles a Maoist campaign in several fundamental aspects (Fewsmith 2014), the hallmark of which is powerful rhetoric, an effective decision-making process, swift and severe punishment, and, above all, the marginalization of the rule of law and civil society. The current anti-corruption campaign builds on that legacy, and reinforces the political dominance of the CCP in the anti-corruption process leading to an unprecedented concentration of political power in the past two decades.

The anti-corruption campaign is also a highly politicized process. Investigations are selective, politically motivated, and aim to achieve particular political consequences. As China transitions to a post-revolutionary state, political leaders generally lack the necessary charisma and legitimacy to hold the country together. State power is increasingly fragmented and the central-local relationship, in particular, has become more delicate, with local states openly or covertly asserting political power. China's unitary state has been strained in the face of expansive local power, defined along political, economic or ethnic lines. Collective leadership in the absence of a cult of individual leadership has created a number of power bases without effective political and constitutional controls. Power may be centred on a policy area (for example, Zhou Yongkang's monopoly over the political-legal system and his influence over oil and gas resources) or a region (for example, Bo Xilai's control in Chongqing), further fragmenting the decision-making process.

A younger generation of authoritarian leaders in twenty-first century China, who are ambitious to push through an aggressive reform agenda, needs to establish the political authority to carry out reforms. Anti-corruption serves that objective well. Firstly, the campaign removes political foes in central ministries and regions. Xi's top-down anti-corruption enforcement is focused, surgical and well-managed, with a clear agenda of excising the empire of Zhou Yongkang. Most high profile detentions to date under Xi's leadership have been people who are directly or indirectly associated with Zhou.

Second, actual or potential political supporters are elevated to powerful positions. By removing political enemies, new leaders are able to create vacancies and thus place their supporters in powerful positions. In China's political system, a change of leadership at the top is not followed by a significant reshuffling of key positions. Because of deeply entrenched factional politics in China, it is more difficult for a new leader in China than it is in democracies to appoint a new team to positions of power in order to implement new policies. Facing with entrenched resistance, state leaders resort to alternative means, including anti-corruption enforcement, to create vacancies in political positions and reward their supporters with those positions. An anti-corruption campaign provides Xi with both sticks and carrots.

Third, Xi's anti-corruption campaign can reaffirm the political loyalty of powerful regional and sectoral leaders in provinces, ministries and SOEs. Anti-corruption enforcement is an entry point into the existing political system to ensure that diverse political interests follow instructions from Beijing. As the Anti-Corruption Action Plan states clearly, one key objective of the anti-corruption campaign is to tighten up overall discipline within the Party so that the whole Party is united in its thoughts and action under Xi's leadership. This 'shock and awe' policy aims to send strong messages to stakeholders and monopoly interests that Xi can remove them if they are deemed disloyal. By using anti-corruption laws as a weapon, Xi can overcome possible obstacles created by entrenched interests in implementing his reform policies set out in the Third Plenum Resolutions. Politicians and bureaucrats may be deeply corrupt, but Xi has to rely on them to implement his reform plan. Deng Xiaoping initiated his reform in the late 1970s and bought bureaucrats' acquiescence to his reform agenda by allowing cadres to enrich themselves; Xi Jinping seeks to achieve his policy goal by threatening to take away everything that they have acquired over the past decades.

Finally, anti-corruption enforcement is instrumental in providing much needed legitimacy and credibility (Naughton 2014). The high profile campaign, particularly the widespread investigation and quick removal of corrupt officials, demonstrates a strong anti-corruption political will and capability. Anti-corruption is extremely popular among the general public and in the private sector; wielding the sword of Damacles over the heads of senior leaders provides much needed legitimacy to Xi. Firm centralization of power, quick decision-making and effective top-down implementation characterize the new campaign and in large part explains its popularity. Xi's sword has been sharp and merciless. Corruption, broadly defined to include any abuse of public power for private gains, has always been ranked as one of the top concerns facing the Chinese political system and once again proves prevalent, deeply embedded, and entrenched in the political structure. There is a moral and political imperative for emerging leaders to launch anti-corruption campaigns. In a country with a revolutionary tradition and communitarian nostalgia which is facing unprecedented inequality (Sicular 2013) and endemic corruption at the same time, the appeal of strong-man anti-corruption campaigns is perhaps overwhelming to the masses and impossible to resist for ambitious leaders. Xi has seized the initiative; however, the real difficulty is not how to augment legitimacy through anti-corruption but how to manage public expectations.

2.   RECENTRALIZATION THROUGH ANTI-CORRUPTION

Xi's anti-corruption campaign has witnessed a centralization of political power in general and the centralization of anti-corruption power in particular. Power steadily shifts towards the centre in three different ways. First, Xi and Wang are re-designing the central-local relationship by transferring corruption investigation powers from provinces, ministries and SOEs to the CCDI, significantly reinforcing central control over regions within the Party structure. Second, the ongoing campaign relies on the Party's political machinery to the degree that it further marginalizes anti-corruption legal institutions. Under Xi's leadership, anti-corruption has been reduced to an intra-party disciplinary matter. Third, while Xi is ruthless in grappling with high-level corruption, he is equally ruthless in clamping down on civil society mobilization against corruption. The censorship of critical voices on the Internet and the harassment and punishment of opinion leaders have been unprecedented, leading to a smothering of bottom-up mobilization against corruption.

Central control is secured through two mechanisms. The first mechanism is to further centralize the anti-corruption power in the hands of the CCDI and the second is to revitalize the central inspection system, which has been in place for nearly a decade and has not been effectively used.

The orthodox explanation is that the Party's disciplinary mechanism has failed to have an impact on corruption because of its lack of independence from local powers and, in particular, its dependence on the Standing Committee of the respective Party Committees, which it is expected to supervise and monitor. Local disciplinary officers are unwilling or unable to investigate local corruption seriously because of institutional design, local politics and social ties. In particular, the line of accountability within the Chinese political system has prevented local disciplinary officials from playing an active role in anti-corruption enforcement.

An essential part of the disciplinary system operates hierarchically and horizontally among three entities: the CCDI, the Provincial Party Committee, and the provincial level disciplinary inspection committee (CDI). Horizontally, a CDI is in charge of anti-corruption enforcement in each province and, as part of the Provincial Party Committee, is accountable to the Provincial Party Committee. Hierarchically, a CDI is also accountable to the CCDI directly. Much of the controversy in anti-corruption enforcement in China relates to this dual, overlapping accountability; and a key concern is whether a provincial CDI has been effectively captured by the Provincial Party Committee or whether the CCDI can exercise effective central control over nationwide anti-corruption work.

The disciplinary system has been partially rejuvenated since 2005 when the CCDI and CDI were respectively authorized to dispatch a disciplinary official to be stationed in the government departments and the SOEs of the respective central and local levels. The intention was to create a degree of external supervision over government departments. For instance, the CCDI sends disciplinary officials to central ministries or SOEs directly under central control, and the dispatched disciplinary officials are directly accountable to the CCDI alone. However, the enforcement of this policy has not been effective. Although the disciplinary official dispatched may be appointed by and accountable to the CCDI, he or she is often effectively co-opted by the government office which he or she supervises. The end result is that the supervisory system is effectively internalized and the system becomes largely self-regulatory leading to a near paralysis of the disciplinary system at the operational level (Xinhua Net, 2 February 2014).

Pilot schemes exist to make CDI supervision more meaningfully independent of the government departments it supervises. For example, instead of sending one CDI head to be stationed in one government department, the CDI in Hubei province set up a supervisory office in 2009 in which a number of disciplinary officials jointly supervise eight provincial government departments without being stationed in any of those departments. The objective of such a policy was to avoid co-option and to concentrate resources for more effective external supervision (ibid.).

A more difficult relationship that has not been effectively managed is the relationship between a CDI and the respective Party Committee, the crucial question being whether the CDI which supervises a Party Committee is structurally part of that Committee or a supervisory body independent of the Committee. According to the CCP Charter, a CDI is a parallel body to the Party Committee, and both are created by and accountable, in theory, to it. The institutional design is such that the Party Committee at each level, being the organ of supreme political power, is watched closely by a disciplinary arm of the Party Congress.

But two institutional mechanisms that effectively reduce and marginalize the supervisory power of a CDI compromise that design. According to the Party's personnel system, a higher Party Committee controls the appointment of key officials of a Party Committee at the next lower level. Significantly, all the officials with the rank of minister/provincial governor are placed on a central list and are accountable directly to the central authority. They are appointed, monitored and removed directly by the Ministry of Organization (MoO). Likewise, they are subject to the control of the CCDI for the purposes of disciplinary matters and anti-corruption investigation (Fu 2013b).

An equally significant difficulty relates to the political practice which renders the CDI an integral part of the provincial political system. The structural rub is that the CDI head is also a member of the Provincial Party Committee standing committee and responsible to the committee. While the provincial CDI has been authorized to supervise the Provincial Party Committee including the Standing Committee members, the CDI operates within the institutional framework of the Provincial Party Committee and the political system places the CDI under the direct control of the Party Committee. Indeed, the disciplinary system places the provincial ranking officials directly under the CCDI control in anti-corruption investigations, and the provincial CDI has no jurisdiction (Shen 2014).

To what degree does the CCDI control a provincial CDI in terms of appointment and operation? Since 2004, CCDI started to exercise the power to appoint the CDI head at the provincial level (Beijing News Net 2013). But there is a degree of uncertainty. As stated above, since 1980 a provincial CDI was simultaneously accountable to both the Provincial Party Committee and the CCDI.

In order to avoid co-option, the Party has adopted three related measures to enhance central control over the provincial level CDIs. The first is the restructuring of the CCDI to enhance its political and operation capacities; the second is to strengthen the control of CCDI over the provincial CDIs; and the third is to revamp *ad hoc* inspections of ministries, provinces and other central entities.

Under Wang Qishan's leadership, the CCDI created two bodies, an Organization Department and a Propaganda Department, to strengthen the overall personnel control and educational functions that are separate from, and independent of, the Party Committee. This serves to make a symbolic statement that, in terms of central-local relations, the CCDI is an independent system outside of the regular Party structure, which exercises independent political power (Li 2014). This is followed by the enhancement of the operational capacity of the CCDI in monitoring provincial level officials. The number of inspection offices that carry out disciplinary inspection has been increased from eight to 12 so that there is a team of disciplinary officials in charge of monitoring high ranking officials in specific ministries or provinces. Even without an increase in the size of the CCDI, more than 100 CCDI officials are said to have been reassigned to this operation. Those disciplinary officials not only have the political power to monitor and control Party officials as the Party rules demand. They also exercise legal powers, if necessary, with the support of police and of the prosecution and courts, allowing them to carry out interrogation, intercept communications, and engage in search, seizure or detention. The CCDI's power in anti-corruption investigations transcends institutional boundaries and is bound by no limits, except those imposed by the Party itself (Mo 2014).

The second strategy is to strengthen the CCDI control over the appointment of provincial CDI heads. The provincial CDI heads have always been accountable to both the Provincial Party Committee and the CCDI, but the current reform seems to tip the balance more decisively towards the CCDI. One mechanism is to parachute a CDI head to a sensitive region, such as the appointment of Hou Kai, who was a core member of the CCDI and also a Deputy Auditor-General, to become Shanghai's CDI head; or laterally to transfer an official from another province such as the appointment of Xu Songnan as the CDI head of Chongqing. Xu was formerly the Organization Chief in Ningxia. It is important to note that this practice of appointing a CDI head at a lower level directly by the CDI at the next higher level is long established. In that sense, although the current wave of parachute appointments and transfers may be unprecedented in terms of scale, it can also be seen as the continuation of a policy that has long been in existence.

Once a centrally appointed head is in place, there is more hands-on control from the centre over operational matters at the provincial level. The new rules provide that in conducting an anti-corruption investigation, investigative work should be placed principally under the leadership of a CDI at the next higher level and that reports to the Party Committee of the same level should also be sent to the CDI at the next higher level. Those new rules necessarily create a more hierarchical disciplinary system with the CCDI at the centre and a clear intention to deprive the local Party Committee of exclusive control over anti-corruption investigations at the equivalent local level (Xinhua Net, 2 February 2014).

This second mechanism of central control has breathed life into the Central Inspection Groups (CIG) in which semi-retired high ranking officials are dispatched to provinces, ministries and SOEs for disciplinary inspection. CIG leaders are principally ministerial ranking officials who have retired from their frontline posts and are under the age of 70 at the time of appointment. This policy was designed in 1996 but did not come to fruition until 2003. It was organized by the CCDI and the Party's Ministry of Organization (MoO), and thus is referred to as the CCDI and MoO Inspection Group. In 2009, the CCID and MoO Inspection Group were renamed the Central Inspection Group to showcase the group's status as an agent of the central committee of the CCP although the core members come from the CCDI and MoO. Xi and Wang have effectively institutionalized the inspection system (CCDI, 15 March 2014a).

The CIG's jurisdiction is broad and goes beyond corruption in the narrow sense. Officially, the CIGs are expected to focus on four issues which are broadly defined to include bribery; collusion with business for self-enrichment; extravagant life styles; and 'political discipline' with a special focus on compliance with central policies and abuse in the appointment of officials (ibid.).

The CIGs' work is divided into three stages during an inspection: discovering problems, reporting these problems, and ensuring that proper action is taken to solve the problems. Because the CIGs do not have disciplinary powers, their principal function is to discover problems and to report their findings to the proper authorities for action. To facilitate their inspection, the CIGs have three general powers exercisable in the course of inspection: (1) to receive reports, hear complaints, organize meetings, and conduct opinion surveys; (2) to organize meetings, visit officials, and review and copy documents; and (3) to conduct confidential interviews with individual officials of varying ranks. Throughout the four rounds of inspection to date, individual interviews are said to have been the most common and effective method of obtaining information (Chu and Luo, 2014). At the end of an inspection, a CIG will report its significant findings to the central authorities. Xi and the entire politburo are debriefed by the CIGs.

Second, the CIGs report their findings in particular cases to relevant organizational or disciplinary authorities for action. The CCDI has undertaken to expedite cases that are referred to it by the CIGs (ibid.). Each inspection has led to the downfall of a number of high-ranking officials in the respective provinces, ministries and enterprises. The CIGs are publicly and specifically instructed to search for 'tigers' and are warned clearly of the potential consequences of negligent investigations. Given the prevalence of corruption, the CIGs are not expected to return to Beijing empty-handed. Naturally, provinces which are to be inspected would experience tremendous consternation and anxiety until a 'tiger' or two have been hunted down and punished (for the example of Jiangxi province, see Guo and Dong 2013). It is unknown whether the CIGs are actually finding new cases during their trips, gathering further evidence on existing cases, or merely implementing decisions that have already been made in a high profile manner. At least, according to Wang Qishan, the central authority is not surprised by the findings of the CIGs, and corruption cases exposed by CIGs largely confirm the central government's suspicions (China News Net, 15 March 2014). After the two rounds of inspection in 2013, the CIGs passed their files to the CCID and MoO leading to investigations of a number of vice-ministerial level officials.

Finally, the CIGs debrief the Party authorities of the provinces, ministries or other organizations inspected. Interestingly, in most debriefing sessions the CIGs are much more forceful and direct in criticizing the inspected departments than might have been expected. The Party secretaries of the provinces duly accept their findings, acknowledge shortcomings in its anti-corruption work and pledge to undertake the necessary action. The meetings, together with the problems identified, are typically published on the front page of the provincial newspapers.

There are further procedural innovations differentiating the four rounds of central inspections from earlier practice. The government emphasizes that each CIG is only temporary; it has been created to carry out one particular inspection and is disbanded immediately afterwards.

Group leaders and their deputies are also appointed on an *ad hoc* basis. The stated intention of this practice is to allow constant change of CIG leaders to avoid the inspectors being corrupted by local and sectoral interests.

There are both highly targeted inspections and routine inspections, with the former focusing on specialist auditing of individual institutions. The key difference is that, while routine inspections aim at discovering corruption through inspection, targeted inspections are proactive investigations of corruption allegations that are known to the CCDI.

CIGs are given additional powers to carry out their inspections. CIGs are given the power to randomly check and verify personal records, especially financial records filed by provincial and ministerial leaders. This practice is not explicitly authorized by the Party's rules but is said to represent a new form of external accountability, indicating a possible shift from self-regulation to external accountability in the controversial area of asset disclosure.

The CIGs not only investigate officials at the provincial level, but also seek to create an environment that will prompt local disciplinary inspection committees to take action. It is the clear intention of the CIGs to deter corruption at the provincial level creating a cascade effect throughout the Party (CCDI, 15 March 2014b). In this sense, the CIGs also aim to create a cascade effect on anti-corruption enforcement.

Through consolidating the leadership of the disciplinary inspection system at the provincial level and the CIGs, power is quietly but quickly shifted from the provinces to Beijing. Indeed, Wang Qishan has specifically asked CIGs to serve as remote eyes for the central authority to discover problems on behalf of the central authority and report them faithfully to the central authority (China Net, 6 June 2013). In the process, provincial leaders are becoming the targets of anti-corruption investigation.

The primary function of the CIGs is not to overcome the agency problem but rather to deal with the loyalty problem. In the factional politics of China, the issue is not the lack of knowledge about what provincial leaders are up to. The central authority clearly has developed effective monitoring mechanisms for its provincial and ministerial level officials. The issue for emerging leaders is to ensure political loyalty from provincial and ministerial leaders and other subordinates. As an authoritarian state, China has designed an anti-corruption campaign combined with periodic CIG inspections that serve that particular objective well.

3. RAISING POPULAR SUPPORT, DIMINISHING PUBLIC PARTICIPATION

A defining characteristic of the on-going anti-corruption campaign is not forceful top-down enforcement—China does not lack for other top-down campaigns; instead, it is diminishing public participation in the control of corruption, in spite of immense public support. The bottom-up anti-corruption initiatives and mobilization that had been growing steadily (Fu 2014b) are now severely restricted as the anti-corruption campaign progresses, and there is a steady decline in civil society participation and citizen involvement. People largely cheer on the sidelines. The new government suppresses civil society at the same time as it cracks down on corruption.

Before 2013 China had been developing a vibrant civil society aimed at exposing corruption through on-line mobilization and off-line action including legal action, political advocacy and street demonstrations. It is important to note that, while political forces across the political spectrum have a common anti-corruption agenda, it is those who are pushing for a more open society who have taken action. When this happens, anti-corruption becomes an integral part of a larger demand for political accountability and democratization.

Online anti-corruption mobilization has been a well-known phenomenon in China. Armed with information technology and the expanded realm of freedom, citizens, acting largely in a spontaneous fashion, have gathered in virtual spaces to identify and to hunt down corrupt officials through on-line mobilization.

Public opinion matters tremendously in China in the resolution of routine political and legal problems. Given the Party's democracy-deficit, its authoritarian leaders may yield to public opinion and seek to appease public demands for further reforms (Gilley 2009; Stockmann 2013). Within this particular context, it is not surprising to find that China has had an unusually active and vibrant online level of activism since the emergence of social media. Supported by the rapid evolution of information technology and a generally tolerant policy from the Party, Chinese Internet users developed an aggressive culture of cyber activism to identify corrupt officials and to expose corruption scandals through a coordinated search commonly referred to as 'human flesh search' (HFS) (Fu 2014b; Yang 2011).

The popularity of HFS may lead to abuse. Anti-corruption is a forceful weapon for the government, but it can also be a useful resource in political competition, in business dealings and for getting revenge in personal and official matters. It is a resource that is being actively exploited and used in political and business competitions. Without strong professionalized political and legal institutions, public opinion in China can more easily swing decision-making and carry more weight than perhaps it ought. Once a potentially corrupt act is exposed and the perpetrators identified, an official investigation follows quickly and the Party soon imposes harsh and swift punishment without careful examination of the case involved. Gradually, online whistle-blowing morphs into online vigilante justice. There are well-known cases in which aggrieved individuals posted allegations to expose corruption scandals leading to prompt investigation and official action with little chance for the accused individuals to defend themselves (Xinhua Net, 10 August 2013).

Anti-corruption mobilization and protests are not new to China. The 1989 democratic movement was in part an anti-corruption movement triggered by official profiteering. Corruption also casts a long shadow in some of the cases of high profile political unrest and public protest over so-called 'land-grabbing'. The Wukan protest, the longest and largest of its kind to date, was triggered by predatory land-grabbing in which corrupt local officials sold or leased village land without properly compensating villagers (Fu 2014a). However, since 1989 there has rarely been an overt concerted anti-corruption movement because the government has become very sensitive to organized anti-corruption mobilization, fearing that such a movement could easily morph into more widespread demonstrations calling for democratic reforms.

Critics and whistleblowers have also been effectively silenced using state laws. Defamation, both civil and criminal, from time to time has been used by officials to silence whistleblowers. The former police chief of Chongqing who sought protection in the US Consulate was infamous for authorizing so-called 'double lawsuits' in 2010 that encouraged defamation proceedings against a newspaper (by the police station) and a journalist (by police officers) (Zhen 2010). After police pursuit of critical journalists became so abusive, the national authorities briefly ordered caution and a stricter adherence to legal rules and procedures (Yan 2011).

Under the Xi government, critics have been systematically silenced in two ways. The first is to target certain popular opinion leaders (the so-called Big V) and to use regular criminal laws to punish them. Well known cases include the prosecution of Charles Xue for visiting a prostitute; Wang Liming for disturbing public order; Dong Rubin (Bian Ming) for falsifying company registration capital, illegal business operations and disturbing public order; Qin Zhihui and Yang Xiuyu for slander and illegal business operations; Liu Hu for defamation; Zhou Lubao for blackmailing, and Chen Yongzhou for defamation (CHRD 2013). From the government's perspective, an 'online pusher team', in collusion with opinions leaders and public intellectuals, creates a virtual 'navy' that fabricates news, disturbs public order, and undermines social stability.[1] The chilling effect of a series of prosecutions is still being strongly felt in the virtual world and beyond.

The second means of criminalizing speech online is explicitly to extend certain criminal offences to the virtual world, in particular through the offence of defamation by making and spreading rumors and disturbing public order. According to a judicial interpretation (Interpretation) passed by the Supreme People's Court (SPC) and Supreme People's Procuratorate (SPP) (SPC and SPP 2013), a person can be convicted of defamation, resulting in a maximum penalty of three years imprisonment, if he or she creates and circulates rumors and the webpage posting these rumors has been visited by more than 5,000 internet users or reposted more than 500 times. The other significant change is an expansion in the scope of public prosecutions for defamation. Defamation depends principally on private prosecution, and public prosecution is possible only when a case 'seriously harms social order and state interest'.[2] The Interpretation provides a list of consequences which qualify for public prosecution and in doing so expands the armory for direct police intervention.[3] In addition, the Interpretation also creates a number of other online offences such as disturbing public order, online blackmailing, and online illegal business operation. Although the police have been cautious in using the new law, the impact on internet activism and online mobilization, including HFS, is palpable.

Efforts have also been made to crackdown on off-line mobilization against corruption. The case of Xu Zhiyong and his New Citizens' Movement illustrates well the vigour of prosecution. Taking cues from Xi's declaration to 'cage the power' and beat 'flies' as well as 'tigers' in a new round of anti-corruption campaigns, citizen activists massed under the banner of a New Citizens' Movement and the leadership of Xu Zhiyong to launch a series of public campaigns and street mobilization demanding

---

[1] For a summary of the official view of the campaign, see, 'The heavy fist must come out to deal with online rumour (written conversation)', available 6 May 2015 at http://chinacopyrightandmedia.wordpress.com/2013/08/31/the-heavy-fist-must-come-out-to-deal-with-online-rumours-written-conversation/.

[2] Article 246 (2), The Criminal Law of People's Republic of China.

[3] Public prosecution is possible in the following circumstances where a case: (1) has caused mass events; (2) has caused public disorder; (3) has caused ethnic or religious conflict; (4) has defamed a large number of persons and led to heinous social impact; (5) has harmed the state image and seriously endangered state interest; (6) has caused heinous international impact; or has caused other serious harm to social order and state interest. Article 3 of the Interpretation.

the creation of a system which imposes a mandatory requirement for the Party and government officials to declare their personal assets. The clarion call received an initial positive response from the government. However, as the popular movement gathered momentum and shifted from online-campaigning to limited street action, the Party-State perceived the risk that the anti-corruption campaign might converge into a more broadly-based democratic movement. In response, the Party used the criminal law to kybosh the movement. The conviction of Xu Zhiyong and his comrades in the New Citizens' Movement for disturbing public order, and the subsequent harassment of lawyers who defended the movement at trials, symbolizes a tragic end to a popular anti-corruption campaign.

The Xi government is committed to anti-corruption enforcement subject to the paramount condition of its monopoly over the entire process. At the same time, the Xi regime has launched the most systemic anti-corruption campaign to date. Xi is able to silence the social media and to diminish if not disable its anti-corruption functions by punishing opinion leaders, de-registering accounts, and crippling civic activism by criminal punishment of the movement's leaders and activists. Xi may look to a 'big society' in providing more cost-effective social services; however, bottom-up anti-corruption activism based on a vibrant civil society advocating social change is another matter altogether (Miller and Lu 2014).

4.   MARGINALIZING LAW

Xi's campaign further shifts power from legal institutions to the Party's disciplinary mechanism. Compared with anti-corruption work under the previous government, the current campaign more decisively bypasses legal procedures and institutions. After a brief moment in which law seemed to be able to play a central role in the anti-corruption process, legal institutions have been effectively marginalized to the role of initiating anti-corruption purges of 'tigers'. There is no longer any meaningful discussion on the end goals and limits of *shuanggui*, the Party's power to detain its own delinquent members and little mention of the creation of a more neutral anti-corruption body (Sapio 2010). Law may provide authority and legitimacy to support the Party's investigation but will emphatically not be tolerated as a hurdle to a concerted anti-corruption campaign. Indeed, the people who bitterly complain about the lack of credibility of anti-corruption investigations are the investigators in China's anti-corruption authority (ACA), with the principal complaints being a lack of independence in initiating investigations and deference to the Party's in-house disciplinary organ.

There are a number of reasons legal institutions are not playing a more meaningful role in the current anti-corruption campaign. First, the campaign is an integral part of a larger political rectification campaign of purges within the ranks of the Communist Party with the ultimate aim of uniting the Party under its new leadership. It is largely a political campaign by the Party and for the Party to entrench Xi's leadership. It was initiated by the highest authority in the Party, carried out in accordance with the Party's internal rules, and presided over principally by the Party's own organization and disciplinary authorities. One of the principal goals of the CIGs is to identify and punish officials who openly defy important policies of the central authority.

Because anti-corruption investigation and disciplinary inspection are tools designed to serve political goals grounded on the shifting sands of political necessity, fixed rules and legal institutions are ill-fitted to play a leading role, if any at all. Pragmatic political calculations loom large in the high profile cases, and there is no place for legality or for that matter morality more broadly (Brown, 2014). During the earlier and most volatile stages of the current anti-corruption campaign, whose end is ultimately unpredictable, law takes a back seat at best.

The political nature of the campaign explains, in part, the extraordinary inertia of the procuracy, which leads China's legal anti-corruption body. As an anti-corruption investigation body, the ACA's jurisdiction is narrowly defined and effectively limited to the investigation of actual crimes. This style of political campaign which has the appearance of casting a wide net without a specific target does not fall under the ACA's criminal investigation remit.

Second, the anti-corruption drive is taking place in the political stratosphere. It reaches the core of the Party's inner sanctum and aims in principal to rein in officials at the highest level. Given how legal institutions are configured in China's political system (Fu 2013a), they are simply not able to play a meaningful role. Under the Party rules, an investigation of a senior Party official and, in particular, a decision to detain or arrest must first be endorsed by the Party Committee at the respective level; and an investigation of corruption at the provincial or ministerial level necessarily requires the approval of, and action by, the central authorities. In practice, the statutory anti-corruption authority is better able to deal with 'flies' for the simple reason that the investigation would not require prior political approval. When the sights of the anti-corruption guns were trained more keenly on those relatively minor officials, as in the past, the legal authority sometimes had a more meaningful role to play. Logically, when an anti-corruption campaign shifts principally to 'tigers', the role of ACA is diminished immediately.

Most of the ACA's investigations are limited to relatively minor corruption cases committed by junior officials. The ACA has concentrated its investigation on corruption that is related to and reported by ordinary people such as corruption in the process of land expropriation, school and university admissions, the provision of medical and health care, employment, public housing, social security, environment, food and drug safety, or poverty reduction. Such cases affect the daily lives of ordinary people and are of significant social concern, but are not on a grand scale. It is interesting to note that the tigers which ACA has investigated in the past year are isolated criminal cases that are not related to the Zhou Yongkang's network.

There are clear signs that, constitutionally, the Party is beginning more openly and forcefully to play a visible and direct role in managing society. The constitutional principle of Party leadership is deeply entrenched, although the Party prefers to hide in the shadows pulling strings to exert political influence through the government and other front organizations. Under Xi, the Party has become more conspicuous and more self-confident. The Party is more assertive in claiming its right to rule directly, bypassing legislative and executive authorities not to mention the judicial authority (Lam, 2014). Because the Party looms increasingly large amidst the increasing marginalization of the legal process in relation to anti-corruption, the relevant legal rules no longer apply to such factors as access to counsels, disclosure and transparency. Coupled with the silencing of social media and the narrowing of the public sphere in China in the immediate aftermath of the Xi take-over, anti-corruption enforcement is more opaque, more secretive and less rule-bound.

5. A CHINESE MODEL FOR ANTI-CORRUPTION ENFORCEMENT?

Like generations of leaders before him, Xi initiated his campaign to enhance the popularity and legitimacy of the government and to pave the ground for his new policy initiatives, which raise questions of how much is new in this current campaign against corruption and to what degree are Xi and Wang able to break with the past.

Each Party Plenary Session seems to have triggered an intensive anti-corruption campaign on 'tigers' and the number of such tigers may have exceeded 40 since Xi came to power. We may reasonably argue that the sheer size of punitive measures dealt out for high-ranking officials is a significant departure. One may argue too that qualitatively Xi's campaign breaks new ground by investigating Zhou Yongkang, a former member of the Standing Committee of the Politburo, and a number of generals in the military.

Another potentially significant departure is a much tighter and consistent control over direct or indirect public spending on the welfare of civil servants, especially the so-called *sangong* spending: in other words public spending on overseas travel, purchase and use of official cars and entertainment. The level of *sangong* spending is staggering, and previous governments all tried to cut back this spending but with only limited success.[4] The Xi government seems to have achieved more than any previous government in limiting government excess. The ambitious Eight Rules of the Party[5] and the Three Measures of the State Council (Xinhua Net, 8 August 2013) have the potential to significantly reduce waste from bureaucratic procedures if rigorously enforced. As usual, the Party is decisive in making new rules. By way of example, the Three Measures require that, within the term of this government, there shall be no new government offices, no new recruitment of civil servants on government payrolls, and no increase in *sangong* spending. This blunt instrument was apparently able to achieve its objective in the first year of the policy's implementation (CCDI, 2 March 2014).

Although Xi has demonstrated a strong determination and achieved more forceful implementation, caution should be exercised not to exaggerate the success of the measures adopted. The senior officials who have been investigated or punished mostly belong to two categories. The first is Xi's political enemies, the investigation of whom is politically motivated and serves an express agenda. Judging by the profiles of the officials who fell from grace, they were primarily officials associated with his political nemesis, Zhou Yongkang, who occupied important offices in security, Sichuan province and oil fields. The purge of Zhou and his associates has been applied over the whole of Zhou's political career, ensnaring his family members and protégés along with businessmen and officials who owed their success to, or had dealings with, him.

Beyond political enemies, Xi's other targets are mixed, but mainly officials who are semi-retired to the 'second line' and no longer holders of real political powers. In point of fact, Xi may not really be after 'tigers', but merely aims to punish officials who hold 'second line' offices with high status but who lack political power, such as deputy chairmen of Provincial

---

[4]   For an over view of illicit public spending, see http://www.baike.com/wiki/% E4%B8%89%E5%85%AC%E6%B6%88%E8%B4%B9 (last accessed 6 May 2015).
[5]   For an introduction of the Eight Rules, see http://fanfu.people.com.cn/ GB/143349/353985/ (last accessed 6 May 2015).

People's Congress Standing Committees or deputy chairmen of Provincial Political Consultative Conferences.

What is the best way to conceptualize Xi's anti-corruption campaign? It is widely recognized that while heavy-handed, top-down campaigns may have a short-term deterrence impact on wide-spread corruption, they do not tackle the root causes which are arguably embedded in the political system. Wang Qishan has famously said that the anti-corruption campaign does more harm to the Party as an organization than to the individuals under investigation. Removal of a large number of senior officials sends a shock wave throughout the Party, and it will take a long while for wounds to heal. The Party is prescribing tough medicine and shock therapy for corruption, and the current campaign in many aspects is extremely destructive (CCDI, 15 March 2014b; Caixin Net, 25 January 2013). The surgical operation that is ongoing and likely to be continuing for several years to come is not aimed at long term anti-corruption capacity building. Again to quote Wang Qishan, shock therapy is used to address the symptoms, that is to stop the further spreading and deepening of corruption, and its intention is to buy time for Xi to tackle the root causes, that is to develop better institutional designs and to improve the overall political accountability (ibid.).

Can the twin imperatives of the political need for short-term impact and the long-term goal of stamping out corruption be reconciled? This remains a tough question that has not been meaningfully debated or carefully researched. Perhaps inevitably the crackdown has to be selective, given the prevalence of CCP corruption and that fact that the crude, ham-fisted approach is intended to achieve a goal that goes beyond anti-corruption itself. As argued above, the anti-corruption campaign is orchestrated to eliminate Xi's political enemies and to overcome real or potential resistance to Xi's reform agenda. By legitimizing the new government and regaining popular support, Xi hopes, through force and discipline, to bring the bureaucracy on board. To do so, Xi needs political patronage and authority, and fighting corruption is an expedient to achieve this end.

The optimistic view holds that once the dust stirred up by the anti-corruption campaign has settled, Xi's government will turn its attention to institutional reforms, including political liberalization, further marketization of the economy and establishing robust anti-corruption institutions based on the rule of law, protection of property rights, freedom of the press and public participation. In contrast, there is an equally persuasive claim that Xi believes that he can establish a Chinese model for fighting corruption that relies on centralizing political power and ruthless, selective enforcement of Party rules. From this perspective, current and future anti-corruption strategies are likely to be predicated on a Party-centric, top-down approach in which a powerful Party-state, through a more effective internal disciplinary mechanism, controls Party members.

From the point of view of the latter, anti-corruption is a delicate political process that needs careful planning, coordination and management. Popular participation risks derailing the grand design. Public support should be solicited while public participation should be curtailed. Xi's and the CCDI's diagnosis assumes that anti-corruption enforcement is not effective because, in part, China lacks a centralized anti-corruption system that can coordinate anti-corruption work without interference in investigative work, which could operate responsibly to this end (Sina News, 2 February 2014).

Thus, a fundamental question remains. What kind of anti-corruption policy can be established given the prevalence of corruption, the deepness of public anger, and the height of public expectations? This boils down to the question of how to control corruption without significantly eroding the monopoly of power by the Party or interfering with other reform objectives.

At root, the choice is between an open-control system and a closed-control system. Best practice necessitates an open system which relies on political accountability, economic competition, effective protection of property rights, the freedom of speech, and a vibrant civil society (Rose-Ackerman 1999). Translated into a Chinese context, the pivot point should be shifted gradually from the center to the local, from the Party to legal institutions and from the state to civil society. However, law and legal institutions in China are, at present, not powerful enough to rein in high-level corruption because of their inferior position in the overall political structure. In a country where law has not traditionally played an effective role, legal institutions cannot be relied on to deal with powerful political figures. In the absence of a will to give up power to the extent necessary to build effective institutions, only the Party is left to clean up the corruption of its own members. To strengthen legal institutions would necessarily submit the Party to more legal control and carry political risks. Bottom up reforms may sound appealing, but equally they can be chaotic and difficult to manage. Civil society mobilization carries an even higher political risk as organizations such as Xu Zhiyong's New Citizens' Movement could mutate into a fully-fledged movement for democracy.

The alternative is to opt for a closed system which depends on internal political control and Party discipline, together with enhanced communist morality, selfless dedication and commitment. Earlier generations of leaders struggled to square this circle and maintain a viable balance between open and closed systems, whereas Xi seems to have decided to shift the balance resolutely toward a closed system. Through strengthening the disciplinary system, especially direct central control over the disciplinary process and the further institutionalization of CIG inspections, Xi aims to rebuild the Party through an overall tightening of central control.

The Party talks much about external supervision and the risk of capture of internal supervision. However, the external supervision that the Party refers to is a very limited one. It merely calls for the further centralization of supervisory power in the hands of the central authority of the CCDI with Xi behind it. Ultimately the proposed reform posits further strengthening the Party as a whole at the cost of genuine external accountability.

Having charted a particular course, the Party is going back to Chinese historical roots to learn from emperors of dynasties who attempted to control their massive bureaucracy with limited means. Ultimately, Xi is trying to build a powerful and self-regulating Party, which is clean and benevolent, enjoys wide popular support, and is effective in controlling corruption. How he will move the Party Leviathan from its present to the future is highly uncertain.

CONCLUSION

Xi's anti-corruption campaign has witnessed an attempted re-concentration of political power that is unprecedented. By designing new and shoring up old anti-corruption mechanisms, the anti-corruption campaign has sought to repatriate powers to the centre in three ways. First, there has been a shift of power from regional governments to the central government as demonstrated by CCDI's direct control of provincial CDIs in personnel and operation matters and by the high-profile CIGs that have been dispatched to a variety of provinces, ministries, universities and SOEs.

Second, power is further shifting from legal institutions to political institutions, particularly the Party's internal disciplinary system. The Party has repeatedly proclaimed its control over anti-corruption work; moreover, due to its top-down nature and a specific focus on senior ranking leaders, the current campaign largely bypasses existing legal procedures and legal institutions, leading to a further marginalization of the rule of law.

Finally, power is shifting from civil society back to the Party. President Xi proves equally harsh and effective in quashing both corruption and civil society mobilization against corruption. In doing so, Xi is undermining the very institutions, such as the freedom of press or public participation, that may prove the most effective in reigning in corruption in the long run. In imposing a monopoly on China's anti-corruption enforcement, Xi has effectively silenced vocal critics bringing the social media practically to its knees through a series of repressive measures.

Of course, anti-corruption is a political necessity that is immensely popular. However, the campaign style, as it is being carried out, can hardly be sustainable, as top anti-corruption leaders such as Wang Qishan readily concede. To quote Wang, the Party is using the anti-corruption campaign to buy the time that the Party needs to develop sound anti-corruption institutions and tackle corruption at its root (Caixin Net, 25 January 2013).

That said, what the CCDI and the Party have in mind in terms of the design of more permanent anti-corruption institutions and what they understand as the root cause of corruption in China are far from clear. The Party has been struggling for decades between internal regulation, self-regulation, and external supervision in designing anti-corruption mechanisms. Notwithstanding, external supervision has acquired a unique meaning in the PRC. Instead of relying on established institutions such as a separation of powers, media scrutiny, the rule of law and a vibrant civil society to supervise political power, the Party seeks a further concentration of power and relies on tougher disciplinary measures and sword-wielding enforcement. The current anti-corruption campaign moves decisively towards this direction.

REFERENCES

Beijing News Net (8 November 2013). 'Reform in the Disciplinary Inspection System Seeking to Go beyond Self-regulation', accessed 28 May 2015 at http://www.bjnews.com.cn/feature/2013/11/08/291603.html.

Brown, Kerry. 2014. 'Xi Jinping Vs Zhou Yongkang', *The Diplomat*, 17 March, available 6 May 2015 at http://thediplomat.com/2014/03/xi-jinping-vs-zhou-yongkang/.

Caixin Net. 25 January 2013. 'Wang Qishan: The Anticorruption Campaign Should Mainly Deal with Symptoms now to Gain Time to Tackle the Root Cause', available 6 May 2015 at http://china.caixin.com/2013-01-25/100486367.html.

CCDI. 2 March 2014. 'Huang Shuxian, CCDI Deputy Secretary and Minister of Supervision Answering Questions from the Press', http://www.ccdi.gov.cn/xwtt/201403/t20140302_19413.html.

CCDI. 15 March, 2014a. 'Background Information', available 6 May 2015 at http://www.ccdi.gov.cn/xwyw/201403/t20140315_20131.html.

CCDI. 15 March 2014b. 'Wang Qishan Speaking on the Role of Inspection in the Party's Anti-corruption Work at the Mobilization and Planning Conference for Central Inspection in 2014', available 6 May 2015 at http://www.ccdi.gov.cn/xwtt/201403/t20140315_20129.html.

CCP Central Committee. 2013. *Establishing a Sound System for Punishing and Preventing Corruption: A Work Plan 2013–2017*, available 6 May 2015 at http://news.xinhuanet.com/politics/2013-12/25/c_118708522_5.htm.

China Net. 6 June 2013. 'Uncovering CIGs: Serving as the Long Distance Eyes for the Central Government and to Expose Tigers and Flies', available 6 May 2015 at http://news.china.com.cn/2013-06/06/content_29043286_2.htm.

China News Net. 15 March 2014. 'Wang Qishan Plans Inspection Work for This Year, and Fourteen Regions and Units will be Inspected', available 6 May 2015 at http://www.chinanews.com/gn/2014/03-15/5954813.shtml.

CHRD. 2013. *A Nightmarish Year Under Xi Jinping's 'Chinese Dream'*. Available 6 May 2015 at http://chrdnet.com/wp-content/uploads/2014/03/FINAL-PDF_2013_CHRD-Report-on-Human-Rights-Defenders-compressed.pdf.

Chu Chaoxin and Luo Ting. 2014. 'How CIGS beating Tigers', available 6 May 2015 at http://www.infzm.com/content/98676.

Fewsmith, Joseph. 2014. 'Mao's Shadow', 43 *China Leadership Monitor*, available 6 May 2015 at http://media.hoover.org/sites/default/files/documents/CLMJF.pdf.

Fu Hualing. 2013a. 'Autonomy, Courts and the Political-Legal Order in Contemporary China', in Cao Liqun, Ivan Sun and Bill Hebeton (eds) *Handbook of Chinese Criminology*. London: Routledge.

Fu Hualing. 2013b. 'The Upward and Downward Spirals in China's Anti-corruption Enforcement', in Mike McConville and Eva Pils, (eds) *Comparative Perspectives on Criminal Justice in China*. Cheltenham, UK and Northampton, MA, USA: Edward Elgar.

Fu Hualing. 2014a. 'What does Wukan Offer? Land-taking, Law, and Dispute Resolution', in Hualing Fu and John Gillespie (eds) *Resolving Land Disputes in East Asia: Exploring the Limits of Law*. Cambridge: Cambridge University Press.

Fu Hualing. 2014b. 'Stability and Anticorruption Initiatives: Is There a Chinese Model?', in Susan Trevaskes, Elisa Nesossi, Sarah Biddulph and Flora Sapio (eds) *The Politics of Law and Stability in China*. Cheltenham, UK and Northampton, MA, USA: Edward Elgar.

Gilley, Bruce. 2009. *The Right to Rules: How State Win and Lose Legitimacy*. New York: Columbia University Press.

Guo Fang and Dong Xianhua. 2013. 'CIGs Searching for Tigers in Jiangxi, the Atmosphere in the Officialdom was Tense', available 6 May 2015 at http://news.qq.com/a/20130723/000658.htm.

Lam, Willy. 2014. 'New High-Level Groups Threaten Line between Party and Government', *China Brief Volume* 14: 7.

Li Yongzhong. 2014. 'Interpreting Departmental Adjustment in CCDI', available 6 May 2015 at http://www.21ccom.net/articles/zgyj/fzyj/article_20140418104617.html.

Manion, Melanie. 2004. *Corruption by Design: Building Clean Government in Mainland China and Hong Kong*. Cambridge, MA: Harvard University Press.

Miller, Tom and Warren Lu. 2014. 'Better Governance through Kung-Fu', GavekalDragonomics, 14 February, available 6 May 2015 at www.gavekal.com.

Mo Yitan. 2014. *Wang Qishan: The Public Enemy of the Officialdom*. Hong Kong: Mirror Books.

Naughton, Barry. 2014. 'After the Third Plenum: Economic Reform Revival Moves toward Implementation', 43 *China Leadership Monitor*, available 6 May 2015 at http://media.hoover.org/sites/default/files/documents/CLM43BN.pdf.

Rose-Akerman, Susan, *Corruption and Government: Causes, Consequences, and Reform*. Cambridge: Cambridge University Press.

Sapio, Flora. 2010. *Sovereign Power and the Law in China*. Leiden: Brill.

Seligson. Mitchell and John Booth. 2009. *The Legitimacy Puzzle: Political Support and Democracy in Latin America*. New York: Cambridge University Press.

Shen Nianzu. 2014. 'Most of the 19 Fallen Officials at the Ministerial and Provincial Level are either Semi-retired or Held Deputy Positions', available 6 May 2015 at http://www.chinasdi.cn/news.aspx?newsid=17981&type=O.

Sicular, Terry. 2013. 'The Challenge of High Inequality in China', *Inequality in Focus*, 2:1–4, available 6 May 2015 at http://www.worldbank.org/content/dam/Worldbank/document/Poverty%20documents/Inequality-In-Focus-0813.pdf.

Sina News, 2 February 2014. 'Research Office of CCDI: Corruption Occurring Frequently in some Places and Accountability Found Lacking', available 6 May 2015 at http://news.sina.com.cn/c/2014-02-02/101629390680.shtml.

SPC and SPP (2013) Interpretation on Several Problems in relation to the Application of Law in Handling Defamation and other Criminal Offences on the Internet (Judicial Interpretation 2013, No 21).

Stockmann, Daniela. 2013. *Media Commercialization and Authoritarian Rule in China*. Cambridge: Cambridge University Press.

Wedeman, Andrew. 2012. *Double Paradox: Rapid Growth and Rising Corruption in China*. Ithaca: Cornell University Press.

Xinhua Net. 8 August 2013. 'Improving Moral Standing, Implementing "Three Measures"', available 6 May 2015 at http://news.xinhuanet.com/politics/2013-08/08/c_116862851.htm.

Xinhua Net. 10 August 2013. 'Whistle-blower Telling the Whole Story of Trailing and Reporting Shanghai Judges' Visiting Prostitutes', available 6 May 2015 at http://news.sina.com.cn/c/2013-08-10/021827911342.shtml.

Xinhua Net. 2 February 2014. 'Research Office of the CCDI on Improving the Disciplinary Inspection System', available 6 May 2015 at http://www.gov.cn/jrzg/2014-02/02/content_2579691.htm.

Yan Meiling. 2011. 'Criminal Defamation in the New Media Environment in the People's Republic of China', *International Journal of Communications Law and Policy* 14: 4–81.

Yang, Guobin. (2011). *The Power of the Internet in China: Citizen Activism Online*. New York: Columbia University Press.

Zhen Zhen. 2010. 'Chongqing Police Chief's "Double Lawsuits" Chills the Media', available 6 May 2015 at http://m.secretchina.com/node/378334.

PART II

Corruption and state performance

6. The story of Paraguayan dams: the long-term consequences of wrongdoing in procurement

Stéphane Straub

1. INTRODUCTION

Public procurement, because it involves the transfer of large amounts of public resources from the public sector to private firms, is an area where wrongdoings and abuses are common. These take many forms, such as collusion and bid rigging, the distortion of specifications, revolving doors, and the use of exception, among many others. They are found both in the purchase of standard goods such as office supplies and milk for school children, and in the procurement of complex projects such as infrastructure. Finally, despite large variations in the quality of institutional frameworks around the world, they hit developing and developed countries alike.

While a large body of contributions, both theoretical and empirical, has addressed these issues, a more neglected aspect has to do with the consequences of systematic wrongdoings in the procurement arena on the long term development trajectory of countries. This chapter aims at illustrating this through the enlightening story of the Paraguayan dams, Itaipú and Yacyretá. These two massive infrastructure projects, started in the 1970s and 1980s, embody most of the ingredients found in the literature, namely widespread corruption and abuses of public money, facilitated by weak or inexistent legal and political institutions, and the long-term adverse effects on the development trajectory of Paraguayan society.

This chapter begins in section 2 by classifying the main results gleaned from this literature, along three main lines: the main channels through which abuses occur, the deep causes of such widespread abuses, and the economic and social consequences of distortions in the procurement process. It divides the consequences into two main parts. First are the static costs, stemming from excess spending and the related under provision of public goods, which are the aspects most often documented. Second are the dynamic costs, for which much less evidence exists, related to distortions in the type of goods and services procured, as well as induced distortions in the number and type of private providers of public goods and services.

Next, in Section 3, the chapter illustrates both static and dynamic abuses, by relating each to episodes of the Paraguayan dams' history. In doing so, it draws on sources from the historical, economic, management, and anthropological literature, as well as journalistic accounts. Section 4 concludes.

2.   CHANNELS, CAUSES, AND CONSEQUENCES

This section aims to set the stage for the main objective of the chapter, which is to illustrate the basic phenomena outlined here with the Paraguayan dams' example.

2.1   Channels

First of all, a large literature analyzes theoretically and documents empirically the numerous channels for wrongdoings in procurement, which can be broadly grouped under the collusion and corruption labels, and include, for example, instances of cartels, bid rigging and other collusive arrangements, as well as the use and abuse of tailored specification, exceptions, and so on. General overviews can be found in the corresponding chapters of Rose-Ackerman (2006), and Rose-Ackerman and Søreide (2012).[1]

A few examples of high-quality recent empirical evidence on corruption in procurement include Di Tella and Schargrodsky (2003), on corruption in Argentinean hospitals, Bandiera, Prat and Valletti (2009), who introduced the idea of passive (inefficiency) versus active waste (corruption) using Italian data, and Mironov and Zhuravskaya (2012) on the link between corruption in procurement and political financing in Russia. On collusion, references include seminal papers by Porter and Zona (1993, 1999), and more recently by Asker (2010), Decarolis and Conley (2013) and Kawai and Nakabayashi (2014), among many others. To some extent, the recent trend towards more transparency in public procurement, and, in particular, the fact that a growing number of countries make the detailed data on their procurement operations public have been key in allowing both researchers and practitioners to document these facts.

---

[1]   See for example chapters 15 and 16 (Part V) in Rose-Ackerman (2006), and Chapters 3 to 5 (Part II) in Rose-Ackerman and Søreide (2012).

2.2 Causes

Many countries nowadays have imported best practices, in the form of modern procurement rules, partly as the consequence of the efforts of international organizations such as the OECD and of the civil society. However, in the presence of deeper flaws in the institutional environment of these countries, good rules (de jure) have not necessarily translated into good practices (de facto), for a number of reasons.

Among these are weak enforcement, slow courts, and the inefficiency or corruption of judicial power, the weakness of auditing institutions, the constraints on contracting forms and information availability (on providers, quality of products) and transmission. These institutional weaknesses often translate into widespread commitment problems, but also, of course, into political instability and opportunism. In that sense, wrongdoing in procurement is but one manifestation of these failures.

2.3 Consequences

Ultimately, we classify the costs associated with wrongdoing into two categories, namely static and dynamic costs.

Static costs are the most obvious and well-documented distortions. They include straightforward instances of overpricing, when the public sector pays excessive prices for the goods or services it procures. A well-known example is found in Olken (2007), where small road projects in Indonesia were shown to give rise to significant missing materials and inflated costs. The other side of this coin is, of course, the under provision of public goods, as a smaller amount can be procured for a given budget, as well as the potentially inferior quality of these goods, and the increased risk of failures or accidents. Most empirical contributions have focused on this type of cost.

An additional class of static costs relates to biases in the types of goods and services procured. For example, Mironov and Zhuraskaya (2012) document the fact that corrupt public officials often overspend on consulting services, which are a convenient way to channel funds to related parties. In terms of the overall public budget, an early paper by Mauro (1998) found that corruption reduced government spending on education in a cross section of countries.

Much less documented are the dynamic costs of wrongdoings in procurement, through the distortions in the incentives facing entrepreneurs. Indeed, in environments where competition is distorted, the set of firms seeking to provide goods and services to the public sector is likely to be distorted.

When success in obtaining public contracts is not related mainly to the efficiency of providers, but, for example, to their ability or willingness to use political connections or to pay bribes, entrepreneurs will adjust their behavior in order to be successful. This phenomenon, described by the early rent-seeking literature, such as Tullock (1967), Buchanan (1980), Krueger (1974) and Baghwati (1982), implies that firms will engage significant resources in wasteful rent-seeking activities. This is, in particular, likely to have consequences on the size of firms, that is, on the intensive margin, as their growth is hampered by this resource diversion.

More recently, Baumol (1990), and Murphy, Shleifer and Vishny (1991) have insisted on a second aspect, which has to do with the potential 'misallocation of talents'. This means that in corrupt environments, entrepreneurs may choose to enter different sectors than they would have selected in a clean environment. Additionally, the set of entrepreneurs may be distorted, as potentially talented ones may end up not entering at all, while less talented ones may benefit from their rent-seeking efforts. These extensive margin effects therefore have a first order impact on the existence, the composition in terms of talent, and the choice of sectors of the entrepreneurial class.

The next section illustrates the interplay of the different elements outlined above in the case of Paraguay and its large investments in hydroelectric dams, focusing in particular in more detail on the dynamic, long-term development costs.[2]

3.   THE STORY OF PARAGUAYAN DAMS

In the 1970s and 1980s, the country decided to build two major hydroelectric power plants, the Itaipú dam on the part of the Paraná River forming the border with Brazil, which would for a long time be the largest one in the world, and the Yacyretá dam, about one-fourth of the production potential of Itaipú, downstream on the same river and jointly owned with Argentina (see Figure 6A.1). The dams were proposed during the ruthless dictatorship of Alfredo Stroessner and the projects were designed to strengthen the regime, first by using these large scale public works to allocate procurement contracts to supporters or to buy allegiance from others, and second to showcase two very large centralized projects which would symbolically validate and reinforce the regime (Folch 2013).

---

[2]   See Auriol, Straub, and Flochel (2012), and Straub (2014) for a broader discussion of the political process and the specific topic of procurement in Paraguay.

The Itaipú project can be traced back to a preliminary agreement signed in 1966 between Brazil and Paraguay although the formal treaty was signed on 26 April 1973. In May 1974 the Itaipú Binacional entity was created to administer the plant's construction and later its operations. Construction started in 1975, and generation began in 1984. The dam, in its final configuration reached in 2007, has 20 turbines and as of 2013 its annual energy generation was 98.6 TWh, which makes it the largest one in the world ahead of the Chinese Three Gorges Dam.

The Yacyretá project has its origin in a 1925 protocol, but the formal treaty was only signed in 1973. Construction started in 1983; the first turbine began operation in 1994, and the full set of 20 turbines came into operation in 1998. At its full capacity, the hydroelectric dam generates approximately 20 TWh annually.

3.1 Building and Operating the Dams: Channels of Wrongdoing

In the case of the dams, the channels for wrongdoing were multiple, covering almost all known forms. In the construction phase, they included everything from outright favoritism through the direct allocation of contracts, to overpricing, direct siphoning of resources without counterpart, and under compliance with contracts requirements such as ignoring mandated environmental studies of the project's impacts.

Although no detailed contract-level information on procurement in either Itaipú or Yacyretá has ever been made public, the systematic practice of favoring a few entrepreneurs and friends with construction, maintenance and related contracts is known to be one of the main channels through which friends of the regime became very rich. A description of this system can be found in Nickson and Lambert (2002), and Auriol, Straub, and Flochel (2011). This last paper documents systematic wrongdoings using public procurement data for the period 2004–2007. Similarly, Straub (2014) uses data covering all the procurement transactions for the period 2004–2011 and shows that political connections to the Colorado party were a major driver of success in obtaining procurement contracts, and that firms linked to high-level regime members lost out on a significant number of contracts after 2008.

Miranda (2000) documents the resulting enrichment of selected families, and reports that most of the biggest Paraguayan fortunes are in some way linked to the dams' history. First and foremost is, of course, the dictator's family. Alfredo Stroessner himself is reported to have accumulated US$ 1.6 billion in funds related to Itaipú, and a recent article in *El País Internacional* claims that the family appears to have hidden the equivalent of US\$ 5 billion in firm holdings and offshore bank accounts.[3] As of 2010, this represented more than twice the stock of external public debt, 27 percent of GDP, and close to 14 times the annual amount received from Brazil in royalties from Itaipú.

Other examples include two subsequent presidents of the country: Juan-Carlos Wasmosy (1993–1998) and Raúl Cubas Grau (1998–1999). Wasmosy is known for being one of the main Itaipú and Yacyretá contractors, through the firms Grupo Consultor Alto Paraná, CONEMPA, and CIE. Between 1975 and 1995, these firms were awarded construction, equipment, and service contracts worth US\$ 3.7 billion. As of 2000, the Wasmosy group was the biggest one in Paraguay with US\$ 1.4 billion in assets. Cubas Grau, also an engineer by training, was the head of several construction firms (Concretmix, 14 de Julio SA, Copac Vial SA) involved in the dams' civil works. He subsequently occupied several ministerial positions before briefly becoming head of state. As of 2000, his personal wealth was estimated to be US\$ 550 million, the most visible asset being the castle-like mansion in the San Lorenzo municipality, worth an estimated US\$ 12 million.

Interestingly, the Paraguayan case calls into question the Murphy, Shleifer and Vishny (1991) empirical argument that the higher the relative share of lawyers versus engineers in a country the more intense the rent-seeking culture. In fact, over the years engineers have benefited from numerous, often inflated public contracts; they have often been the main winners in the local rent-seeking game.

Of course, this state of affairs has had as corollary a string of problems with the cost, quality and timing of the works themselves. Initially projected at US\$ 3.4 billion, the final construction cost of Itaipú is estimated to be US\$19.6 billion, equivalent to 4.3 times the value of 1989 Paraguayan GDP. Despite this huge cost overrun, the construction work displays a rather dismal record on works security, with an official workers' death toll over the construction process of 149.

As for Yacyretá, Carlos Menem, who was Argentine President from 1989–1999, famously (and perhaps knowingly) said that it was a 'monument to corruption'. A World Bank report later estimated cost overruns of around US\$ 8 billion. The final construction cost was estimated to reach 15 billion, equivalent to 3.3 times the value of 1989 GDP.

The building of the dam itself took approximately ten years. However, the project managers failed to meet the environmental and resettlement

---

[3]   http://internacional.elpais.com/internacional/2012/02/21/actualidad/ 1329855402_524683.html (last accessed 7 May 2015).

requirements imposed by the international funders, the World Bank and the Inter-American Development Bank (IDB). As a result, the reservoir was only filled up to 76 meters, and energy generation was only 60 percent of the dam's potential. This situation lasted for almost 20 more years, during which there was relatively little evolution. The top height, initially planned to be 83 meters above sea level, was only reached in 2011, 28 years after the start of construction. The enduring mismatch between costs that were much higher than initially envisioned and benefits that were reduced by the dam's inability to operate at full capacity, has, of course, a first order bearing on the direct cost of the project's mismanagement.

The environmental record, a particularly sensitive aspect in the case of dams, is not much better. In 2004, two independent panels, the Yacyretá Inspection Panel (World Bank), and the Panel of The Independent Investigation Mechanism on Yacyretá Hydroelectric Project 760/OC-RG (IDB) were established following the complaints of the *Paraguayan Federación de Afectados por Yacyretá de Itapúa y Misiones* (FEDAYIM). These reports stressed that most of the claims for irregularities were justified and that the environmental and social assessments were in several respects inadequate.

The 2004 'Final Report of the Panel of the Independent Investigation Mechanism on Yacyretá Hydroelectric Project 760/OC-RG', is particularly revealing. This panel 'was formally established in November, 2003 and was given the task of analyzing the extent to which four sets of claims, totaling 12 individual claims, were valid and if IDB operational policies, particularly those on involuntary settlements and the environment, were violated'. It concluded that all 12 claims submitted, which included flooding, health, contamination and vector control issues, were valid. It also concluded that both the IDB's Involuntary Settlement and environmental policies had been violated in the process of reaching the 76 meters level. Similarly, a World Bank's Inspection Panel concluded that the project violated four separate World Bank policies on 14 different counts.[4]

The second aspect of wrongdoings that is often prevalent in large scale infrastructure projects, especially those that imply a long-lasting operational phase, is the routine mismanagement and the abuse of the institution's resources for objectives that differ from its main purpose. Again, Paraguayans hydroelectric binational companies are first-rate examples of this.

---

[4]   See http://www.internationalrivers.org/resources/world-bank-investigation-confirms-serious-problems-at-yacyret%C3%A1-dam-3892 (last accessed 7 May 2015).

Their procurement practices have always been particularly opaque, but scandals and leaks have occasionally permitted a glimpse of the excesses going on behind the curtains. One such episode occurred in 2008 after the Colorado party lost power to former catholic bishop Fernando Lugo. Itaipú's Tesai Foundation, created in 1997 to provide health services to Itaipú's workers and their families, was revealed to have been systematically used to siphon resources out of the binational company to finance undertakings such as political campaigns. Although several numbers have circulated, a 2008 audit mentioned that US$ 23 million never appeared on Tesai's books, out of a total of 70 million that Itaipú injected into the foundation. Tesai apparently had been actively looted during the 2008 presidential campaign, when elected Colorado officials dipped into Tesai for 'medical expenditures' on average once every four days. In the first semester of that year alone, a US$2.4 million lump sum transfer from Itaipú was left unaccounted for.[5]

As he took charge of Itaipú after Lugo's election in 2008, the new executive director Carlos Mateo Balmelli famously commissioned a seal which said '*Pague de su bolsillo*' (pay out of your own pocket), in order to respond to the daily avalanche of financing requests that were arriving on his desk for anything from national and international travel and hotels, donations of freezers and outboard engines, cash, patrols, paving neighborhoods, building plazas, sports and religious travel, travel for beauty queens, to scholarships to study in Europe (see Figure 6A.2). In that same period, employees of the hydroelectric firm intentionally set fire to a number of archives and documents, falsely arguing that they were responding to an executive order. Destroyed in the fire were papers referring to political financing requests and pictures of the Colorado party's candidate campaign (see Figure 6A.3).[6] Initial charges against the perpetrators were dropped two years later.

Both companies have for years been used by politicians as a reservoir of employment for friends, political supporters, as well as activists during political campaigns. In November 2013, Itaipú had 1,861 employees on the Paraguayan side, to be compared to 1,441 on the Brazilian side. The exact list of employees as well as the salary structure was for a long time a well-protected secret. In early 2013, the Paraguayan Supreme Court issued a resolution making it mandatory for public institutions to make public

---

[5]   See for example Diario ABC Color, 12 May 2008, and 19 October 2008.

[6]   See Diario Ultima Hora, 17 November 2008, and 22 December 2010: http://www.ultimahora.com/itaipu-empleados-sorprendidos-quema-varios-archivos-n171996.html and http://www.ultimahora.com/sobreseen-funcionarios-quema-archivos-n388921.html (both accessed 7 May 2015).

details concerning their employees and their remuneration, giving rise to a wave of scandals when double remunerations and widespread abuse by high level politicians involving their close family, among others, came to light.

However, Itaipú and Yacyretá resisted this obligation, arguing that their binational nature did not allow them to comply. Finally in August 2014, following pressure from the newly elected president Horacio Cartes, these lists were published. The structure of salaries and added benefits came as a shock to the public, as it was revealed for example that unskilled employees acting as drivers, receptionist or cleaning staff were making between US$ 2,000 and 8,000 a month, from 5 to 20 times the Paraguayan minimum salary, while counselors, political appointees that form the administration council and usually gather every two months, were receiving monthly compensation of US$ 18,000 in Yacyretá and US$ 25,000 in Itaipú.[7]

These points clearly illustrate the type of excess (static) cost potentially involved in the corrupt procurement process of large scale infrastructure. Next we briefly outline the causes or facilitating circumstances of such excesses, before analyzing their consequences.

3.2 The Causes: Paraguay Institutional Framework[8]

The set of excesses described above was clearly made easier by the fact that both projects were initially built under dictatorial regimes, on all sides of the river borders.[9] The military regimes that prevailed at the turn of the 1970s in Argentina, Brazil, and Paraguay obviously did not allow for independent judiciary powers, not to speak of public audit or comptroller units.

To different extents across the three countries, the shortcomings inherited from this period had implications for the set of institutions that prevailed after they returned to democracy. In the case of Paraguay, the fact that Stroessner's Colorado party remained in power after the 1989 coup

---

[7] See for example Diario Ultima Hora, 2, 3 and 6 August 2014. Links to the lists of employees, wages, and travel benefits can be found at http://www.itaipu.gov.py/es/recursos-humanos/datos-de-empleados-y-estructura-salarial and http://www.ultimahora.com/eby-publica-nomina-funcionarios-sus-respectivos-salarios-n816822.html (both accessed 7 May 2015).

[8] See Straub (2014) and references herein for a description of the political and institutional environment in Paraguay since the rise to power of Stroessner in 1954.

[9] Dictatorships spanned the 1954–1989 period in Paraguay, 1964–1985 in Brazil, and 1976–1983 in Argentina.

until 2008 implied that the issues of public sector inefficiency, corruption, and lack of transparency in the operation of public companies such as the hydroelectric dams if anything became worse (Pérez-Liñán et al. 2006; Richards 2008).[10]

This was partly because the once monolithic system developed by Stroessner broke down into many feuding factions, with each local power or official trying to maximize the bribes extracted over their often short public tenures. This is in essence the prediction of the Shleifer and Vishny (1993) model, in which uncoordinated bribe extraction by several layers of corrupt bureaucrats generates a bigger deadweight loss than coordinated corruption by agents acting as a monopolist.

In the case of the dams, the fact that their legal status was binational made things even more complicated, as the Paraguayan government always used this pretext to refuse to allow independent auditing of the internal practices or to answer any request for information, as in the November 2013 supreme court ruling mentioned above, in which the dams companies were the only ones not to comply. In that sense, Paraguay clearly exhibits most of the institutional weaknesses listed above, with an especially weak judicial system that has always been captured by leading politicians.

3.3 Consequences

Beyond their huge static cost, the distortions described above also had profound consequences for the long-term development prospect of the Paraguayan economy. Today Paraguay is one of the countries in the world with the highest per capita generation of electricity, yet the resources it gets from this are small, and this electricity bonanza reaches few of the country's people and firms.

In terms of resources, Paraguay's hydroelectricity production makes it a resource-rich country, very much like some oil or gas producing countries. The electricity from Yacyretá and other smaller dams makes Paraguay one of the world's highest hydroelectric power producers in per capita terms, and the third exporter overall (Nickson, 2010). The Itaipú hydro-electric dam's 20 turbines produce close to 100 TWh yearly. Although Paraguay owns ten of these turbines, the production of only one and a half of them exceeds all the energy needs of the country. As a result, it transfers the energy it does not use to Brazil, under the 50-year Itaipú treaty signed in 1973.

---

[10]   The Colorado party retained power for 61 straight years, from 1947–2008.

The terms of this treaty have historically proven to be very unfavorable to Paraguay, and have been criticized by many internal and external observers as unfair.[11] First of all, the price fixed in the treaty is disconnected from the market price. For example, Nickson (2010) mentions a price equivalent to US$ 2.70 per MWh, while the corresponding wholesale prices at which Electrobras sells electricity varies between US$ 60 for Brazilian distribution companies and US$ 100 for Argentine electricity companies. VCC (2013) perform computations which lead to an estimate of lost earnings of almost US$ 750 million in 2012, despite the fact that in 2009, Fernando Lugo agreed with its Brazilian counterpart to a significant revision of the conditions of the treaty, which tripled the royalties.

Moreover, no sale to a third country is allowed until the end of the treaty in 2023. As a result, Paraguay gives most of its production away to its partner Brazil, in exchange for yearly royalties plus compensation payments. In the decade of the 2000s for example, this amounted to US$ 366 million in 2005 (US$ 553 million in 2006), equivalent to 4.9 percent (5.8 percent in 2006) of GDP, corresponding to close to half of the total government tax collection (Auriol et al. 2011). So although revenues from hydroelectricity may be unfairly low, they are also quite significant for a country in which tax collection has been hovering around 12 percent of GDP at best, compared with a Latin American average of more than 20 percent.

This free flow of resources could at first sight be considered as an opportunity for the country, but it has, in fact, arguably had the reverse effect, sustaining the rent-seeking system initiated under the Stroessner dictatorship. Indeed, most of this money is actually spent on salaries for low-productivity public sector workers (two-thirds of total government revenues) and public consumption purchases, and very little on investment goods such as infrastructure. No reserve fund has ever been created.

Moreover, bureaucrats and politicians in power have systematically allocated public contracts to friends and relatives. One of the main channels described in Auriol, et al. (2011) is precisely the allocation of public contracts to firms that in most cases are created for the purpose of supplying the state.[12] These are in the majority importers, but also construction and some service firms that often supply the government with a wide variety of goods and services. This is where the distortion

---

[11] See for example the recent Earth institute report on Paraguay on this topic (VCC, 2013).

[12] These are sometimes called 'empresas maletas' (private communication from a former Itaipú official).

of entrepreneurship towards rent-seeking mostly occurs. Additionally, the existence of this exogenous source of rent implied that governments did not have to worry about preserving a healthy productive sector from which they could raise taxes to finance their activities. This certainly had a reinforcing effect on the corrupt behavior of public institutions, since they were never at risk of seriously undermining their resource base.

Corrupt behavior in the allocation of public contracts is a key channel for rent-seeking. This large-scale network of favoritism, sometimes coined in Spanish '*la patria contratista*', in turn has deeply damaging economic consequences: public institutions buy goods and services at inflated prices, the incentives facing potential entrepreneurs are distorted towards unproductive activities, and this ultimately limits the dynamism of the economy, explaining, in part, why Paraguay has had, over the last quarter century, a constantly declining industrial sector with dismal exporting performance, a booming import sector and sluggish growth.

Specifically, Paraguay is in this respect a perfect example of 'misallocation of talents', à la Baumol (1990), and Murphy, Shleifer and Vishny (1991). As shown in Auriol et al. (2011), throughout the last decades prospective entrepreneurs mostly entered rent-seeking sectors where profits were higher, such as import activities, construction and consulting services oriented to doing business with the government. In contrast, export and innovation-oriented sectors, which were poorly rewarded, did not attract the country's talents, with long term growth consequences.

Straub (2014) reveals evidence of this process by looking at how until 2008 political connections mattered if one sought to obtain government procurement contracts. Among large providers, connections to the Colorado party were pivotal until 2008. Unfortunately, however, the Lugo government was significantly constrained after the 2008 democratization shock; the long-term monopolization of power by Colorados had left few alternative providers to respond to the push for transparency and increased efficiency in public purchases.

In the long run, the fact that Paraguayan authorities had access to an important exogenous source of revenue that allowed them to disregard the negative consequence of their policies for their productive sector is, therefore, probably one of the main causes of the country's underdevelopment. In this, its situation is similar to other Latin American countries that experienced large inflows of cash as a result of natural resource abundance in a context of pervasive corruption, such as oil-rich Venezuela, gas-rich Bolivia, and, analogously, Panama, whose economy is largely dependent on its canal.

Because of these structural distortions, the energy produced from the dams did not translate into an improvement of living and working conditions, mostly because these were significantly constrained by the lack of adequate transmission and distribution capacity. Deficient transmission lines, the bad quality of connections when available, and the lack of coverage in many areas, led to important welfare losses to households and to profound distortions in the productive structure.

In particular, there is a mismatch between Paraguay's energy production capacity and its productive development. In a sense, electricity has not reached the firms: data from the World Bank Enterprise Survey (WBES) from 2010 indicates that 21 percent of firms expect to have to give gifts to get an electrical connection, compared with 4 percent in Latin America on average. Outages are frequent and 38 percent of firms identify electricity as a major constraint to their business operation.

This situation likely added to the adverse entrepreneurial incentives prevailing in the country. Indeed, Alby, Dethier and Straub (2013) show, using firm-level data from 87 countries, that electricity-intensive sectors in countries with frequent power outages are characterized by a significantly lower share of small firms. Existing enterprises often opt for self-generation and therefore operate inside the technological frontier.

As argued in Auriol et al. (2011), these distortions have produced an entrepreneurial class that is predominantly oriented toward imports (in the 2000s, over 90 percent of the top 500 taxpayers were importers) and the public sector, and a systematically negative commercial balance (average deficit of 8.5 percent of GDP between 1996 and 2005). As a result, the burst of growth which followed the dams' construction in the 1970s and early 1980s did not endure into the 1990s and 2000s, and per capita GDP growth was negative over this period (−0.1 percent in the 1990s and −0.6 percent in the 2000s), leading to a lower level of real per capita income lower in 2005 than at the end of the 1970s (see Figure 6A.4).

4. CONCLUSION

In many developing countries, corruption is the product of a systematic organization of political and economic relationships rather than a simple collection of acts. Moreover, it is often locked-in by important past public choices, such as large infrastructure investments. As such, it may be resistant to anti-corruption measures aimed at specific wrongdoing, and it may also have long-term adverse effects, even after major political transitions.

This chapter has illustrated this in the Paraguayan case by looking at the history of two major investments in large-scale hydroelectric dams, Itaipú and Yacyretá. Beyond the direct wrongdoings and abuse in the construction and then in the operation of these undertakings, it has tried to illustrate how these projects have shaped the rent-seeking nature of the economy over several decades and well into the twenty-first century.

Of particular concern are the dynamic distortions that perverse incentives have generated among the population and potential entrepreneurs. The free-flowing resources to the state budget from excess energy production meant that successive rulers did not need to foster the development of a healthy private productive sector. Added to the widespread diversion of resources, which left the physical infrastructure—in particular the transport and energy networks—underdeveloped, the result was productive stagnation and low growth.

In that sense, the seeds of current underdevelopment were already present in the planning of the large scale hydroelectric infrastructure projects in a country characterized by the absence of democratic oversight and weak institutions. Whether these procurement choices were willingly distorted towards projects that were more open to manipulation but were arguably not a priority for the country, or whether these were potentially good projects gone bad because of the context in which they were decided and the way they were implemented remains an open question.

REFERENCES

Alby, P., J.J. Dethier and S. Straub. 2013. 'Firms Operating under Electricity Constraints in Developing Countries', *The World Bank Economic Review* 27(1): 109–32.

Asker, J. 2010. 'A Study of the Internal Organization of a Bidding Cartel', *American Economic Review* 100(3): 724–62.

Auriol, E., S. Straub and T. Flochel. 2011. 'Public Procurement and Rent-Seeking: The Case of Paraguay', TSE Working Paper, n°11-224, Toulouse.

Bandiera O., A. Prat and T. Valletti. 2008. 'Active and Passive Waste in Government Spending: Evidence from a Policy Experiment', *American Economic Review* 99: 1278–308.

Baumol, W.J. 1990. 'Entrepreneurship: Productive, Unproductive, and Destructive', *Journal of Political Economy* 98(5): 893–921.

Bhagwati, J. 1982. 'Directly Unproductive, Profit seeking (DUP) Activities', *Journal of Political Economy* 90: 998–1002.

Buchanan, J. M. 1980. 'Rent-seeking and profit-seeking', in J.M. Buchanan, R.D. Tollison and G. Tullock (eds), *Towards a Theory of the Rent-Seeking Society*, 3–15. College Station: Texas A&M University Press.

Decarolis, F. and T. Conley. 2013. 'Detecting Bidders Groups in Collusive Auctions', mimeo.

Di Tella, R. and E. Schargrodsky. 2003. 'The Role of Wages and Auditing during a Crackdown on Corruption in the City of Buenos Aires', *Journal of Law and Economics* 46(1): 269–92.

Folch, C. 2013. 'Surveillance and State Violence in Stroessner's Paraguay: Itaipu Hydroelectric Dam, Archive of Terror', *American Anthropologist* 115(1): 44–57.

Kawai, K. and J. Nakabayashi. 2014. 'Detecting Large-Scale Collusion in Procurement Auctions', mimeo.

Krueger, Anne. 1974. 'The political economy of the rent seeking society', *American Economic Review* 64: 291–303.

Leal Filho, W., J.R. Murrieta and A. Heyman. 2004. 'FINAL REPORT of the Panel of the Independent Investigation Mechanism on Yacyretá Hydroelectric Project 760/OC-RG', 27 February.

Mauro, P. 1998. 'Corruption and the Composition of Government Expenditure', *Journal of Public Economics* 69: 263–79.

Miranda, A., 2000. *Dossier Paraguay – Los Duenos de Grandes Fortunas*. AR Impresiones, Asuncion, Paraguay.

Mironov, M. and E. Zhuravskaya. 2012. 'Corruption in Procurement and Shadow Campaign Financing: Evidence from Russia', mimeo.

Murphy, K., A. Shleifer and R. Vishny. 1991. The Allocation of Talent: The Implications for Growth, *Quarterly Journal of Economics* 106: 503–30.

Nickson, R.A. 2010. 'Revising the past: The Paraguayan energy sector in perspective' in Tanya Harmer and Guy Burton (eds), *Powering Up: Latin America's Energy* Challenges, 29–37. London: LSE Ideas Latin America International Affairs Programme, London School of Economics, 2010.

Nickson, A. and P. Lambert. 2002. 'State Reform and the Privatized State in Paraguay', *Public Administration and Development* 22(2): 163–74.

Olken, B. 2007. 'Monitoring Corruption: Evidence from a Field Experiment in Indonesia', *Journal of Political Economy* 115(2): 200–249.

Pérez-Liñán, A., J. Molinas, M. Montero and S. Saiegh. 2006. 'Political Institutions, Policymaking Processes and Policy Outcomes in Paraguay, 1954–2003', Inter-American Development Bank, Research Network Working Papers R-502.

Porter, R. and D. Zona. 1993. 'Detection of Bid Rigging in Procurement Auctions', *Journal of Political Economy*, 101(3): 518–38.

Porter, R. and D. Zona. 1999. 'Ohio School Milk Markets: An Analysis of Bidding', *RAND Journal of Economics*, 30(2): 263–88.

Richards, D. G., 2008. 'Transition and Reform in a Predatory State: the Case of Paraguay', *Journal of Economic Policy Reform* 11(2): 31, 101–14.

Rose-Ackerman, S. 2006. *International Handbook on the Economics of Corruption*. Cheltenham, UK and Northampton, MA, USA: Edward Elgar.

Rose-Ackerman, S. and T Søreide. 2012. *International Handbook on the Economics of Corruption*, vol 2. Cheltenham, UK and Northampton, MA, USA: Edward Elgar.

Shleifer, A. and R.W. Vishny. 1993. 'Corruption', *Quarterly Journal of Economics* 108(3) 599–617.

Straub, S. 2014. 'Political Firms, Public Procurement, and the Democratization Process', TSE Working Paper, n°14-461.

Tullock, G. 1967. 'The Welfare Costs of Tariffs, Monopolies, and Theft', *Western Economic Journal*, 5: 224–32.

VCC (Vale Columbia Center for Sustainable International Investment). 2013. 'Leveraging Paraguay's Hydropower for Sustainable Economic Development', Final report.

APPENDIX

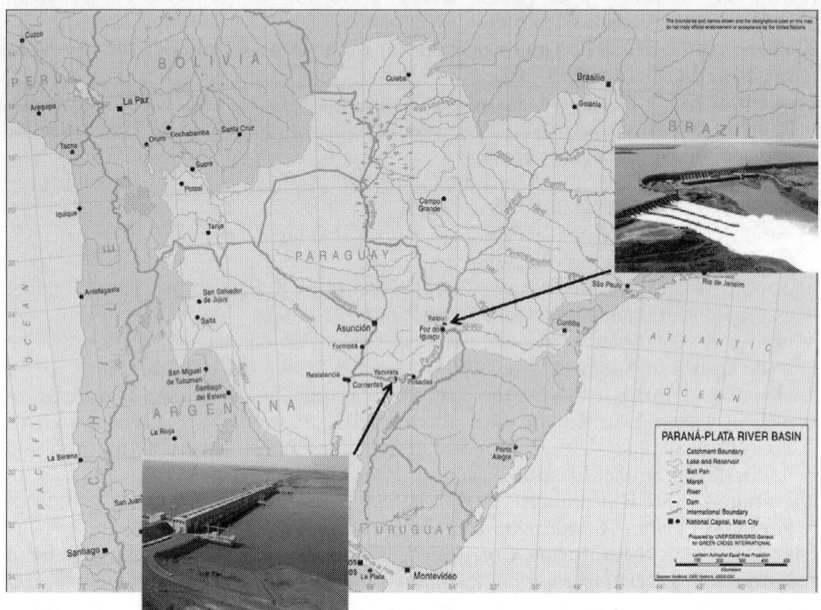

Figure 6A.1   Itaipú and Yacyretá location

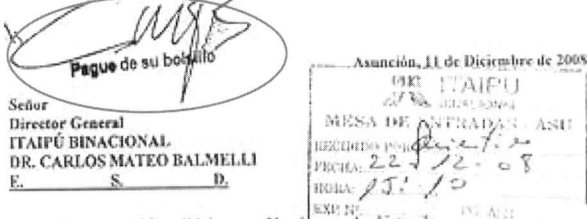

Señor
Director General
ITAIPÚ BINACIONAL
DR. CARLOS MATEO BALMELLI
E.   S.   D.

Asunción, 11 de Diciembre de 2008

Tenemos a bien dirigimos a Usted con el objeto de conocimiento que el 14° Festival Nacional y el 9° Festival Internacional la ciudad Itacurubi del Rosario, mediante la ardua gestión de su COMISIÓN CENTRAL ORGANIZADORA, DEPENDIENTE DE LA FUNDACIÓN POR EL ARTE, LA CULTURA Y EL DEPORTE, DECRETO 386 DEL AÑO 2008, está en plena etapa preparatoria, con vista a su próxima edición a cumplirse los días 24, 25, 26, 27, 28, 29, 30 y 31 de Enero del 2009, en nuestra comunidad Itacurubi del Rosario, Departamento de San Pedro, declarado de interés Cultural y Turístico hace 13 años.

Queremos destacar que, además de rescatar, defender y difundir las genuinas manifestaciones Folklórica de nuestra Patria, el Festival Ykuá Salas, anualmente, dedica su mejor objetivo a la solidaria ayuda a Instituciones Educativas, de Salud y Socio-Deportivas de la zona.

Sin embargo, es imperativo reconocer que la organización y realización global del evento demanda inversiones cuyas cifras están ajenas al modesto alcance y capacidad de nuestra comunidad.

Solicitamos respetuosamente a esta Identidad para cubrir parte de los gastos, que demanda la Organización, que incluye entre otros, pasajes, estadías, comida, transporte y artistas (nacionales y extranjeros), elaboración de afiches, tripticos, publicidad, equipos de sonidos e iluminación, maestros de ceremonia entre otros, la suma de Gs. 30.000.000 (treinta millones de guaraníes). Ajuntamos presupuesto General del Festival.

Atendiendo a los nobles objetivos culturales y sociales de nuestro Festival, respetuosamente nos permitimos solicitar a la ITAIPÚ BINACIONAL, su apoyo económico, a fin de facilitar el cumplimiento del Cronograma de Actividades previsto por la comisión.

Sabemos que la ITAIPÚ BINACIONAL está cumpliendo una labor ejemplar, después de tanto tiempo en nuestro país, para devolver al pueblo las expresiones más puras de su paraguayidad, y permitirle un permanente encuentro con sus raíces y la esencia misma de su ser y sentir nacionales.

Señor Director, nuestro festival es una fiesta popular, cumple una misión cultural, es un atractivo turístico en el Segundo Departamento San Pedro y se convierte en puente coadyuvante para asistir a los necesitados que preserva orgullosamente las tradiciones más vivas de la Patria.

Por todo lo expuesto, rogamos a la ITAIPÚ BINACIONAL a su dignísimo cargo, tenga a bien conceder este pedido, de todo el pueblo de Itacurubi del Rosario, que año tras año, redobla esfuerzos a pesar de las precariedades, para mantener encendida la llama emotiva de las más sentidas tradiciones Paraguayas.

Con el eslogan TRABAJO Y CULTURA, busquemos la reactivación económica para Itacurubi del Rosario, con el apoyo de Usted Señor Director.

Atentamente

Sra. Ignacia Martens
Coordinadora General

Estela Mareco
Presidenta

Dra. Estela Mary Mareco
Directora y Organizadora General

Wilma de Escalante
Tesorera

Dr. Carlos Mateo Balmelli
Director General Paraguayo

Figure 6A.2   Itaipú's director seal 'pague de su bolsillo'

Greed, corruption, and the modern state

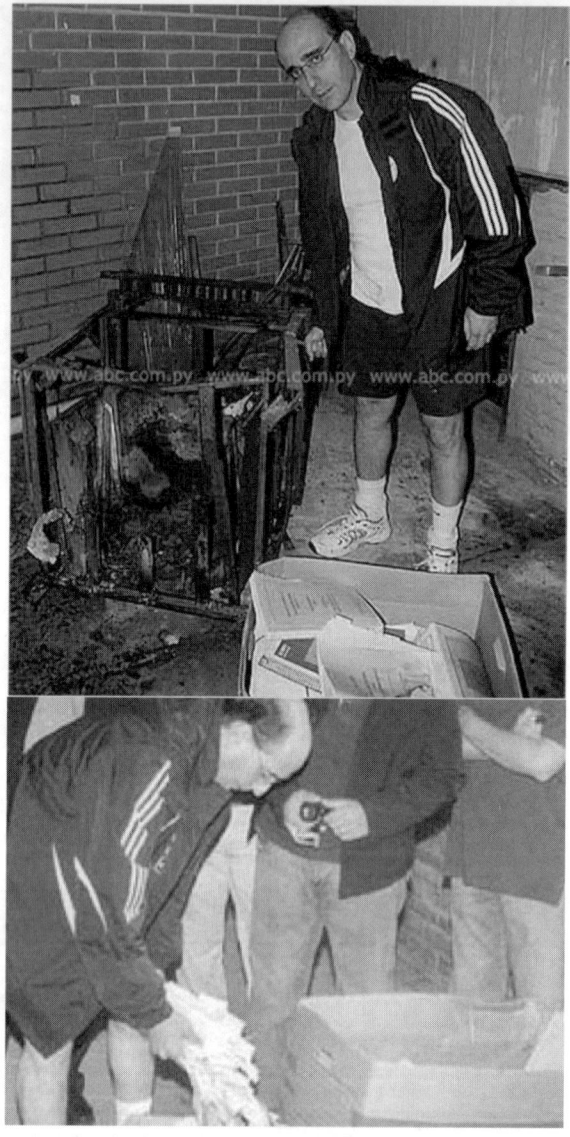

Source: Diario Ultima Hora, 17 November 2008 (http://www.ultimahora.com/itaipu-
empleados-sorprendidos-quema-varios-archivos-n171996.html), Diario ABC Color,
18 November 2008 (http://www.abc.com.py/edicion-impresa/politica/fiscala-imputa-a-tres-
funcionarios-por-la-quema-de-papeles-de-itaipu-1121968.html) (both accessed 7 May 2015).

Figure 6A.3   *Itaipú's director Carlos Mateo Balmelli inspects burned
documents (November 2008)*

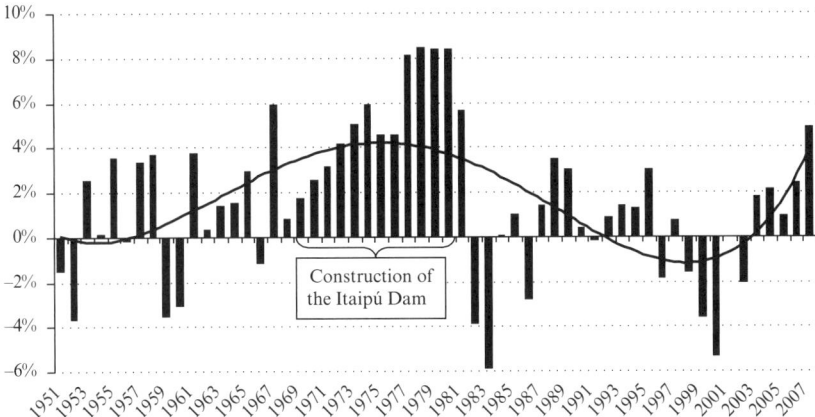

Figure 6A.4   Per capita GDP growth, 1950–2007

7. Saving Gotham: fighting corruption in New York City's property tax system*

Paul Lagunes and Rongyao Huang

The Department of Finance collects vital revenue for the City of New York. One of its major responsibilities is determining the value of more than one million properties spread across the city's five boroughs (NYC Finance 2014). To accomplish this task Finance's Real Property Assessment Unit relies on property tax assessors.

Property tax assessors are front-line bureaucrats responsible for determining the rate at which property owners should be taxed. They perform three important tasks: First, property tax assessors ensure that properties are assigned to the appropriate tax categories; second, they verify that the characteristics of both building and land are correct; and third, they value properties in accordance with the existing guidelines (NYC Finance 2014).

The role that property tax assessors play in New York City's public administration supports the thesis that bureaucrats often have considerable bearing on citizen's lives (Weber 1958; Wilson 1978; Lipsky 1980; Woll 2009). In carrying out their responsibilities, they have access to privileged information and wield broad discretionary powers, which place them at an advantage vis-à-vis the voting public (Dodd and Schott 1979; Ferejohn 1999; Rose-Ackerman 1999; Stiglitz 2002).

The information asymmetry that gives bureaucrats, in general, and property tax assessors, in particular, relative power over the citizenry can lead to abuse. It is an institutional flaw that a free and active press (Gentzkow, Glaeser and Goldin 2006: 188; Schiffrin 2014), independent

* We would like to thank Nicola Bonucci and Gautam Nair for their useful comments to an early draft of this chapter. Participants at the Conference on Grand and Petty Corruption in Developing States at Yale also made suggestions that guided our revisions. Finally, we are especially thankful that Milica Koscica, Lise Martina and Jennifer Rodgers were willing to provide detailed edits to an advanced draft of our work. Any remaining mistakes are our own.

accounting offices (Manin, Przeworski and Stokes 1999: 24), freedom of information procedures (Ackerman and Sandoval-Ballesteros 2006: 93; Banisar 2006), and anti-corruption agencies endeavor to correct (Winslow and Burke 1993; Manion 2004). Still, the information asymmetry is sufficiently entrenched that bureaucrats continue to find opportunities to abuse their power. To illustrate, we provide a case study that examines a scandal involving New York City property tax assessors.[1]

In February of 2002, shortly after Mayor Michael Bloomberg first took office, federal prosecutors arrested 18 current and former tax assessors. They were charged with participating in an over-three-decades-old corruption scheme that involved more than 500 properties and cost the city an estimated $40 million in revenue a year (Bagli and Rashbaum 2002b). The total loss amounted to approximately one billion dollars (Committee on Real Property Taxation 2002: 57–8).

Mayor Bloomberg captured the case's significance by referring to it as the 'largest and most damaging corruption scheme ever conducted within the city' (Seifman 2004). A spokesman for the New York City Department of Investigation (DOI) went so far as to state that it knew of no larger municipal fraud case in US history (Mcgurk 2002). If these assertions are correct, then this property tax assessment scheme had a greater negative impact on the city than the 1970s affair involving corruption in the police and buildings departments (for further details refer to: Knapp Commission 1973; Maas 1973; Gardiner and Lyman 1978); the 1986 Democratic party machine fiasco (Newfield and Barrett 1988); and the 1994 'Dirty Thirty' case of drug dealing cops (Treaster 1994; Anechiarico and Jacobs 1996: 164–70).

In any case, this study is the first scholarly effort to examine corruption in New York City's property tax system. We interviewed Charles V. Bagli, a veteran *New York Times* reporter who has covered the intersection of politics and real estate since 1987.[2] We also spoke with

---

[1]   There are those who view case studies as beset by a degree-of-freedom problem and as vulnerable to selection bias (King, Keohane and Verba 1994: 119–20, 128; McKeown 1999; Geddes 2006: 89). Although we acknowledge the method's limitations, we also view case studies as a useful tool for identifying testable hypotheses and exploring the intricacies of extreme cases (Van Evera 1997: 55; Sambanis 2004: 260; George and Bennett 2005: 19). In this chapter, we use the case study approach to achieve the latter objective, but also to motivate future empirical work.

[2]   Charles V. Bagli is the author of, *Other People's Money*, a book that details the dynamics that led to the recent US real estate meltdown. Bagli first caught wind of the problem in the City's Property Assessment Office thanks to an anonymous call. He wrote over 12 news articles on the topic.

Sharon L. McCarthy, one of the three prosecutors in the criminal case resulting from the tax assessor scandal.[3] In addition to the in-person interviews, we corresponded with Rose Gill Hearn.[4] Between 2002 and 2013, Gill Hearn served as DOI Commissioner. Prior to her appointment at DOI, Gill Hearn was a federal prosecutor for ten years in the US Attorney's Office for the Southern District of New York. Finally, to complement the perspectives gathered through direct communications, we studied government reports, news articles, legal documents in the public domain, and transcripts from the hearings held by the New York State Assembly Standing Committee on Real Property Taxation.

Part I reviews key conceptual issues in the study of corruption. In this section we address questions such as: What are the institutional structures that sustain bureaucratic corruption? How are corruption and inefficiency related, and why do anti-corruption agencies tend to target both phenomena? What distinguishes New York City's Department of Investigation from other such agencies, and what do we know about this particular agency's history, statutory powers, legal obligations, institutional capacity and track record? Part II introduces the reader to the structure of urban property taxation. Part III is the heart of the chapter. There we provide a close examination of the 2002 corruption scandal. Finally, we conclude with a summary and a brief description of a collaborative research project with DOI. This partnership is ongoing and should serve to evaluate distinct anti-corruption mechanisms through a randomized control trial.

I. A CONCEPTUAL APPROACH TO URBAN CORRUPTION

There is much that the voting public, and even elected and appointed officials, do not know about the workings of government and the bureaucracy. To some extent, their ignorance is justified. Elected and appointed officials often hold vast responsibilities and are, thus, personally incapable of overseeing the work of every agent under their charge. Similarly, the electorate dedicates a majority of its time to private, non-governmental

---

³   Sharon L. McCarthy is a partner at the law firm Kostelanetz & Fink, LLP. She represents individuals and corporations in civil and white-collar criminal litigation and tax controversies and trials. Before rejoining the private sector in 2006, she served for 12 years in the US Attorney's Office for the Southern District of New York.

⁴   Rose Gill Hearn is a Principal at Bloomberg Associates, which is a pro-bono consulting group that advises city governments in the United States and around the world on governance, economic and other issues.

affairs. When citizens do engage their government as individuals petitioning for assistance, they are often confused and repelled by legal and procedural complexities. This is not to say that every citizen petition is just; however, democracy is founded on the idea that government serves society. The members of the voting public are government officials' *de jure* principals, and government officials are reminded of the voting public's supremacy on Election Day. In other words, an electoral connection exists between the citizenry and the officials who populate government, but the connecting thread becomes thinner the deeper it pierces into the layers of public administration. An example from local government illustrates this point.

Citizens elect a mayor. The mayor is the city government's highest-ranking executive and by extension most bureaucrats' *de facto* principal. If the mayor is interested in running for re-election or higher office, she faces institutional incentives to serve the public. These same career incentives might reasonably motivate the mayor to appoint cabinet members who seem willing and capable of serving the citizenry, and yet these appointed high-level officials are two steps removed from the ballot box. Being invited to serve as the secretary of a local ministry or department hinges on the electorate's choice of mayor, and on the elected mayor's choice of close collaborators.

Following the mayor's example, the top leadership of city government fills select positions with agents of their choosing. These appointed officials, however, generally rely on the existing corps of lower-level officials to carry out the lion's share of operations. This dynamic presents an advantage: a level of continuity is ensured from one mayoral administration to the next. Everything does not stop when the outgoing mayor and her close collaborators pack their bags, and the incoming mayor and her staff find their way around city hall. From the standpoint of democratic accountability, however, this setup poses two significant challenges. First, the officials who join government in the wake of an election often depend on the experience and technical knowledge of bureaucrats. Second, these bureaucrats are at minimum three degrees removed from the power of the ballot box, and are, therefore, significantly less sensitive to the interests of the voting public.

Being removed from the electorate grants bureaucrats considerable discretion, and this discretionary power is subject to abuse. However, influence over a state activity, such as deciding whether a property owner receives an illegitimate tax cut, is a necessary but not sufficient condition for corruption. Other factors, including personal values, prevailing social norms, job satisfaction, probability of detection, and severity of the penalty, help determine whether an official becomes corrupt.

A bureaucrat who values personal integrity may avoid acting corruptly for fear of incurring a psychological penalty in the form of guilt. The likelihood that a bureaucrat will be corrupt also depends on the bureaucrat's expectations regarding the behavior of others. If corruption is prevalent, she can hide her malfeasance within the mix of other corrupt acts. Job satisfaction, driven in large part by remuneration, is another variable of potential interest. A competitive public sector wage may reduce the probability that a bureaucrat will participate in corruption by eliminating her incentive to supplement an inadequate salary with illegal rents. Additionally, given the employment alternatives in the labor market, a competitive public sector wage raises a bureaucrat's opportunity costs of losing her current job in government because of malfeasance. However, the idea of losing a public sector job or being penalized in some other way for corruption depends on the probability of detection, and corruption detection is anything but a simple endeavor.

Corruption is difficult to identify, in part, because it is often confused with inefficiency, a seemingly lesser ill. Crucially, corruption and inefficiency are related pathologies—an institution affected by corruption is often also inefficient, and vice versa. Corruption and inefficiency may enjoy a mutually reinforcing relationship. For instance, red tape in the form of excessive bureaucratic delays creates an incentive for corrupt payments. Similarly, we assume that corruption breeds an environment where bureaucrats are unmotivated to work energetically to advance the government's official, public-oriented goals. After all, corruption is by definition an act that places individual interests above those of the collective.

The key difference between the two is that corruption commonly promises material gain or the avoidance of material loss by at least one of the parties involved in a transaction. In contrast, inefficiency implies waste. Inefficiency occurs when resources—such as time, energy, or capital—are not expended in a manner that most directly furthers an agency's official goals.

Inefficiency may be caused by an agent's lack of competence, drive, or focus, or by an agency's poor organizational structure. Similar to corruption, inefficiency produces suboptimal outcomes from a public interest perspective. This is precisely why anti-corruption agencies, such as New York City's Department of Investigation, tend to target *both* phenomena (City of New York 2004). Indeed, DOI is meant to promote better management in NYC, whether or not linked to corrupt acts (Seidman 1941).

DOI was originally known as the Office of the Commissioners of Accounts, and is one of the oldest law enforcement agencies in the United States dedicated to fighting corruption (Department of Investigation

2014b). It was founded in 1873 to oppose Tammany Hall's influence (Winslow and Burke 1993: 1–4). In this sense, 'The creation of DOI was through a reactive process, as opposed to a proactive process' (Green 2013: 12). Be that as it may, by the mid-1950s, the agency had evolved into a strong, nonpartisan watchdog for the municipal government in New York City (Anechiarico and Jacobs 1996: 76–81; Department of Investigation 2014a).

DOI stands today as an independent department supported by an annual budget of approximately \$22 million and a staff of about 470 members (Green 2013: 14; Peters 2014a: 4). The agency employs attorneys, investigators, forensic auditors, computer forensic specialists and administrative personnel (Graycar and Villa 2011: 423; Peters 2014b: 2). DOI holds significant powers (including the power to subpoena and conduct arrests), and is responsible for investigating and referring for criminal prosecution cases of unethical behavior by local officials, contractors and others who receive benefits from or conduct business with the city (Department of Investigation 2014b).[5] Based on recent data, a vast majority of DOI's investigations appear to focus on New York City's Housing Authority (Dobkin 2014). However, DOI also conducts numerous investigations within the Department of Correction, the Department of Buildings, the Fire Department and the School Construction Authority, among other agencies (ibid.).[6] Importantly, a majority of these cases involve a threat to the city's capacity to meet requirements set by legislation (Graycar and Villa 2011).

On the question of efficacy, Anechiarico and Jacobs (1996) find important instances in DOI's history where it failed to prevent corruption. However, Anechiarico and Smith (2008) also note that, 'serious cases [of corruption] have been cut by almost two-thirds in recent years'.[7] Other metrics reveal that, since 2002, DOI investigations have led to more than 6,400 arrests and the recovery of more than \$500 million (Gill Hearn 2008;

---

[5] As described by local statutes, DOI is responsible for 'the investigation and elimination of corrupt or other criminal activity, conflict of interest, unethical conduct, misconduct and incompetence (i) by City agencies, (ii) by City officers and employees, and (iii) by persons regulated by, doing business with or receiving funds directly or indirectly from the City . . .' (see Mayoral Executive Order No. 16 for more information).

[6] The Department of Finance in particular is the 12th most investigated agency in New York City (Dobkin 2014).

[7] Based on a different sample (in other words, one that is not solely looking at 'significant cases'), a reporter applauds DOI's efforts during Mayor Bloomberg's administration because it made a record 6,773 municipal corruption arrests (Smith 2013).

Adams Otis 2013; Department of Investigation 2013).[8] These numbers are of course noteworthy in absolute terms, but their relative significance depends on the unknown quantity of actual corruption events and financial losses due to corruption. Therefore, given what information we have available, the most we are able to say is that DOI's success in recouping hundreds of millions of dollars signals a positive and dutiful effort to fend against the theft of public resources. This is an issue that is particularly relevant given the topic at hand.

As we discuss at length in Part III, the 2002 corruption scandal involving New York City property tax assessors hit soon after the September 11 terrorist attacks. This is a period during which the city faced a \$4 billion budget gap (Bagli 2002a). In court, Sharon McCarthy argued that the tax assessors involved in the corruption scheme abused their power and, 'in doing so deflated assessments, denying the city of certain tax revenue' (*USA v. Marino* 2000: 8).[9] The prevailing estimate is that the city lost a total of approximately one billion dollars over the course of more than three decades. This is precisely why Rose Gill Hearn (2014), the commissioner of the Department of Investigation during Bloomberg's administration, considers the property tax assessment scheme to be one of the two most costly corruption events in the city's recent history.[10] The other significant case involved fraud in a payroll modernization project that cost taxpayers more than \$600 million (Gross 2011; Weiser 2014).

---

[8] In addition to searching for statistics, we also reviewed multiple news articles to see how the media evaluated the level of government integrity during Bloomberg's administration. No single article or quote in *The New York Times*, *The Economist* or *The Wall Street Journal* offered a clear and direct assessment. Most articles focused on specific events related to the issue (scandals, increased oversight, etc.), but none evaluated the overall state of government integrity in New York City. However, taken together, the articles paint a picture that the Bloomberg administration struggled with several integrity issues, but that it also attempted to implement procedures to overcome them.

[9] Agreeing with McCarthy's assessment, the judge observed that, '[the scheme] went on for quite a number of years. My problem is', he continued, 'we are talking about \$4.1 million in bribes. We are not talking about a small amount. I don't accept the suggestion that there was no substantial loss. I mean, I cannot believe that someone would pay \$4.1 million unless he was getting something substantial in return' (*USA v. Marino* 2000a: 17).

[10] In the interviewee's own words: 'The only other case that comes to mind as comparable in relation to its direct monetary impact is the CityTime case, which we also investigated and brought to a successful conclusion with the U.S. Attorney's Office for the Southern District of New York' (Gill Hearn 2014).

II. MUNICIPAL PROPERTY TAX ASSESSMENT

Property taxation has been the major source of tax revenue for US munici-palities since the seventeenth century (Netzer 1966: 3). It is also an impor-tant source of local government revenue in Britain, Ireland, South Africa, Australia, and New Zealand (11). But our focus is on the United States, where state and local governments collected an estimated $488 billion in property taxes in 2013 (US Census Bureau 2013). This considerable amount represents more than a third of all state and local government revenue for that year (Entrikin 2014: 289).

In New York City, property taxes account for approximately $18.4 billion of its budget, or about 40 percent of all the city tax revenue collected in fiscal year 2013 (Office of Management and Budget 2014). It is the city's single largest and most stable source of funding. The property tax is, moreover, a source of revenue that has been growing since fiscal year 2002, a fact that we highlight in Figure 7.1, where the x-axis stands for fiscal year and the y-axis represents the adopted tax revenue budget in million US dollars. The light grey ribbon shows the property tax revenue from 2002 to 2014; the dark grey ribbon shows all other tax revenue. Together, they constitute the total tax revenue for New York City.

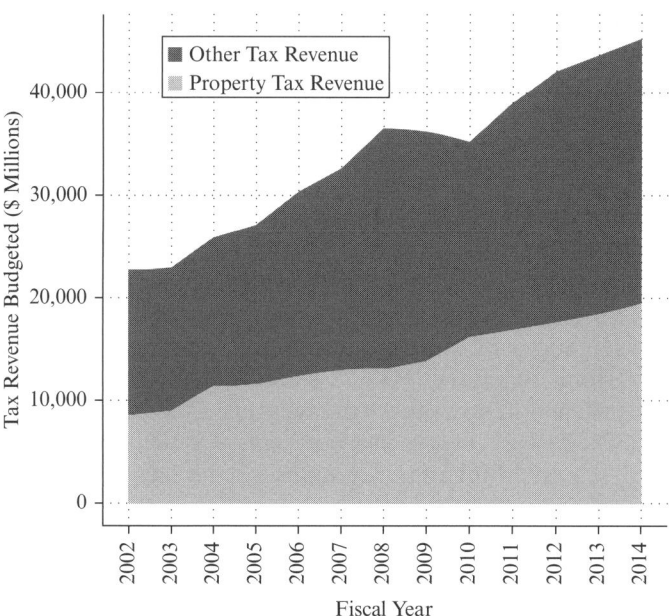

Figure 7.1   The importance of property tax revenue for New York City

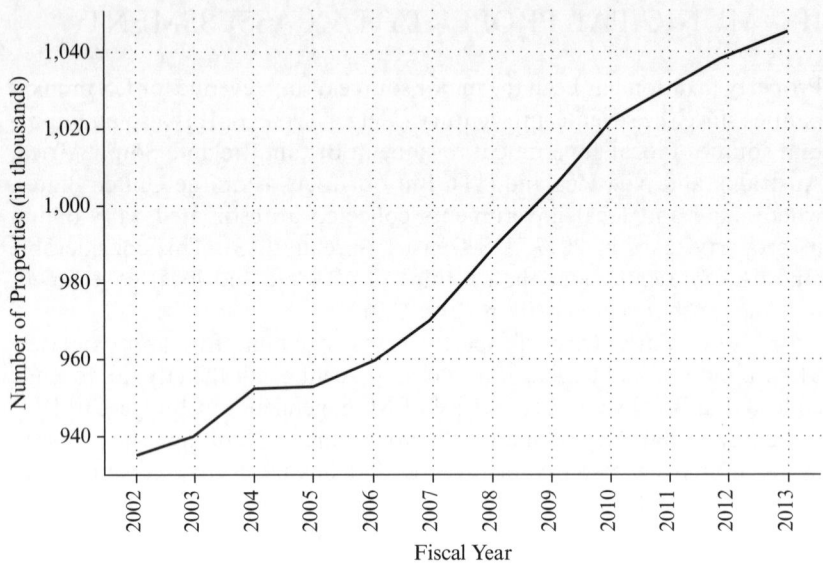

Note: The graph includes partially taxable and fully taxable properties. It excludes fully exempt properties.

Figure 7.2   Number of taxable properties in NYC

The Department of Finance (DOF) is responsible for collecting property taxes in New York City. As noted in the introduction, the task is one of monumental proportions. In fact, as Figure 7.2 reveals, the number of properties in New York City has been growing rapidly since fiscal year 2002, and now exceeds one million (NYC Finance 2013).

DOF has an office known as Real Property Assessments. This is the specific unit that assesses[11] the value of properties in the city, issues Notices of Assessment to taxpayers, and collects property taxes from taxpayers (NYC Finance 2014). The Real Property Assessments Unit employs approximately 119 assessors and has offices in each of New York City's five boroughs. Of the five boroughs, as Figure 7.3 shows, Manhattan accounts for the largest taxable value.

---

[11]   The term 'assessment' refers to the, 'whole statutory mode of imposing the [property tax]. It embraces all the proceedings for raising money by the exercise of the power of taxation from the inception to the conclusion of the proceedings' (*Jackson Lumber Co. v. McCrimmon* in Entrikin 2014: 5).

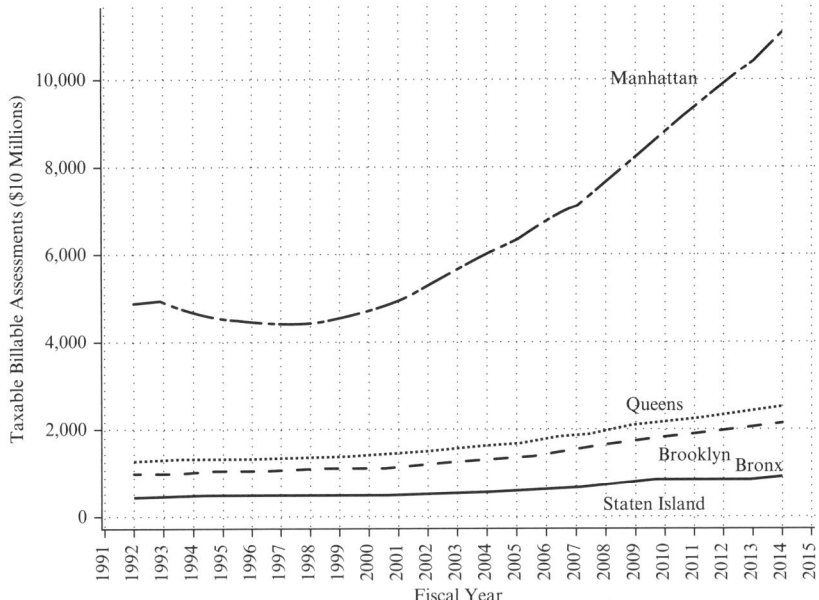

Figure 7.3   Property taxable billable assessments by borough

Moreover, the borough's taxable value has been growing rapidly since fiscal year 2002.

Another aspect of the New York City property tax system that merits attention is its subdivision by property types. Before 1981, New York City's properties were divided into ten non-housing tax classes (Netzer et al. 1980: I–20). It was a complex system with even greater room for bureaucratic discretion. In particular, the rates of tax for each class were determined by assessors in combination with the Tax Commission and the courts (I–2). Then, in 1981, the New York State legislature enacted S7000A. This statute created a system with four classes of property, each class being taxed on a different share of its market value. Following is a description of each tax class:

- Class 1 encompasses one- to three-unit residential properties.
- Class 2 refers to residential properties with more than 3 units, including cooperatives and condominiums.
- Class 3 is meant for utility company equipment and special franchise properties.
- Class 4 captures all other properties, including office buildings and hotels.

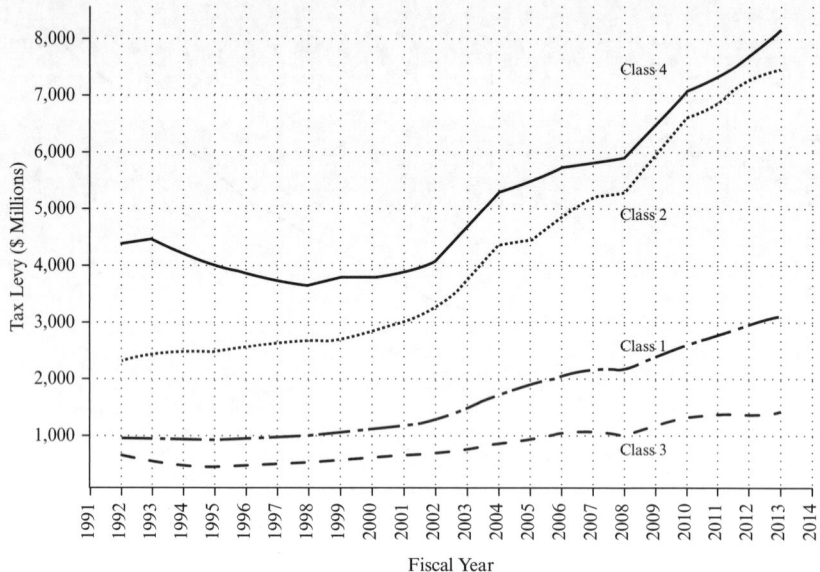

Figure 7.4   Tax levy by tax class

Figure 7.4 compares the tax levy for the four tax classes. The data reveal that, across all of New York City, tax class 4 has the largest share of tax collections among the tax classes.

All properties—regardless of the tax class or borough they belong to—are assessed on a yearly basis. The assessment process follows a set timeline. On 5 January, DOF determines the taxable status of each parcel of real property in New York City. Ten days later, on 15 January, DOF makes public the tentative assessed values for every parcel of real property. It does so by mailing a Notice of Assessment to every property owner, but also by publishing the Tentative Tax Roll. The Tentative Tax Roll is open for public inspection from 16 January to 16 March of each year. Property owners who disagree with DOF's assessment may file an appeal with the Tax Commission. After the Tentative Tax Roll is closed to public inspection and after DOF and the Tax Commission have made their corrections, the annual roll is made final on 25 May. Then, on 1 July, a new fiscal year begins.

Thus far we have described property taxation as it is supposed to work. However, Diane B. Paul, a scholar who has written about property taxation in the U.S. describes the activity as one of 'the most corrupt of urban functions' (Paul 1975: 7). The author of *The Politics of the Property Tax* further explains that:

[T]he actual work of valuing property is done by 'street level bureaucrats' over whom there is generally little effective supervision. The decisions made by urban assessors are sometimes of great importance to taxpayers, particularly owners of apartment buildings and commercial and industrial property, and it is precisely for these kinds of property that well-defined standards of assessment are lacking. Assessing, like police work, is both discretionary and subjective, combining constant temptation with minimal likelihood of exposure . . . (8).

This last problem—specifically, imperfect monitoring in taxation—is analyzed by Das-Gupta and Mookherjee (1998) and by Flatters and Macleod (1995). Moreover, it is a problem that local news coverage has recently exposed in Los Angeles (Dolan 2013), Cayahoga County (Caniglia 2013), and Cook County (Meisner 2013).

In summary, property tax assessment is a vital but imperfectly monitored government activity that relies on bureaucratic discretion. This is true even for agencies that have come to rely on new technology, such as computer modeling. Data analytics allows government auditors to identify individuals or firms who are paying less in taxes compared to others showing similar characteristics. During David Frankel's tenure as commissioner, DOF created the Data Intelligence Group in order to improve the efficiency of its auditing activities (Goldsmith 2014). In spite of these efforts, however, the property tax system continues to rely on assessors to conduct field inspections and interpret property tax laws. Herein lies the risk.

III. THE 2002 PROPERTY TAX SCANDAL

Large and small property owners may seek relief from property taxes by hiring consultants. Tax consultants are middlemen whose compensation often comes in the form of a fraction (typically, 30 to 50 percent) of the tax savings obtained for a property owner (Entrikin 2014: 300). Many property tax consultants follow ethical and professional standards, but there are also those who rely on questionable methods to influence tax officials. This explains why tax consultants are sometimes painted in a negative light as bureaucratic lobbyists. As stated by a New York City real estate executive, 'We pay lobbyists. That's the system we live in. Sometimes you get one that's crooked' (Rashbaum and Bagli 2002).

Enter Albert Schussler. After 30 years of working as a tax assessor for the City of New York, Schussler left government in 1967 to begin a career as a private sector consultant (Bagli and Rashbaum 2002b; Entrikin 2014: 318). Schussler aimed to capitalize on his knowledge about and contacts within the real estate industry. For the next 35 years, he charged property owners substantial fees[12] in exchange for contriving to reduce their property taxes.[13]

In 2002, authorities accused Schussler of masterminding a massive corruption scheme (US District Court 2002). According to the indictment, Schussler had paid a total of $10 million in bribes so that tax assessors would undervalue some 562 properties (ibid.).[14] The bribes ranged from expensive dinners to thousands of dollars in cash payments. In exchange, assessors—whose official salaries ranged from $46,000 to $68,000 a year[15]—agreed to show Schussler their valuations before assessments were made public (Newman 2002: 73). Schussler would then provide a counter-assessment. In some cases, assessments dropped. In other cases, they stayed the same as the previous year or did not increase as much as they should have under normal circumstances (ibid.).[16]

When the scandal hit, the President of the Real Estate Board of New York responded by focusing the blame on the indicted tax assessors, and by defending the reputation of the city's real estate industry (Committee on Real Property Taxation 2002: 106).[17] This is an industry with significant political influence in the city (Bagli 2014; Craig, Raushbaum and Kaplan 2014), and yet the interests of its members are not always aligned. As a case in point, the corruption scheme described here hurt many more landlords than it helped. This explains why nearly 1,000

---

[12]   According to one report, Albert Schussler charged his customers a flat retainer of $200,000 to $400,000 (Bagli and Rashbaum 2002b).

[13]   Schussler's influence grew to the point that he became an active figure in the Real Estate Board of New York. He also purchased and managed properties, including the iconic Ansonia Hotel (US District Court 2002 4; Bagli 2003a).

[14]   The exact number of undervalued properties is unclear. One report, for example, has the number at 545 (Bagli 2002b).

[15]   During the State Assembly hearings the union representative for tax assessors suggested that, 'Assessors should be better compensated and receive financial incentives for obtaining professional designations and higher education' (Committee on Real Property Taxation 2002: 73).

[16]   In alphabetical order and according to news reports, a few of the real estate firms whose property taxes were lowered as a result of Schussler's intervention were: Cohen Brothers Realty, Glenwood Management, Helmsley Spear, Jack Resnick and Sons, Lefferts-Fore and SL Green Realty (Danis 2002; Bagli 2002a; Bagli and Rashbaum 2002a; Bagli 2002c).

[17]   'As an industry', the President of the Real Estate Board asserted, 'we have a proud history of [. . .] contributing our time, energy, and money to causes, cultural, social, educational, enhancing the quality of life and the image of our City around the world, despite the baseless accusations of reckless editorials who have commented on this episode' (Committee on Real Property Taxation 2002: 106).

property owners sued the city on the basis that they had been forced to pay higher taxes to make up for the losses caused by tax assessor corruption (Bagli 2002e; Bagli 2003b).

In spite of the mounting pressure due to the lawsuits and media coverage, not a single property owner was criminally charged. Reflecting on this outcome, one of the prosecutors expressed the following statement:

> [Y]ou'd love to follow the rainbow to its very end, and get every single person along the way who has been committing crimes, but, unfortunately, it's not possible. You need evidence, and in a case like this the best way to get evidence is from people who dealt directly with the property owners. The person who dealt directly with the property owners is Albert Schussler, and he passed away, and, so [we lost the] ability to go after anyone else. And, you know, [. . .] there was no clear evidence that any of the property owners knew that Albert Schussler was paying bribes. So, none of the Tax Assessors, at least none of the witnesses that we worked with, had ever met directly with the property owners (McCarthy 2014).

In other words, by relying on a tax consultant property owners managed to advance their financial interests, while maintaining a safe distance from the actual assessment process.

Now, in order to better comprehend the tax scheme itself it is worth reviewing what we know about a tax assessor who served as Schussler's closest collaborator, Joseph Marino. A reporter describes Marino as a 'real tough guy . . . [often] smoking Camel cigarettes, and when he did come in the office he'd snap his fingers, and there was this other guy who didn't go out into the field anymore because he'd gotten beat up once, he'd bring him over his cup of espresso' (Bagli 2014). Standing before a judge, Marino admitted that he received as much as $4.1 million in bribes from Schussler between 1991 and 1997 (*USA v. Marino* 2000: 13). These bribe payments flowed as checks from Schussler's firm to that of one of Marino's relatives. The latter then declared the payments as taxable income (ibid.).

In terms of the number of officials implicated, around 40 percent of the city's 38 Manhattan assessors were directly involved in the corruption scheme (Bagli and Rashbaum 2002b). Two more officials, Roberta C. Hand and Aldo Macina, were arrested a year later (Friedman 2003; Saulny 2003).

There is much we can also learn from studying the information contained in the original indictment (see: U.S. District Court 2002). Our review of the bribes paid to tax assessors in Manhattan between 1997 and 2002 shows that corruption was a particular risk in the months of

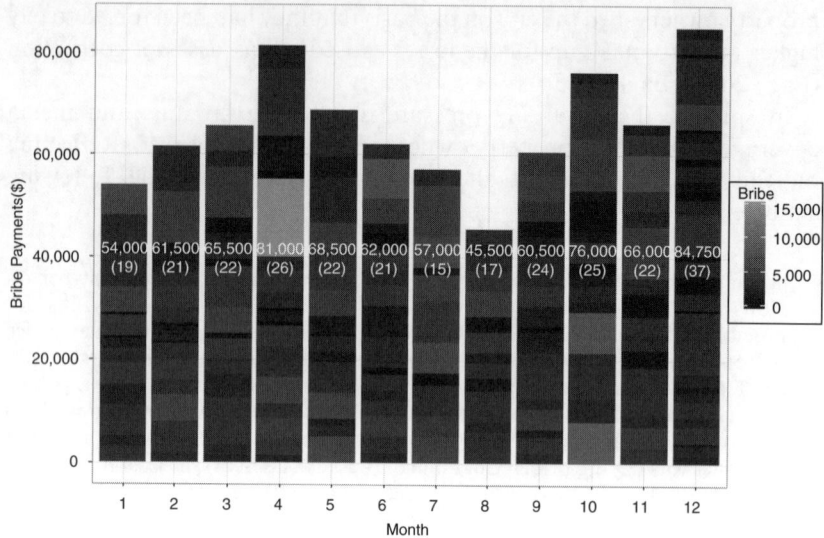

Note: The first number represents the total amount of bribes paid; the second number in parenthesis represents the number of bribe payments.

Figure 7.5   Bribe payments by month

December and April—that is, before the tentative and final tax rolls were published. Figure 7.5 illustrates our finding. The x-axis represents months in a year (1=January, 2=February, and so on) and the y-axis captures bribe data in US dollars. The height of a bar signals the total amount of bribes paid on a given month over the course of five years. Each colored block in a bar is a bribe payment. The block's tone and size signals the bribe's magnitude.

The corruption scheme's proportions are evident when examining the geographical area affected, the number of tax assessors involved, and the amount of bribes paid and tax revenue lost. Reports show that the scheme extended from Lower Manhattan through the Upper East Side to Harlem. It also covered the area between West 41st Street and West 96th Street, west of Eighth Avenue/Central Park West (Bagli 2002a; Bagli and Rashbaum 2002a). The following map pinpoints a partial sample (N=198) of these properties.

Finally, we turn to the question of bribes and revenue. Figure 7.7 summarizes key information about the known illicit payments made to 16 of the assessors implicated in the corruption scheme. The x-axis represents bribe amount in US dollars, and the y-axis lists the name of assessors. The

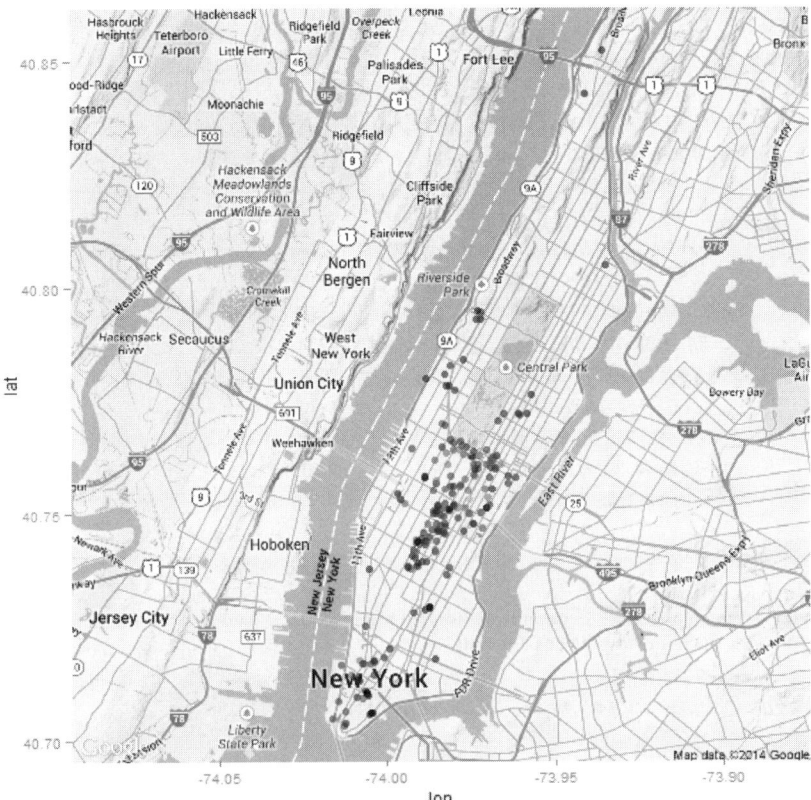

Note: * The map includes 198 properties with their values assessed Fiscal Year 2009.

Figure 7.6   Map: properties involved in the 2002 scandal

most corrupt assessor is shown at the top, and the least corrupt is shown at the bottom. The size of a bar signals the total amount of bribes received between 1997 and 2002. Each shaded block in a bar is one bribe payment. The block's tone and size signals the bribe's magnitude. The numbers shown with each bar are: (1) the average amount of bribes, and (2) the number of bribes recorded for each assessor. The top three assessors in terms of total amount of bribes received are Joseph Iovino, Vatchara Vachiraprapun, and Howard Habler. Figure 7.8 suggests a correlation between hierarchy and corrupt returns: the higher the position, the greater the bribes.

On the question of revenue, it is difficult to calculate exactly how much was lost because of corruption. That said, prosecutors estimated that the

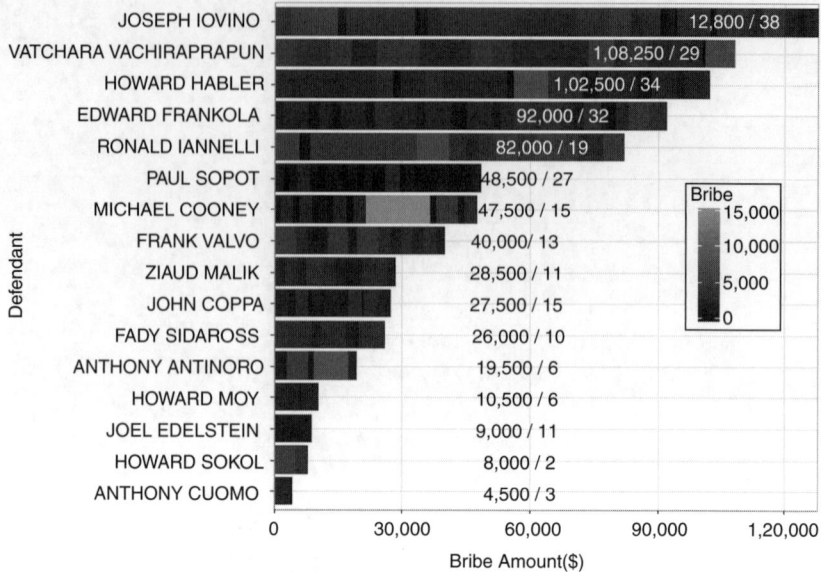

Note: The first number represents the total amount of bribes paid; the second number represents the number of bribe payments.

Figure 7.7 Bribe payments by defendant

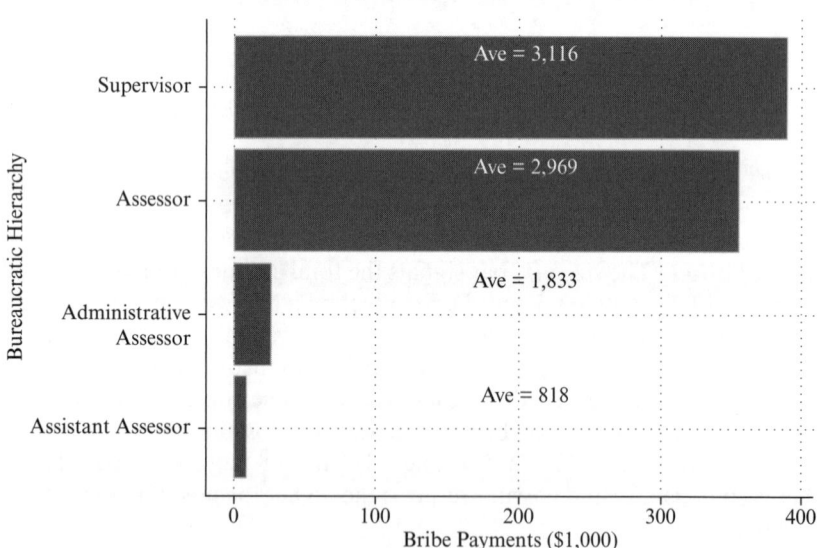

Figure 7.8 Bribe by position in the bureaucracy's hierarchy

scheme cost the city $40 million a year in tax income, or $160 million between 1997 and 2002 (Bagli 2002d). Considering that the scheme went on for approximately 35 years, the city may have lost up to one billion dollars (Committee on Real Property Taxation 2002: 57–8).

As the engineer of the corruption scheme, Schussler risked spending 25 years in prison (Miller 2003). However, shortly before his trial, in early 2003, the tax-assessor-turned-consultant suffered a lethal stroke at the age of 85 (Bagli 2003a). 'So we had given [Schussler] a deadline', the interviewed prosecutor explained, 'in which to tell us whether he was going to proceed to trial, or enter a guilty plea. And he died that day, the day that we were expecting his answer. [. . .] I was shocked when he died, of course. I was shocked. He seemed to be in fine health. I didn't have any concerns about his health; his lawyers didn't raise any health concerns. But I imagine he was under quite a bit of stress' (McCarthy 2014).[18] Needless to say, Schussler's passing was an important setback for the prosecution— one that perhaps could have been avoided had the corruption scheme been detected sooner. On the subject of timing, Mayor Bloomberg complained that fraud in property taxation had 'gone on through six mayors, innumerable commissioners of finance' (Danis 2002).

There had been earlier signs. A former president of the city's Tax Commission, David Goldstein, claimed to have written an urgent letter in 1993 to DOI alerting it to possible corruption in the tax assessor's office. The letter apparently made explicit references to Albert Schussler and one of his associates, Thomas McArdle (Bagli 2002f). Aware of these suspicions, DOI launched a focused investigation into the question of corruption in property tax assessment around 1997. As part of its investigation, DOI twice inserted undercover agents into the Manhattan

---

[18]   Bagli (2014) tells the following story to suggest that Schussler's death was surprising:

> At one point, while I'm writing this story, I'm waiting outside [the courthouse] and [Schussler] comes out and his lawyer, whom I'd gotten to know, comes over to me and says, 'Would you like to meet Mr. Schussler?' And I was kind of surprised . . . So he came over, and we shook hands, and he congratulated me on my reporting. Kind of weird. So, ultimately, at a certain point I knew that he was going [to court] in January, I forget whether it was . . . it must have been January of 2003, he was supposed to go in to talk to the US prosecutor, and he was going to Florida for the holidays. Upon his return he was scheduled for a meeting. The night before the meeting he died. This shook the hell out of his lawyer, as well as everybody else. You began to hear and think of those stories of Russian spies and getting stabbed underneath a bridge in London with an umbrella. . . . Well, I know that when I talked to his lawyer the next day, he was really shaken [sic]. And it sort of took the wind out of the sails because the hope or the expectation was that he was going to name names.

property valuations unit (Rashbaum and Bagli 2002). However, DOI's search faced three significant obstacles:

- The city's tax assessors worked as a tightly knit group, which some described as 'clannish' and akin to 'an organized crime family' (ibid.).
- The assessment process was fraught with complexities that helped hide the corruption.[19]
- One of DOI's undercover agents, Nancy Sidaross, leaked confidential information about the investigation to the assessors (Seifman 2002).

In spite of these significant hurdles, a news article claims that DOI had a lucky break while conducting an interview about corruption allegations involving Brooklyn assessors. The interviewee misunderstood his questioners and began disclosing information about corruption in the Real Property Assessment's Manhattan office (Rashbaum and Bagli 2002). This helped authorities close in on Joseph Marino.

When Marino pleaded guilty in September of 2000, Albert Schussler dropped out of the corruption scheme. In July of 2001, however, Alan Edelstein, age 52, took Schussler's place in a revived version of the operation (2002f). Evidently, Edelstein did not realize that the investigation was ongoing. In fact, by this point, investigators had the cooperation of Marino and two other individuals—specifically, Thomas and Stephen McArdle—who also participated in the corruption scheme (Bagli 2002f). Stephen McCardle, in particular, was crucial, because, in cooperating with the investigation, later recorded tax assessors' descriptions of their involvement in the tax scheme (McCarthy 2014).

In the end, the accumulated evidence enabled authorities to prosecute a total of 20 individuals. It also made it possible for authorities to seize $17,597,842 of Schussler's ill-gotten assets (Gearty 2004; Gill Hearn 2004). This offered a degree of closure to a major case of urban fraud. Some might even see these actions by the authorities as inhibiting a similar corruption scheme from arising in the future. However, the fact that not everyone who benefited from Schussler's shady operations was disciplined might have generated a moral hazard problem. Property tax assessment

---

[19]   In the words of a law enforcement official, 'It's one thing to have the allegations. But the target can always come back and say, "This is why we ranked this building at a lower assessment than the guy next door"' (Rashbaum and Bagli 2002).

remains a complicated process with significant financial implications in the hands of modestly paid bureaucrats. Gotham, thus, needs DOI's unceasing vigilance.

IV.   CONCLUSION AND RESEARCH AGENDA

In this chapter we examined a corruption scandal in New York City's recent history. The case involved a fraudulent scheme in property tax assessment that lasted over three decades and may have cost the city as much as one billion dollars in revenue. Approximately 40 percent of the city's Manhattan assessors were directly implicated. Even global news agencies—from *The New York Times* to *The Guardian*—reported on the story, and yet only a short period after the criminal case ended few people seem to remember the event.

Even fewer realize that a similar scheme had been uncovered in California a few decades before (Phelan 1966). Albert Schussler's counterpart in that earlier scheme was James C. Tooke. Like Schussler, Tooke was a former tax assessor turned consultant who knew how to grease the wheels of bureaucracy. Another parallel between the cases is that not a single individual or firm that hired Tooke was charged with wrongdoing or complicity. Thus, there appears to exist a pattern, and scholars writing on administrative corruption summarize that pattern with the following: 'Delinquent taxpayers are practically never prosecuted' (Flatters and Macleod 1995: 398).

However, beyond the question of prosecution, as researchers, what we are most interested in is corruption prevention. It is, thus, worth reviewing some of the reforms that DOF implemented after the 2002 scandal. These reforms included:

- Reducing the amount of contact between assessors and property owners.
- Engaging in random assessment reviews, and restructuring the Internal Audit and Department Advocate's Units.
- Requiring that assessors file financial disclosure forms.
- Implementing new technology to enhance the assessment process (NYC Finance 2004).

In spite of these innovations, however, there have been new, if sporadic, reports of property tax evasion (Bagli 2012; Gonzalez 2014). Corruption hazards continue to exist in the city's tax system; however, DOI has reaffirmed its commitment to effective monitoring. As a sign of this commitment, the agency opened itself up to a collaborative research project that tests ways to curb corruption in property taxation.

As was noted earlier, according to an independent assessment, DOI has reduced serious cases of corruption by almost two-thirds in recent years (Anechiarico and Smith 2008: 76). This finding, nonetheless, is based on observational data and is, therefore, vulnerable to certain forms of measurement bias. Indeed, given the nature of the data, we are unable to distinguish whether the reduction in cases of corruption is explained by DOI's enhanced efforts or some other factor, such as inhibited corruption reporting or heightened sophistication among those who partake in corruption. But even if we grant that DOI has raised the level of government integrity in New York City, the existing data does not help us evaluate the effectiveness across DOI's different anti-corruption strategies. Therefore, we conducted a randomized control trial (or RCT) in order to answer two questions. First, does monitoring by DOI help ensure that property assessments are conducted with greater integrity and efficiency? Second, which is more effective in ensuring that property assessments are performed in an honest and efficient manner: proactive or reactive audits?

RCTs are a powerful tool for advancing scientific knowledge, especially when applied to real-world situations. As case in point, Lawrence Sherman and coauthors (1995) conducted an RCT on deterrence in criminal justice. Similarly, in 2009, criminologists from Temple University collaborated with the city of Philadelphia in order to conduct an RCT that tested the effectiveness of foot patrols in fighting crime. Their finding that patrolling city blocks by foot reduces violent crime by 23 percent overturned conventional views about policing (Ratcliffe et al. 2011).

In the realm of corruption studies, RCTs are also increasingly popular (Peisakhin 2011). For instance, in Indonesia, Ben Olken (2007) tested whether grassroots versus centralized monitoring is more effective in reducing corruption. In another study, Ferraz and Finan (2011) analyzed data from local corruption audits in Brazil. Their results show that corruption is less common among mayors seeking re-election. Following a similar approach, Lagunes conducted an RCT in Querétaro, one of Mexico's most populous cities. In this study a random sample of construction permit applications were entered into a treatment group. Plan Examiners (that is, the low-level officials responsible for reviewing building permit applications) and the Permits Office Director were made aware that an independent anti-corruption auditor was reviewing all the physical documentation (for example, title deeds, blue prints, and tax receipts) for applications within this group. Simultaneously, these same officials were unaware that the auditor was reviewing another set of randomly selected applications via the government's computer network. With implications for law enforcement, the study's results reveal that monitoring spurs greater diligence and stringency among bureaucrats, but *only* when they sense the risk of a top-down sanction.

In this new and independently funded RCT the main hypothesis is that the threat of an audit will stimulate local tax assessors to perform their duty in a more efficient and honest manner. An additional hypothesis is that, compared to the threat of post-hoc or reactive audits, proactive monitoring by DOI will have a stronger and positive effect on government officials' behavior. This chapter, however, is not about that RCT, which—as of this writing—is in the analysis stage. Instead, this chapter is about an extraordinary case of municipal fraud that begs practitioners and academics alike to persevere in their effort to prevent corruption.

REFERENCES

Ackerman, John M. and Irma E. Sandoval-Ballesteros. 2006. 'The Global Explosion of Freedom of Information Laws', *Administrative Law Review* 58(1): 85.

Adams Otis, Ginger. 2013. 'NYC Has a Dedicated Watchdog in Rose Gill Hearn', *Daily News* 10 July, sec. New York.

Anechiarico, Frank and James B. Jacobs. 1996. *The Pursuit of Absolute Integrity: How Corruption Control Makes Government Ineffective*. Chicago, Il.: The University of Chicago Press.

Anechiarico, Frank, and Dennis Smith. 2008. 'Evaluation of the New York City Integrity System', in Leo Huberts, Frank Anechiarico and Frédérique Six (eds), *Local Integrity Systems: World Cities Fighting Corruption and Safeguarding Integrity*. The Hague: BJU Legal Publishers, 69–77.

Bagli, Charles V. 2002a. 'Clients Reel at Indictments in Tax Scheme: A Network of Friends Own Affected Properties', *The New York Times* 1 March 1, sec. B: 2.

Bagli, Charles V. 2002b. 'Tax Bills to Rise for Scheme's Beneficiaries', *The New York Times* 13 March.

Bagli, Charles V. 2002c. 'Tax-Plot Case against Executive Is Tightening', *The New York Times* 4 October.

Bagli, Charles V. 2002d. 'Jail for Former Tax Assessor Involved in Bribery Scheme', *The New York Times* 26 October.

Bagli, Charles V. 2002e. 'Trump Sues City, Saying Scheme by Assessors Hurt Condo Values', *The New York Times* 8 November.

Bagli, Charles V. 2002f. 'Scandal over Property Tax Bribes May Extend to Lawyers and Firms', *The New York Times* 7 December, sec. B.

Bagli, Charles V. 2003a. 'Man at Center of Bribe Case Dies of Stroke', *The New York Times* 8 January.

Bagli, Charles V. 2003b. 'Hundreds of Property Owners Sue City over Tax Scheme', *The New York Times* 13 February 13, sec. Archives.

Bagli, Charles V. 2012. 'Property Tax Evasion in City Is Widespread, Report Suggests', *The New York Times* 1 August.

Bagli, Charles V. 2014. 'Personal Interview: Veteran New York Times Reporter', Interviewed with consent in New York City ed.

Bagli, Charles V. and William K. Rashbaum. 2002a. 'Grand Jury Examines Allegations Tax Assessors Took Bribes', *The New York Times* 14 January.

Bagli, Charles V. and William K. Rashbaum. 2002b. '18 City Tax Assessors Indicted in Decades-Long Bribe Scheme', *The New York Times* 26 February.

Banisar, David. 2006. *Freedom of Information around the World 2006*. Privacy International.

Caniglia, J. 2013. 'Cayahoga County Corruption Investigation Winds Down to the Finish as Bulk of Case Completed'. Ceveland.com. 20 April 2014, available 7 May 2015 at http://www.cleveland.com/countyincrisis/index.ssf/2013/01/cuyahoga_county_corruption_inv.html.

City of New York. 2004. 'New York City Charter'. 34th edn. New York State Legislature. Vol. 801–7.

Committee on Real Property Taxation. 2002. 'Real Property Tax Assessor Practices in New York City'. Ed. Assembly Standing Committee on Real Property Taxation. New York, 191.

Craig, Susanne, William K. Raushbaum, and Thomas Kaplan. 2014. 'Cuomo's Office Hobbled Ehtics Inquiries by Moreland Commission', *The New York Times* 23 July, sec. N.Y./Region.

Danis, Kirsten 2002. 'Fed Indictments Kick Assessors: Property-Tax Bigs Ran Scam for 35 Years, Authorities Say', *New York Post* 26 February.

Das-Gupta, Arindam, and Dilip Mookherjee. 1998. *Incentives and Institutional Reform in Tax Enforcement: An Analysis of Developing Country Experiences*. New Dehli, India: Oxford University Press.

Department of Investigation. 2013. 'City's Corruption Watchdog Releases Year-End Stats Closes out 2013 with Significant Impacts'. Ed. Department of Investigation. New York City, 8.

Department of Investigation. 2014a. 'DOI History'. Online. The City of New York 30 November available 7 May 2015 at http://www.nyc.gov/html/doi/html/about/history.shtml.

Department of Investigation. 2014b. 'Our Mission'. Online. The City of New York 30 November, available 7 May 2015 at http://www.nyc.gov/html/doi/html/about/mission.shtml.

Dobkin, Jake 2014. 'Which Nyc Government Agencies Are the Most Corrupt', 14 May, available 7 May 2015 at http://gothamist.com/2014/05/14/nyc_government_corruption.php.

Dodd, Lawrence C., and Richard L. Schott. 1979. *Congress and the Administrative State*. New York: Wiley.

Dolan, J. 2013. 'New Corruption Charges Filed against Noguez', *Los Angeles Times* 9 March.

Entrikin, J. Lyn. 2014. 'Tax Ferrets, Tax Consultants, Bounty Hunters, and Hired Guns: The Property Tax Netherworld Fueled by Contingency Fees and Champertous Agreements', *Chicago-Kent Law Review* 89(1): 289–352.

Ferejohn, John. 1999. 'Accountability and Authority: Toward a Theory of Political Accountability', in Adam Przeworski, Susan Stokes and Bernard Manin (eds), *Democracy, Accountability, and Representation*. Cambridge, MA: Cambridge University Press, 131–53.

Ferraz, Claudio and Frederico Finan. 2011. 'Electoral Accountability and Corruption: Evidence from the Audits of Local Governments', *American Economic Review* 101(4): 1274–311.

Flatters, Frank and W. Bentley Macleod. 1995. 'Administrative Corruption and Taxation', *International Tax and Public Finance* 2: 397–417.

Friedman, Stefan C. 2003. 'City Staffer Guilty in Tax-Assess Bribe Case', *New York Post* 27 June.

Gardiner, John A. and Theodore R. Lyman. 1978. *Decisions for Sale: Corruption and Reform in Land-Use and Building Regulation*. New York: Praeger Publishers.

Gearty, Robert. 2004. 'City to Get 17m out of Dead Mogul', *New York Daily News* 4 August.

Geddes, Barbara. 2006. *Paradigms and Sand Castles*. Ann Arbor, MI: University of Michigan Press.

Gentzkow, Matthew, Edward L. Glaeser and Claudia Goldin. 2006. 'The Rise of the Fourth Estate: How Newspapers Became Informative and Why It Mattered', in Edward L. Glaeser and Claudia Goldin (eds), *Corruption and Reform: Lessons from America's Economic History*. Chicago: NBER and Chicago University Press, 187–230.

George, Alexander L. and Andrew Bennett. 2005. *Case Studies and Theory Development in the Social Sciences*. Cambridge, MA: MIT Press.

Gill Hearn, Rose. 2004. 'DOI Recovers $17.5 Million for New York City: Estate of Defendant in a Criminal Case Pays $17.6 Million in Restitution'. Ed. Department of Investigation. New York, 1.

Gill Hearn, Rose. 2008. 'The New York City Integrity System', in Leo Huberts, Frank Anechiarico and Frédérique Six (eds), *Local Integrity Systems: World Cities Fighting Corruption and Safeguarding Integrity*. The Hague: BJU Legal Publishers, 55–68.

Gill Hearn, Rose. 2014. 'Personal Correspondence: Former Doi Commissioner'. 2014.

Goldsmith, Stephen. 2015. 'Making Data Matter in Administrative Systems'. Online, 2014. Data-Smart City Solutions 14 January, available 7 May 2015 at http://datasmart.ash.harvard.edu/news/article/making-data-matter-in-administrative-systems-504.

Gonzalez, Juan. 2014. 'City Overrules Its Own Assessors and Lowers Google's Real Estate Taxes by $21 Million', *New York Daily News* 16 January.

Graycar, Adam and Diego Villa. 2011. 'The Loss of Governance Capacity through Corruption', *Governance: An International Journal of Policy, Administration, and Institutions* 24(3): 419–38.

Green, Vincent E. 2013. *Corruption in the Twenty-First Century*. Bloomington, IN: iUniverse, Inc.

Gross, Samantha. 2011. 'Citytime Was "Corrupted to Its Core", Cost Taxpayers $600m: DA', *The Huffington Post* 20 June, sec. New York.

King, Gary, Robert O. Keohane, and Sidney Verba. 1994. *Designing Social Inquiry*. Princeton, NJ: Princeton University Press.

Knapp Comission. 1973. *The Knapp Commission Report on Police Corruption*. New York: George Braziller, Inc.

Lipsky, Michael. 1980. *Street Level Bureaucracy*. New York: Russell Sage Foundation.

Maas, Peter. 1973. *Serpico*. New York: Viking Press.

Manin, Bernard, Adam Przeworski, and Susan Stokes. 1999. 'Introduction', in Adam Przeworski, Susan Stokes and Bernard Manin (eds), *Democracy, Accountability, and Representation*. Cambridge, MA: Cambridge University Press, 1–26.

Manion, Melanie. 2004. *Corruption by Design: Building Clean Government in Mainland China and Hong Kong*. Cambridge, MA: Harvard University Press.

McCarthy, Sharon. 2014. 'Personal Interview: Former Assistant United States Attorney for the Southern District of New York'.

Mcgurk, Joe. 2002. 'Assess This, Pal: Bribe Guy Must Pay $160m', *New York Post* 26 October.

McKeown, Timothy J. 1999. Review of 'Designing Social Inquiry: Scientific Inference in Qualitative Research', *International Organization* 53(1): 161–90.

Meisner, J. 2013. 'Assessor Berrios' Name Emerges in Bribery Trial', *Chicago Tribune* 23 October.

Miller, Adam. 2003. 'Death Won't Halt Tax-Assess Probe', *New York Post* 9 January.

Netzer, Dick. 1966. *Economics of the Property Tax*. Washington, DC: The Brookings Institution.

Netzer, Dick, et al. 1980. *Real Property Tax Policy for New York City: A Study Conducted under Contract with the Department of Finance, City of New York*. Graduate School of Public Administration, New York University.

Newfield, Jack, and Wayne Barrett. 1988. *City for Sale: Ed Koch and the Betrayal of New York*. New York: Harper & Row.

Newman, Andy. 2002. 'Records Show Wide Variety in Lifestyles of Assessors', *The New York Times* 28 February.

NYC Finance. 2004. *Department of Finance, Department of Investigation Release Final Report on Assessor Reform; Fy05 Tentative Property Assessment Roll Published*. New York, NY: Department of Finance, 2004.

NYC Finance. 2013. *The New York City Property Tax Fy 2014: Market and Assessed Value Summary Tables*. New York: Department of Finance.

NYC Finance. 2014. 'Nyc Residential Property Taxes'. Ed. Property Division. New York, 13.

Office of Management and Budget. 2014. *Expense Revenue Contract*. New York, NY.

Olken, Benjamin. 2007. 'Monitoring Corruption: Evidence from a Field Experiment in Indonesia', *Journal of Political Economy* 115(2): 200–249.

Paul, Diane B. 1975. *The Politics of the Property Tax*. Lexington, MA: Lexington Books.

Peisakhin, Leonid V. 2011. 'Field Experimentation and the Study of Corruption', in Susan Rose-Ackerman and Tina Soreide (eds), *International Handbook on the Economics of Corruption, Volume Two*. Cheltenham, UK and Northampton, MA, USA: Edward Elgar.

Peters, Mark G. 2014a. *Testimony of Mark G. Peters (Commissioner, New York City Department of Investigation) Concerning the Executive Budget for Fiscal Year 2015*. New York City Council Committee on Oversight and Investigations Jointly with the Committee on Finance.

Peters, Mark G. 2014b. *DOI Commissioner Mark G. Peters Delivers Opening Remarks at Association of Inspectors General Fall Training Conference in New Jersey*. The City of New York: Department of Investigation.

Phelan, James. 1966. 'When I Looked in Those Files, My Eyes Popped', *Saturday Evening Post*.

Rashbaum, William K., and Charles V. Bagli. 2002. 'Tax Agency Was Suspected for a Decade', *The New York Times* 27 February, sec. B: 1.

Ratcliffe, Jerry H., et al. 2011. 'The Philadelphia Foot Patrol Experiment:

A Randomized Controlled Trial of Police Effectiveness in Violent Crime Hotspots', *Criminology* 49(3): 795–831.

Rose-Ackerman, Susan. 1999. *Corruption and Government*. New York: Cambridge University Press.

Sambanis, Nicholas. 2004. 'Using Case Studies to Expand Economic Models of Civil War', *Perspectives on Politics* 2: 259–79.

Saulny, Susan. 2003. 'Ex-Assessor Pleads Guilty to Bribery in Tax Scheme', *The New York Times* 21 June.

Schiffrin, Anya, (ed.). 2014. *Global Muckraking*. New York: The New Press.

Seidman, Harold. 1941. *Investigating Municipal Corruption A Study of New York City Department of Investigation*. New York City: Institute of Public Administration, Columbia University.

Seifman, David. 2002. 'Prober Spilled Beans in Tax Scam', *New York Post* 25 July.

Seifman, David. 2004. '$17m Fraud Was Dead Wrong', New York Post.

Sherman, Lawrence W., et al. 1995. 'Deterrent Effects of Police Raids on Crack Houses: A Randomized, Controlled Experiment', *Justice Quarterly* 12(4): 755–81.

Smith, Greg B. 2013. 'Bloomberg Leaves Office Having Set Record for Most Municipal Corruption Busts', *Daily News* 29 December.

Stiglitz, Joseph. 2002. 'Transparency in Government', in *The Right to Tell: The Role of Mass Media in Economic Development*. Washington, DC: The World Bank, 27–44.

Treaster, Joseph B. 1994. 'Convicted Police Officer Receives a Sentence of at Least 11 Years', *The New York Times* 12 July.

U.S. Census Bureau. 2013. *Latest National Totals of State & Local Taxes*.

U.S. District Court. 2002. 'United States v. Alberth Schussler Et Al.' Ed. Southern District of New York.

USA v. Marino. 2000. *United States of America v. Joseph Marino*. 1:00-cr-00361-DC. Ed. United States District Court of New York. New York, 25.

Van Evera, Stephen. 1997. *What Are Case Studies? How Should They Be Performed?*. Ithaca, NY: Cornell University Press.

Weber, Max. 1958. *From Max Weber*. C. Wright Mills and H. H. Gerth (eds). New York: Oxford University Press.

Weiser, Benjamin. 2014. 'Three Contractors Sentenced to 20 Years in CityTime Corruption Case', *The New York Times* 28 April, sec. N.Y./Region.

Wilson, James Q. 1978. 'The Rise of the Bureaucratic State', in Francis E. Rourke (ed.), *Bureaucratic Power in National Politics*. 3rd edn. Boston: Little, Brown, 54–78.

Winslow, Richard S. and David W. Burke. 1993. *Rogues, Rascals, and Heroes*. New York: Department of Investigation, 1993.

Woll, Peter. 2009. 'Constitutional Democracy and Bureaucratic Power', in Peter Woll (ed.), *American Government: Readings and Cases*. 19th edn. New York: Longman Publishing Group, 2009.

8.   Corruption and trade costs

Sandra Sequeira

1.   THE DETERMINANTS OF TRADE COSTS

An established literature argues that reducing trade costs can substantially increase income and improve welfare in trading countries (Frankel and Romer 1999; Rodrik and Rodriguez 2000; Limao and Venables 2001; Obstfeld and Rogoff 2001). Although the standard approach to measuring trade costs focuses on tariff barriers, recent rounds of tariff liberalization led by the WTO have significantly reduced the impact of tariffs on the cost of trade. As a result, attention has shifted to other forms of non-tariff barriers to trade such as the costs associated with the transport of goods across space (Anderson and Wincoop 2004; Donaldson forthcoming). Decades of substantial investments in road, rail and port infrastructure have not yet led to a substantial decline in transport costs, particularly in Sub-Saharan Africa where these costs are highest.[1] Hummels (2008) documents how high transport costs currently generate a higher effective rate of protection than tariffs in most of the developing world and Limao and Venables (2001) argue that the low quality of transport infrastructure accounts for an important part of the developing world's poor trade performance.[2]

In 2011, shipping a container from a firm in the African sub-continent was still almost twice as expensive as shipping it from India, and six times more time-consuming than shipping it from the US (World Bank 2011). It also took an average of 31 days for a firm in Sub-Saharan Africa to take a standard 20ft container from its warehouse through the closest port, with potential implications for the structure of trade in the region. In fact,

---

[1]   In 2008 alone, approximately 20 percent of the World Bank's budget was spent on transport infrastructure projects, constituting the largest category of expenditures for the organization and a larger share than that of education, health and social services combined.

[2]   The authors suggest that improving transport infrastructure from the bottom quarter of countries—primarily from SSA—to that of the median country in their sample, could increase trade by 50 percent.

Djankov, Freund and Phan (2010) find that each day cargo is delayed reduces a country's trade by 1 percent and distorts the ratio of trade in time-sensitive to time-insensitive goods by 6 percent.

The dismal performance of investments in transport infrastructure suggests that reducing transport costs to promote international trade is more challenging than initially envisioned. For one, returns to investments in physical infrastructure are highly dependent on the institutional infrastructure that supports it, such as the bureaucracies that manage ports, roads and railroads. As monopolies in the supply of an essential public good, transport bureaucracies are often plagued with corruption. Bribe-taking is, however, both hard to measure and highly variable across different institutional and bureaucratic settings, which has challenged our ability to test predictions from standard corruption models and to establish important empirical regularities on the impact of corruption in transport on trade. And yet, if the economic costs of corruption in the transport system are large enough, not only can they directly affect both the intensive and the extensive margins of international trade by altering the relative prices of imports but, by potentially affecting demand for transport services, they can also either amplify or dampen the returns to investments in physical transport infrastructure that are currently underway throughout the developing world. This can represent, in the long-run, an additional indirect channel through which corruption can affect trade.

The goal of this chapter is twofold: to contribute to the literature on corruption by first reviewing new evidence on the institutional determinants of corruption in transport, and second, by discussing how corruption can affect trade patterns, as firms adjust the intensive and extensive margins of international trade in response to different types of corruption-induced trade costs.

2. CORRUPTION AND THE COST OF TRADE

Although anti-corruption policies have been an increasingly important part of trade facilitation programs, they are not yet based on a clear understanding of the nature, the magnitude and the dynamics of corruption in the movement of goods across international borders. There is still limited empirical evidence on the interaction between institutional and agent-level determinants of corrupt behavior, on the types of corruption that can emerge in equilibrium and ultimately, on how firms respond to corruption costs.

In theory, patterns of corruption can be determined by opportunities for bribe extraction created by the institutions and bureaucracies that regulate and manage the movement of goods across international borders. The institutional features of transport and clearing bureaucracies that can affect the extent and the nature of corrupt practices include opaque pricing strategies (for example: rail or port management parastatals will often rely on ad hoc negotiation with private users to determine how rail slots get distributed, how port equipment is assigned to shipments and how transport prices are set); bureaucratic mandates (for example: port bureaucracies can devolve more or less bureaucratic authority to different frontline agents in charge of overseeing the movement of cargo, which they can then exercise to extract bribes); and policies for monitoring and sanctioning frontline agents who engage in corrupt practices.

Shaped by these institutional incentives, corruption in transport networks can then take different forms. First, bribes may be set to allow private agents to overcome cumbersome regulations, while creating direct incentives for bureaucrats to perform (Lui 1995).[3] Examples of this type of corruption are bribes to avoid tariffs (Fisman and Wei 2004; Javorcik and Narciso 2008; Mishra et al 2008) or speed money to jump long queues. This could in principle result in a reduction in trade costs, though corruption may still distort trade patterns if it rewards firms that are simply better at navigating corrupt schemes. Alternatively, bribes can be set according to the strategic preferences of bureaucrats, which may not be aligned with the interests of firms. Examples of this type of corruption occur when officials purposefully generate red tape in order to extract a bribe from firms using the transport network, above the official clearing fees. In these cases, corruption is cost-increasing for firms. The impact of corruption on firm-level trade costs is therefore theoretically uncertain: corruption can increase firm-level trade costs if bribes increase the final price of clearing services, or corruption can decrease firm-level trade costs if bribes allow firms to avoid significant clearing fees such as tariff duties.

Finally, firms may respond to either type of corruption-induced trade costs by adjusting decisions on the location of production, the sourcing of inputs, inventory strategies and on their participation in international trade.[4] If bribes are predictable, then firms may factor them in as a normal

---

[3]　This will guarantee allocation efficiency if corrupt officials can perfectly discriminate based on the time-preferences of shippers and/or their ability to pay a bribe. If this is the case, they will award access to the transport slot to the highest bidder, which in principle will be the low-cost, most efficient firm. These queuing models can however be complicated under conditions of imperfect information and strategic considerations, as argued by Bardhan (1997) and Rose-Ackerman (1978).

[4]　Anderson and Wincoop (2004) estimate that transport costs can place up to a 21 percent markup over an average firm's production costs in industrialized

cost of doing business across borders, similar to any other type of cost that introduces a wedge between domestic and international prices of goods. Firms may then adjust their decisions in the same way as they would respond to the price effects of other factors of production. Alternatively, an important way in which corruption may differ from a standard tax or fee is by introducing an element of risk and uncertainty in international trade. Uncertainty as to the final cost of trade due to the variability of bribes or biased beliefs about the extent of corruption can lead firms to sub-optimally over or under-adjust their import and export behavior (Olken 2009). Given the secrecy associated with corrupt deals, understanding how firms perceive the cost of corruption—both its mean and variance—may be as important as understanding actual corruption costs in order to identify the trade distortions introduced by corruption in transport networks.

3. BUREAUCRATIC STRUCTURES OF INTERNATIONAL BORDERS AND INCENTIVES FOR CORRUPT BEHAVIOR: EVIDENCE FROM SOUTHERN AFRICA

This section examines how international border bureaucracies can create opportunities and constraints for frontline officials to extract bribes. It draws on evidence from a detailed comparison between two competing port bureaucracies in Southern Africa discussed in Sequeira and Djankov (2014). The authors identify two types of port officials involved in the movement of goods through ports: customs officials and regular port operators. These two groups differ in their bureaucratic mandates and in the level of information they can access on each shipment and each shipper at any given time. Customs officials have significant discretion to stop cargo, a broader bureaucratic toolkit from which to draw on to justify delays and unanticipated hurdles, and they have full information on both the shipment and the shipper at all times. Port operators have a narrower bureaucratic

---

countries, while suggesting that this number may be even higher for firms operating in developing economies. Eifert et al (2008) provide cross-country evidence on how indirect costs of inputs like transport create a major barrier for the competitiveness of firms in Sub-Saharan Africa. In particular, the authors show that when indirect costs such as transport are taken into account, the net total factor value of African firms is 20 to 40 percent lower than that of comparable firms in China. Total Factor Value corresponds to a firm's ability to generate revenue from a given value of inputs. Corruption in transport networks, by directly affecting transport costs, is therefore likely to have a significant impact on the cost structure of firms.

mandate, fewer bureaucratic reasons to stop cargo, and limited information on the characteristics of each shipment and shipper. Relative to a regular port operator, customs officials can therefore be considered the high extractive types, conditional on the opportunity to extract a bribe.

A third important player in the clearance process is the clearing agent. These are private agents who by law each firm has to hire to clear goods through borders on their behalf. The role of the clearing agent was initially created to limit the possibility of firms attempting to engage in bribery deals directly with border officials, and they are now a common fixture of clearance processes throughout the developing world.

The organizational structure of port bureaucracies can then create opportunities and incentives for each of these types of public officials to extract bribes from clearing agents. An often necessary condition for bribery to take place is that there is frequent and direct contact between clearing agents and port officials. This level of contact is determined by specific organizational features of port bureaucracies, such as the type of terminal management at the port, the clearance technology and the monitoring and punishment schemes in place to deter corrupt behavior.

4.   PORT OPERATIONS: THE IMPORTANCE OF BUREAUCRATIC MANAGEMENT

Sequeira and Djankov (2014) discuss corruption patterns of two types of port management schemes: public and private. While their analysis is restricted to two data points only—the ports of Maputo in Mozambique and Durban in South Africa—it provides some suggestive evidence on the dynamics associated with each management type.

In the early 2000s, fast-paced technological change in the form of containerization and IT container tracking systems significantly altered the production function of ports worldwide. Port operators, who in the past were responsible for coordinating complex processes of cargo loading and off-loading on the docks, began to be substantially less important for harbor operations. These changes facilitated the privatization of port operations, particularly in places like Mozambique that did not have a long tradition of unionized labor. As a result, all terminals and port operations in Maputo were outsourced to the private sector by the government of Mozambique in 2004.[5] Private management of the port of Maputo

---

[5]   Privatization was a necessary condition for Mozambique to receive partial funding from the IFIs to rehabilitate its broader transport network in

resulted in a centralized delivery of cargo handling services and in the automation of port operations, which limited interactions between private clearing agents and any given port operator. Problems concerning cargo movements were often dealt with at the central level, as clearing agents were less able to approach individual port operators in an attempt to 'grease' the process. The limited contact between clearing agents and port operators was associated with very low and infrequent bribe payments for regular port services at the port of Maputo. Moreover, privatization appears to have been associated with more stringent monitoring and punishment for corrupt behavior as the objective function of private ownership shifted toward increased efficiency and competitive prices that could attract customers to the port.

In the port of Durban, terminals are under a decentralized form of public management and port operators can more easily be approached by individual clearing agents in order to facilitate a shipment. Historically, privatization has been resisted in Durban due to the strength of dockworker unions.[6] The retrenchments that might ensue carried a high political risk of conflict with labor, which was politically unappealing given the location of Durban in a swing political province.

Durban is also a larger and more congested port, where space availability is at a premium. This created opportunities for port officials overseeing the movement of cargo to extract bribes by threatening to move cargo from the main docks where they are stored at no cost into expensive private depots.

the early 2000s. The fall of Apartheid in neighboring South Africa in the early 1990s led donors and multilaterals to focus on transnational economic initiatives that would sustain regional peace through economic integration. For the government of Mozambique, the only way to access international funding for infrastructure was to propose transnational investments that would promote regional integration, such as the Maputo corridor linking South Africa to the port of Maputo.

[6] The privatization and automation of port operations presented the South African government with several political and financial challenges. For one, ports represented the most profitable branch of the transport business. Revenue from port activities in South Africa was locked into a complex cross-subsidization scheme to support the under-performing railway network.

4.1 Corruption and the Automation of Service Delivery

While the degree of red tape was similar across the ports at the time of the study, the level of automation of critical phases of the clearance process differed significantly.[7]

In Durban, customs officials had limited contact with clearing agents given that all shipment documentation was processed online and customs offices were located outside the port area. While corruption in customs was still possible in Durban, transaction costs were higher as they required tampering with the online system where tracing would be possible.

In Maputo, clearance documentation was processed in-person by the clearing agent and the customs building was located inside the port. This created opportunities for clearing agents to frequently interact with customs officials during work hours or during their breaks. The close interaction between clearing agents and port officials with high extractive capacity resulted in increased opportunities for corrupt behavior to take place. The potential for corrupt deals was exacerbated by the fact that Mozambican customs adopted a policy of frequent rotation of customs officials across terminals with varying degrees of 'bribe profitability'. Given the uncertainty surrounding future opportunities for rent extraction and the short time horizons, this practice appears to have had the unintended effect of increasing the probability of customs officials front-loading bribe payments, as they failed to internalize negative demand elasticities across time (Campante et al 2009).[8]

Although this analysis is limited to only two data points, the correlations discussed are suggestive of how different organizational features of transport bureaucracies can lead to very different patterns of corruption. Bribes were higher and more prevalent in the port with public oversight of officials with the most bureaucratic discretion to extract bribes, and with the least sophisticated technology to limit interactions between bribers and bribees. Further research is, however, warranted to firmly establish

---

[7]   South Africa and Mozambique require the same number of documents to process the clearing of goods through their ports (Doing Business, 2007).

[8]   The bribe tracking study reported in Sequeira and Djankov (2014) revealed that customs' agents stayed in a given post at times for less than a month, and at most for up to 6 months. For a random sample of 20 shipments, clearing agents were asked when they had last interacted with the customs' official in charge of clearing their cargo. All clearing agents declared either that they had never interacted with the official before (80 percent of the times) or that they had not done so for at least a month (20 percent of the times).

causal links between different bureaucratic arrangements and opportunities for corrupt behavior.

5. INDIVIDUAL INCENTIVES FOR BRIBE-TAKING AND CORRUPTION TYPES

While an extensive theoretical literature has argued that low wages are an important driver of corrupt behavior, conclusive evidence remains elusive (Becker and Stigler 1974; Besley and McLaren 1993). In Sequeira and Djankov (2014), the median bribe observed in Maputo was equivalent to approximately 24 percent of the monthly salary of a customs official, while in Durban, it was equivalent to 4 percent of the monthly salary of a regular port operator (CPI adjusted to 2005 US dollars).[9] The authors then conduct a back of the envelope calculation to estimate that corruption could increase monthly salaries by over 600 percent for customs officials in Maputo and up to 144 percent for port operators in Durban. Surprisingly, the salary of a customs official in Maputo is one of the highest in public administration in the country and is equivalent to that of a port operator in South Africa, when adjusted for each country's CPI index.

On the other hand, punishment for corrupt behavior was limited for both port operators in Durban and customs officials in Maputo. The authors note that in 2006–2007, both ports averaged less than six reports denouncing a corrupt transaction, which was substantially lower than the frequency of bribery transactions detected by Sequeira and Djankov (2014). Though the authors have no hard data on the actual disciplinary procedures that ensued, the Mozambican customs agency and the port management parastatal in Durban reported that the standard operating procedure was to simply transfer the corrupt official to another terminal or border post. All things considered, corruption in the ports of Durban and Maputo appears to have been less correlated with wage incentives than with the bureaucratic 'opportunity' to extract bribes.

Sequeira and Djankov (2014) also provide a window into public officials' bribe-setting strategies. In both Durban and Maputo, officials appear to set bribes using as exogenous reference points identifiable costs the private agent is trying to avoid, so as to minimize both the informational costs associated with bribe-setting and the risk associated with the illicit transaction. In Maputo, bribes were an increasing function of tariff rates as this represented common knowledge of how much the private

---

[9]   See Table 8.1 for a description of corruption patterns across the two ports.

Table 8.1   Corruption patterns across Maputo and Durban

	MAPUTO	DURBAN
Probability of Paying a Bribe	52.75%	36.09%
Mean Bribe Amount (USD)	275.3	95
Mean Bribe as a % of port costs	129%	32%
Mean Bribe as a % of overland costs	25%	9%
Mean Bribe as a % of ocean shipping to/from the Far East	46%	37%
Mean Bribe as a % of total shipping costs (overland, port and ocean shipping)	14%	4%
Monthly salary increase of port official	600%	144%
Real monthly wage of port official in USD (CPI adjusted)	692	699

Source: Adapted from Sequeira and Djankov (2014).

agent could benefit from the illicit transaction. Customs' officials would thus avoid lengthy and risky attempts to elicit firms' reservation bribe prices based on the time sensitivity of a shipment or a firm's ability to pay. Associating the bribe with tariff evasion had the additional benefit of lowering the risk of detection of the illicit transaction by implicating both parties in the illicit transaction. In Durban, a similar rule of thumb was employed, with the reference point for bribe-setting centering on storage costs at the port. This is a clear cost that firms will try to avoid and it further allows port operators to exploit an important asymmetry of information: private agents are unable to directly observe congestion levels at the port and therefore the urgency with which cargo would have to be moved from the general docks where it stayed for free to expensive private depots. Understanding rules of thumb for bribe-setting is important since it can guide the design of more targeted anti-corruption policies.

Sequeira and Djankov (2014) further document how port officials engaged in one of two types of bribe-taking with important implications for the cost of trade. 'Collusive' forms of corruption emerged when there was an element of rent-sharing between public officials and private agents, as they would split the surplus of the illicit transaction. The main example for collusive corruption was the payment of a bribe for tariff evasion: the official would receive the bribe and in return the private agent would be able to pay lower tariff duties. In most reported instances, this was achieved by the underreporting of quantities or the undervaluation of goods. 'Coercive' forms of corruption emerged when the surplus of the illicit transaction was exclusively captured by the official. Private agents were requested to pay a bribe, above and beyond the official clearance fees, simply to move the clearance process forward. An example of coercive corruption would be when a port operator holds back a container in exchange for a bribe. By definition, collusive forms of corruption can be harder to detect given that neither party to the deal has an incentive to denounce the transaction (Schelling 1956). It is also potentially more profitable for the public official as the private agent should in principle have a higher willingness to pay a bribe when the payoff for the illicit transaction is positive.

In Maputo, customs' officials were the primary recipients of bribes, mostly to sell tariff evasion in a collusive form of corruption. In Durban, the majority of bribes were paid to port operators such as clerks in the document department and security agents overseeing idle cargo on the docks. The main reason for bribe payments was to prevent cargo from being arbitrarily moved from the general docks to expensive depots while waiting for clearance. Given that cargo was entitled to stay in the general docks for a full three days and that most bribes were paid well before this deadline expired, port operators in Durban appear to have been engaging in coercive forms of corruption. The distinction between coercive and collusive corruption is important insofar as it helps understand which bribes are cost-reducing and which ones are cost-increasing for firms. It also suggests the extent to which bribers and bribees have an incentive to enforce anti-corruption policies and denounce corrupt practices, depending on the size of the rent they manage to capture from the illicit transaction.

6. CORRUPTION, TRADE COSTS AND FIRM BEHAVIOR: EVIDENCE FROM SOUTHERN AFRICA

The following sections discuss the existing evidence on how firms respond to different types of corruption-induced changes in trade costs, by adjusting three important margins of behavior: transport, inventory management and sourcing strategies.

6.1 Transport Strategies

A firm's choice of which transport corridor and which port to use is an important determinant of trade costs given that cargo in Sub-Saharan Africa will often travel long distances between centres of production or consumption and ports, at very high prices of overland transport. In fact, over one-third of countries in the sub-continent are landlocked and have the option of shipping their exports and imports through more than one port, at times located in more than one country. Given that both the type and extent of corruption may vary across institutional settings and transport bureaucracies, corruption can play an important role in firms' choice of which port to use. Sequeira and Djankov (2014) show that coercive forms of corruption applied to cargo in transit through the port of Maputo caused South African firms to re-route their imports to the port of Durban, even when the diversion increased transport costs significantly more than the cost of the bribe itself (by a factor of 2).[10] The authors argue that this puzzling result could be explained by the high variability of bribes in Maputo. Given the structure of the transport industry, uncertainty in bribe levels can create short-run liquidity constraints and exacerbate agency problems between firms and clearing agents, as the latter make non-verifiable last-minute requests to the former in order to meet demands for higher bribes.

The study also reports that when firms re-route to Durban, they create imbalanced flows of cargo in the transport network. This imbalance translates into higher transport prices on the corridor leading to the more corrupt port of Maputo, even though the actual costs of transporting goods are identical across corridors. While there are many structural determinants of imbalanced flows of cargo in the region, the data suggest that corruption may also play a role and generate deadweight loss (Campos, Lien and Pradhan 1999).

6.2 Inventory Management

A firm's ability to manage inventories productively can directly affect sales profitability and cash flow. Unneeded inventory to mitigate supply risk is often associated with higher costs of warehousing, security, spoilage and tied up capital.[11] Low inventories on the other hand can interfere with the efficiency of the production process due to stockouts (Kremer et al. 2013).

Actual or perceived corruption at ports and border posts can directly affect firms' decision on the level of input inventory they decide to carry, particularly for imported inputs with low degree of substitutability for

---

[10]   See Figure 8.1 for the layout of the road network connecting the hub of economic activity in Southern Africa to the competing ports of Durban and Maputo.

[11]   Fafchamps et al. (2000) show that Zimbabwean firms hedge against uncertain transport delivery times and costs by building higher than average input inventories. According to this study, safety stocks due to uncertain transport delivery can even reach one year of expected sales. This represents tied up capital that negatively affects business growth.

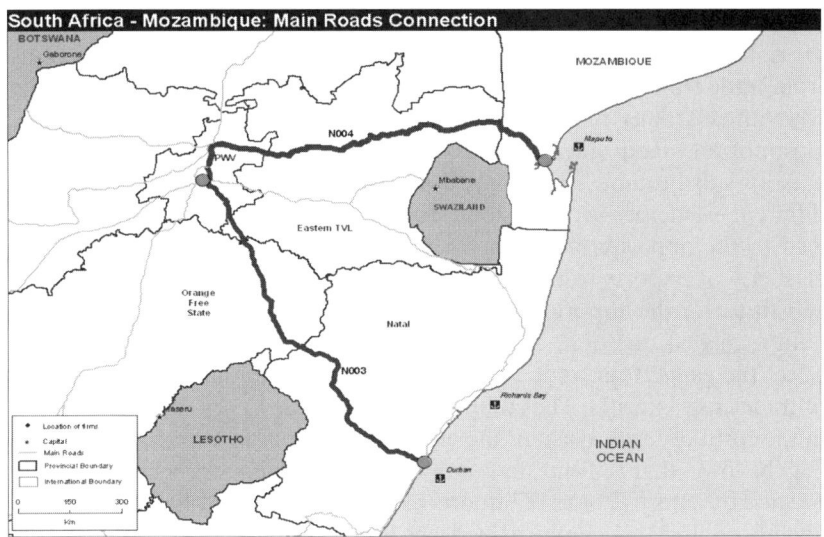

Source: Reproduced from Sequeira and Djankov (2014).

Figure 8.1 *Road connection between the hub of economic activity in Gauteng, South Africa, to the Ports of Maputo and Durban*

domestic inputs. While this is a potentially important channel through which different corruption patterns can affect firm growth, it is one that has remained fairly unexplored in the literature.

6.3 Corruption, Import Behavior and Gains from Trade

A growing literature has begun to document how imports can be an important channel of total factor productivity growth (Feenstra, Markusen and Zeile 1992; Halpern, Koren and Szeidl 2005; Amiti and Konings 2007; Goldberg et al. 2010; Bloom, Draca and Van Reenen 2011) and international technology transfer (Acharya and Keller 2009).[12] The

---

[12] This empirical literature was motivated by earlier theoretical work by Ethier (1982) and Grossman and Helpman (1991). In these models, lower input tariffs are associated with higher firm productivity due to access to a greater variety of high quality inputs, and potentially through learning effects due to the technology embodied in foreign inputs. Amiti and Konings (2007) estimate that a 10 percent decline in input tariffs leads to a 12 percent productivity gain for importing firms and Halpern, Koren and Szeidl (2011) show that imports contributed in 30 percent to TFP growth in Hungary in the 1990s.

relationship between corruption, trade costs and firm-level import behavior is, however, theoretically ambiguous. In standard trade models, gains from trade from a reduction in trade costs such as corruption can be large when the elasticity of trade with regard to trade costs is low (Arkolakis, Costinot and Rodriguez-Clare 2012). The intuition is that all goods are equally substitutable, including domestically sourced goods. Assuming different elasticities between domestic and foreign goods, would, however, lead to the opposite prediction: gains from trade would be larger if the elasticity of imports to trade costs was high because there is no domestic substitute for the imported good.

In a related question, Sequeira (2015) looks at how corruption could affect the gains from trade resulting from a reduction in a particular type of trade costs—tariffs. The study suggests that due to pervasive corruption in the form of tariff evasion, the elasticity of imports to changes in tariffs may be low—that is, firms do not re-optimize their import behavior simply because the effective price of imports remains unchanged following the tariff liberalization. More empirical evidence is needed to test predictions on how corruption may affect gains from trade following changes in trade costs.

6.4   Tackling Corruption and Reducing Trade Costs

While the range of anti-corruption programs has proliferated in recent decades, the evidence of their success is still scant. More often than not, the main challenge is one of implementation. Attempts to reform transport bureaucracies have often been met with institutional and political resistance; changes in clearance technology to reduce the level of contact between border officials and private agents have faced several technical challenges; the introduction of hotlines for users to denounce corrupt officials have experienced limited uptake; and changes to the incentive structure of public officials through salary increases or stronger punishment face several political and bureaucratic hurdles. Moreover, it is possible that the type of corruption observed amongst frontline officials is replicated throughout the hierarchical chain of each transport bureaucracy, raising further obstacles to top-down reform.

Sequeira (2015) examines how an indirect type of reform—the simplification and reduction of tariff barriers through regional liberalization schemes—affected corruption at borders in Mozambique.[13] The

---

[13]   The need to reduce opportunities and incentives for corruption in the form of tariff evasion is a long-standing argument in favor of tariff liberalization and free trade agreements (Gatti 1999). Several countries have moved in this direc-

identification strategy relies on the fact that the tariff liberalization scheme—both in terms of its timing and content—was determined in the early 1990s, and is therefore uncorrelated to corruption levels observed today. The tariff liberalization scheme had the further advantage of reducing tariffs in a sequence of waves between 2008 and 2012, creating significant variation in the magnitude of tariff reductions both across products and time. Given the existence of an identifiable subset of products that did not change tariffs—a comparison group—the study is able to detect the impact of different types of tariff reductions on corruption patterns, while holding constant overall trends in corruption and any changes in enforcement capabilities that could occur during this time.

The results were striking. Products that experienced a tariff reduction recorded a 30 percent decline in the probability of paying a bribe at the border. The amount of bribe paid was also significantly lower (0.4 standard deviations) relative to products that did not experience a tariff reduction. Products that remained in a high tariff category continued to pay bribes to reduce the amount of tariff duties they were required to pay.

An important question when assessing the long-term impact of any type of reform on corruption is whether bribe-taking was simply displaced away from the activity targeted by the reform, into other forms of illicit activity that can occur during the delivery of the public service. In the case of the movement of goods across borders, tariff evasion is just a subset of the bribe extraction methods available to border officials.[14] In fact, Sequeira (2014) identifies displacement effects following the tariff change. For products that experienced a reduction in tariffs, customs' officials switched from selling tariff evasion to trying to extract bribes by claiming irregularities with documentation, or by selling faster clearance against claims of increased congestion. Interestingly, the main products targeted were those that prior to the tariff change were paying higher bribes. A possible reason for the apparent stickiness of bribe payments is that shippers of products who were paying high bribes for tariff evasion had already

---

tion such as Chile in the 1970s, Mexico and Bolivia in the 1980s. The simplification of tariff rates is often an important goal in the trade liberalization agenda.

[14] While an extensive literature discusses the potential for corruption to be displaced across methods of illicit activities (Reppetto 1976; Chaiken, Lawless and Stevenson 1974; McPheters, Mann, and Schlagenhauf 1984; Ayres and Levitt 1998; Levitt 1998; Di Tella and Schargrodsky 2004), with the exception of Yang (2008a; 2008b), displacement effects in the context of trade policy and trade costs have remained largely unexplored. Should these displacement effects be sizable and economically meaningful, they could however dampen the impact of any policy intervention on corruption.

signalled their willingness to engage in corrupt behavior and pay a price higher than the official clearance fee.

In the setting discussed in Sequeira (2015), the displacement effects dampened the effect of the tariff change on corruption by only 10 percent. While small, these displacement effects represented a shift both in the level and in the composition of bribes. First, there was a shift from collusive to coercive forms of corruption: if before the tariff change private firms were paying bribes to avoid tariffs and thus reduce their trade costs, following the tariff change bribes were being paid just to move the clearance process forward. On net, this could represent an increase in firm-level trade costs, if the implicit counterfactual is an environment of low tariffs without corruption. Assessing the net effect of any policy reform on the users of the service requires a clear understanding of not only changes in the magnitude of bribes but also changes in the type of bribes that are being paid and how they may affect the cost structure of firms.

While in the case examined in Sequeira (2015) the magnitude of the displacement effects does not fully offset the reduction in corruption triggered by the tariff liberalization scheme, it still suggests policy complementarities between anti-corruption and trade facilitation policies. It also underlines the critical importance of understanding the context of public service delivery so as to monitor potential displacement effects caused by public officials attempting to protect their bribe rents, and private agents seeking to further reduce trade costs.

7.   CONCLUSIONS

This chapter examines how corruption can affect firm-level trade costs, and consequently firm behavior. It does so by drawing on novel evidence from two studies of bribe payments at international ports and border posts along two major transport corridors in Southern Africa (Sequeira and Djankov 2014; Sequeira 2014).

The first key lesson is that bureaucratic and organizational structures can affect the magnitude and type of corruption observed, by creating different sets of opportunities for frontline public officials to extract bribes. In this particular setting, corruption patterns were driven by the degree of face-to-face interactions between public officials and private agents; by the level of bureaucratic discretion delegated to frontline officials overseeing different stages of the clearance process and by officials' time horizons on the job.

Second, corruption can either increase or reduce firm-level trade costs, depending on whether agents engage in collusive or coercive forms of bribe extraction. Understanding how rents from illicit transactions are split between bribers and bribees is important insofar as it can determine the way in which corruption affects trade costs, while at the same time, suggesting anti-corruption policies that are incentive-compatible for those trusted with enforcing them.

Third, corruption-induced trade costs are not always equivalent to the costs associated with other factors of production. For one, corruption costs may be more unpredictable or firms may hold biased beliefs about actual corruption patterns. This suggests that it is important to measure both actual and perceived costs of corruption to more accurately predict firm behavior.

The fourth lesson is that the cost of corruption can go beyond the simple transfer between a briber and a bribee. Sequeira and Djankov (2014) provide an example of how corruption in Southern Africa led firms to avoid the most corrupt port available as an import channel, thus altering the balance of import and export flows in the entire regional transport network. This imbalance translated into increased costs for transport services in the corridor leading to the most corrupt port and added congestion to the least corrupt port.

The fifth lesson is that policy interventions that mitigate incentives for private agents to pay bribes and that create fewer opportunities for public officials to extract them can succeed. A tariff liberalization scheme was shown to significantly reduce the overall level of bribes paid for tariff evasion. To assess the overall impact of reform on corruption, it is however important to examine whether the policy interventions end up simply displacing corruption across different types of illicit activities associated with the delivery of the public service, as public officials attempt to preserve their bribe rents and private agents attempt to further reduce trade costs. Although in the case discussed in Sequeira (2015) these displacement effects were relatively small, they changed the nature of corruption patterns, with potential long-term implications for growth.

Understanding the dynamic implications of changes in corruption patterns for firms remains an exciting future research agenda on corruption.

REFERENCES

Acharya, Ram and Wolfgang Keller. 2009. 'Technology Transfer through Imports', *Canadian Journal of Economics* 42(4): 1411–48.

Amiti, Mary and Jozef Konings. 2007. 'Trade Liberalization, Intermediate Inputs, and Productivity: Evidence from Indonesia', *American Economic Review* 97(5): 1611–38.

Anderson, J and Eric Wincoop. 2004. 'Trade Costs', *Journal of Economic Literature*, 42: 691–751.

Arkokalis, Costas, Arnaud Costinot and Andres Rodriguez-Clare. 2012. 'New Trade Models, Same Old Gains?', *American Economic Review* 102(1): 94–130.

Ayres, Ian and Steve Levitt. 1998. 'Measuring Positive Externalities from Unobservable Victim Precaution: An Empirical Analysis of Lojack', *Quarterly Journal of Economics*, 113(1): 43–77.

Bardhan, Pranab. 1997. 'Corruption and Development: A Review of Issues', *Journal of Economic Literature* 35(3): 1320–21.

Becker, Gary S. and George J. Stigler. 1974. 'Law Enforcement, Malfeasance and Compensation of Enforcers', *Journal of Legal Studies* 3(1): 1–18.

Besley, Timothy and John McLaren. 1993. 'Taxes and Bribery: The Role of Wage Incentives', *Economic Journal* 103(416): 119–41.

Bloom, Nick, Mirko Draca and John Van Reenen. 2011. 'Trade Induced Technical Change? The Impact of Chinese Imports on Innovation, IT and Productivity', CEP Discussion Paper 1000.

Campante, Filipe, Davin Chor, and Quoc-Anh Do. 2009. 'Instability and the Incentives for Corruption', *Economics and Politics* 21(1): 42–92.

Campos, J. Edgardo, D. Lien and S. Pradhan. 1999. 'The Impact of Corruption on Investment: Predictability Matters', *World Development* 27(6): 1059–67.

Chaiken, Jan, Michael Lawless and Keith Stevenson. 1974. *The Impact of Police Activity on Crime: Robberies on the New York City Subway System.* New York City: Rand Institute.

Di Tella, Rafael and Ernesto Schargrodsky. 2004. 'Do Police Reduce Crime? Estimates using the Allocation of Police Forces after a Terrorist Attack', *American Economic Review*, 94(1): 115–33.

Djankov, Simeon, Caroline Freund, and Cong S. Pham. 2010. 'Trading on Time', *Review of Economics and Statistics* 92(1): 166–73.

Donaldson, David. Forthcoming. 'Railroads of the Raj: Estimating the Impact of Transportation Infrastructure', *American Economic Review*.

Eifert, Benn, Alan Gelb and Vijaya Ramachadran. 2008. 'The Cost of Doing Business in Africa: Evidence from Enterprise Survey Data', *World Development* 36(9): 1531–46.

Ethier, Wilfred. 1982. 'National and International Returns to Scale in the Modern Theory of International Trade', *American Economic Review* 72(3): 389–405.

Fafchamps, Marcel, Jan Willem Gunning and Remco Oostendorp. 2000. 'Inventories and Risk in African Manufacturing', *Economic Journal* 110(466): 861–93.

Feenstra, Robert C, Markusen, James R and William Zeile. 1992. 'Accounting for Growth with New Inputs: Theory and Evidence', *American Economic Review* 82(2): 415–21.

Fisman, Ray and Shang-ji Wei. 2004. 'Tax Rates and Tax Evasion: Evidence from Missing Imports in China', *Journal of Political Economy* 112(2): 471–500.

Frankel, Jefffrey and David Romer. 1999. 'Does Trade Cause Growth?', *American Economic Review* 89(3): 379–99.

Gatti, Roberta. 1999. 'Corruption and Trade Tariffs, or a Case for Uniform Tariffs', *World Bank Policy Research Working Paper* n. 2216.

Goldberg, Pinelopi K., Amit Khandelwal, Nina Pavcnik, and Petia Topalova. 2010. 'Imported Intermediate Inputs and Domestic Product Growth: Evidence from India', *Quarterly Journal of Economics* 125(4): 1727–67.

Grossman, Gene and Elhanan Helpman, (1991) *Innovation and Growth in the Global Economy*, Cambridge, MA: MIT Press.

Halpern, Laszlo, Miklos Koren and Adam Szeidl. 2011. 'Imported Inputs and Productivity', mimeo CEPR.

Hummels, David. 2008. 'Transportation Costs and International Trade Over Time', *Journal of Economic Perspectives* 21(3): 131–54.

Javorcik, Beata S. and Gaia Narciso. 2008. 'Differentiated Products and Evasion of Import Tariffs', *Journal of International Economics* 76(2): 208–22.

Kremer, Michael, Jean Lee, Jonathan Robinson and Olga Rostapshova. 2013. 'Behavioral Biases and Firm Behavior: Evidence from Kenyan Retail Shops', *American Economic Review* 103(3): 362–68.

Levitt, Steve. 1998. 'Why do Increased Arrest Rates Appear to Reduce Crime: Deterrence, Incapacitation, or Measurement Error?', *Economic Inquiry* 36: 353–72.

Limao, N. and A. Venables. 2001. 'Infrastructure, Geographical Disadvantage, Transport Costs and Trade', *World Bank Economic Review* 15: 451–79.

Lui, Francis. 1985. 'An Equilibrium Queuing Model of Bribery', *Journal of Political Economy* 93: 760–81.

McPheters, Lee, Robert Mann and Don Schlagenhauf. 1984. 'Economic Response to a Crime Deterrence Program: Mandatory Sentencing for Robbery with a Firearm', *Economic Inquiry* 22(4): 550–70.

Mishra, Prachi, Arvind Subramanian and Petia Topalova. 2008. 'Tariffs, Enforcement, and Customs Evasion: Evidence from India', *Journal of Public Economics* 92(10): 1907–25.

Obstfeld, Maurice and Kenneth Rogoff. 2000. 'The Six Major Puzzles in International Macroeconomics: Is There a Common Cause?' *NBER Macroeconomics Annual*, Vol. 15. Cambridge, MA: NBER, pp. 339–90.

Olken, Benjamin A. 2009. 'Corruption Perceptions vs. Corruption Reality', *Journal of Public Economics* 93(7–8): 950–64.

Reppetto, Thomas. 1976. 'Crime Prevention and the Displacement Phenomenon', *Crime and Deliquency*, 166–77.

Rodriguez, Francisco and Dani Rodrik. 2001. 'Trade Policy and Economic Growth: A Skeptic's Guide to the Cross-National Evidence', in Ben S. Bernanke and Kenneth Rogoff (eds), *NBER Macroeconomics Annual*, Vol. 15. Cambridge, MA: MIT Press.

Rose-Ackerman, Susan. 1978. *Corruption: A Study in Political Economy*, New York: Academic Press.

Schelling, Thomas. 1956. 'An Essay on Bargaining', *American Economic Review* 46(3): 281–306.

Sequeira, Sandra. 2015. 'Corruption, Trade Costs and Gains from Tariff Liberalization: Evidence from Southern Africa', London School of Economics, mimeo.

Sequeira, Sandra and Simeon Djankov. 2014. 'Corruption and Firm Behavior: Evidence from African Ports', *Journal of International Economics* 94(2): 277–94.

Yang, Dean. 2008a. 'Integrity for Hire: An Analysis of a Widespread Customs Reform', *Journal of Law and Economics* 51(1): 25–57.

Yang, Dean. 2008b. 'Can Enforcement Backfire? Crime Displacement in the Context of Customs Reform in the Philippines', *Review of Economics and Statistics* 90(1): 1–14.

World Bank. 2007. *Doing Business Report*, World Bank Group.

World Bank. 2011. *Doing Business Report*, World Bank Group.

9. A corruption, military procurement and FDI nexus?

Nancy Hite-Rubin

Corruption in military procurement is a very serious problem (see, for example, Willett 2009; Auriol 2006; Gupta, de Mello and Sharan 2001),[1] particularly for developing economies that have experienced the greatest increase in military spending since the Cold War. Corruption of any form arguably stifles economic development. Yet, a recent paper by Daniel Drezner and Nancy Hite-Rubin (2014) provides a possible refutation of this notion. In their global analysis of post-Cold War military spending, they find that countries that are perceived to be corrupt actually attract more foreign direct investment (FDI) when they spend more on their military. The authors attribute their robust empirical finding to the geo-economic favoritism hypothesis. This is the idea that military spending signals to foreign investors that FDI property rights are more secure. Could it also be the case that military procurement, a key component of military spending, stimulates FDI?

Drezner and Hite-Rubin's finding that military spending attracts foreign capital only into corrupt economies is worth further discussion. In this chapter, I explore the relationship between corruption and FDI with an emphasis on how corruption may play a role in arms procurement. I build from Drezner and Hite-Rubin's previous finding that aggregate military spending leads to higher FDI, and look more closely at the relationship between major arms transfers and subsequent FDI in corrupt states. I show that the purchase of major arms on the international market is also linked to greater FDI, even when controlling for total military spending. This is important, as it means that both the level of overall military spending and the composition of that spending each help to determine foreign investment. In this chapter I explore the possibility that military

---

[1] Transparency International (TI) has also done extensive work on this issue, including issuing a Government Defence Anti-corruption Index (Cover et al. 2013). See also 'Defence and Security', Transparency International, available 8 May 2015 at http://www.transparency.org/topic/detail/defence_security.

contracting creates rent-seeking opportunities that actually encourage the flow of foreign capital into corrupt states.

Military procurement is highly prone to corruption for several reasons. First, for security reasons, governments tend to be least transparent in their spending on defense. This alone creates opportunities for rent seeking and project misallocation. Furthermore, military equipment is usually highly specialized, which reduces market entry and competition among suppliers as well as buyers. Finally, because major arms are expensive and complicated, prices vary highly and thus provide a window for corruption. The highly specialized nature of military goods, large profit margins and lack of market competition sets the stage for bribe-taking, collusion and misallocation. Indeed, research using firm-level data indicates that purchases of military equipment are more prone to corruption, and that bribes usurp nearly twice the contract value of any other sector (Cole and Tran 2011). Certainly, corruption in military spending results in losses and is market-distorting. How, then, can it be the case that military spending in relatively corrupt markets actually corresponds to higher investment?

The following section reviews literature on corruption and foreign direct investment, discussing how the Drezner and Hite-Rubin article contributes to this debate. I then provide an overview of trends in military spending and arms transfers in the post-Cold War era. Here, I describe the phenomenon of military offset agreements and how they have become increasingly more common, especially in connection with the sale of major arms from wealthy to developing countries. The empirical section of this chapter establishes two findings. First, when corrupt countries spend more on their military they attract foreign capital, whereas non-corrupt countries that spend more do not. Second, arms procurement from foreign sources also significantly attracts FDI, even when controlling for total military spending. This empirical evidence sheds light on the curious triangular relationship between military procurement, foreign capital investment and corruption. The chapter concludes with a discussion on the role of corruption in military procurement, and how it may distort the composition of investment at the same time as it attracts larger dollar totals.

1. CORRUPTION, INSTITUTIONAL QUALITY AND FDI

Many influential studies have demonstrated that corruption stifles foreign investment and thus growth (Mauro 1995; Keefer and Knack 1997; Wei 2000; Habib and Zurawicki 2002; Dreher and Herzfeld 2005; Hsu 2008; Castro and Nunes 2013). This is based on the idea that the institutional quality of the host country is the paramount factor determining the riskiness, and ultimately the profitability, of foreign investment. As Raymond Vernon (1971) observed more than four decades ago, the 'obsolescing bargain' of FDI means that companies must be concerned about the ability of host countries to credibly commit when it comes to maintaining the foreign investment climate. A country's ability to signal to investors that its commitments are credible is inversely related to the degree that it is perceived as being corrupt.

The attractiveness of a host country to foreign investors is deeply intertwined with institutional quality. For example, in recent years a fair amount of empirical research has been devoted to examining the effect that investment-specific institutions, such as bilateral investment treaties (BITs) and preferential trade agreements, have on FDI (Tobin and Rose-Ackerman 2005; Neumeyer and Spess 2005; Kerner 2009; Büthe and Milner 2008). Neumeyer and Spess ran an empirical analysis looking at the relationship between BITs and foreign direct investment inflows and found a robust, positive correlation. They contend that BITs can function as a substitute for poor institutional quality. Alternatively, Tobin and Rose-Ackerman are more cautious in interpreting this correlation. They find that this BIT-FDI relationship is only robust for countries that already have a stable institutional environment, and caution against asserting any substituting function. Kerner adds to the debate by providing a more refined model, asserting that BITs attract FDI through indirect channels. Finally Büthe and Milner investigate the empirical relationship with FDI inflows across a multitude of international political institutions, contending that these international institutional agreements (including BITs) allow host governments to make more credible commitments and thus attract more investment. All of these papers share an implicit assumption that corruption is a sign of institutional shortcomings, which sends negative signals to foreign investors.

In addition to exploring the role of international agreements, other scholars argue that due to their inherent institutional checks, democracies are more capable of committing credibly to investors and thus attracting greater FDI. States with democratic regimes are perceived to be more likely to honor their contracts (North and Weingast 1989; Schultz and Weingast 2003; Besley and Persson 2007; Acemoğlu and Robinson 2012). Relatedly, foreign investors are thought to be more vulnerable to the development of 'extractive', non-democratic political institutions where politically powerful actors can exploit the coercive apparatus of the state to reward members of the selectorate with private goods, rather than providing the general population with the public goods necessary to attract inward capital flows (Bueno de Mesquita et al. 2003). As Daron Acemoğlu and James Robinson (2012) have observed, countries that rely on extrac-tive institutions are more likely to possess comparatively more sclerotic economies. Finally, Nathan Jensen (2006) argues that because of the higher 'domestic audience costs' of democratic institutions, democratic leaders are more geared to policies that facilitate the operations of multinationals.

Although most scholars view corruption as an institutional problem, there is not an overwhelming consensus that such corruption deters foreign direct investment. Egger and Winner argue that corruption is actu-ally a stimulus for FDI (Egger and Winner 2005). They base this claim on their empirical analysis of 73 countries between 1995 and 1999, wherein they find a strong statistical correlation between positive corruption levels and FDI. From this evidence they assert that corruption is associated with more direct investment in low-income economies, due to its being utilized as a means to circumvent bureaucratic inefficiencies and obstacles. Egger and Winner's paper complements the 'efficient grease' view of cor-ruption under which it facilitates rather than deters economic activities (Kaufmann and Wei 1999; Méon and Weill 2009).

Egger and Winner's empirical strategy is, however, seriously flawed. First and foremost, the mere existence of a robust statistical correlation does not provide sufficient grounds to make causal claims. In this chapter, I utilize cross-sectional time series data from 90 countries (1990–2008) and also find that the correlation between corruption and FDI inflows is significant and positive (across a multitude of similarly conservative specifications). However, I attribute this global relationship to the fact that since the end of the Cold War, the most rapid growth in the world economy has occurred in developing markets. The Global South is also significantly more corrupt than the Global North. Therefore, a cross-sectional empirical model—even one using lags and country-fixed effects as Egger and Winner did—would likely still produce a significant beta coefficient for corruption as a predictor of FDI (due to cross-sectional variation). This does not mean that FDI will increase if corruption levels rise within an individual country, nor does it explain the growth in foreign investment in any particular country. Indeed, when I split the sample of countries between 'corrupt' and 'non-corrupt' states, the statistical cor-respondence between corruption and FDI vanishes.[2] In other words, if

---

[2] See the empirical analysis presented in Tables 9.1, 9.3 and 9.4, wherein I split the sample according to level of corruption. The impact of corruption thus vanishes. This is because the significance of the coefficient picks up on differences across the Global South and North, rather than how volatility of an individual country's corruption score predicts FDI. Although fixed effects helps to correct

the corruption level in the Philippines (and similarly 'corrupt' countries) is perceived to rise or fall from one year to the next, this change does not affect expected FDI.

Our recent paper on military spending and foreign direct investment demonstrates that military spending is linked to foreign direct investment, but more importantly this link is contingent upon corruption levels (Drezner and Hite-Rubin 2014). We are not suggesting that corruption causes a particular change in FDI. There are numerous factors that correspond with corruption levels that would make the investment climate and political economy of a host country distinct. For this reason, I use the rather simple technique of sample splitting the countries in terms of their corruption levels.[3] In doing so I hope to advance the debate on whether corruption helps or hinders FDI, by showing that military spending only attracts investment into corrupt countries. The purpose of this chapter is to explore why that is the case.

'Military spending' is a measure of all spending on state defense, which includes maintenance, personnel, domestic production of military equipment, and the purchase of major weapons from foreign entities. The measure for 'arms transfers' is but one component of military spending, and arguably the only component that involves purchases in the international market. When I analyze the relationship between military spending (excluding arms imports) and FDI, military spending alone is still strongly linked to FDI. I attribute this to the geo-economic favoritism mechanism, whereby domestic investment in security signals to foreign investors that the institutional environment is secure.

In this chapter, I pay close attention to an auxiliary finding from our previous article; namely, that the volume of major arms transfers into corrupt countries appears to increase FDI. The relationship between arms procurement and the attraction of foreign capital is statistically independent of the relationship between overall military spending and FDI. Whereas the tendency of aggregate military spending to attract FDI is explained by the logic of geo-economic favoritism as stated earlier (Drezner and Hite-Rubin 2014), the nature of military procurement in international markets merits further consideration. The following section explores trends in

---

for this problem (by estimating individual intercepts for each country), it is not sufficient. Simply splitting the sample enables an empirical analyst to check for these differentials in the impact of corruption on FDI.

[3] We can learn a lot more from doing this, than running more elaborate models which require implausible assumptions. However it is also important to justify the dimensions by which to split categories and not split into very small groups.

military expenditures, focusing on arms transfers. The purpose here is to begin a discussion on whether military procurement in corrupt countries can actually be beneficial to these economies. Alternatively, is there something about military purchases and offset agreements that could distort local markets, while still resulting in a net increase in FDI inflows?

2. MILITARY SPENDING, PROCUREMENT AND OFFSET AGREEMENTS

Global military expenditures are currently at an all-time high, estimated to be 1.7 trillion US dollars per year (Archer and Willi 2012). Although the United States still outspends the rest of the world, its relative share is diminishing as other countries (mostly middle-income) are quickly catching up. Although North America and Western and Central Europe have scaled back military spending since 2004, spending has more than doubled (even quadrupled) in many countries throughout the rest of the world (Perlo-Freeman and Solmirano 2014: 6). Much of this increase is attributable to major weapons purchases in the world market. According to the Stockholm International Peace Research Institute (SIPRI), the volume of international arms trade has increased considerably in the last ten years. The world's top importers of major weapons are India, China, Pakistan, the UAE and Saudi Arabia. SIPRI identified over 150 countries that imported weapons since 2009, and finds that sales are growing everywhere except for European states (Perlo-Freeman and Solmirano 2014).

The following two figures illustrate which countries spent the most on their militaries and imported the highest volumes of major weapons per year. Figure 9.1 covers the period from the post-Cold war era through 1999, and Figure 9.2 covers trends in the 2000s. The sample has been censored to only include 'corrupt' countries,[4] purposely excluding countries such as the US and Western European countries in which the link between military spending and attracting FDI does not apply. During the 1990s, the greatest quantities of arms were transferred to countries in the Middle East, northern Africa and Asia. Saudi Arabia had the highest annual level of transfers during the 1990s, closely followed by Turkey and Japan. No Latin American countries stood out, nor did any of the sub-Saharan

---

[4]   This means the chart is censored to only include countries that are considered to be corrupt. In this case, I used a PRS score of under 4 to make this determination.

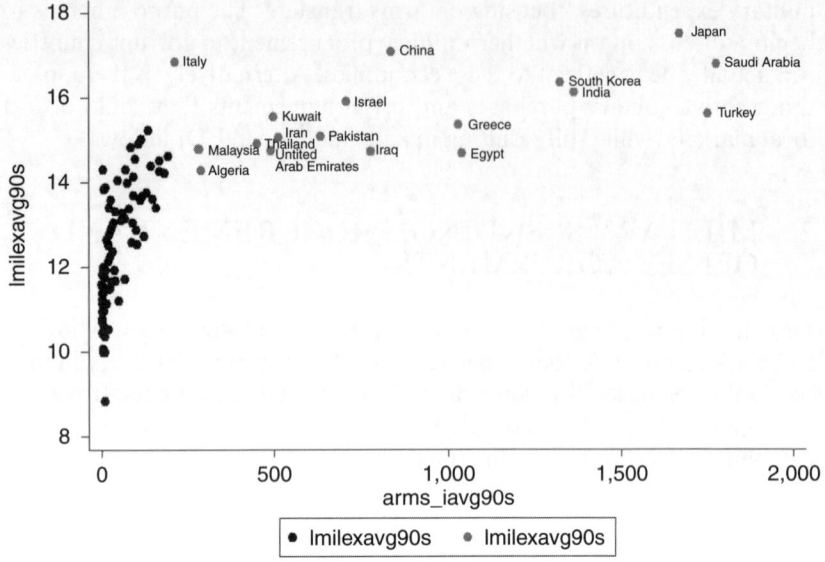

Notes:

Notes: The scatter plot depicts logged military expenditures on the y-axis and average arms spending (between 2000 and 2008) on the x-axis. 'Corrupt' countries that acquired major weapons at markedly high rates are labeled within the plot. These countries, from order of highest import to lowest are Saudi Arabia, Turkey, Japan, India, South Korea, Egypt, Greece, China, Iraq, Israel, Pakistan, Iran, Kuwait, the United Arab Emirates, Thailand, Algeria, Malaysia and Italy.

Figure 9.1   Military spending and weapons transfers into corrupt countries, 1990–1999

African states have major weapons transfers that were above average at that time.

Between 2000 and 2008 the international sale volume of major arms nearly doubled, as evidenced by the country averages in Figure 9.2. Comparing across the two charts illustrates several important points. First, the composition of arms transfers has changed considerably. From the Cold War until the 1990s, there was a shift away from Western Europe. This shift continued into the 2000s and, in fact, there was even more of a pivot towards developing states. Latin American countries such as Chile and Venezuela imported major arms at unprecedented rates, and South Africa became a major player. During the 2000s, arms production and military service companies found profitable consumer bases throughout the developing world. China has dramatically increased its defense spending as well as its importation of major arms, more than quadrupling

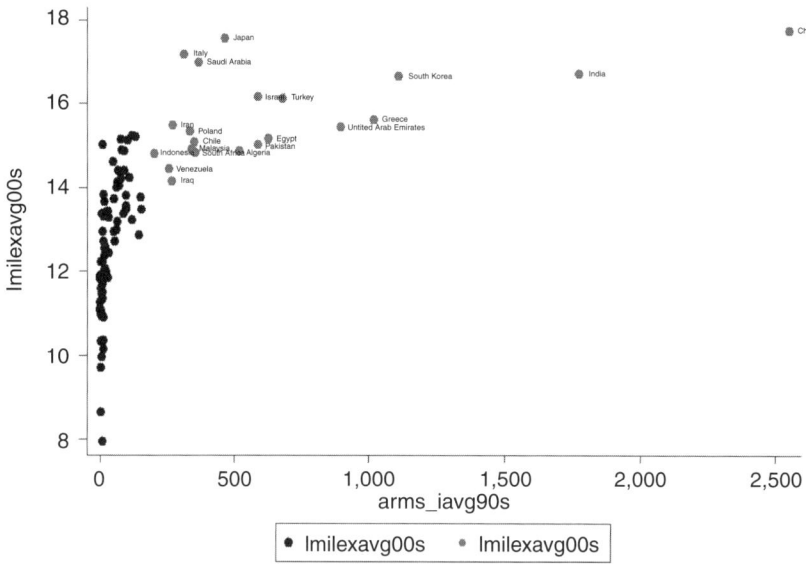

Notes: The scatter plot depicts logged military expenditures on the y-axis and average arms spending (between 2000 and 2008) on the x-axis. Corrupt countries that acquired major weapons at markedly high rates are labeled in the plot. These countries, from order of highest import to lowest are: China, India, South Korea, Greece, United Arab Emirates, Turkey, Egypt, Israel, Pakistan, Algeria, Japan, Saudi Arabia, South Africa, Chile, Malaysia, Poland, Italy, Iran, Iraq, Venezuela and Indonesia.

Figure 9.2   *Military spending and weapons transfers into corrupt countries, 2000–2008*

the former and more than tripling the latter during this decade. Since the end of the Cold War, there has been a marked rise in military spending, as well as arms procurement by countries with lower institutional credibility and political stability.

The SIPRI measure of arms transfers is an annual, country-level estimate of the volume of military weapons purchased (or transferred) on the international market. The values displayed in Figure 9.3 show the aggregate volume of 'major conventional weapons and components' that are tracked by SIPRI. This includes expensive and complicated items such as missiles, reconnaissance satellites, ships and large artillery (both new and old).[5] The measure does not account for major weapons transferred

5   'Coverage', SIPRI Arms Transfers Database, available 8 May 2015 at http://www.sipri.org/databases/armstransfers/background/coverage/.

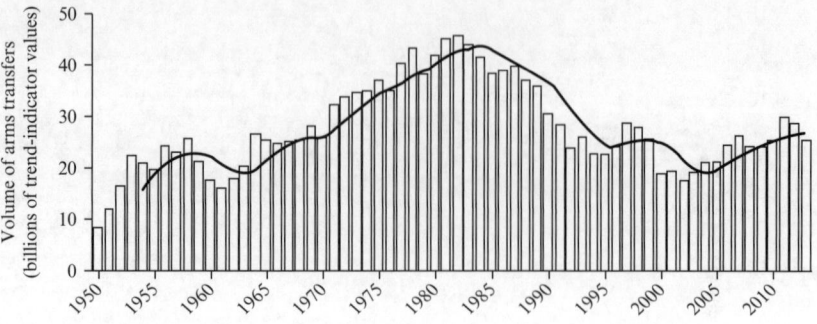

Source: Wezeman and Wezeman (2014: 1).

Figure 9.3 *The trend in international transfers of major weapons,*
1950–2013

or sold to non-state actors, nor does it cover smaller items such as trucks, guns and life vests. SIPRI collects its information directly from arms suppliers and indirectly from the US Congressional Research Service's (CRS) annual report, *Conventional Arms Transfers to Developing Nations*. SIPRI claims to receive data regarding arms transfers from non-US countries from CRS sources (Holtom, Bromley and Simmel 2012); however, it is not entirely clear how complete this information is because many of the details are classified.[6]

The sale of defense equipment has been notoriously associated with corruption (Willett 2009; Auriol 2006; Gupta, de Mello and Sharan 2001).[7] Such corruption ranges from bribes deposited into personal offshore accounts to generally opaque and non-competitive procurement contracts. Military purchases are particularly non-transparent because government defense ministries can invoke national security as a plausible excuse to prevent oversight. Military procurement is prone to rent seeking for economic reasons. Namely, major arms are difficult to price fairly because of product complexity, uniqueness and variation in size. Additionally, the market for international defense equipment is extremely opaque, due in

---

[6] For example, CSR reports rely only on unclassified information and estimated data (see Grimmett and Kerr 2012: 1, 69–75; Holtom, Bromley and Simmel 2012: 4; Federation of American Scientists 1991).

[7] Transparency International (TI) has also done extensive work on this issue, including issuing a Government Defence Anti-corruption Index (Cover et al. 2013). See also 'Defence and Security', Transparency International, available 8 May 2015 at http://www.transparency.org/topic/detail/defence_security.

part to national security considerations. Finally, since the end of the Cold War arms procurement has become a 'buyers' market', meaning that arms sellers clamor to sell equipment and generate elaborate schemes to win contracts. The phenomenon of military offsets in procurement contracts, increasingly prevalent in the wake of the Cold War, is arguably the result of the shadowy incentives of this arms economy.

A military offset is a reciprocal economic agreement associated with large arms and/or infrastructure purchases from foreign countries. They are the result of negotiations between large suppliers and governments and a typical part of such agreements (Economist Intelligence Unit 2013).[8] According to the US Defense Procurement and Acquisition Policy, the term 'offset' refers to:

> . . . the entire range of industrial and commercial benefits provided to foreign governments as an inducement or condition to purchase military goods or services, including benefits such as co-production, licensed production, subcontracting, technology transfer, in-county procurement, marketing and financial assistance, and joint ventures. (Defense Offsets Disclosure Act of 1999, Pub. L. 106–113, section 1243(3))[9]

The broad definition reflects the general diversity that exists across offset arrangements, as well as the fact that little systematic information exists. There are two types of offsets: direct offsets relating to the primary military arms transactions, and indirect offsets, which can be entirely unrelated to security (Ungaro 2013). Another classification relates to whether offset contracts entail 'countertrade', 'local content requirements' or 'bundling' (Markowski and Hall 2006). A 'countertrade' provision in an offset agreement refers to the major arms supplier being compensated with goods from the purchasing nation; for example, if part of the contract for military jets is financed with palm oil. Such arrangements are argued to be beneficial to host countries because they are export-creating. 'Local content requirements' refer to offset stipulations whereby the arms supplier sub-contracts, licenses production or directly finances activities according to the preferences of the arms-importing country. Finally,

---

[8] For further information on countertrade and offsets, see 'FAQs' issued by the Global Offset and Countertrade Association at http://www.globaloffset. org/faqs.php or read about offsets on the EPICOS website at http://www.epicos. com/Portal/Main/AerospaceDefence/ICOffset/Pages/default.aspx (both available 8 May 2015).

[9] For more information about the US law, see Defense Procurement and Acquisition Policy (DPAP), accessed 28 May 2015 at http://www.acq.osd.mil/ dpap/sitemap.html.

Markowski and Hall refer to 'bundling' as supplying products and services that represent bonuses to the primary arms acquisition. This often takes the form of technology transfers.

Some argue that offset agreements facilitate trade and spill over positively in other sectors unrelated to security (Taylor 2011; Grieve n.d.; Khaitan 2013). Many governments explicitly require offset agreements for all military procurement. In some countries, such as India, the general culture embraces offsets as a means of developing local capacities through technology transfer, creating export markets, and even stimulating foreign investment (Khaitan 2013).

The US Department of Commerce Bureau of Industry and Security (BIS) reports that American defense firms entered into defense export sales contracts worth $122.67 billion from 1993 to 2011. Of these contracts, associated offset agreements were valued at $83.73 billion (approximately 68 percent of all contract value) (BIS 2013). The majority of global sales of arms originate from US suppliers. According to a 2012 Congressional Research Service Report, between 2004 and 2011 US-origin conventional arms transfers totaled $145.2 million. This was twice the amount of arms transfers from the next highest supplier country (Russia, which contracted for $72.5 million), and nearly six times the amount of transfers from the following two suppliers (France and the United Kingdom, at $25.7 and $23.2 million, respectively) (Grimmett and Kerr 2012: 41).[10]

Importantly, offsets agreements are not illegal bribes, and the act of offsetting military spending does not explicitly defy international law[11] or anti-corruption regimes. Despite criticisms, offsets do not necessarily entail bribery. However, the negotiations involved in order to arrive at an offset agreement may provide avenues for corrupt rent seeking. According to a Transparency International research report, offset agreements are particularly prone to corruption in three specific channels (Muravska et al. 2010). The lucrative incentives presented in offset packages may influence leaders to procure arms that they would otherwise not. Second, officials involved in the offset negotiation and competition may exploit

---

[10]   Interestingly, the US supply of offset contracts especially took off between 2008 and 2011. Between 2004 and 2007, Russia led the world in supply of offset contracts, nearly doubling those of the US in contract value (Grimmett and Kerr 2012, 40).

[11]   According to WTO's Agreement on Government Procurement (GPA) Article XXIII, procurements that the acquiring country views as 'necessary for the protection of its essential security interests' are exempt from the GPA general ban on offset agreements. Yet when national security interests are involved, private influence may affect the outcome of procurement decisions (Piga 2011: 146).

their influence for personal gain. Third, private sector corruption may also play a nefarious role if private companies collude with the arms supplier to unfairly extract gains from the offset provisions. The authors' broad categories for corruption in defense offsets highlight just some of the ways that non-competitive, highly secretive and exceedingly complex market for major arms could be rife with rent seeking.

The following statistical analysis is not able to determine whether offset agreements lead to more corruption than arms procurement that does not involve offsets. Unfortunately, it cannot determine if the counter-trade, local context requirements and procurement bundling provisions in offset packages induce corrupt governments to buy unnecessary equipment. Nor will I show definitively whether the complexity and secrecy of military procurement directly feeds political patronage and generates economic losses. Rather, the analysis does establish that there is an empirical link between major arms procurement and subsequent foreign investment, which is stronger the higher the levels of perceived corruption.

3. EMPIRICAL METHODS AND DATA

The analysis presented here extends the earlier empirical strategy, utilizing some of the same model specifications as the previous article (Drezner and Hite-Rubin 2014). I first revisit the correlation between foreign direct investment and military spending to show how the relationship is tied to perceptions of corruption. In addition to looking at military spending, I narrow the focus to arms transfers (a component of military spending). As discussed in the previous section, these arms transfers are often tied to military offset agreements. Such agreements are becoming increasingly more complex, and may in their own right produce avenues for FDI. Through this empirical analysis, I explore the possible connection between arms purchases and FDI.

The data are organized in pooled time-series cross-sectional format (TSCS), covering 92 countries from the end of the Cold War (1990) through 2008. The results presented account for heteroskedasticity, auto-correlation and cross-sectional dependence of the data. All of the variables utilized in this analysis are described in Table 9.1.

3.1 Corruption

I utilize two independent index measures of corruption. The primary measure (*corr*) is a measure of 'corruption within the political system ... [that is] a threat to foreign investment', determined annually and published

Table 9.1 Data appendix: variable descriptions and source

Variable	Description	Source*	Index/Scale	Mean (Not Corrupt)	Mean (Corrupt)	Mean (Very Corrupt)	p-value test with Corruption
lfdi_WB*	Logged FDI inflows	(PRS)	$billions	1.266	0.016	−0.284	(−)***
lmilex	Logged Military Expenditures	(COW)	$ thousand current USD	14.383	13.140	12.852	(−)***
larms_i_	Logged Arms Transfers	(SIPRI)	5-year moving avg, trendv value	4.581	4.039	3.927	(−)***
corr_	Corruption	(PRS)	0 to 6	4.696	2.893	1.675	1
lgdp	Logged GDP	(PRS)	(Nominal, $bn)	18.767	17.804	17.556	(−)***
ltpop	Logged Total Population	(COW)	thousands	9.387	9.272	9.479	(+)*
bit_	# Bilateral Investment Treaties	Hite 2013	cumulative annual measure	24.805	17.339	12.327	(−)***
riskr_	Investor Risk Rating	(PRS)	0 to 50	36.682	34.245	32.256	(−)***
f_debt_gdp_	Gross Foreign Debt as % GDP	(PRS)		44.747	54.404	61.278	(+)***
bb_gdp_	Budget Balance as % GDP	(PRS)		−1.958	−3.377	−3.035	(−)***

Variable	Description	Source	Units				Sign
lpec	Primary Energy Consumption	(COW)	Thousand Coal-Ton	10.914	9.814	9.647	(−)***
law_o_	Law & Order	(PRS)	0 to 6	4.897	3.649	2.961	(−)***
NATO	NATO membership status	Ulfelder International Organization Database	0 to 2	0.650	0.261	0.078	(−)***
GATTWTO	GATT/WTO membership status		0 or 1	0.892	0.888	0.728	(−)***
pwt_gsg	Govt Spending as % GDP	(Penn World Tables)		96.324	73.934	60.778	(−)***
wdi_aid	Net Development Assistance and Aid	World Bank Development Indicators	(Constant USD)	5.38E+08	5.29E+08	6.85E+08	(+)***
ucdp_count	Number of Conflicts	UCDP/PRIO Armed Conflict Dataset	cumulative annual measure (1988–2005)	0.181	0.405	0.479	(+)***
fh_polity2	Democracy Score	Freedom House/Polity	0 to 10	8.084	6.317	4.851	(−)***
p_durable	Regime Durability	Polity	# years since regime change	47.943	21.058	16.900	(−)***

as part of the ICRG.[12] This indicator measures country-level corruption on a 0–6 relative scale: 6 is considered a perfect score and 0 is considered extremely corrupt. To insure robustness the analysis is retested using Transparency International's Corruption Perceptions Index (TI's CPI) as an alternative measure (*ti_cpi*). The two corruption indices have a correlation coefficient of .837. The ICRG measure is arguably a more appropriate measure for this analysis, because of its balance with respect to the data set and focus on foreign investor incentives.[13]

3.2   FDI Inflows

The dependent variable is a measure of net FDI inflows into the host country in a given year, measured in current US dollars. There are two measures of FDI inflows: one relying on Political Risk Services (PRS) Group data, and one relying on World Bank data. The PRS Group's International Country Risk Guide (ICRG) is a subscription-based service that provides data on foreign investment and country-specific political and economic factors.[14] Both sources utilize the same definition and measure for FDI inflows, with the two sources co-varying at over 90 percent.

3.3   Military Spending

Military expenditure data are from the National Material Capabilities (NMC) data set, which is part of the Correlates of War Project at the University of Michigan. Its variable *milex* is a country-year measure of military expenditures, measured in current US dollars. This project utilizes the most recent version (4.0) that covers 158 countries from 1990 to 2007.

---

[12]   The *ICRG Methodology* explains more fully that this is an assessment of corruption within the political system. Such corruption is a threat to foreign investment for several reasons: it distorts the economic and financial environment; it reduces the efficiency of government and business by enabling people to assume positions of power through patronage rather than ability; and, last but not least, it introduces an inherent instability into the political process. (PRS Group 2014) The *ICRG Methodology* also contains maximum points for these variable and related formulas for calculating risk.

[13]   'Balance' refers to the consistency in coverage of country-year observations over the post–Cold War data set. The PRS Group provides data as an investment-focused consumer service. The data it covers are most complete for middle income and emerging market countries.

[14]   More information about PRS Group's data is available at http://www.prs-group.com/ICRG.aspx and http://www.prsgroup.com/CountryData.aspx (both available 8 May 2015).

3.4 Arms Purchases (From Abroad)

This logged variable utilizes SIPRI's five-year moving average of arms transfers, a measure that aims to account for year-to-year fluctuations in arms delivery given the often significant variation in total annual transfers (Wezeman and Wezeman 2014, 1). The value is a trend indicator value, designed by SIPRI as a roughly equivalent in estimate of the current dollar value of arms import volumes. The value is not to be confused as an exact value, and thus relative comparisons are more meaningful than absolute figures. Notice in Table 9.1, that both logged military expenditures (lmilex) and arms imports (larms_i_) are both negatively associated with corruption. This descriptive statistic indicates that both arms imports and military spending tend to be higher in less corrupt countries. Similarly, the raw correlation test statistic across FDI and corruption is also negative and significant. FDI inflows are lower on average the more corrupt a country is perceived to be.

3.5 Core Political and Economic Controls

Many institutional, economic and political factors account for changes in FDI inflows from one year to the next. The data set is constructed to comprehensively control for these competing explanations, ensuring that relationships between military spending and FDI inflows are not spurious. The following measures are utilized throughout the findings section. Later, the number of controls is increased in order to verify the robustness of the findings.

Economic Controls. I use two measures control for market size. Logged population (*lpop*) is taken from the Composite Index of National Capability (CINC)[15] version 4.0, which is based on the NMC data set. In addition, CINC's measure for logged primary energy consumption (*lpec*) provides a fairly good proxy for the size of the domestic market within a country in a given year. This energy consumption variable is measured in thousand coal-tons by country-year. In additional to market size, level of economic development is another key control and is measured here as the

---

[15]   This data set is part of the Correlates of War Project, established in 1963 by J. David Singer, a political scientist at the University of Michigan. The Project's goal has been 'the systematic accumulation of scientific knowledge about war'. See 'Project History', Correlates of War, available 8 May 2015 at http://www. correlatesofwar.org. The CINC covers the period from 1816 to 2007 and is 'the most widely used indicator of national capability' (see 'Available Data Sets' on the Project's website).

log of GDP per capita in constant, 2005 US dollars (*lgdp_percap*). This measure is calculated by taking the log of GDP (*gdppcwb05*). The control for economic growth is the annual change in estimated GDP, at constant 1990 prices (*gdp_grow*). Finally, a measure from the Penn World Tables (*pst_gsg*) controls for the role of government size in attracting foreign capital, measuring total government spending as a percentage of GDP.

Political risk. The PRS Group's ICRG political risk measures are also used as control variables. The ICRG collects political and economic information and converts these into annual 'risk points', or indexed assessments of financial risk in a given country, along several dimensions. Five of these dimensions are used in the data set. The first is corruption (*corr*), which the ICRG measures annually on a 0–6 scale. Another dimension is foreign debt (*f_debt_gdp*), an annual measure of gross foreign debt expressed as a percentage of GDP. The third dimension is an annual measure of government budget balance (*bb_gdp*), expressed as a percentage of GDP. Fourth, the ICRG provides a 6-point index measure of 'law and order'[16] (*law_o_*). The ICRG calculates this risk point based on a combined score that measures the strength and impartiality of the legal system, along with an assessment of the observance of law in practice. Finally, the ICRG's combined economic risk rating (*riskr_*) rates investor risk for each country yearly from 0 (highest risk) to 50 (least risk).[17]

International organizations and treaties. Another major factor that can explain FDI flows is BITs (Tobin and Rose-Ackerman 2011, 2005). In order to control for the role of bilateral investment treaties, I generated a unique variable *bit*, which, is a country-year measure of the number of active BITs a particular country has with other countries. The intuition

---

[16] These two measures comprise one risk component, with each sub-component equaling half of the total. The 'law' sub-component assesses the strength and impartiality of the legal system, and the 'order' sub-component assesses popular observance of the law. (Refer to ICRG Methodology regarding maximum points for these variable and related formulas for calculating risk.)

[17] 'Economic risk rating' is a means of assessing a country's current economic strengths and weaknesses. In general, where strengths outweigh weaknesses a country will show low risk, and where weaknesses outweigh strengths the economic risk will be high. To ensure comparability between countries, risk components are based on accepted ratios between the measured data within the national economic/financial structure, and then the ratios are compared rather than the data. Risk points are assessed for each of the component factors of GDP per head of population, real annual GDP growth, annual inflation rate, budget balance as a percentage of GDP, and current account balance as a percentage of GDP. Risk ratings range from a high of 50 (least risk) to a low of 0 (highest risk), though the lowest de facto ratings are generally near 15.

behind the measure is that the greater the number of active BITs a country has in a given year, the more capital investment is likely to follow. The variable is constructed with 4,199 country-year observations, with countries averaging 14 treaties in any given year. The model specifications also include two control variables to account for the role of institutionalization upon both attracting FDI and (possibly) stimulating military spending. Formal membership in GATT or WTO is an independent variable to control for the effect of trade alliances. This measure (*GATTWTO*) comes from the Ulfelder International Organizations database. This is a dichotomous measure, coded as a 1 for every year that a given country is a member of either GATT or WTO. In addition, Ulfelder's measure for NATO membership accounts for the possible role of security alliances. *NATO* is a categorical variable, also country-year level of analysis, coded as 0 (neither a member nor formally invited to join), 1 (formally invited to join but not a member), or 2 (member). Both of these control variables cover 160 countries over the 1990–2008 timeframe.

Institutional environment. In addition to political risk factors and international relations variables, I include additional controls for the domestic institutional environment. One such control is the size of government (pwt_gsp), a measure of aggregate government spending as a percentage of GDP. The logic behind this being that official government spending tends to be rather low in more corrupt countries, and military spending (and thus arms procurement spending) is but one component of the overall government budget. I control for size of government, so to avoid spuriously attributing the impact of increasing the size of the public sector to the effects at hand. Similarly, I also control for net development aid (wdi_aid), a measure of foreign financial assistance from abroad. I also employ the Freedom House democracy score (fh_polity2) and two measures of political stability (ucdp_count, p_durability). The ucdp_count is a measure of the number of conflicts a country is involved in, and p_durability is a count of the number of years since a country had undergone a regime change. Unsurprisingly, on Table 9.1, we see that more 'corrupt' countries have significantly lower democracy scores, less durable regimes and have experienced more conflicts during the (1990–2008) time frame.

4.   MILITARY SPENDING AND FDI IN 'CORRUPT COUNTRIES'

The analysis shows that countries riddled by corruption tend to attract greater foreign capital when their military spending rises. Although a link between military spending and FDI does not hold in less corrupt economies, the relationship is positive and significant for the emerging market economies (EMEs) in the sample. I demonstrate this by first testing for the relationship among all countries in the global sample and then 'splitting' the analysis by corruption levels.

The results presented in Table 9.2 demonstrate that the relationship across FDI and military spending hinges significantly upon perceptions of corruption. Here, I split the sample by corruption measure to see if military spending relates to FDI differently for corrupt states. The ICRG measures corruption annually with a relative scale, assigning 75 percent of countries to a score of 4.0 or lower. I coded countries with a score of 4.5 or higher as 'Low Corruption' and countries scoring 4.0 or lower as 'Corrupt'. The split analysis above compares countries that are perceived as corrupt (model 3) to those not perceived by international investors as being corrupt (model 2). What is striking in this analysis is that the relationship between military spending (*lmilex*)[18] and FDI is significant and negative for the subsample of non-corrupt states. This negative relationship for non-corrupt countries is striking in comparison to the robust positive relationship seen in corrupt countries. In countries where corruption does not detract from investor confidence, perhaps military spending is a signal of waste. The relationship for country-year observations that fall at or below 4.0 on the corruption scale is robust and positive, in the same manner as the full sample.[19]

One possible explanation for why countries with higher levels of

---

[18]   This logged variable utilizes SIPRI's military expenditure data. This data aggregates (where possible) all current and capital expenditure on:
- the armed forces, including peacekeeping forces,
- defence ministries and other government agencies engaged in defense projects,
- paramilitary forces, when judged to be trained and equipped for military operations, and
- military space activities

Such expenditure should include:
- military and civil personnel, including retirement pensions of military personnel and social services for personnel,
- operations and maintenance,
- procurement, military research and development, and
- military aid (in the military expenditure of the donor country (Perlo-Freeman and Solmirano 2014: 8)).

[19]   Note that the cut off point of 4, is selected as a conceptual benchmark in line with the ICRG's 75 percentile ranking. In our forthcoming article, we employ marginal-effects analysis to demonstrate that the relationship is insensitive to this arbitrary cut-off.

Table 9.2   Military spending and FDI, by level of corruption

Net FDI Inflows (PRS)	ALL	Low Corruption	Corrupt
	Model 1	Model 2	Model 3
lmilex_percap	0.271**	−0.235**	0.322**
	0.104	0.0923	0.117
lgdp_pc	1.952***	3.458***	1.819***
	0.267	0.367	0.446
gdp_grow_	0.0485***	0.0474***	0.0454**
	0.0149	0.0106	0.0175
bit_	0.0219***	0.0167***	0.0333***
	0.004	0.00473	0.00626
corr_	−0.069	−0.0252	−0.0449
	0.0624	0.0841	0.104
riskr_	0.0316***	0.012	0.0276**
	0.00868	0.0124	0.0107
f_debt_gdp_	−0.00291***	−0.000417	−0.00431***
	0.000752	0.00196	0.00143
bb_gdp_	0.00724	0.0150**	0.00715
	0.0049	0.00602	0.00478
lpec	0.17	−0.402	0.287*
	0.114	0.311	0.15
law_o_	0.104**	0.0704	0.114*
	0.0487	0.0545	0.0625
NATO	0.147*	0.0484	0.423***
	0.0709	0.0884	0.0831
GATTWTO	0.330**	0.950***	0.202
	0.121	0.226	0.142
pwt_gsg	−0.00319***	−0.00367	−0.00276**
	0.000965	0.00399	0.00103
Constant	−22.21***	−28.32***	−21.86***
	2.387	4.827	3.644
Observations	1,362	503	859
Number of groups	88	55	74

Notes: Split analysis of military spending and FDI inflows, over corruption level. Estimation of pooled OLS/WLS and fixed effects (within) regression models with Driscoll and Kraay (1998) standard errors. *** $p<0.01$, ** $p<0.05$, * $p<0.1$. Note that the number of groups refers to the number of countries in the model specification. Since corruption scores vary from year to year, the 'low corruption' and 'corrupt' country groups overlap.

corruption benefit from military spending is that it may signal to international investors that their assets are more secure. This interpretation comports with the geo-economic favoritism hypothesis that military spending attracts foreign investment. Countries that are corrupt have inherently insecure institutional environments, and thus require the expensive signal of military spending to demonstrate to investors that the risk of seizure or conflict is minimized. The primary analysis in Figure 9.1 supports the claim that military spending may send a favorable signal to foreign investors in such environments. Yet, is it possible that another factor may explain this divergence?

To address the relationship across military procurement, corruption and FDI, I need to 'unpack' the measure of military spending. In doing so, I investigate whether military procurement, a component of aggregate military spending, explains the FDI increases in corrupt economies. I look at the potential role of corruption as a factor independently resulting in kickbacks and offsets that may increase the level of FDI. In the preceding analysis, I utilized a measure for aggregate military spending, which is seen to reflect military *power* and thus enables testing of the geo-economic favoritism hypothesis. I find support for geo-economic favoritism only in countries with moderate to high levels of corruption. The question at hand, then, is twofold. First, is it possible that military offsets are driving the finding? In other words, when military procurement costs are removed from the aggregate military spending measure, do the initial results still hold? Second, in addition to testing for the robustness of the geo-economic favoritism interpretation I analyse the role of arms transfers alone. Here, I ask whether military purchases on the international market correspond to higher FDI.

The regressions presented in Table 9.3 are consistent with the preceding analysis. The inclusion of arms imports as a control variable appears to bolster, rather than challenge, the main finding. Increased military spending is associated with higher FDI for corrupt states and lower FDI for non-corrupt states.[20] The analysis in Table 9.3 therefore supports the geo-economic favoritism hypothesis that an increase in aggregate military spending signals to foreign investors that the country is more capable of protecting the assets of foreign investors. However, the results also strikingly show that, while the core finding remains robust, arms imports also appear to predict FDI inflows. Notice that this relationship is only significant for the subsample of countries that are 'corrupt'. Specifically, arms imports (*larms_i_*)[21] are positively and significantly associated with FDI for countries that are perceived as moderately to very corrupt. In other

---

[20]   One could simply subtract arms imports from aggregate military spending, but SIPRI advises against combining these two measures into one factor because the data for the two measures are unbalanced.

[21]   This logged variable utilizes SIPRI's five-year moving average of arms transfers, a measure which aims to account for year-to-year fluctuations in arms

Table 9.3 Military spending, arms imports and FDI

	FULL SAMPLE	Lowest Corruption	Medium Corruption	Highest Corruption
	Model 1	Model 2	Model 3	Model 4
lmilex	0.233**	−0.393*	0.347**	0.208**
	0.106	0.208	0.121	0.0972
larms_imports	0.0422	−0.00988	0.121*	0.183**
	0.0281	0.028	0.0591	0.0783
corr_	−0.062	0.0282	0.00586	0.0695
	0.0512	0.102	0.12	0.109
lgdp	1.973***	3.115***	2.072***	2.878***
	0.231	0.478	0.426	0.411
ltpop	1.751***	−1.420*	1.710**	3.344***
	0.517	0.772	0.67	0.939
bit_	0.0215***	0.0193***	0.0223**	−0.0209***
	0.00433	0.00463	0.0079	0.00533
riskr_	0.0180*	0.0226	0.0162	0.00859
	0.01	0.0162	0.0101	0.0141
f_debt_gdp_	−0.000999	0.00371	−0.00124	0.000383
	0.00195	0.00385	0.00233	0.00166
bb_gdp_	0.0311***	0.0194*	0.0318***	0.0256**
	0.00646	0.0095	0.0106	0.00957
lpec	−0.652***	−0.557	−0.515	−0.392
	0.201	0.398	0.359	0.304
law_o_	0.0473	0.0662	0.0289	0.0328
	0.0314	0.0473	0.0408	0.0515
Constant	−51.96***	−35.11***	−57.03***	−89.03***
	5.468	4.585	7.775	8.143
Observations	1,091	455	547	289
Number of groups	86	51	68	53

Notes: Estimation of pooled OLS/WLS and fixed effects (within) regression models with Driscoll and Kraay standard errors. *** $p<0.01$, ** $p<0.05$, * $p<0.1$

words, the more corrupt a country is perceived to be, the higher the likelihood that an increase in arms imports corresponds to an increase in FDI inflows. This empirical finding may provide a first glimpse at the prevalence of military offsets and kickbacks associated with arms purchases.

---

delivery given the often significant variation in total annual transfers (Wezeman and Wezeman 2014: 1).

To further explore the relationship between arms procurement in corrupt countries and FDI, I have excluded military spending and expanded the model specifications. Table 9.4 presents the results after extending the analysis to control for conflict-related factors, and isolating the relationship between arms imports and net foreign direct investment inflows. The relationship across arms imports and FDI is quite similar to the relationship across military expenditures and FDI. However, there is one key distinction: arms sales appear to more strongly predict FDI the more corrupt the country is perceived to be. In addition to the core set of controls, I also included measures for international organization membership (NATO, GATTWTO), size of government (pwt_gsp), net development aid (wdi_aid), democracy score (fh_polity2), and two measures of political stability (ucdp_count, p_durability).[22] The relationship between the controls and the dependent variable (net FDI inflows) are interesting in their own right and warrant further consideration beyond this chapter. What is perhaps most striking is that the number of conflicts a corrupt state has been involved in since the Cold War (ucdp_count) positively predicts FDI inflows. Also, relative democracy level (fh_polity2) among corrupt and very corrupt states does not seem to make a difference when it comes to attracting FDI. Net development aid flowing into countries corresponds to higher FDI, regardless of corruption level. Most importantly, the inclusion of these controls shows us that the volume of arms transfers corresponds to higher FDI, when holding a multitude of important political and economic factors constant.

5.   CONCLUSION

The findings present us with an empirical puzzle that inspires more questions than answers. How can it be the case that countries such as the Philippines or South Africa, or even the Democratic Republic of Congo, tend to acquire an influx of foreign investment following major military purchases?

An optimistic take on this could be that the offset agreements are making it possible for foreign investors to enter markets that were deemed too risky. In other words, we see that the increase in FDI associated with

---

[22]   These controls were also utilized in (Drezner and Hite-Rubin 2014) as part of additional robustness checks and specifications for testing the relationship across aggregate military spending and FDI. The findings from both analyses discussed in this chapter and the related paper are robust to additional controls and alternative regression estimators.

Table 9.4   Arms imports and FDI

	FULL SAMPLE	Lowest Corruption	Medium Corruption	Highest Corruption
	Model 1	Model 2	Model 3	Model 4
larms_i_	0.0643	−0.0871**	0.181***	0.321***
	0.0417	0.0364	0.0599	0.0617
corr_	0.0288	0.258*	0.029	0.0595
	−0.0713	−0.129	−0.0805	−0.13
lgdp	1.628***	0.920*	2.371***	2.911**
	−0.42	−0.43	−0.716	−1.123
ltpop	2.074*	0.632	1.325	2.273**
	−0.983	−1.293	−0.958	−0.897
bit_	0.0274***	0.0183*	0.0266**	−0.0171
	−0.00449	−0.00907	−0.0121	−0.0134
riskr_	0.0222**	0.0144	0.0124	0.00724
	−0.00932	−0.0137	−0.01	−0.0184
f_debt_gdp_	−0.00545**	0.000561	−0.00754**	−0.00343**
	−0.00197	−0.00338	−0.00313	−0.00149
bb_gdp_	0.0233*	0.0500***	0.00719	−0.0263
	−0.0122	−0.015	−0.0147	−0.0176
lpec	−0.701***	−0.374	−0.388	−0.306
	−0.147	−0.32	−0.297	−0.622
law_o_	0.126**	0.0878	0.115	0.0689
	−0.0506	−0.0788	−0.0687	−0.0736
NATO	0.274*	−0.0779	0.603**	−0.575***
	−0.141	−0.109	−0.249	−0.133
GATTWTO	−0.378**	1.380***	−0.494***	−0.897***
	−0.148	−0.29	−0.156	−0.199
pwt_gsg	0.000345	0.0131**	0.000339	0.000344
	−0.000516	−0.0061	−0.000759	−0.00104
wdi_aid	2.25e-10***	1.75e-10***	2.40e-10***	1.67e-10***
	0	−5.31E-11	−7.07E-11	0
ucdp_count	0.145**	0.0797	0.158***	0.155***
	−0.0557	−0.362	−0.045	−0.0375
fh_polity2	0.0619	0.633***	0.0273	−0.0567
	−0.073	−0.195	−0.0676	−0.0768
p_durable	−0.0028	0.0824**	−0.0223	0.0136
	−0.0131	−0.0279	−0.0189	−0.0218
Constant	−45.80***	−28.81**	−54.88***	−76.93***
	−4.984	−10.97	−7.757	−16.54
Observations	593	143	397	207
Number	61	30	58	43

Notes: Estimation of pooled OLS/WLS and fixed effects (within) regression models with Driscoll and Kraay standard errors. *** $p<0.01$, ** $p<0.05$, * $p<0.1$

arms procurement is higher the more corrupt the state is. The observed bump in FDI inflows could be a function of contract 'bundling', as well as, spill over from opening new streams for foreign investment. Consider for example, a scenario wherein a company such as Pepsi invests in Indonesia as part of the offset package for purchasing fighter jets from Lockheed, an American company. Lockheed distributes some of the expected profits to Pepsi, and all colluding parties profit on both the supplier and purchasing end. The success of this contract inspires other MNCs to invest in Indonesia, and thus FDI further increases.

Unfortunately, the rosy scenario is likely to be incomplete. First, we do not know if the Indonesian government would have bought fighter jets, but for the offset package inducements. Second, it may also be unclear if the winning contract was most beneficial to the Indonesian government and economy, or if there were side payments involved. Finally, even if the sale of major weapons to Indonesia corresponds to a boost in FDI, it is not obvious that this is welfare enhancing. In other words, foreign investment for a 'bridge to nowhere' could register as FDI but actually undermine the host country's development prospects and international profile.

The preceding analysis demonstrates that a robust correlation exists across arms procurement and FDI, while controlling for economic, geopolitical and institutional factors. The finding that arms procurement corresponds to higher FDI, at an increasing rate on the axis of corruption, is critical. The question for future research is *why*? One interpretation is that the purchase of major arms, and associated military offsets, may act a springboard for opening broader foreign investment into corrupt markets. The economic, political and security implications of this cannot be understated.

REFERENCES

Acemoğlu, Daron, and James A. Robinson. 2012. *Why Nations Fail: The Origins of Power, Prosperity, and Poverty*. New York: Crown.

Archer, Colin, and Annette Willi. 2012. 'Opportunity Costs: Military Spending and the UN's Development Agenda'. Geneva: International Peace Bureau. Available 8 May 2015 at http://www.ipb.org/uploads/tbl_noticies_web/169/documents/Opportunity%20Costs_text%20only.pdf.

Auriol, Emmanuelle. 2006. 'Corruption in Procurement and Public Purchase', *International Journal of Industrial Organization* 24(5): 867–85.

Besley, Timothy, and Torsten Persson. 2007. 'The Origins of State Capacity: Property Rights, Taxation, and Politics'. NBER Working Paper, no. 13028, April.

BIS. 2012. 'Offsets in Defense Trade: Sixteenth Study'. Conducted pursuant to section 723 of the Defense Production Act of 1950, as amended (January).

Available 8 May 2015 at https://www.bis.doc.gov/index.php/forms-documents/doc_view/396-offsets-in-defense-trade-sixteenth-study.

BIS. 2013. 'Offsets in Defense Trade: Seventeenth Study'. Conducted pursuant to section 723 of the Defense Production Act of 1950, as amended (February). Available 8 May 2015 at https://www.bis.doc.gov/index.php/forms-documents/doc_view/687-seventeenth-report-to-congress.

Bueno de Mesquita, Bruce, Alistair Smith, Randolph M. Siverson and James D. Morrow. 2003. *The Logic of Political Survival*. Cambridge, MA: MIT Press.

Büthe, Tim and Helen V. Milner. 2008. 'The Politics of Foreign Direct Investment into Developing Countries: Increasing FDI through International Trade Agreements?', *American Journal of Political Science* 2(4): 741–62.

Castro, Conceição, and Pedro Nunes. 2013. 'Does Corruption Inhibit Foreign Direct Investment?', *Política* 51(1): 61–83.

Cole, Shawn and Anh Tran. 2011. 'Evidence from the Firm: A New Approach to Understanding Corruption', in Susan Rose-Ackerman and Tina Søreide (eds) *International Handbook on the Economics of Corruption*, vol 2. Cheltenham, UK, and Northampton, MA, US: Edward Elgar, pp. 408–27.

Corruption Watch. n.d. 'The Arms Deal—What You Need to Know'. Available 8 May 2015 at http://www.corruptionwatch.org.za/content/arms-deal-what-you-need-know.

Cover, Oliver, Tehmina Abbas, Leah Wawro and Anne-Christine Wegener. 2013. *Government Defence Anti-corruption Index 2013*. London: Transparency International UK.

Dreher, Axel and Thomas Herzfeld. 2005. 'The Economic Costs of Corruption: A Survey and New Evidence', Social Science Research Network working paper. Available 8 May 2015 at http://papers.ssrn.com/sol3/papers.cfm?abstract_id=734184.

Drezner, Daniel W. and Nancy Hite-Rubin. 2014. 'Does Military Spending Attract (Corrupt) Foreign Investment? An Empirical Investigation'. Working paper prepared for presentation at the American Political Science Association annual meeting, Washington, DC, August.

Driscoll, John C. and Aart C. Kraay. 1998. 'Consistent Covariance Matrix Estimation with Spatially Dependent Panel Data', *Review of Economics and Statistics* 80(4): 549–60.

Economist Intelligence Unit. 2013. 'The Defence Industry: Guns and Sugar'. *Economist Intelligence Unit* (May 25). Available 8 May 2015 at http://www.economist.com/news/business/21578400-more-governments-are-insisting-weapons-sellers-invest-side-deals-help-them-develop.

Egger, Peter and Hannes Winner. 2005. 'Evidence on Corruption as an Incentive for Foreign Direct Investment', *European Journal of Political Economy* 21: 932–52.

Federation of American Scientists. 1991. 'Literature Review: CRS' Conventional Arms Transfers to the Third World', *Arms Sales Monitor* 6 (August).

Grieve, Chuck. n.d. 'Why It's Good to Switch on to Offsets', *Defence* 53–6. Available 8 May 2015 at http://www.offsets2000.com/wp-content/uploads/2013/07/Offsets-2000-Roger-Bulgin-Defence-Interview.pdf.

Grimmett, Richard E. and Paul K. Kerr. 2012. *Conventional Arms Transfers to Developing Nations, 2004–2011*. US Library of Congress, CSR Report R42678, August 24. Washington, DC: Congressional Research Service.

Gupta, Sanjeev, Luiz de Mello and Raju Sharan. 2001. 'Corruption and Military Spending', *European Journal of Political Economy* 17(4): 749–77.

Habib, Mohsin and Leon Zurawicki. 2002. 'Corruption and Foreign Direct Investment', *Journal of International Business Studies* 33(2): 291–307.

Holtom, Paul, Mark Bromley and Verena Simmel. 2012. 'Measuring International Arms Transfers'. SIPRI Fact Sheet (December). Available 8 May 2015 at http://books.sipri.org/product_info?c_product_id=450.

Hsu, Yuan-Ho. 2008. 'Is Corruption a Grabbing Hand? A Panel Data Study of FDI'. Program for Encouraging Academic Research, National Cheng Kung University, Tainan, Taiwan.

Jensen, Nathan M. 2006. *Nation States and the Multinational Corporation: A Political Economy of Foreign Direct Investment*. Princeton, NJ: Princeton University Press.

Kaufmann, Daniel and Shang-Jin Wei. 1999. 'Does "Grease Money" Speed Up the Wheels of Commerce?' NBER Working Paper 7093. Washington, DC: National Bureau of Economic Research. Available 8 May 2015 at http://www.nber.org/papers/w7093.

Keefer, Philip and Stephen Knack. 1997. 'Why Don't Poor Countries Catch Up: A Cross-national Test of an Institutional Explanation', *Economic Inquiry* 35(3): 590–602.

Kerner, Andrew. 2009. 'Why Should I Believe You? The Costs and Consequences of Bilateral Investment Treaties', *International Studies Quarterly* 53(1): 73–102.

Khaitan, Rajiv. 2013. 'Indian Defence Industry and Defence Offset'. Seminar on Practical Aspects of Doing Business with India, Hotel Herods, Tel Aviv, February 14. Available 8 May 2015 at http://www.indembassy.co.il/admin-part/resimages/68090Indian%20Defence%20Industry%20and%20Defence%20Offset%20-%20Khaitan%20(14%20February%202013).pdf.

Markowski, Stefan, and Peter Hall. 2014. 'Mandated Defence Offsets: Can They Ever Deliver?' *Defense & Security Analysis* 30(2): 148–62.

Mauro, Paolo. 1995. 'Corruption and Growth', *Quarterly Journal of Economics* 110(3): 681–712.

Méon, Pierre-Guillaume and Laurent Weill. 2009. 'Is Corruption an Efficient Grease?', *World Development* 38(3): 244–59.

Muravska, Julia, Mark Pyman and Francisco Vihena da Cunha. 2010. 'Corruption Risks in Defence Offset Contracts' presentation for Global Revolution V Conference. Copenhagen, September 9–10, 2010.

Neumayer, Eric and Laura Spess. 2005. 'Do Bilateral Investment Treaties Increase Foreign Direct Investment to Developing Countries?', *World Development* 33(10): 1567–85.

North, Douglass and Barry Weingast. 1989. 'Constitutions and Commitment: The Evolution of Institutions Governing Public Choice in Seventeenth Century England', *Journal of Economic History* 49(4): 803–32.

Perlo-Freeman, Sam and Carina Solmirano. 2014. 'Trends in World Military Expenditure, 2013'. SIPRI Fact Sheet (April). http://books.sipri.org/files/FS/SIPRIFS1404.pdf.

Piga, Gustavo. 2011. 'A Fighting Chance against Corruption in Public Procurement?', in Susan Rose-Ackerman and Tina Søreide (eds), *International Handbook on the Economics of Corruption*, vol. 2. Cheltenham, UK, and Northampton, MA, USA: Edward Elgar, pp. 141–81.

PRS Group. 2014. *IGRG Methodology*. East Syracuse, NY: PRS Group. Available

8 May 2015 at http://www.prsgroup.com/wp-content/uploads/2014/08/icrg-methodology.pdf.

Schultz, Kenneth and Barry Weingast. 2003. 'The Democratic Advantage: Institutional Foundations of Financial Power in International Competition', *International Organization* 57(1): 3–42.

Taylor, Travis K. 2011. 'Countertrade Offsets in International Procurement: Theory and Evidence', in Murat A. Yülek and Travis K. Taylor (eds), *Designing Public Procurement Policy in Developing Countries: How to Foster Technology Transfer and Industrialization in the Global Economy*. New York, Dordrecht, Heidelberg and London: Springer, pp. 15–34.

Tobin, Jennifer and Susan Rose-Ackerman. 2005. 'Foreign Direct Investment and the Business Environment in Developing Countries: The Impact of Bilateral Investment Treaties'. Yale Law School Center for Law, Economics and Public Policy Research Paper No. 293. Available 8 May 2015 at http://papers.ssrn.com/sol3/papers.cfm?abstract_id=557121.

Tobin, Jennifer and Susan Rose-Ackerman. 2011. 'When BITs Have Some Bite: The Political-Economic Environment for Bilateral Investment Treaties?', *Review of International Organizations* 6(1): 1–32.

Ungaro, Alessandro R. 2013. 'Trends in the Defence Offsets Market'. 17th Annual International Conference on Economics and Security (ICES), SIPRI, Stockholm, 14–15 June. Available 8 May 2015 at http://www.sipri.org/research/armaments/milex/ICES2013/papers/archive/ungaro-trends-in-the-defence-offsets-market.

Vernon, Raymond. 1971. *Sovereignty at Bay*. Boston: Longman.

Wei, Shang-Jin. 2000. 'Local Corruption and Global Capital Flows'. Brookings Papers on Economic Activity 2: 303–46.

Wezeman, Siemon T. and Pieter D. Wezeman. 2014. 'Trends in International Arms Transfers, 2013'. SIPRI Fact Sheet (March). Available 8 May 2015 at http://books.sipri.org/files/FS/SIPRIFS1403.pdf.

Willett, Susan. 2009. 'Defence Expenditures, Arms Procurement and Corruption in Sub-Saharan Africa', *Review of African Political Economy* 36(121): 335–51.

10. Caught in the crossfire: the geography of extortion and police corruption in Mexico*

Alberto Diaz-Cayeros, Beatriz Magaloni and Vidal Romero

El narco está en la sociedad, arraigado como la corrupción.
El Mayo Zambada

1. INTRODUCTION

When Mexican president Felipe Calderón took office in December 2006 he declared a war on the nation's drug traffic organizations (Ríos and Shirk 2011). Violence escalated as criminal organizations became increasingly fragmented and disputed their territories (Killebrew and Bernal 2010; Beittel 2013). The main strategy followed by the federal government involved capturing leaders and lieutenants of criminal organizations (Calderón et al. forthcoming). This seemed to provoke even more violence, by making the competition over territorial control fiercer and providing incentives for many gangs to make extortion and protection fees (*derecho de piso*) an additional source of revenue (Guerrero-Gutiérrez 2011). Given the absence of legal (and peaceful) rules and enforcement mechanisms for competitors in the illegal drug market, disagreements

* Preliminary versions of this chapter were presented at the conference Grand and Petty Corruption in Developing States: Business, Citizens, and the State, Yale University, May 1–2, 2014 and at the V Conferencia Anticorrupción Internacional—CAAI 2014, Lima, Perú, 24 and 25 September 2014. Comments by Paul Lagunes, Natalia Bueno and Susan Rose-Ackerman are gratefully acknowledged. We thank Rafael Giménez and Lorena Becerra from the polling unit of the Mexican Office of the President for collecting the Survey on Public Safety and Governance in Mexico (SPSGM) used in this research. Neither those individuals, nor the institutions they are affiliated to, are responsible for the opinions and analysis contained in this chapter. All errors remain our own.

were usually solved violently. Under the pressure of the crackdown by the federal police, the navy and the army, contracts among criminal gangs were often disrupted, leading to even more violence.[1] Competition over the strategic routes towards the market in the United States was settled by literally eliminating rivals (Dell 2012).

The wide availability of illegal guns crossing from the US border (Dube et al. 2013) turned firearm deaths into the main cause of death among young men in Mexico. Meanwhile, citizens became caught in the crossfire of rival drug cartels and extortion at the hands of criminal gangs. A highly visible example of this was the case of two students in the prestigious private university Tecnológico de Monterrey who were killed in 2010 in the midst of a military attack on suspected members of a criminal gang. The case became particularly controversial due to the excessive use of force by the army and their effort to cover up the case by planting evidence on the students.[2]

During the late 1990s and early 2000s Mexico gradually changed from being a transit territory for drugs heading to the United States market to a place of increasing consumption (Castañeda and Aguilar, 2010). This transformation was partially driven by a change in the way that wholesale drug importers were paying for services; they switched from payments only in cash to payments with part of the same drug they were distributing (Grillo, 2011: 80). The change from a transportation to a retail distribution business implied that drug cartels had to increase the number of personnel. Having a larger full-time workforce, the cartels could now count on small armies of salaried criminals at their disposal.

The perfect complement to this new industrial organization was an easily corruptible police and judicial system at all levels of government. Increasingly fragmented criminal organizations began to diversify their illegal activities—to extortion of small businesses, kidnappings of middle-class individuals, racketeering and control of retail trade in their territories, and extortion of migrant workers—perhaps in association with police departments. Although it is difficult to provide evidence on how much real progress has been made, there is no question that efforts at

---

[1]   Drug traffic organizations in Mexico often work on the basis of subcontracting transit agreements, in which an organization controlling a trade route or specific city (*plaza*) allows other criminal organizations to go through, provided they pay a transit fee. These arrangements became very unstable as federal and joint operations were expanded throughout the country.

[2]   See Amnesty International memorandum AMR 41/070/2010.

reforming the police forces in Mexico face a momentous challenge in such an environment.

Although a new federal police force was created after 2006 and, in principle, all police had to comply with background checks and other administrative procedures, in fact, state and municipal police forces remain not just corrupt but also keep on using excessive force and violating human rights.[3] This became patently clear in the case of the 43 Ayotzinapa missing students, who in October 2014 were detained by the municipal police of the city of Iguala, only to be handed over to the killers employed by a drug traffic organization. The police force of Iguala is not alone in having been penetrated by organized crime and having failed to protect citizens.

This chapter explores the connection between police distrust, corruption and extortion. Despite the difficulty in measuring these phenomena through conventional public opinion polls and citizen or firm level surveys, much can be learned from the variation across geographic units in reported victimization and corruption. We use a list experiment collected through the Survey on Public Safety and Governance in Mexico (SPSGM), to study the practices of extortion by both police forces and criminal organizations.[4] Using a Bayesian spatial estimation method, we provide a mapping of the geographic distribution of police extortion.

Our findings suggest that weak state institutions in vast regions within Mexico have become captured, through corruption, by competing drug traffic organizations. Extortion prevails either because police forces have become agents of criminal organizations or because criminals can engage in racketeering without any police intervention. We conclude with a discussion of the emergence of self-defense groups as a strategy for coping with extortion; a strategy that while effective at protecting citizens, may further undermine state capacity.

The chapter is not a direct test of the effect of police corruption on extortion and criminal violence, but it assembles evidence of how organized crime can prey on citizens with police complicity creating a generalized environment of fear. In some regions in Mexico the state has become so

---

[3]   See a Human Rights Watch Report: *Mexico's Disappeared: The Enduring Cost of a Crisis Ignored.* 20 February 2013. Available 8 May 2015 at http://www. hrw.org/reports/2013/02/20/mexicos-disappeared.

[4]   List experiments provide better measures of the prevalence of extortion, mitigating potential biases emerging from social desirability and citizens fears of truthful revelation of information (Blair and Imai 2012; Bullock et al. 2011; Imai 2011; Glynn 2013).

closely identified with criminal gangs and drug cartels that these criminal organizations do not need to corrupt the state—they essentially 'are' part of the state. Our account by no means provides a full depiction of the relationship between organized crime, police corruption, and state power. But we provide at least some understanding of the way in which citizens can cease to be protected by the state when police forces are corrupt and penetrated by crime; and how fear and citizen distrust can render police action even less effective.

The embeddedness of criminal organizations in everyday life and the failure to provide public safety due to corruption explain why the current state of affairs is so difficult to change. In the words of one of Mexico's most notorious drug traffickers, el Mayo Zambada, to the late journalist Julio Scherer, 'Drug traffickers are in society, deep-rooted like corruption'.[5] Our results are consistent with his view. But they also point to where solutions are more likely to succeed: if the connection between corrupt police forces and criminal organizations is broken, citizens are more likely to report crime and seek out the protection and help of legitimate public forces, rather than turning to self-defense groups and other forms of collective protection from crime and extortion.

The chapter is organized as follows. The next section provides an overview of the fight against drug cartels and organized crime in Mexico. We provide some evidence of the levels of victimization and distrust among both citizens and firms. We complement the analysis with an overview of the territorial variation in citizen perceptions of police corruption at various levels of government. The section is followed by a brief discussion the problem of social desirability bias and the design of list experiments in our survey. We present the stratification of the survey that was meant to ensure coverage in places of high levels of violence, as well as being able to differentiate between situations occurring in urban and rural localities. We then present the results of the list experiments measuring the extent of extortion by both the police and drug traffic organizations. A mapping of the territorial extent of extortion is also estimated. The final section concludes with some reflections on the industrial organization of extortion in Mexico.

---

[5]   *Proceso*, 1744, 6 April 2010, cited in Tajonar (2011), our translation.

2.   ORGANIZED CRIME, VIOLENCE AND POLICE DISTRUST

(a)   Firm Extortion

On 25 and 26 May 2012 a drug trafficking organization called the Knights Templar attacked several facilities of Sabritas, the Mexican subsidiary of Pepsico in the states of Michoacán and Guanajuato. The incident was notorious because it was a visible sign of how emboldened criminal organizations had become in the extortion business. Drug traffic organizations were known to commit killings of their enemies and even innocent bystanders. But by 2012 it was clear that they were involved in human trafficking, extortion and kidnapping in what can only be described as a diversified portfolio of criminal activities. The *Sabritas* incident was unusual in that private corporations in Mexico generally seem to be able to prevent such dramatic displays of force from taking place, most likely by regularly paying protection money in the form of what is usually referred to as '*derecho de piso*'.

The challenge of doing business when organized crime has taken over vast areas of the country is not just that violence may disrupt economic activity (see Robles et al. 2013), but that criminal organizations begin commanding economic activity and collecting 'taxes' from private businesses in the territories they control.[6] The extortion situation gets compounded when police forces and bureaucrats also demand bribes or other payments. Within Mexico the Sabritas arson incident is perhaps the most notorious case of a company caught in a web of extortion. Note that it was not related to typical forms of extortion by, for example, public officials withholding the issuing of permits. Corruption watchers around the world have paid attention to the Walmart bribery case in Mexico because it exhibited a global company in its day-today business practices (Barstow, 2012 and Barstow and von Bertrab, 2012). Mexican public officials were all too eager to extort money from the multinational corporation, while Walmart all too easily provided bribes to expedite the issuing of permits. But it is possible that the most important forms of off-the-book payments made by multinational corporations in Mexico are now in the form of protection fees paid to organized crime.

---

[6]   To give an example from the state of Michoacán, criminal organizations may control both illegal logging and legal lemon production.

Table 10.1 Self-declared victimization and fear rates

	Actual victims	Afraid of being a victim
Kidnapping	1.0	81.8
Kidnapping (express*)	1.3	82.8
Affected by criminals crossfire	3.1	83.4
Car robbery	5.8	68.6
Public transportation assault	7.4	80.6
House robbery	10.1	84.2
Street assault	10.8	83.0
Car accessories robbery	11.2	65.7
Phone extortion	25.7	81.3

Note: Express Kidnapping refers to an all too common practice of detaining individuals for a few hours or overnight in order to get them to withdraw funds from ATMs after midnight.

Source: Survey on Public Safety and Governance in Mexico (2011).

(b) Fear and Victimization

Fear is perhaps the word that best describes Mexicans' current mood. All opinion polls and surveys consistently show similar results.[7] However, the proportion of self-reported victims in Mexico is not especially high by international standards, and has not changed much since the early 2000s (Bailey et al. 2011). Nonetheless most Mexicans fear becoming victims of crime: According to the Survey on Public Safety and Governance in Mexico (SPSGM, discussed in more detail below), collected in 2011, eight out of ten citizens are afraid of suffering various types of crime. A breakdown by specific crimes compared to actual victimization rates is provided in Table 10.1.

Individuals' estimation of their likelihood of becoming a victim seems to be independent of the victimization rate. For instance, citizens are equally afraid of being kidnapped as of being blackmailed over the phone, even though the prevalence of those two incidents is very different: according

---

[7] Guerrero-Gutiérrez (2011) reports the following data coming from surveys: 65 percent of people according to ICESI surveys do not feel safe in the state they inhabit. In a Buendía and Laredo poll from 2011 he reports that 76 percent of the respondents are worried about kidnapping, drug cartel violence and robbery. And he quotes a Consulta Mitofsky polls showing that since January 2010 the most worrisome topics for Mexicans have shifted from the economy to security issues.

to the SPSGM survey, one percent of Mexicans have been kidnapped, and one out of every four has been the victim of extortion over the phone. If we suppose that the 'objective' probability of being victim of a crime is related to the current victimization rate, then, the gap between the actual rate of victimization and the proportion of individuals who are afraid of being a victim could be thought of as the 'subjective' probability of becoming a victim. This large gap suggests that Mexicans feel afraid and vulnerable. Regardless of whether these perceptions match the actual victimization rates closely, the perception-based data is a real depiction of the prevalent climate of fear affecting Mexican society.

(c) Distrust of the Police

This sentiment of fear is most likely fed by the lack of confidence in the work of state and municipal police forces. Mexico is organized as a federal system characterized by concurrent jurisdiction in most issue areas. Security is one of them. Although federal police have exclusive jurisdiction over organized crime, in practice, all police forces are involved in the fight against drug trafficking. From the point of view of citizens' perceptions security is provided by the fused efforts of federal, state and municipal forces. According to the above-mentioned survey, only 25 to 27 percent of citizens evaluate the performance of municipal and state police as 'good'. Citizens feel caught in a crossfire: in addition to fearing criminals, according to the SPSGM survey almost half of the population fears being subject to abuse from municipal or state police. They have no one to ask for protection.

Further evidence on the perception of police forces is presented in Table 10.2, drawing from the two largest national surveys collected by the Mexican national statistical office (Instituto Nacional de Estadistica, Geografia e Informatica, INEGI) reflecting two distinct targets of crime, firms and individual citizens.

These victimization surveys of the business community (ENVE for 2012 and 2014) and the general population (ENVIPE, most recent results for 2014) exhibit a remarkable degree of agreement regarding the corruption of various public safety forces. Local police forces are perceived to be the most corrupt, and the least corruption is presumably found in the military and the navy. Coercive forces from the state governments, including the state attorney (*Ministerio Publico*) are perceived at an intermediate level of corruption, but somewhat closer to local officials than to the federal ones.[8]

---

[8]   The SPSGM survey also asked respondents to judge the corruption of

Table 10.2   Percentage that perceives that (. . .) is corrupt

	Firms 2012	Firms 2014	Citizens 2014
Traffic Police	78.2	73.5	77.3
Municipal Police	70.1	66.2	66.3
Attorney General	66.8	64.6	57.2
Judicial Police (MP)	69.9	64.3	61.6
Judges	62.1	61.6	65.0
State Police	63.8	60.1	61.9
Federal Police	56.8	52.2	52.6
Army	23.1	17.6	20.3
Navy	15.0	13.2	13.7

Source: INEGI, *Encuesta Nacional de Victimización de Empresas* (ENVE) 2014 and *Encuesta Nacional de Victimización y Percepción Sobre Seguridad Pública* (ENVIPE) 2014.

The National Survey on Victimization (ENVIPE) provides subnational evidence of the trust that is inspired by the police in each state.[9] This level of trust varies according to the corporations being evaluated. A simple metric that summarizes citizen assessments of their police forces is the net difference between citizens that trust their police (a lot or some) minus those who distrust the security forces (a lot or some). This net police trust can be either negative or positive depending on whether a majority is on each side of the assessment. In Mexico virtually all levels of trust of police corporations are negative.

Figure 10.1 shows citizens' assessment of local and state police forces. The horizontal axis is the degree of trust in municipal police forces (preventive, not the traffic police); while the vertical one shows the level

---

different law enforcement agents and the army. According to the respondents, municipal police are perceived as the most corrupt, regardless of levels of violence. However, in high violence places, the federal police are perceived to be just as corrupt as the municipal police − 45 and 48 percent evaluate the federal corps and the municipal police respectively as 'very corrupt' in high violence places. In contrast, only between 10 and 16 percent (in low and high violence areas respectively) perceive that the military is very corrupt. The data suggest that despite the fact that the military is not completely trusted by some segments of the population, it is perceived by far as the least corrupt option. The army has a much better evaluation than all other coercive corporations: 68 percent believes that it is doing a good job in protecting citizens according to the SPSGM; but with an important caveat: four out of every ten respondents in that survey feared being abused by the military.

[9]   The sample is large enough and designed to ensure statistical significance at the state level.

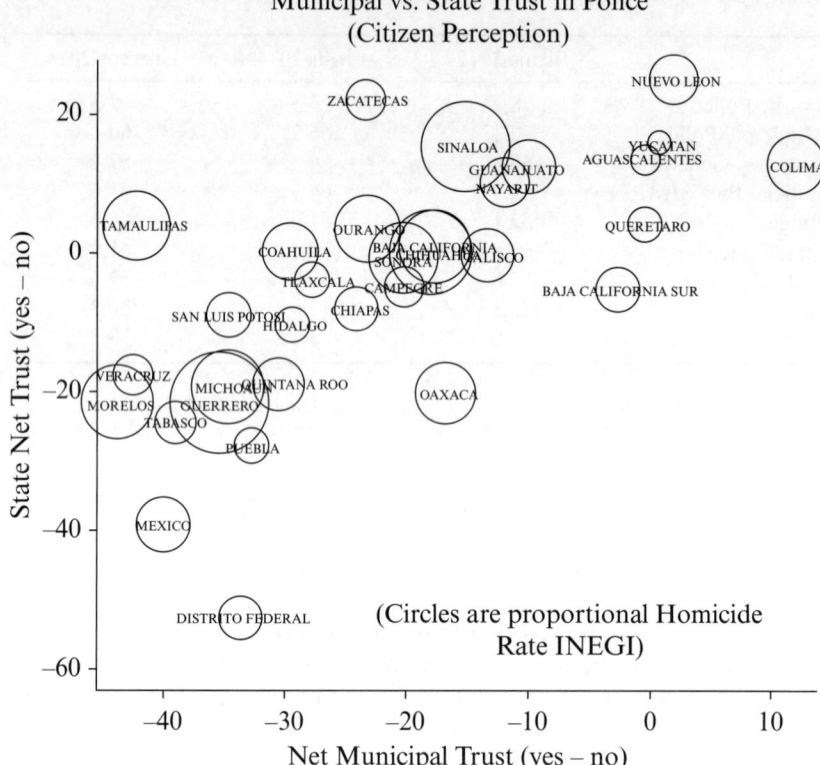

Source: Calculations based on INEGI ENVIPE 2014.

Figure 10.1   Police distrust by state

of trust in the state police. The size of each circle indicates the degree of insecurity in each state, proxied by the murder rate according to the state attorney offices for 2014 (until October) as provided by the Executive Secretariat of the National System of Public Safety.[10]

It is clear that, except for the case of the small state of Colima, in most states a majority believes police are not to be trusted. The worst negative values (denoting distrust) are found in the states of Morelos, Veracruz, Tamaulipas and Mexico state. The distrust is higher for municipal corporations, but it is similar for state police forces, where only slightly

---

[10]   Dataset available 8 May 2015 at http://secretariadoejecutivo.gob.mx/incidencia-delictiva/incidencia-delictiva.php#.

more than a third of the states have positive values. But perhaps the most striking feature in the graph is the almost perfect alignment of citizen perceptions along a diagonal. This indicates that the distrust of each police corporation is highly correlated within each state.

It is possible that citizens may not quite understand under which command within the federal system of government each police force in their state falls, but there are many visible signs that exhibit the differences between corporations: the federal police usually has the best equipment, vehicles and distinctive uniforms; the state police follows in its display of high power firearms, although their uniforms are often worn out and their vehicles somewhat beaten down; while the municipal police are visibly ill-equipped. Citizens can distinguish between these police forces, but they nonetheless believe that when their police forces are not to be trusted at the municipal level, they also have that same perception at the state level.

In order to improve police performance in the country, both the Calderón and Enrique Peña Nieto administrations attempted to eliminate municipal police corporations.[11] But the issue is not that Mexico ought to eliminate its municipal police forces in order to generate a trustworthy police, but rather that it needs to establish why some states have been able to achieve a much higher position along the diagonal line. The largest variation is not between corporations, but among states.

(d)   Drug-related Violence

The war on drug traffic organizations unleashed violence of a new kind in Mexico. Although homicide rates had been declining steadily since the 1990s, the new forms of violence expressed themselves through gruesome killings where criminal organizations were not worried about displaying their behavior in public. In fact, the publicity of their actions was one of the ways in which they successfully instilled fear in and silent complicity from the civilian population.[12] Since the beginning of the drug violence in 2007, Mexican newspapers kept track of the upsurge in violence and provided comprehensive information on the location of deaths. *Reforma* newspaper reports, in particular, have been used by the Trans-Border

---

[11]   See the study prepared by the Chamber of Deputies for the initiative by President Calderón in 2010 (available 8 May 2015 at http://www.diputados.gob. mx/sedia/sia/spi/SPI-ISS-30-10.pdf) and the initiative submitted by President Peña Nieto to the Senate in 2014 available 8 May 2015 at http://embamex.sre.gob.mx/ italia/images/pdf/politicos/reforma-constitucional-policia-unica.pdf.

[12]   On the signalling effects of visible killings see Walter (2009).

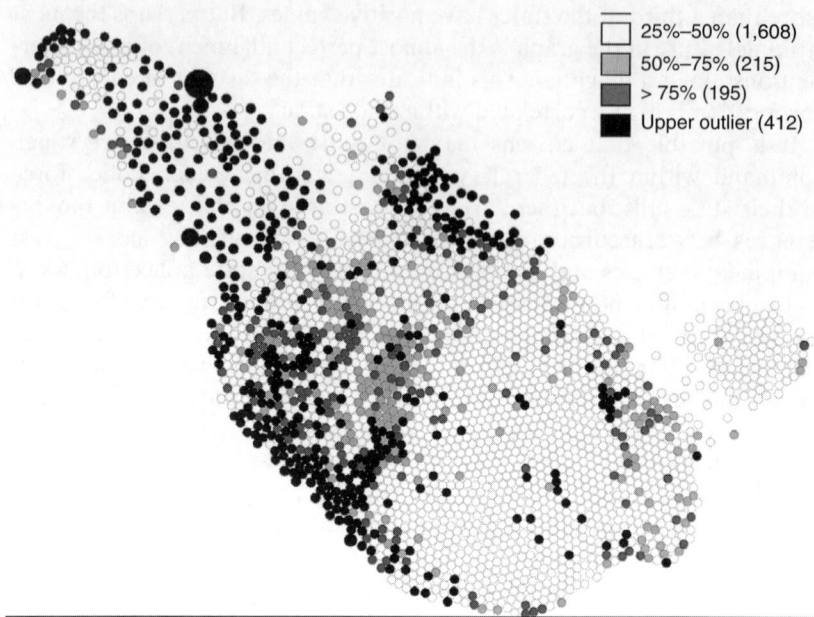

☐	25%–50% (1,608)
▨	50%–75% (215)
▪	> 75% (195)
■	Upper outlier (412)

Source: Own calculations based on Base de Datos de Fallecimientos de Presunta Rivalidad Delincuencial.

Figure 10.2　Cartogram of drug related violence in Mexican municipalities

Institute (TBI), for example, to provide a general overview of state-level trends in violence.[13] In 2011 the federal government released what has become the most analyzed dataset of drug related homicides, within the Sistema Nacional de Seguridad Publica.

Figure 10.2 displays a visualization by means of a cartogram of homicides presumably related to rivalry between criminal organizations, across the Mexican territory, from 2008 to 2011 according to that source.[14] A cartogram is a type of map that depicts municipalities proportionally to their relative size not in terms of land area, but according to the variable of interest, in this case deaths. The cartograms were prepared using the GeoDa software. The dots depict all the municipalities, shaded and sized

---

[13] For a comprehensive discussion of drug related homicide data and trends see the report prepared for the Trans-Border Institute (TBI) by Ríos and Shirk (2011).
[14] The data was downloaded from http://www.cisen.gob.mx/espanol/base-datos-homicidios1.htm (last accessed 8 May 2015).

according to the ranking in drug related violence. The cartogram depicts in grey municipalities where criminal organization murders are registered; but highlights in black those places where the murder rates are particularly high. White dots are the municipalities where drug related murders do not occur. The size of the circle denotes a ranking by number of deaths, where the largest dot in the North corresponds to Ciudad Juárez. Dots for each municipality are placed as close as possible to their geographic coordinates.

Most of the Mexican population is concentrated in the central highlands. Beyond the core areas around Mexico City and Guadalajara, the coastlines and the border region also have large urban concentrations. The North is sparsely populated. In terms of poverty, the vast majority of the poor in Mexico are concentrated in the Southern regions. The cartogram suggests that drug violence deaths have a unique pattern, which is not related to population or poverty, but rather to the entry and exit points of the drug trade and the logistics network for merchandise shipment.[15]

This violence dataset possibly underestimates the true count of drug related deaths. Local newspapers might be more reliable sources than either the *Reforma* newspaper or this count; and the SNSP data may be biased downwards because it privileges counting deaths resulting from clashes between drug trafficking organizations.[16] The dataset does not include clandestine graves which might also contribute to under-counting. But the data do reflect the overall spatial pattern of violence related to drug trafficking. The vast majority of Mexican municipalities do not have drug violence. The phenomenon is concentrated in the Northeast, the border regions, and some of the corridors running from the port of Lázaro Cárdenas on the Pacific Coast and along the Gulf of Mexico.

3.   THE GEOGRAPHY OF EXTORTION

(a)   Motivation for List Experiments

Elsewhere (Magaloni, et al. 2014) we have shown that fear and intimidation may generate tacit support for criminal organizations. In that paper we explore the ways in which Drug Traffic Organizations (DTOs) are present in society. These criminal organizations may not only provide

---

[15]   See Guerrero-Gutiérrez (2011) and Dell (forthcoming).
[16]   We thank Guillermo Trejo for this insight.

employment (Ríos, 2009), but also insure against hard times and provide public goods. Although we are unable to gauge the relative frequency with which *Narcotraficantes* (*narcos*, for short) may fix the local church or provide money for public services in small towns, some insight comes from the willingness of citizens to seek out their help, which is one of the issues we explore in that paper. We also explored how much citizens reported being extorted by *narcos*, and compared this extortion with the protection payment demands made by the police. In that research we assessed how *narcos* often operated unhindered across the Mexican territory. In short, we explored the presence of DTOs in society and the degree to which criminal organizations have become an integral part of Mexican society. Social integration includes both actions that intimidate citizens—like extortion or kidnapping—as well as actions that somehow assist citizens—such as lending money or providing protection from other DTOs. The greatest challenge in this research was to obtain truthful answers regarding questions that may be difficult to answer.

How best to elicit truthful responses from citizens when there are good reasons for them to lie because of fear or social desirability biases? Eliciting truthful responses from citizens for behavior that is not socially acceptable, or where there is a social norm of 'proper' behavior, is a challenge that has been faced in many contexts. List experiments are a device of indirect questioning in which sensitive issues can be mixed in with innocuous questions in order to protect respondents' answers. Respondents need not admit to any specific behavior. Instead, they consider a list and simply report how many items on the list they have done. The approach is called an experiment because the lists are randomized across respondents. A control group receives no sensitive items. The treatment group receives the innocuous items plus the treatment. If randomization has succeeded, the differences in responses can be used as a proxy for the sensitive behavior, such as bribing a policeman.[17]

In the questionnaire of the SPSGM we embedded list experiments seeking to understand the prevalence of DTOs activity in Mexico. Individuals were randomly selected to create control and treatment groups. Since the selection of the individuals in the sample was done randomly, there is no reason to suspect bias in the sub-samples in every group.[18] The lists were directly read by the interviewee from cards given

---

[17] For a discussion of methodological issues in list experiments see Blair and Imai (2011) and Glynn (2013).

[18] There were three different types of questionnaires. Balance tests were performed to check whether the compliance with randomization was achieved. All baseline sociodemographic variables were balanced between groups.

Table 10.3 List experiment item design

Introduction	Please tell me how many of these things you have done in the past 6 months. We just want to know how many you have done, do not tell me which.
Control Group (n=900) 3 ITEMS	• I have received benefits from the Oportunidades program • I have participated in a tanda* • I gave charity (*limosna*) in church or the street
EXPERIMENT 1 Treatment Group (n=900) 4 ITEMS	• I have received benefits from the Oportunidades program • I have participated in a tanda • **I have given money to the police so that they protect me** • I gave charity (*limosna*) in church or the street
Control Group (n=900) 3 ITEMS	• I got drunk in a party I went to • I did some exercise outdoors • I attended church almost every Sunday
EXPERIMENT 2 Treatment Group (n=900) 4 ITEMS	• I got drunk in a party I went to • I did some exercise outdoors • **I have given money to drug or criminal organizations so that they do not harm me** • I attended church almost every Sunday

Note: The treatment item is NOT bold in the actual experiment. Here it is emphasized to highlight the experimental intervention. Respondents are randomly assigned to a flashcard of EITHER the control or the experimental treatment.
* Tanda is a rotating savings and credit informal association.

Source: Survey on Public Safety and Governance in Mexico (2011).

by the interviewer. Each interviewee received a total of three different cards. Table 10.3 describes the exact wording, and the cards that were given to the experimental group. The control group received all items listed in the first row. The treatment groups also received those items, plus the additional sensitive events of extortion from either the police or the *narcos*.

(b) Survey Sample

The SPSGM survey was made up of 2,700 face-to-face interviews with adults aged 18 or older interviewed at their homes. A two-stage stratified sampling method was used on the basis of federal electoral precincts, as defined by the Federal Electoral Institute (IFE) in the last update of the voter registration (2010). The sample frame excluded the state of Tamaulipas, that was deemed unsafe for the enumerators. City, town or

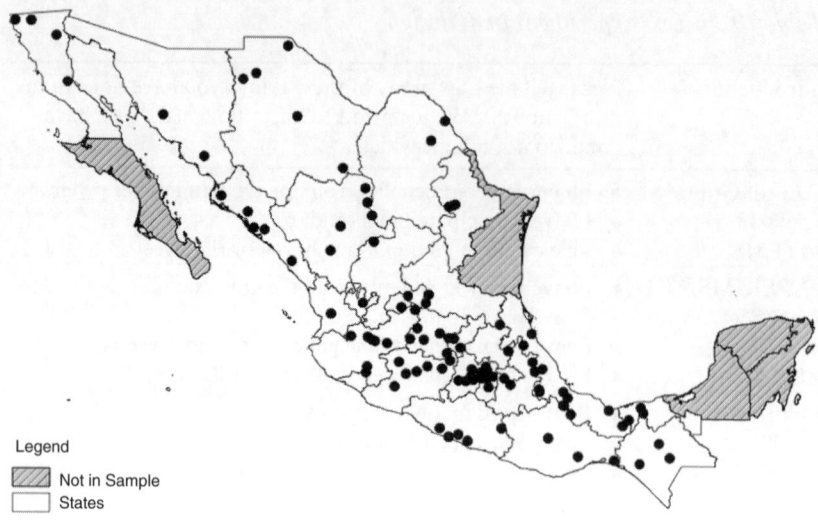

Legend

Not in Sample
States

Source: Survey on Public Safety and Governance in Mexico (2011).

Figure 10.3   Sample polling points

village blocks in each electoral section were chosen randomly starting from the address of the polling booth, selecting at random three homes in each block. Rejection rates were tallied by the enumerators. An adjustment of quotas was made to reflect the population by age and gender, according to official census data. The margin of error for the full sample is 1.89 percent at the 95 percent confidence interval. Figure 10.3 indicates the locations of the surveyed polling places.

The team collecting the survey was trained to understand how to ask the questions related to the list experiments. Questionnaires were randomized by polling point and enumerator, and lists were handed in to respondents as cards, so respondents could read them by themselves. The mechanics of handling cards and questionnaires were pretested before the survey. Several sensitive and control items in the lists were pretested in a nationally representative survey two weeks before the collection of the dataset. The survey was collected from 9 to 17 July 2011.

The SNSP dataset of drug-related violence was used to construct three strata of municipalities according to their levels of violence in the first semester of 2011. The high violence strata is made up of the municipalities where drug-related violence has been pervasive, with more than 75 drug-related murders per year. The medium violence strata has had between 3 and 75 murders per year; while the low violence strata, where most of the municipalities in the country lie, had less than 3 drug-related murders per year since December 2007. The states of Baja California Sur, Campeche, Yucatán and Quintana Roo ended up with no sample points, due to their relative small size and because the stratification caused their municipalities to fall in the low violence stratum.

The sample is also stratified by the size of the locality, because we wanted to know whether rural areas in high violence locations have a different pattern of interaction with DTOs than urban locations. The population stratification is done on the basis of the Federal Electoral Institute (IFE) distinction between urban electoral precincts and rural (plus semi-urban) ones. All the high violence polling points fell in only four municipalities: Chihuahua, Juarez, Durango and Acapulco. But it is important to note that half of those points fall in rural locations outside of the main urban conglomeration. Hence the survey has a small component of non-violent locations, and an oversampling of violent places.

(c) Social Desirability Bias

The list experiments provide insight into the prevalence of drug related activities, extortion and citizen responses to them. Table 10.4 shows the difference in means between the treated and the control groups in our lists. A sizable 10 percent report being extorted by criminal organizations. The extortion rate is close to the one observed in the list experiment for police shakedowns, which is 11 percent. This is a rather disturbing figure, but it seems consistent with the daily life of many Mexicans.

The stratification in the sample allows for a breakdown of the responses to the treatments in the list experiments according to the level of violence in the municipality and the urban or non-urban character of the specific sampling point. Hence, we can gain some understanding about when criminal organizations are more likely to practice extortion vis-à-vis police forces.

Table 10.5 reveals the patterns regarding citizen extortion by DTOs and

Table 10.4   Average treatment on the treated (test of means)

Treatment	Average Effect	Standard Error
DTO Extortion	0.10	(0.04) ***
Police Extortion	0.11	(0.04) ***

Source: Survey on Public Safety and Governance in Mexico (2011).

Table 10.5   Extortion by police and narcos treatment

Level of Violence	Police Extortion		Narcos Extortion	
	Urban	Non-urban	Urban	Non-urban
High	0.11 (0.09)	0.19 (0.09)**	0.23 (0.09)***	0.22 (0.10)**
Medium	0.08 (0.09)	0.00 (0.10)	0.01 (0.08)	0.15 (0.09)*
Low	0.17 (0.09)**	0.09 (0.09)	0.12 (0.09)	0.16 (0.10)

Source: Survey on Public Safety and Governance in Mexico (2011).

the police. *Narcos* extortion seems to be more prevalent in high violence places (more than 20 percent), both urban and non-urban, and police extortion occurs in both high violence non-urban places (19 percent) and low violence urban places (17 percent). The results thus indicate that *narcos* prey on citizens more where violence is high. However, in low violence places the police prey on citizens.

The extent to which both sides prey on ordinary citizens, asking them for money in exchange for protection, is somewhat limited. Although *narcos* extort citizens the most in high violence regions and the police in low violence ones, an important question that emerges is whether police forces may be extorting on behalf of criminal organizations. The generalized practice of extortion allows drug gangs to signal unambiguously that they are in control and will punish anyone who opposes them, while the police cannot credibly signal that they can regain control of the streets because they are often part of the extortion problem. In low violence regions it is possible that criminal organizations have successfully established a monopoly in their activity, so that police forces perform some of their coercive functions for them.

Table 10.6 disaggregates extortion by four occupation groups: 'informal/self-employed', 'private' and 'public' sectors, and 'housewives'. According to the survey results, criminal organizations prey mostly on people in

Table 10.6   Extortion by occupation

	Informal/ Self-employed	Private Sector	Public Sector	Housewife
Extorted by *Narcos*	.10	.16**	.28**	.08*
Extorted by the Police	.22***	.08	.17	.08*

Source: Survey on Public Safety and Governance in Mexico (2011).

the public sector, followed by private sector workers and housewives. By contrast, the police prey mostly on the informal/self-employed sector, although they also target housewives.

(d) Territoriality of Police Extortion

It is possible to reconstruct the geography of DTO activity across the Mexican territory making use of advances in geostatistics. In particular, we construct, on the basis of the spatial distribution of polling points in our survey, spatially smoothed surfaces that provide a glimpse at the most likely parts of the country where the embeddedness of drug activity is more prevalent.

The mapping exercise is similar to geospatial public health applications or geo-mining, seeking to leverage the spatial character of the data to generate smooth prevalence rates. In this case we seek to provide a smooth difference of means between the treated and the control groups in the experiments we conducted throughout Mexico. In order to do this we proceed in two steps. First, we use spatial proximity of contiguous data to create groups of individuals, calculating the average treatment effect of the list experiment.[19] We weight individuals using a Bayesian model.

Following Anselin et al. (2006) we assume that the prior distribution is characterized by mean θ and variance φ. The Bayesian estimate for the difference of means is the weighted average of the raw difference of means, di, and the prior, with weights inversely related to the variance. The difference of means in our survey can be calculated as:

$$di = ((\sum_t iLi - \sum_c iLi)/Pi) \tag{1}$$

where Li is the sum of the items in the list experiment, for either the treated t or the control c groups; i is a specific location of a polling point and P is the total number of treated and control individuals in that survey point.

A standard empirical Bayesian estimator δi is known to be:

---

[19]   The difference in means was calculated through an empirical Bayes estimator with an n of at least 42. In the most rural, sparsely populated polling points, we collected nine questionnaires, of which one-third were randomly assigned to each of the treatment groups. Therefore, with 6 polling points * 3 treated individuals (plus 6 polling points * 3 control), in addition to the 6 observations from the polling point itself, the mean calculated at any point has at least 42 observations.

$$\delta i = \omega i d i + (1 - \omega i)\theta \tag{2}$$

where:

$$\omega i = \varphi/[\varphi + (\theta/P i)] \tag{3}$$

This means that when the population is large in the given polling point, most of the weight goes to the raw estimate of the difference in means. This Bayesian approach is *empirical* because the priors are taken from the distribution of the data in the neighborhood of the point (that is, the six closest polling locations). We calculated these rates for each polling point using GeoDA. The results are obviously sensitive to the choice of the reference region. In general, this approach means that for our survey, in densely populated areas of Central Mexico, the contiguous locations are within a 50 km radius, arguably close enough to think of them as regionally contiguous.

The second step which is meant to improve the visualization consists of generating a smooth interpolated difference in the unknown territory. We used the simplest interpolation technique, which is an Inverse Distance Weighted (IDW) method implemented through ArcGIS. Thus, we can think of this as a moving window that calculates the mean difference between treatment and control, already smoothed spatially in each data point, but that takes into account the distance as a discounting factor, so that far away observations take a lower weight.

Figure 10.4 displays the spatial distribution of police extortion as estimated with our spatial smoothing method. The highest prevalence rates are observed in Southern Mexico, specifically in the state of Chiapas and Tabasco, and in a region bordering Michoacán and the Estado de México. Surprisingly, in the Northern regions with large DTO violence and presence, our method indicates that there is a very low prevalence of police extortion.

Our findings suggest that—even though it may be necessary in the short-run given the absence of trustworthy police forces—public strategies emphasizing military action are not likely to affect the social embeddedness that protects drug gangs and criminal organizations. This is particularly true because the Mexican state cannot count on police forces that can offer an alternative over the *narcos* to ordinary citizens. The police lack citizen trust within communities because they engage in behavior similar to that of the drug gangs.

Furthermore, our list experiments demonstrate that the police prey on the most uneducated citizens. This is quite consistent with the findings of the creative experimental study of corruption in Mexico by Fried et al.

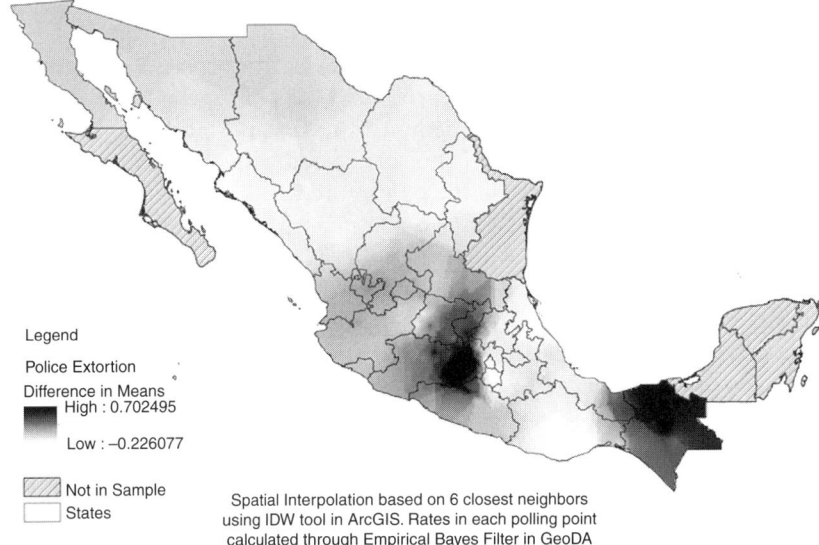

Legend

Police Extortion
Difference in Means
High : 0.702495

Low : −0.226077

Not in Sample
States

Spatial Interpolation based on 6 closest neighbors
using IDW tool in ArcGIS. Rates in each polling point
calculated through Empirical Bayes Filter in GeoDA

Source: Own calculations using data from the Survey on Public Safety and Governance in Mexico (2011).

Figure 10.4   The territorial extent of police extortion

(2010), which demonstrates that bribery and extortion by traffic policemen is mediated by socioeconomic status. Richer offenders of traffic violations are more likely to get away with breaking the law while officers are more likely to prey on less well-to-do drivers, probably because officials do not fear any retaliatory response or defensive measures from the poor. Finally, linking the results with those presented in the previous section, our lists show that the states where the police were perceived to be the most corrupt are places where they are more likely to extort citizens.

As long as law enforcement agents are perceived as incapable and unwilling to protect their citizens because of corruption, citizens are likely to continue to live in fear and tacitly protect the *narcos*. A strategy for sustainable peace in the long-run requires strengthening the social fabric by enhancing citizens' trust within communities and upgrading the reputation of police forces while improving the adjudication of justice.

4. CONCLUSIONS

This chapter has shown that citizens in Mexico are trapped in between two illegitimate forces—the drug cartels and the police who are in charge of protecting them. Our results demonstrate that the problem of extortion cannot be understood if it is not connected with the corruption and distrust that citizens perceive in the police forces.

The organization of extortion is a complex challenge for both participants and a government seeking to fight it. The issue can be understood in the context of a principal-agent framework. From the point of view of Mexican Drug Traffic Organizations, their core economic activity is logistics, namely moving drugs from the sites of production or the entry ports towards the US border. DTOs have a comparative advantage in the use of force, particularly when competition has pushed them towards a militarization of their organizations. This comparative advantage in using violence in a coherent and synchronized manner may be eroded when the federal government decapitates a criminal organization, but that does not reduce the comparative advantage of gangs and smaller criminal groups acting in local environments.

The investment of criminal organizations in violence potential can tempt them to use those inputs for other illegal activities, such as human trafficking, extortion or kidnapping. This temptation will be tempered by the risk that diversification may undermine the core competence of DTOs which is primarily in the control of territories for the shipment and transport of illegal merchandise. The alternative for DTOs, like any business firm, is to hire out the services of specialists in violence, particularly if these specialists can provide a reliable and credible use of force when required. The most obvious supplier of violence is a corrupt police force. This does not mean that all police forces will be penetrated by criminal organizations, but they are the most natural organizations that may provide violent services. The DTOs will compare the net benefits of hiring police forces to the costs and benefits of providing coercive resources internally to their organization. The greatest challenge for a criminal organization is that any external contracting process generates a principal-agent problem. The police forces may work for them, but they could also be co-opted by a competing organization or even start enforcing the laws or the federal strategy against DTOs. This means that the enforcement of extortion contract for criminal activity is in its own nature quite unstable. That very instability could lead to an escalation of violence or more optimistically, could be an opening for the reform of the system of law enforcement and domestic security.

Some changes are already apparent, but they come from an unexpected source. In the last few years Mexico has witnessed the emergence of self-defense groups that are providing public safety. These self-defense groups substitute the police and directly face criminal organizations. In many indigenous regions with traditional communitarian arrangements, the self-defense groups have become an effective police and violence has been curbed. In other settings, self-defense groups might evolve in ways similar to Colombia, becoming paramilitary organizations or private militias. And in still other regions state and local governments are collaborating and incorporating these organizations to their efforts in policing. But none of these emerging organizations will be able to substitute the fact that, in the end, Mexico needs to reform its state, municipal and federal police forces so that they may be trusted by citizens and actually defend them from criminals, while ensuring their respect for human rights and due process.

REFERENCES

Anselin, Luc, Ibnu Syabri and Youngihn Kho. 2006. 'GeoDa: an introduction to spatial data analysis', *Geographical Analysis* 38(1): 5–22.

Bailey, John; Paras, Pablo and Vargas Dinorah. 2011. 'Army as Police? Correlates of Public Confidence in the Police, Justice System, and the Military: Mexico in Comparative Context'. Available 8 May 2015 at http://pdba.georgetown.edu/Security/referencematerials/LAPOPCIDE.pdf.

Barstow, David. 2012. 'Wal-Mart Hushed up a Vast Mexican Bribery Case', *The New York Times* 21 April, sec. Business.

Barstow, David, and Alejandra Xanic von Bertrab. 2012. 'How Wal-Mart Used Payoffs to Get Its Way in Mexico', *The New York Times* 17 December, sec. Business.

Beittel, June S. 2013. 'Mexico's Drug Trafficking Organizations: Source and Scope of the Violence'. United States Congressional Research Service, 7-5700.

Blair, Graeme and Kosuke Imai. 2012. 'Statistical Analysis of List Experiments', *Political Analysis* 20(1): 47–77.

Bullock, Will, Kosuke Imai and Jacob N. Shapiro. 2011. Measuring Political Support and Issue Ownership using Endorsement Experiments, with Applications to Militant Groups in Pakistan. Available 8 May 2015 at http://polmeth.wustl.edu/media/Paper/support.pdf.

Calderón, Gabriela, Gustavo Robles, Beatriz Magaloni and Alberto Diaz-Cayeros. Forthcoming. 'The Beheading of Criminal Organizations and the Dynamics of Violence in Mexico's Drug War'. *Journal of Conflict Resolution*.

Castañeda, Jorge and Rubén Aguilar. 2010. *El Narco: La Guerra Fallida*. Mexico: Punto de Lectura.

Dell, Melissa. Forthcoming. 'Trafficking Networks and the Mexican Drug War', *American Economic Review*.

Dube, Arindrajit, Oeindrila Dube and Omar García-Ponce. 2013. 'Cross-border

Spillover: US Gun Laws and Violence in Mexico', *American Political Science Review* 107(3): 397–417.

Fried, Brian, Paul Lagunes and Atheendar Venkataramani. 2010. 'Inequality and Corruption at the Crossroads: A Multi-Method Study of Bribery and Discrimination in Latin America', *Latin American Research Review* 45(1): 76–97.

Glynn, Adam N. 2013. 'What can we Learn with Statistical Truth Serum? Design and Analysis of the List Experiment', *Public Opinion Quarterly* 77(S1): 159–72.

Grillo, Ioan (2011). *El Narco: the Bloody Rise of Mexican Drug Cartels*. London: Bloomsbury Publishing.

Guerrero-Gutiérrez, Eduardo. 2011, October. 'Security, Drugs, and Violence in Mexico: A Survey'. In 7th North American Forum, Washington DC.

Imai, Kosuke. 2011. 'Multivariate Regression Analysis for the Item Count Technique', *Journal of the American Statistical Association* 106(494): 407–16.

INEGI, Instituto Nacional de Estadistica, Geografia e Informatica. 2014. Encuesta Nacional de Victimización de Empresas (ENVE). Aguascalientes: INEGI.

INEGI, Instituto Nacional de Estadistica, Geografia e Informatica. 2014. Encuesta Nacional de Victimización y Percepción Sobre Seguridad Publica (ENVIPE). Aguascalientes: INEGI.

Killebrew, Bob, and Jennifer Bernal. 2010. 'Crime Wars: Crimes, Cartels and US National Security'. Center for New American Security. Available 8 May 2015 at http://www.cnas.org/files/documents/publications/CNAS_CrimeWars_KillebrewBernal.pdf.

Magaloni, Beatriz, Aila M. Matanock, Vidal Romero and Alberto Díaz-Cayeros. 2014. 'Living in Fear: The Dynamics of Extortion in Mexico's Criminal Insurgency'. Typescript, Stanford University.

Presidencia de la República. 2011. *Survey on Public Safety and Governance in Mexico* (SPSGM). Mexico.

Ríos, Viridiana. 2009. 'To Be or not To Be a Drug Trafficker: Modeling Criminal Occupational Choices'. Paper presented at the Midwest Political Science Association Meeting. Available 8 May 2015 at http://www.gov.harvard.edu/files/Rios_MPSA2010_TobeOrNotToBe.pdf.

Ríos, Viridiana and David Shirk. 2011. *Drug Violence in Mexico: Data and Analysis through 2010*. San Diego: Trans Border Institute.

Robles, Gustavo, Gabriela Calderón and Beatriz Magaloni. 2013. 'Las Consecuencias Económicas de la Violencia del Narcotráfico en México'. Documento de trabajo del BID # IDB-WP-426. Washington: Interamerican Development Bank.

Sistema Nacional de Seguridad Pública. 2012. Base de Datos de Fallecimientos de Presunta Rivalidad Delincuencial. Available 8 May 2015 at http://calderon.presidencia.gob.mx/base-de-datos-de-fallecimientos/

Tajonar, Héctor. 2011. 'La máscara y el botín. obstáculos para la consolidación democrática en México'. Typescript, Center for US Mexican Studies.

Walter, Barbara. 2009. *Reputation and Civil War: Why Separatist Conflicts Are So Violent*. Cambridge: Cambridge University Press.

PART III

Controlling corruption across international borders

11. Bribing abroad

Dimitris Batzilis[1]

The prevalence of corruption varies widely across countries, and the causes of this variation have been the subject of extensive research. Corruption has been connected to a variety of institutional and cultural factors that are usually difficult to disentangle. To isolate the cultural component of corruption, researchers have provided evidence that cultural norms persist even when individuals, or their families, move to a society with different formal institutions. Fisman and Miguel (2007) find that UN diplomats from more corrupt countries were more likely to take advantage of their diplomatic immunity, and leave parking tickets unpaid in the city of New York. Barr and Serra (2010) find that international college students' willingness to bribe when playing a game in a lab setting depends on the level of corruption at their home country, while Cameron et al. (2009) find mixed results. Simpser (2013) documents that individuals whose ancestors came to the United States from high corruption countries are less likely to consider it 'wrong for a public official to solicit bribes in return for a service'.[2]

Similarly, the evidence suggests that companies from corrupt countries tend to bribe more often even when they operate abroad. The major source of information on the behavior of firms that invest or trade abroad is the Bribe Payers Index (Transparency International, 1999–2011), which is based on local businessmen's evaluation of the corporate conduct of foreign firms in their country. The Index summarizes the propensity of

---

[1] I would like to thank Transparency International for providing the Bribe Payers Index survey data, and seminar participants at the Conference on Grand and Petty Corruption in Developing States at Yale and the Political Economy Lunch at the University of Chicago for their comments.
[2] Social capital in general survives changes in the institutional environment. Algan and Cahuc (2010) provide evidence that trust tends to persist for generations after immigration. Bloom et al (2012) find that companies from countries where individuals trust each other tend to have a more decentralized structure. The same holds for multinationals' subsidiaries when there is strong bilateral trust between the origin (headquarters) and destination (subsidiary) countries.

firms to bribe in international transactions by country of headquarters, and it is highly correlated with the Corruption Perceptions Index. This fact has been highlighted in Transparency International's reports, and it is reproduced in Figure 11A.1 in the Appendix.

However, the correlation between corruption in the home country and the propensity of firms to bribe abroad does not necessarily provide evidence for the persistence of cultural norms. Formal institutions in the country of origin can also influence the behavior of companies when they do business abroad, because many countries prohibit companies headquartered within their borders from bribing *foreign* public officials in *foreign* territory. The US Congress passed the first such law, the Foreign Corrupt Practices Act (1977), in response to scandals that involved US-based companies bribing foreign officials.[3] The Act prohibits 'U.S. persons and businesses ... U.S. and foreign public companies listed on stock exchanges in the United States ... and certain foreign persons and businesses acting while in the territory of the United States ... from making corrupt payments to foreign officials to obtain or retain business' (DoJ's guide to FCPA). Getting caught for bribing abroad is rather costly: Karpoff et al (2012) find that the day after the announcement that a firm is prosecuted for foreign bribery, its stock value falls by 3.11 percent. In perhaps one of the most prominent cases of FCPA violations, Siemens was fined USD 450 million for bribes paid by its subsidiaries in Argentina, Venezuela, and Bangladesh.

Several other countries, including OECD members, have recently adopted foreign bribery laws. As of 2013, 40 countries have signed the Convention on Combating Bribery of Foreign Public Officials in International Business Transactions of 1997, more commonly known as the OECD Anti-Bribery Convention. The members of the treaty have agreed to treat foreign bribery as an offense. Furthermore, the signatories are required to extradite offenders, and provide legal assistance to each other. Considering that until the mid-1990s many countries accepted foreign bribes as deductible expenses (Moran 2006), this is significant progress. But, problems remain, as the enforcement of the conventions is left to the national governments, and it is often lacking (Heimman and Dell 2012).[4]

---

[3]   An example of such a scandal that attracted a lot of attention is the aptly named 'Bananagate' scandal, where Chiquita bribed the Honduran dictator in 1975 to lower the tariff on banana exports. The FCPA was further amended in 1998 by the International Anti-Bribery Act.

[4]   Other international conventions that have attempted to tackle foreign bribery are the United Nations Convention Against Corruption of 2003, the

The evidence on the effect of foreign bribery laws on corporate conduct is mixed. Using the Bribe Payers Index, Baughn et al. (2010) find that companies from countries that are part of the OECD Anti-Bribery Convention are less likely to engage in corruption while doing business abroad. On the other hand, Hellman et al. (2002) use bribery data based on self-reports and find that prohibiting foreign bribery had no effect on firms' behavior.

The shortcoming of the above evidence is that the results can be at least partially driven by selection. To the extent that companies head-quartered in corrupt countries prefer to play by the rules they know, they may be more likely to trade, invest, or compete for public contracts in other corrupt countries. Indeed, there is ample empirical evidence that institutional distance reduces foreign direct investment (FDI) (Habib and Zurawicki 2002; Cuervo-Cazurra 2006; Benassy-Quere et al. 2007; Ledyaeva et al. 2013) and trade flows (Linders et al. 2005). Cultural differences also affect the companies' choice of entry (Kogut and Singh 1988) and organization (Bloom et al. 2012). Laws against foreign bribery can affect the location choice of investment as well. Hines (1995) finds that after the Foreign Corrupt Practices Act was passed, there was a reduction in the economic activity of US companies in more corrupt countries. This is not surprising: from the first moment, the FCPA raised concerns that US companies would lose competitiveness abroad (Krever 2007), because at the time no other sovereign constrained its companies and citizens with similar laws. Cuervo-Cazzura (2006) also finds that signing the OECD Anti-Bribery Convention led to lower investment flows from the signatories towards corrupt countries. D'Souza (2010) finds a similar effect of the Convention on trade.

Because the quantity of economic interaction between two countries determines if and how many respondents from the destination country give an opinion on the behavior of firms from the origin country, the selection channel can be important in explaining the correlation between corruption at home and the Bribe Payers Index. That is, firms from corrupt countries may appear to be bribing more when they go abroad only because they invest in more corrupt countries, and not because they bribe more than firms from low corruption countries when they are working under the same set of host-country institutions. Similarly, firms from countries that prohibit foreign bribery may appear to bribe less only because they invest in less corrupt countries.

Inter-American Convention Against Corruption of 1996, and the African Union Convention on Preventing and Combating Corruption of 2003.

Using the full micro data from the Bribe Payers Index surveys allows me to eliminate any bias caused by selection on the observables by controlling for variables that describe corruption and levels of development at both nodes of each origin-destination country pair. Furthermore, I control for variables that measure cultural distance and historical ties, because they could have an effect both on the quantity of economic interaction and on the propensity to bribe.[5] Furthermore, by using the full survey data, I can look into a variety of different types of corrupt activities, and perform a set of robustness tests that would be impossible to do using only the aggregate index.

I find that firms headquartered in high corruption countries are more likely to bribe foreign public officials, compared to firms from low corruption countries, even when they operate in equally corrupt destination countries. The level of corruption in the country where firms trade, invest, or bid for public procurement contracts is also associated with more bribery. The corruption level of the origin country tends to matter less in high corruption destinations, suggesting that even companies from low corruption countries are somewhat forced to play according to the rules of the game in corrupt countries. Perhaps counterintuitively, speaking a common language does not appear to facilitate bribery. Concerning the effect of historical ties, bribe frequency is higher in pairs of countries that once used to be part of the same entity, but not in pairs of countries that have had a colonial relationship.

Companies from countries that are part of the OECD Anti-Bribery Convention bribe less when they do business abroad. However, this is likely to be a spurious result as the apparent effect is the same for types of corruption that fall within the scope of foreign bribery laws and types that are not. This suggests that the foreign bribery law variable probably picks up some unobserved aspect and not the effect of the Convention itself. Looking at the effect of foreign bribery laws using the full set of countries that prohibit foreign bribery, whether they are part of the Convention or not, I find no association between the laws and corporate conduct. The effect of corruption in the country of a firm's headquarters on foreign bribery remains the same after controlling for the presence of foreign bribery laws, and it is the same for all different types of corruption as well.

Because the difference in the behavior of firms cannot be attributed to the different formal institutions (foreign bribery laws) of their home

---

[5]   Another possibility is that the results are biased due to selection on unobservables. Using the Heckman correction procedure (Heckman 1979), though, gives identical results.

countries, only cultural differences could rationalize my findings. Firms are owned and run by people, whose values (or lack of) could shape the way they behave. Investors from countries where bribery is common might simply find it more acceptable to offer a gift to a foreign public official or politician in exchange for a contract or some other favor. Investors from high corruption countries may also be better at bribing, as they have acquired skills that allow them to navigate the institutional environment of their home countries. For example, construction companies in high corruption countries need to develop relations with politicians and parties to win public procurement contracts, while their colleagues in low corruption countries need to minimize costs and to place the lowest bid. To the extent that such 'corruption skills' are transferrable, a company from a high corruption country will be more likely to bribe abroad (and more successful), compared to an otherwise identical company from a low corruption country.

1. EMPIRICAL EVIDENCE

Data on perceptions of bribe frequency in international transactions come from Transparency International's Bribe Payers Index (BPI) surveys, which have been conducted five times the last 15 years (in 1999, 2002, 2006, 2008 and 2011). The surveys asked businessmen from a large number of countries to evaluate the extent to which foreign companies bribe when they do business in the respondents' countries. For most of the empirical analysis, I use the 2006 survey, which was part of the World Economic Forum's Executive Opinion Survey, because it has the most extended coverage: 30 origin and 125 destination countries. The relevant questions on foreign bribery read as follows:

> 'From the list of countries below, please select those nationalities of the foreign-owned companies doing most business in your country'

and

> 'In your experience, to what extent do firms from the countries you have selected make undocumented extra payments or bribes?'

The original responses ranged from 1 (common) to 7 (never), and were rescaled so that higher values indicate higher frequency. The phrasing of the questions in the other surveys was similar, but not identical. Data on distance, historical ties, and common language come from the GeoDist database (Mayer and Zignago, 2011). I use the control of corruption measure from the World Governance Indicators, which is also rescaled so that higher values indicate more corruption. For a short description and summary statistics of the variables used, see Tables 11A.1 and 11A.2 in the Appendix.

1.1 The Effect of Corruption at Home

For each pair of countries, I computed the average of the responses to the bribe frequency question. Then, I standardized the averages so that their mean is zero and their standard deviation is one, to facilitate the interpretation of the results. I also dropped the pairs where the origin and destination country are the same. Data are available for 3,648 out of the 3,751 origin-destination country pairs. For the other 103 pairs, no respondent gave a rating. The first goal of the analysis is to identify the impact of corruption at both nodes of the pair on bribe frequency, allowing for the possibility that there is an interaction effect. The specification of the main regressions takes the following form:

$$bribe_{ij} = \beta_0 + \beta_1 corr_i + \beta_2 corr_j + \beta_3 corr_i \times corr_j + \beta_4 X_{ij} + \varepsilon_{ij}$$

where i indexes the destination country, j indexes the origin country, X is the vector of the other covariates, and ε_{ij} is the error term. $bribe_{ij}$ measures how much companies from country j bribe in country i. Because I am running the analysis at the level of country pairs, errors are likely to be correlated both at the home country and the destination country level. To account for that, I report non-nested clustered standard errors (Cameron et al. 2011).[6]

The corruption level of the origin country has a positive, large, and statistically significant effect on the extent of bribery abroad (Table 11A.3, col. 1). In a destination country that has an average (zero) level of corruption, a one standard deviation increase in the corruption level of the origin country is associated with an increase in bribery equal to .437 of a standard deviation. The corruption level of the destination country also matters. For companies from an origin country with average corruption,

---

[6] In STATA, this is implemented by cgmreg.ado. Cameron et al. (2011) summarize their procedure as follows: 'In the two-way clustering case, we obtain three different cluster-robust "variance" matrices for the estimator by one-way clustering in, respectively, the first dimension, the second dimension, and by the intersection of the first and second dimensions . . . Then we add the first two variance matrices and subtract the third.'

a one standard deviation increase in the corruption level at destination is associated with an increase in bribery equal to .259 of a standard deviation. After the addition of extra control variables in column 2, the destination coefficient becomes .383, the origin coefficient falls to .306, and they both remain significant. The coefficient of the interaction term is negative and significant, suggesting that the effect of corruption at the origin diminishes in high corruption destination countries. Equivalently, the effect of corruption at destination is smaller when the origin country is very corrupt.[7]

Regarding the effects of the other controls on the dependent variable, companies from poorer countries are more likely to bribe, even when we hold corruption constant. An increase in GDP per capita by 100 percent, approximately equal to the distance between Argentina and Germany, is associated with a reduction in the propensity to bribe that is close to .14 of a standard deviation. The *Colonial Relationship* binary variable, which takes the value 1 if one of the two countries has ever colonized the other, does not have an effect on bribery. This might contradict the reader's priors, as we would naturally expect companies from former colonizers to know their way around the bureaucracy better than other foreign competitors. The *Same Country* variable, which equals 1 if the countries have been part of the same entity in the past, has a positive, large and statistically significant coefficient. This could possibly capture either cultural similarities, or better knowledge of the destination country's politics and public sector. Country break-ups, though, are not random and it is possible that the variable simply proxies for other unobserved institutional deficiencies of the two countries in the pair. Finally, speaking the same language does not seem to facilitate bribery. The coefficient of the *Common Language* variable, which equals 1 if more than 9 percent of both countries' population speak the same language, is indistinguishable from zero.

Figures 11A.2 and 11A.3 present some examples that visualize the main results. Figure 11A.2 plots the extent of bribery abroad by US and Russian companies, against the corruption of the destination country. Russian companies seem to bribe more overall, regardless of the level of corruption of the destination country. This is consistent with the positive coefficient on corruption in the country of origin. As the corruption of the destination country increases, bribe frequency goes up for both US and Russian businesses, just as the positive coefficient of the destination's

---

[7]   Note that the interaction effect is small compared to the coefficients of corruption at the origin and the destination. The marginal effects of the two corruption variables are positive and significant across the board.

corruption suggests. However, there is some convergence, as the difference in bribe frequency becomes smaller in high corruption destination countries, possibly because bribing is a precondition for doing business in such environments. In other words, the slope of the linear prediction for Russian businesses is smaller, in accordance with the negative interaction coefficient. Figure 11A.3 plots the bribe frequency in Switzerland and Indonesia for companies headquartered abroad, against the corruption level at the country of the companies' origin. In accordance with the results from Table 11A.3, bribe frequency is higher in Indonesia, and it goes up as corruption at the origin goes up. The negative interaction coefficient implies that the slope is smaller for high corruption countries, which is evident in this graph as well.

Next, I drop the country-pairs for which there are less than 20 responses available in the survey, reducing the number of available observations from 3,648 to 1,071. Column 3 of Table 11A.3 presents the results from the smaller sample. The results are not much changed compared to column 2, except for the interaction term that is smaller 2 and statistically insignificant. Because the results in the restricted sample are similar to those in the larger sample, I will use second column as the main specification for the rest of the empirical analysis. To control for selection in unobservables, I used a correction model with kilometric distance as the excluded variable. The results are very similar and are not presented here.

1.2   Foreign Bribery Laws

To investigate the effect of formal institutions on bribe frequency, I first add a binary variable that equals to 1 if the origin country was part of the OECD Convention as of 2006 (OECD FBL 2006), and 0 otherwise. The first column of Table 11A.4 presents the results from the 2006 survey with the addition of the OECD FBL binary variable, whose coefficient is negative and significant, suggesting that the foreign bribery laws that were passed as a result of the Convention had an effect.

However, the societies that punish foreign bribery may have stronger anti-corruption attitudes compared to those that do not. So, it is possible that the negative coefficient on the OECD FBL variable only captures some unobserved cultural component. To test this, I compare the coefficients on the foreign bribery laws variable on different types of corruption, some of whom are covered by the laws and some that are usually outside their scope. The 2008 Bribe Payers Index survey contains information on the propensity of foreign companies to engage in the following types of corruption: bribery of politicians and parties; facilitating payments towards public sector employees; and contracts awarded 'because of personal or familiar relationships rather than on a competitive bidding basis'. Laws against the bribery of foreign public officials often allow for facilitating payments, whose purpose is to expedite the bureaucratic procedures.[8] Also, the development of personal relationships with local politicians is hard to regulate and is often a way for companies to avoid the restrictions on foreign bribery.[9] So, the laws should have a bigger effect on direct bribery towards high-ranking politicians, compared to other types of corruption. The next four columns of Table 11A.4 use data from the 2008 survey on the frequency of bribes in general (col. 2), bribes towards politicians (col. 3), facilitating payments towards officials (col. 4), and the use of connections to win contracts (col. 5). The coefficients of the OECD FBL variable are all negative and statistically indistinguishable from each other, which casts doubt on the effectiveness of the laws.

Next, I repeat the same analysis, but this time I shift the focus towards the full set of countries where foreign bribery is prohibited, whether they are part of the Convention or not. I add a binary variable (FBL) that equals 1 if the origin country had prohibited foreign bribery as of 2006. Data were collected based on the information that OECD provides on the status of the ratification and implementation of the Anti-Bribery Convention, the reports from 'Getting the Deal Through: Anti-Corruption Regulation' (GTD 2010), and Norton Rose Group's 'Anti-Corruption Laws in Asia Pacific' (2012). There are several grey-area cases, where there is no special law against foreign bribery, but the existing legislation is phrased in a way that does not discriminate between domestic and foreign bribery. When the sources give a clear interpretation that foreign bribery is de facto illegal, even though it is not explicitly mentioned in the laws, the country is classified as having a foreign bribery law. The first column of Table 11A.5 presents the results from the 2006 survey with the addition of the FBL binary variable, whose coefficient is small and significant only at the 10 percent level. In the rest of Table 11A.5, the FBL variable appears to have no effect on the outcome variables. The difference in the results between Tables 4 and 5 is mostly due to the re-classification of Hong Kong and Singapore, that are not part of the Convention but de facto prohibit bribery according to the sources mentioned above. The evidence overall

---

[8] The FCPA, for example, does not prohibit payments whose purpose is to grease the bureaucracy in order to expedite a permit, or in general to perform its legal duties faster. South Korea's Foreign Public Officials Act also 'allows payments that are made to foreign officials in order to facilitate official functions' (Norton Rose Group 2012: 66).

[9] Investors often disguise bribes by forming partnerships with politicians' friends or relatives (Moran 2006).

does not seem to support the hypothesis that foreign bribery laws change the behavior of domestic firms when they invest abroad. Also note that controlling for the presence of foreign bribery laws did not alter the effect of the corruption at the origin on the firms' propensity to bribe.

Whether the comparison across different categories of corruption is a good test for the effectiveness of the laws depends on the crucial assumption that the laws affect only the direct bribery of politicians. This need not be true if the laws serve as signals that overall corrupt behavior is not tolerated. Also, the increase in the oversight by the home country may discourage all types of corruption. So, if the firms are forced to re-examine their corporate conduct as a whole, and drastically revise the way they do business, then foreign bribery laws may have an effect across the board.

1.3   Robustness Checks

An important concern with the Bribe Payers Index data is that the respondents may simply reproduce stereotypes that do not necessarily reflect the behavior of foreign investors in the respondents' country. For example, respondents from Brazil may claim that investors from Russia bribe more than investors from the US, only because they have heard that bribes are more common in Russia. In this case, the problem is not that perceptions might be generally inaccurate measures of true corruption.[10] The problem is that the perceptions expressed in the survey might be the wrong ones. The survey questions, however, were carefully phrased so that respondents are directed to evaluate corrupt behavior based on their own personal observations in their own country. In the 2006 survey, the question specifically asked for a rating based on the respondents' experience. In the 2002 survey, the interviewees were asked to focus on the sectors that they know well. In the 2008 and 2011 surveys, the respondents were instructed to single out the origin countries of the companies with whom they have business relationships ('as a supplier, client, partner, or competitor'). The structure of the survey questions mitigates concerns regarding the quality of the data.

It is still reasonable, though, to worry that the respondents do not pay enough attention to the wording and misunderstand the purpose of the questions. According to Transparency International's report on the 2006 survey, many respondents gave their opinion on companies from all—or

---

[10]   For a discussion on the use of perceptions to measure government performance, see Kaufmann et al (2010). In a field experiment in Indonesia, Olken (2009) finds that perceptions are indeed correlated with actual corruption.

almost all—origin countries. This raises doubts about the quality of the data. In the authors' words, 'It can be argued that these respondents may not have precise experience of how companies from so many countries do business. Indeed, it could be that these respondents misunderstood the question, believing that they were being asked to give their impression of all countries rather than their experience of just those with which they were familiar.' As a robustness check, I dropped all respondents who gave answers for 10 countries of origin or more, and redid the analysis.[11] The number of respondents decreased by about 15 percent, and the available country-pairs dropped from 3,618 to 2,838. The results are presented in the second column of Table 11A.6 (the first column reproduces the main results to facilitate comparison). The coefficients of the corruption variables are smaller, but they remain large and statistically significant. The coefficient of the interaction of the corruption variables and the coefficient of the logarithm of GDP per capita of the destination country lose their significance.

Even the respondents who seem to follow the questions' guidelines, though, could possibly be influenced by their general knowledge of the prevalence of corruption around the world. For example, the respondents might be aware that poorer countries have higher levels of corruption, and they might 'profile' them accordingly. If that was the case, we would expect the results to weaken after controlling for GDP per capita. However, this does not happen (Table 11A.3, col. 2). The second possibility is that the respondents' priors come from reading the newspaper or watching the news. Corruption indices very often receive attention in the media, and they likely shape the public's perception of corruption in other parts of the world. Consequently, respondents who are familiar with Transparency International's Corruption Perceptions Index are more likely to base their responses on their perception of corruption in the origin countries. As an additional robustness check, I separated the respondents of the 2006 survey into those who know of the Index and those who do not.[12] The coefficients of the corruption levels at both nodes of the pair are only slightly smaller when we look at the respondents who are not familiar with the CPI (Table 11A.6, cols. 3 and 4), and the difference is insignificant.

---

[11] In the 2006 report, the authors drop those who gave answers for more than 20 countries, and find that the new BPI index is very highly correlated with the original one.

[12] The related question read: '12.02 How well do you know Transparency International's annual Corruption Perceptions Index?', with possible responses ranging from 1 ('Unknown') to 7 ('Well known'). I classify the respondents whose answer is 4 or above as those who are familiar.

Furthermore, the data derived from the local businessmen's perceptions are strongly correlated with the data from the Business Environment and Enterprise Performance Survey, as reproduced in Hellman et al. (2002). Russian companies investing in transition economies reported paying bribes equal on average to 6 percent of their revenues, compared to 1.3 percent for Swedish companies, or 2.5 percent for German companies. Overall, the correlation between bribes paid as a percentage of revenue and the 2006 Bribe Payers Index is −.79 (N=11). So, the evidence presented in this chapter is corroborated by evidence from surveys based on self-reported behavior.

I performed several other robustness checks, but I do not present here to conserve space. Variables that measure contiguity, common legal origins, common official language, colonial relationship after 1945 (GeoDist), bilateral trust (Guiso et al. 2009), and cultural distance were added as controls. In all cases, the extra controls had no effect on the dependent variable, and did not alter the main results either. Also using the CPI instead of the WGI measure of corruption, adding region dummies, weighting each observation by the number of responses, or using the 2002 survey data did not make a difference. Finally, adding dummies for the countries of destination did not affect much the coefficient of corruption at the country of origin, and vice versa.

2. FURTHER DISCUSSION AND CONCLUSION

My results provide evidence that companies from high corruption countries that do business abroad tend to bribe more often than companies from low corruption countries, even when they operate in equally corrupt destination countries. Quite expectedly, the corruption level of the destination country also increases the propensity of foreign firms to bribe. The results are robust to the exclusion of respondents whose evaluations of foreign bribery might be heavily influenced by their knowledge of the prevalence of corruption across the world. This lends confidence to the quality of the perceptions data used in this study.

There is some evidence that companies from countries that are part of the OECD Convention engage less in corrupt activities. However, this effect is statistically the same for types of corruption that are within the scope of the law and types that are not. Therefore, it is possible that the apparent negative effect of the foreign bribery laws simply reflects some other unobserved factor, perhaps a general interest in limiting corruption in their business dealings that is reflected in their support for the goals of the OECD Convention. So, even though research suggests that foreign bribery laws result in less investment towards corrupt destination countries (Hines 2014), it seems that they do not lead to an adjustment of corporate conduct when we hold the corruption level of the destination country constant. These findings suggest that it is necessary to bribe in high-corruption countries, and that firms respond to foreign bribery laws either by exiting or by continuing their business as before.

Most important, the effect of corruption at the origin on bribe frequency does not fall when I control for the presence of foreign bribery laws, and it is the same across different types of corruption. This suggests that culture and 'corruption skills' have an important explanatory role in explaining the behavior of the firms abroad.

REFERENCES

Algan, Yann and Pierre Cahuc. 2010. 'Inherited Trust and Growth', *American Economic Review* 100(5): 2060–92.

Barr, Abigail and Danila Serra. 2010. 'Corruption and Culture: An Experimental Analysis', *Journal of Public Economics* 94(11–12): 862–9.

Baughn, Christopher, Nancy Bodie, Mark Buchanan, and Michael Bixby. 2010. 'Bribery in International Business Transactions', *Journal of Business Ethics* 95: 15–32.

Benassy-Quere, Agnes Maylis Coupet and Thierry Mayer. 2007. 'Institutional Determinants of Foreign Direct Investment', *The World Economy* 30(5): 764–82.

Bloom, Nicholas, Raffaella Sadun and John Van Reenen. 2012. 'The Organization of Firms Across Countries', *Quarterly Journal of Economics* 127(4): 1663–705.

Cameron, Lisa, Ananish Chaudhuri and Nisvan Erkal. 2009. 'Propensities to Engage in and Punish Corrupt Behavior: Experimental Evidence from Australia, India, Indonesia and Singapore', *Journal of Public Economics* 93: 843–951.

Cameron, Colin, Jonah Gelbach and Douglas Miller. 2011. 'Robust Inference With Multiway Clustering', Journal of Business & Economic Statistics 29(2): 238–49.

Cuervo-Cazurra, Alvaro. 2006. 'Who Cares about Corruption', *Journal of International Business Studies* 37: 807–22.

Department of Justice, 'A Resource Guide to the U.S. Foreign Corrupt Practices Act', available 11 May 2015 at http://www.justice.gov/criminal/fraud/fcpa/guidance/guide.pdf.

D'Souza, Anna. 2010. 'The OECD Anti-Bribery Convention: Changing the Currents of Trade', *Journal of Development Economics* 97: 73–87.

Fisman, Raymond and Edward Miguel. 2007. 'Corruption, Norms, and Legal Enforcement: Evidence from Diplomatic Parking Tickets', *Journal of Political Economy* 115(6) 1020–48.

Guiso, Luigi, Paola Sapienza and Luigi Zingales. 2009. 'Cultural Biases in Economic Exchange?', *Quarterly Journal of Economics* 124(3): 1095–131.

Habib, Mohsin and Leon Zurawicki. 2002. 'Corruption and Foreign Direct Investment', *Journal of International Business Studies* 33(2): 291–307.

Heckman, James. 1979. 'Sample Selection Bias as a Specification Error', *Econometrica* 47(1): 153–61.

Heimann, Fritz and Gillian Dell. 2012. *Exporting Corruption? Country Enforcement* of the OECD Anti-Bribery Convention. Progress Report 2012. Transparency International.

Hellman, Joel, Geraint Jones and Daniel Kaufmann. 2002. 'Far from Home: Do Foreign Investors Import Higher Standards of Governance in Transition Economies?'. The World Bank, Policy Research Working Paper.

Hines, James. 1995. 'Forbidden Payment: Foreign Bribery and American Business After 1977', NBER Working Paper 5266.

Hines, James. 2014. 'Competitive Considerations in Combating Corruption'. Working Paper. Conference on Grand and Petty Corruption in Developing States: Business, Citizens, and the State: Yale University.

IMF World Economic Outlook Database (April, 2012).

Karpoff, Jonathan, Scott Lee and Gerald Martin. 2012. 'The Impact of Anti-Bribery Enforcement Actions on Targeted Firms', Working Paper.

Kaufmann, Daniel, Aart Kraay and Massimo Mastruzzi. 2010. 'The Worldwide Governance Indicators: Methodology and Analytical Issues', World Bank Policy Research Working Paper 5430.

Kogut, Bruce and Harbir Singh. 1988. 'The Effect of National Culture on the Choice of Entry', *Journal of International Business Studies* 19(3): 411–32.

Krever, Tor. 2007. 'Curbing Corruption? The Efficacy of the Foreign Corrupt Practices Act', *North Carolina Journal of International Law and Commercial Regulation* 33(1): 83–103.

Ledyaeva, Svetlana, Paivi; Karhunen and Riita Kosonen. 2013. 'Birds of a Feather: Evidence on Commonality of Corruption and Democracy in the Origin and Location of Foreign Investment in Russian Regions', *European Journal of Political Economy* 32: 1–25.

Linders, Gert-Jan, Sjoerd, Beugelsdijk, Henri de Groot and Arjen Slangen. 2005. 'Cultural and Institutional Determinants of Bilateral Trade Flows', Tinbergen Institute Discussion Paper.

Mayer, Thierry, Soledad Zignago. 2011. 'Notes on CEPII's Distances Measures: The GeoDist Database', CEPII Working Paper 2011-25.

Moran, Theodore (2006) 'How Multinational Investors Evade Developed Country Laws', Center for Global Development, Working Paper No. 79.

Norton Rose Group. 2012. *Anti-Corruption Laws in Asia Pacific.*

OECD (1997) Convention on Combating Bribery of Foreign Public Officials in International Business Transactions.

Olken, Benjamin. 2009. 'Corruption Perceptions vs. Corruption Reality', *Journal of Public Economics* 93: 950–64.

Simpser, Alberto. 2013. 'The Intergenerational Transmission of Attitudes Toward Corruption', Working Paper.

Transparency International (1999–) Bribe Payers Index & BPI Analysis Reports.

Transparency International (1999–) Corruption Perceptions Index.

APPENDIX

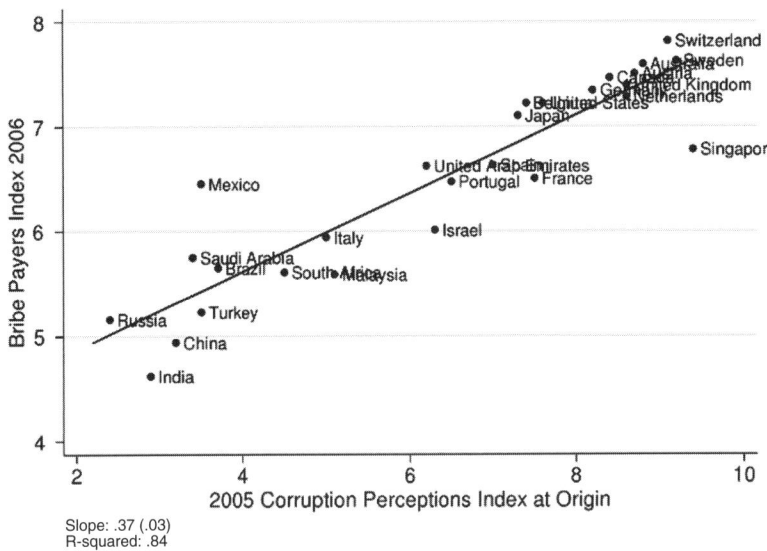

Slope: .37 (.03)
R-squared: .84

Source: Transparency International.

Figure 11A.1   Bribe Payers Index vs. CPI at the origin

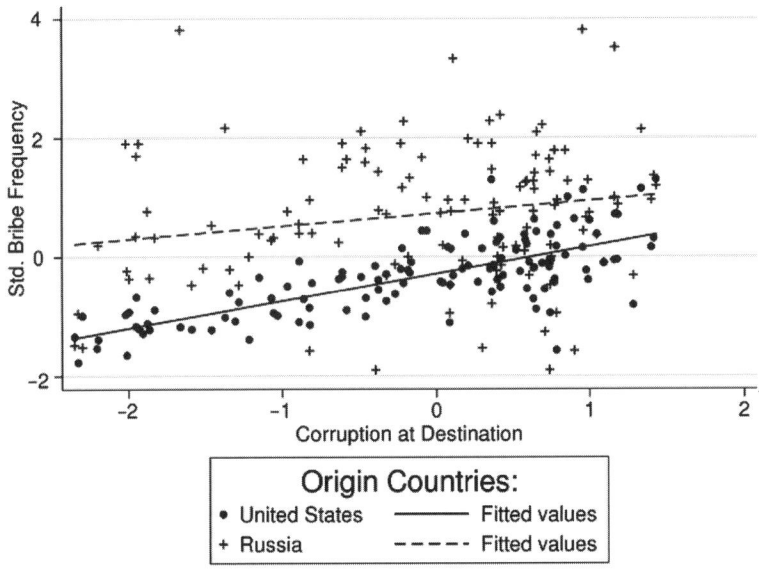

Figure 11A.2   Bribe frequency vs. corruption at the destination

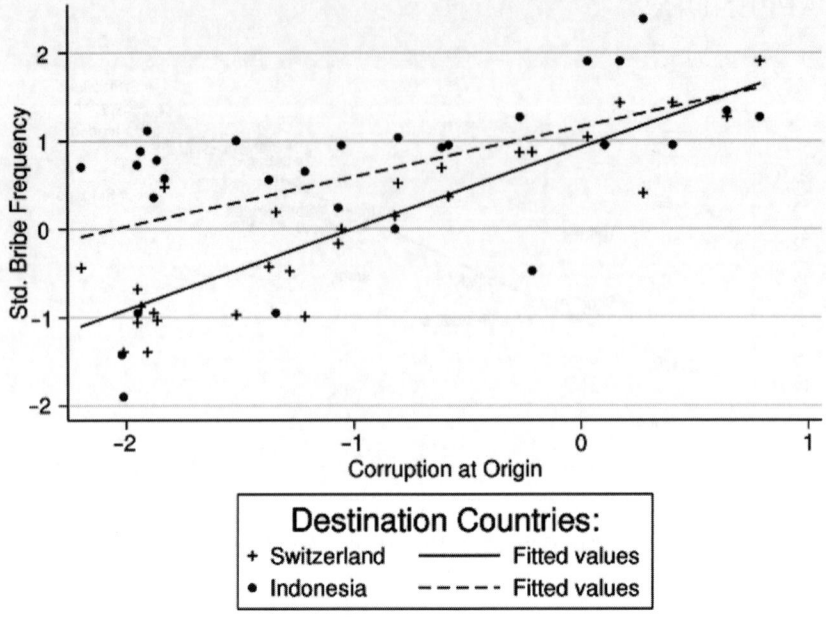

Figure 11A.3   Bribe frequency vs. corruption at the origin

Table 11A.1   Variables and their sources

Variable Name	Variable Description and Source
Bribe Frequency	Standardized. Higher values indicate higher frequency. Source: Transparency International
Corruption	WGI's Control of Corruption in 2005. Rescaled so that higher values indicate more corruption
Log GDP pc	Log GDP per capita in 2005. Source: IMF World Economic Outlook (April 2012)
FBL in 2006	Foreign Bribery Law in 2006. 1 if bribery of foreign public officials is prohibited, 0 otherwise
Common Language	'1 if a language is spoken by at least 9% of the population in both countries', 0 otherwise. Source: GeoDist
Colonial Relationship	'1 for pairs ever in colonial relationship', 0 otherwise. Source: GeoDist
Same Country	'1 if countries were or are the same country', 0 otherwise. Source: Geodist
Distance	Weighted distance between major cities. Source: GeoDist

Table 11A.2 Summary statistics

Variable	Mean	Std. Dev.	Min.	Max.	N
Std. Bribery in 2006	0.002	1	−1.901	3.806	3648
Corruption at Destination	−0.095	1.002	−2.355	1.432	3648
Corruption at Origin	−0.982	0.904	−2.2	0.786	3648
Log GDP pc at Destination	8.25	1.636	5.005	11.304	3648
Log GDP pc at Origin	9.773	1.031	6.591	10.821	3648
Colonial Relationship	0.037	0.188	0	1	3618
Same Country	0.005	0.07	0	1	3618
Common Language	0.144	0.351	0	1	3618
FBL in 2006 – Destination	0.705	0.456	0	1	1818
FBL in 2006 – Origin	0.794	0.405	0	1	3526

Table 11A.3 Corruption at home and the propensity to bribe abroad

	(1) OLS All	(2) OLS All	(4) OLS count>20
Corruption at Destination	0.259***	0.383***	0.422***
	(0.06)	(0.09)	(0.11)
Corruption at Origin	0.437***	0.306***	0.323***
	(0.05)	(0.07)	(0.06)
Corruption at Or. X Dest.	−0.057**	−0.056**	−0.022
	(0.02)	(0.02)	(0.05)
Log GDP pc at Destination		0.091*	0.012
		(0.05)	(0.05)
Log GDP pc at Origin		−0.141***	−0.146***
		(0.04)	(0.04)
Colonial Relationship		0.118	0.133
		(0.12)	(0.11)
Same Country		0.366**	0.349**
		(0.15)	(0.15)
Common Language		−0.039	−0.024
		(0.06)	(0.07)
Constant	0.461***	0.968	1.751***
	(0.07)	(0.61)	(0.49)
Observations	3,648	3,618	1,071
Adjusted R-sq.	0.263	0.276	0.540

Note: Dependent variable: Std. Bribe Frequency. Standard errors in parentheses, clustered at both the origin and destination country levels. *,**, and *** indicate significance at the 10%, 5%, and 1% level respectively.

Table 11A.4   OECD Convention and foreign bribery

Survey Year: Dependent Variable:	(1) 2006 General	(2) 2008 General	(3) 2008 Politicians	(4) 2008 Officials	(5) 2008 Connections
Corruption at Destination	0.380***	0.032	−0.261	−0.229	−0.144
	(0.09)	(0.21)	(0.16)	(0.15)	(0.18)
Corruption at Origin	0.296***	0.514***	0.447***	0.450***	0.481***
	(0.05)	(0.04)	(0.07)	(0.06)	(0.08)
Corruption at Or. X Dest.	−0.057**	−0.085***	−0.167***	−0.147***	−0.089***
	(0.02)	(0.03)	(0.04)	(0.03)	(0.03)
Log GDP pc at Destination	0.091*	0.128	−0.017	0.014	0.051
	(0.05)	(0.15)	(0.12)	(0.11)	(0.13)
Log GDP pc at Origin	−0.093***	0.082**	0.145	0.077	0.142*
	(0.03)	(0.04)	(0.11)	(0.10)	(0.08)
Colonial Relationship	0.176	0.179***	0.129	0.087	0.158
	(0.12)	(0.07)	(0.09)	(0.13)	(0.12)
Same Country	0.317***	1.017***	1.315***	0.882***	1.026***
	(0.12)	(0.19)	(0.28)	(0.31)	(0.21)
Common Language	−0.063	0.156	0.139	0.176	0.214
	(0.07)	(0.12)	(0.12)	(0.14)	(0.16)
OECD FBL in 2006	−0.285***	−0.468***	−0.385**	−0.277*	−0.234**
	(0.08)	(0.09)	(0.19)	(0.16)	(0.10)
Observations	3,497	515	455	472	461
Adjusted R-sq.	0.294	0.310	0.205	0.223	0.169

Note: Dependent variable: Std. Bribe Frequency. Standard errors in parentheses, clustered at both the origin and destination country levels. *,**, and *** indicate significance at the 10%, 5%, and 1% level respectively.

Table 11A.5   Foreign bribery laws

	(1) 2006 General	(2) 2008 General	(3) 2008 Politicians	(4) 2008 Officials	(5) 2008 Connections
Survey Year: Dependent Variable:					
Corruption at Destination	0.382***	0.032	−0.267	−0.237	−0.148
	(0.09)	(0.21)	(0.16)	(0.15)	(0.18)
Corruption at Origin	0.293***	0.422***	0.378***	0.406***	0.438***
	(0.08)	(0.08)	(0.10)	(0.10)	(0.10)
Corruption at Or. X Dest.	−0.056**	−0.087***	−0.174***	−0.155***	−0.094***
	(0.02)	(0.03)	(0.05)	(0.03)	(0.03)
Log GDP pc at Destination	0.092*	0.133	−0.011	0.020	0.056
	(0.05)	(0.14)	(0.12)	(0.12)	(0.13)
Log GDP pc at Origin	−0.127***	−0.030	0.008	−0.056	0.057
	(0.05)	(0.09)	(0.13)	(0.11)	(0.09)
Colonial Relationship	0.132	0.124*	0.092	0.065	0.130
	(0.12)	(0.07)	(0.11)	(0.14)	(0.12)
Same Country	0.313**	0.952***	1.288***	0.891***	1.017***
	(0.13)	(0.20)	(0.24)	(0.27)	(0.20)
Common Language	−0.036	0.185	0.159	0.182	0.223
	(0.06)	(0.12)	(0.12)	(0.12)	(0.15)
FBL in 2006	−0.111*	−0.213	0.018	0.169	0.018
	(0.07)	(0.23)	(0.33)	(0.32)	(0.26)
Observations	3,497	515	455	472	461
Adjusted R-sq.	0.282	0.288	0.190	0.216	0.164

Note: Dependent variable: Std. Bribe Frequency. Standard errors in parentheses, clustered at both the origin and destination country levels. *,**, and *** indicate significance at the 10%, 5%, and 1% level respectively.

Table 11A.6   Robustness checks

	(1) All	(2) <10 answers	(3) Knows TI	(4) Doesn't Know TI
Corruption at Destination	0.383***	0.248***	0.323***	0.260***
	(0.09)	(0.08)	(0.10)	(0.09)
Corruption at Origin	0.306***	0.224***	0.305***	0.246***
	(0.07)	(0.07)	(0.07)	(0.06)
Corruption at Or. X Dest.	−0.056**	−0.037	−0.069**	−0.057**
	(0.02)	(0.03)	(0.03)	(0.03)
Log GDP pc at Destination	0.091*	−0.037	0.111**	0.040
	(0.05)	(0.05)	(0.06)	(0.05)
Log GDP pc at Origin	−0.141***	−0.104***	−0.110**	−0.138***
	(0.04)	(0.04)	(0.05)	(0.04)
Colonial Relationship	0.118	0.036	0.093	0.093
	(0.12)	(0.09)	(0.09)	(0.12)
Same Country	0.366**	0.270*	0.374***	0.305*
	(0.15)	(0.14)	(0.13)	(0.17)
Common Language	−0.039	0.021	0.028	−0.091
	(0.06)	(0.07)	(0.06)	(0.06)
Observations	3,618	2,838	3,418	3,294
Adjusted R-sq.	0.276	0.220	0.211	0.202

Note: Dependent variable: Std. Bribe Frequency. Standard errors in parentheses, clustered at both the origin and destination country levels. *,**, and *** indicate significance at the 10%, 5%, and 1% level respectively.

12. Regulation of foreign bribery: the FCPA enforcement model

Kevin E. Davis*

INTRODUCTION

The first phase in the global campaign to regulate foreign bribery is nearly complete. There is now a broad international consensus in favor of prohibiting bribery of foreign public officials, as evidenced by the OECD Convention on Combating Bribery of Foreign Public Officials in International Business Transactions and the United Nations Convention against Corruption. The next phase of the campaign requires analysts to step back to analyze the impact of these prohibitions with a view to determining whether additional interventions are required (see for example, Hines 1995; Cuervo-Cazurra 2008).

It seems intuitive that the effects of prohibitions on foreign bribery depend on the strategies used to enforce them, that is, the cases pursued and the sanctions imposed. Those strategies are undoubtedly determined to some extent by the amount of resources devoted to enforcement as well as, of course, the strategies that firms adopt in response. What is less well understood, especially outside of legal circles, is that basic features of the underlying legal system also influence enforcement strategies in subtle yet important ways. This chapter examines how distinctive features of the US legal system have shaped the overall approach to enforcement of the prohibition on foreign bribery found in the United States' Foreign Corrupt Practices Act of 1977 (FCPA). Understanding the implications of the US enforcement model is important because there are signs that it exerts

* I am grateful to Nicholas McLean, Susan Rose-Ackerman and participants in the Conference on Grand and Petty Corruption in Developing States: Business, Citizens, and the State for helpful comments on previous drafts of this chapter. An earlier version was delivered as lectures at the Fundação Getulio Vargas in São Paulo and Rio de Janeiro and benefited from comments from the audience on those occasions. Financial support from the Filomen D'Agostino and Max E. Greenberg Research Fund is acknowledged with thanks.

significant influence over other anti-corruption regimes. More generally, analysis of enforcement strategies represents a critical step towards a comprehensive analysis of the overall foreign bribery enforcement game, a game whose players include US and non-US enforcement agencies as well as the firms subject to their jurisdiction.

The first section of this chapter provides a typology of enforcement strategies, showing that they can be motivated by very different concerns and can seek to achieve very different objectives. The motivations range from self-interest to cosmopolitanism to altruism, and the key objectives are retribution, prevention and compensation. The number of combinations of these motivations and objectives—at least nine, assuming no overlaps—shows the wide variety of potential enforcement strategies. That variety underscores the importance of determining the enforcement strategies that any given regime is actually pursuing.

The next section describes the FCPA and the most distinctive features of the legal framework that governs its enforcement. It focuses on four key elements of the FCPA enforcement model: (1) prosecutors in the US Department of Justice (DOJ) and Securities and Exchange Commission (SEC) dominate decision-making; (2) sanctions are routinely imposed on corporations whose employees or agents pay bribes; (3) extra-territorial jurisdiction is asserted over a broad range of actors and transactions; and (4) high-powered punitive sanctions are common. The section concludes by discussing indications that authorities in other countries, as well as at the supra-national level, are adopting elements of the FCPA model.

The following section contains the core of the analysis. It begins by surveying the existing empirical literature. It then sets out conjectures about how each element of the FCPA enforcement model might, based on theoretical considerations, influence the strategies that US authorities adopt. The final section concludes.

A TYPOLOGY OF ENFORCEMENT STRATEGIES

The strategies used to enforce a prohibition on foreign bribery consist of a set of decisions about which cases to pursue and what sanctions to impose in those cases. Enforcement strategies can respond to different motivations and be designed to achieve different objectives. The motivations consist of different ideas about why foreign bribery is a problem. The objectives embody different conceptions of the role legal sanctions ought to play in responding to social problems.

The legislative history of the FCPA reveals several distinct motivations, each of which reflects a different idea about why foreign bribery is a problem (Davis 2012). First is the idea that foreign bribery is of concern because it is inherently reprehensible, just like bribery of domestic public officials. A second concern is that foreign bribery places honest US firms at a competitive disadvantage. Third, foreign bribery might be of concern primarily because of the harm it causes to the people represented by the officials who have been bribed. For convenience we can refer to these motivations as cosmopolitanism (since it places equal weight on the welfare of foreign and domestic victims of corruption), self-interest and altruism.

Each of these motivations points to different conclusions about what forms of foreign bribery are most problematic and suggests different ways of measuring the culpability of actors who engage in foreign bribery. Take cosmopolitanism. This view suggests that whatever factors are used to select cases for investigation and to determine the culpability of any given bribe-payer, those factors generally should not include the nationality of the defendant or the victims. The caveat 'generally' is there because if the US wants to make a credible statement that it takes foreign bribery as seriously as domestic bribery and is not biased in favor of local firms and local victims, it may have to go out of its way to prosecute US firms.

Self-interest, conceived in narrow economic terms, suggests that bribes paid by foreign firms that compete with US firms pose the greatest problems and should be the focus of enforcement efforts. For these purposes the extent to which a firm is foreign or domestic does not turn on where it is incorporated or where its headquarters are located. The most critical factor is the extent to which the welfare of US citizens is linked to the welfare of the firm. This will depend on the extent to which its shareholders, creditors, employees, suppliers and customers are US nationals.

Altruism suggests that culpability should depend on the magnitude of the threat that a given instance of bribery poses to people represented by the public officials implicated in the scheme, especially if other anticorruption institutions are incapable of protecting them. In principle, this analysis should take into account any benefits generated by the corrupt transaction. This implies that enforcement efforts should be concentrated on cases involving payment of bribes in relatively vulnerable countries.

FCPA enforcement strategies may vary according to their objectives as well as their motivations. Authorities can use legal sanctions to achieve retribution, prevention (which includes both deterrence and incapacitation) or compensation. Each objective points to a different set of enforcement strategies. For instance, if retribution is the objective, then sanctions in individual cases should depend solely on culpability, however conceived. Pursuing retribution also arguably implies that authorities should select cases to maximize the amount of harm that is sanctioned, subject to resource constraints. This in turn implies that the likelihood of any given case being pursued should be an increasing function of the defendant's culpability and a decreasing function of the cost of imposing a sanction (which will depend on the cost of securing relevant evidence).

If prevention is the objective then authorities ought to design an enforcement strategy that not only responds to the defendant's misconduct, but that also seeks to influence the behavior of actors that might become involved in misconduct in the future. The most important form of prevention involves deterrence. The deterrent effects of sanctions will depend on how they affect prevailing values, beliefs about the likelihood of being sanctioned, and beliefs about the kinds of sanctions that will be imposed. Formulating an appropriate deterrence-oriented enforcement strategy is a complex task. If potential wrongdoers focus on the expected penalty, it makes sense to adjust sanctions upwards in cases in which the perceived likelihood of detecting the misconduct is low. If more salient cases disproportionately influence potential wrongdoers, it might be appropriate to target especially prominent defendants. Alternatively, if potential wrongdoers are especially sensitive to the probability of being sanctioned, it might be appropriate to allocate resources to maximize the number of defendants sanctioned, regardless of their culpability.

Prevention can also involve incapacitation, that is, making it physically impossible for certain actors to engage in misconduct. This typically involves incarcerating individual wrongdoers. The appointment of a monitor serves a comparable purpose in the corporate context.

Finally, if the objective is to ensure compensation for some class of victims then it makes sense to take into account defendants' ability to provide compensation when choosing cases. In this case the sanctions imposed should either include compensatory remedies, such as restitution, or serve to facilitate efforts to secure compensation through other means.

Combining three distinct motivations for enforcement and three distinctive objectives yields at least nine distinct enforcement strategies: cosmopolitan retribution, self-interested prevention, altruistic compensation, and so on. A regime may also give weight to several motivations or objectives and pursue them simultaneously. This increases the number of possible strategies to include combinations such as 'cosmopolitan retribution and prevention, with greater weight given to retribution'. The size of the range of possible enforcement strategies underscores the importance of trying to identify which strategy any given regime is pursuing during any given period of time.

THE FCPA AND ITS ENFORCEMENT MODEL

Overview of the FCPA

The FCPA was the earliest significant effort to regulate foreign bribery. At its core are the anti-bribery provisions, which prohibit bribery of foreign officials designed to assist the bribe-payer in 'obtaining or retaining business for or with, or directing business to, any person'. The FCPA also contains so-called 'accounting provisions' which impose liability on listed firms that fail to maintain accurate books and records (the 'books and records' provision) or adequate internal controls (the 'internal controls' provision) over their assets and transactions (see generally Criminal Division of the US Department of Justice and Enforcement Division of the US Securities and Exchange Commission 2012, hereinafter 'DOJ/SEC Guide').

The FCPA defines the bounds of the conduct subject to its provisions in three different ways. The first is nationality of the wrongdoer: the FCPA covers violations committed anywhere in the world by US entities, including firms organized under US law and individuals who are US nationals. The second basis for determining the scope of the FCPA is territoriality. The FCPA also applies to any violations committed 'while in the territory of the United States'. Third, the FCPA applies to violations committed by firms that have issued securities under US law so long as they 'make use of the mails or any means or instrumentality of interstate commerce' in the course of the offence. The FCPA also applies to a wide range of actors affiliated with the firms or individuals that fall into these three categories. It expressly applies to officers, directors, employees, agents and shareholders (if they are acting on behalf of a firm) otherwise subject to the FCPA. The DOJ has also asserted the right to apply the FCPA to foreign actors on the basis that they have conspired with or aided or abetted firms that are subject to the statute, even if those actors have no other connection to the US (DOJ/SEC Guide: 34).

Violations of the FCPA can lead to criminal prosecution by the DOJ. In the case of US issuers and the individuals or firms associated with them, FCPA violations can also lead to civil or administrative proceedings instituted by the SEC.

There are four distinctive features of the US approach to enforcement of the FCPA's basic prohibitions.

- Dominance of enforcement policy by prosecutors.
- Liberal rules for attributing liability to organizations.
- Broad assertions of extraterritorial jurisdiction.
- High-powered sanctions.

The following sections explain each of these features.

Dominance by Prosecutors

FCPA enforcement strategy is controlled primarily by investigators and attorneys located in specialized units of the DOJ, the SEC and the FBI. These units decide both which firms will be prosecuted and what sanctions ought to be imposed.

In recent years virtually all FCPA cases aimed at organizational defendants have been resolved through pre-trial agreements between prosecutors and the target firms with very little oversight from the courts. The agreements typically involve assent to written statements of facts as well as requirements that the firm take various measures to prevent future violations. Sometimes firms are even required to appoint an independent monitor. These agreements come in three forms: non-prosecution agreements (NPAs), deferred prosecutions agreements (DPAs) and guilty pleas. DPAs and guilty pleas must be approved by the court. To date, however, there has been relatively little judicial scrutiny of their terms.

Why so many pre-trial agreements? Because going to trial is costly for both prosecutors and firms. Going to trial is typically costly for firms because in addition to the direct costs of trial there is also the cost of the associated negative publicity. Going to trial will be costly for prosecutors if they have to collect and present evidence of corrupt payments, especially when witnesses and records have to be brought in from foreign countries. Given the magnitude of trial costs, defendants can agree to significantly harsher sanctions than they expect to receive at trial and still be better off than going to trial. Similarly, prosecutors can agree to less severe sanctions than they expect to be imposed after a trial and still be better off. Moreover, there is little room for disagreement about the outcome of an FCPA case at trial as firms have relatively few defenses and the US Sentencing Guidelines constrain judges' discretion over sentencing. All of these factors serve to enhance the likelihood of pre-trial agreements (Priest and Klein 1984).

Organizational Liability

US federal common law holds that a firm is liable 'when its directors, officers, employees, or agents, acting within the scope of their employment, commit FCPA violations intended, at least in part, to benefit the company'. As a result, no matter how lowly the employee, regardless of whether their conduct was consistent with company policy, and regardless of the efforts the firm has taken to prevent misconduct, the firm can still be liable (DOJ/SEC Guide, 27). The DOJ and SEC also appear to define the concept of an agent quite broadly; on occasion parent companies have been held liable for bribes paid by employees of subsidiary companies on the theory that the subsidiary was an agent of the parent company (DOJ/SEC Guide, 27–28).

Extraterritoriality

One of the most remarkable features of the FCPA is the extent to which it permits the US to assert jurisdiction over bribe-paying firms whose activities have very little obvious connection to the United States. To recap, the FCPA does this by providing for US jurisdiction over:

- All firms organized under US law and individual citizens, regardless of where their conduct takes place.
- Non-US firms and individuals, and especially firms listed on a US stock exchange, if any part of the conduct takes place in the US, including transfers of money through the US.
- Officers, directors, employees, agents and shareholders acting on behalf of the above, regardless of whether they have any other connection to the US.
- Actors that would not ordinarily be subject to US jurisdiction but which conspire with firms that are subject to US jurisdiction.

High-powered Sanctions

At first glance the potential sanctions for violation of the FCPA's anti-bribery provisions are not exorbitant. Organizations face criminal fines of up to $2 million and civil penalties of up to $16,000 per violation. Individuals may be fined up to $250,000 or imprisoned for five years, or both. These limits are misleading, however, because other legislative provisions dramatically increase the potential sanctions for bribe-payers. First, the Alternatives Fines Act overrides the FCPA's limits on criminal fines and permits fines to range up to two times the gross gain or the gross loss resulting from the offense. Second, an individual or organization that pays a bribe often will have violated the FCPA's accounting provisions. Under the accounting provisions criminal penalties can range up to $25 million for organizations and $5 million for individuals. Individuals may also be imprisoned for up to 20 years. Maximum civil penalties for each violation of the FCPA's accounting provisions are the greater of gross pecuniary gains and either $150,000, in the case of an individual, or $725,000, in the case of an organization. A third consideration is that the

SEC routinely orders disgorgement of profits derived from violations of the FCPA.

The DOJ and the SEC take the position that sanctions for violations of the FCPA should generally accord with the US Sentencing Guidelines. Those Guidelines identify multiple criteria to be used in determining sanctions. Some of those criteria relate to the nature of the misconduct, including the amount of the bribe paid, the resulting loss and the level of the public official. In the case of an organizational offender it matters whether high-level personnel were involved in or tolerated the misconduct. The characteristics of the offender also matter, including its prior misconduct and, in the case of an organization, its size. The Guidelines also give credit to actors that voluntary disclose wrongdoing, cooperate in an investigation, and accept responsibility.

Diffusion of the FCPA Model

Each of these elements of the US enforcement model represents only one approach among several alternatives. Although prosecutors necessarily play an important role in decisions about enforcement, specialized anti-corruption regulators, civil plaintiffs or judges could certainly be more involved than they have been in the process of FCPA enforcement. Instead of focusing on firms whose employees or agents have paid bribes to foreign officials, enforcement could focus on individual employees, agents or officials. While FCPA enforcement currently extends to firms with only tenuous connections to the United States, it could certainly be limited to firms with more substantial connections. Finally, monetary sanctions for FCPA violations are high, but there is no reason why they could not be either higher or lower. They could also be re-oriented toward compensating victims of corruption rather than punishing bribe-payers.

Despite the range of possible enforcement models, there are indications that other anti-corruption authorities have been influenced by the FCPA model. The World Bank's sanctions process is a good example of this phenomenon (see generally Leroy and Fariello 2012). As a result of reforms adopted in 2010, the Integrity Vice-Presidency of the World Bank, its prosecutorial branch, has considerable authority to negotiate settlements (World Bank Sanctions Procedures, Article XI). The process is used to debar not only individuals but also corporations and even entire corporate groups (see MDB Harmonized Principles on Treatment of Corporate Groups). The concept of extraterritoriality is not applicable in the context of the World Bank's sanctions process because it has always applied to World Bank-sponsored projects around the world. But in 2010 the World

Bank signed a cross-debarment agreement with several other multilateral development banks (Agreement for Mutual Enforcement of Debarment Decisions) which significantly enhanced the scope and potency of the participating institutions' sanctions processes.

Elements of the FCPA model are also being adopted in national legal systems. For example, in 2010 the United Kingdom adopted the Bribery Act 2010. One of its most striking features is that it permits organizations to be held liable for failing to prevent agents from committing foreign bribery. Under prior law an organization could only be held liable for the misconduct of relatively high level officials. (Unlike under US federal law, however, firms can avoid liability under the Bribery Act if they demonstrate that they had adequate procedures in place to prevent bribery.) The Bribery Act also has an extremely broad jurisdictional scope. If a firm 'carries on a business, or part of a business, in any part of the United Kingdom' it can be held liable for failing to prevent bribery in any part of the world (Bribery Act 2010, ss. 7 and 12(5)). More recently, UK law was amended to grant prosecutors in England and Wales authority to negotiate deferred prosecution agreements of the kind pioneered in the United States with commercial organizations (Crime and Courts Act 2013, Schedule 17).

The influence of the FCPA model has spread beyond the members of the OECD. In 2013 Brazil adopted a remarkably tough new anti-corruption law that covers foreign as well as domestic bribery (Law 12.846 of August 1, 2013). The law does not explicitly expand prosecutorial authority, although it does provide for adjudication through an expedited administrative process which can be initiated by the responsible administrative authority. The law does not formally depart from the Brazilian tradition which eschews corporate criminal liability, but it does permit administrative sanctions to be imposed on organizations without proof of subjective fault. Those sanctions are severe, including a monetary penalty of up to 20 percent of the organization's gross turnover in the year before the commencement of the investigation and temporary suspension of various privileges.

The influence of the FCPA model appears to be amplified by the work of the OECD Working Group on Bribery in International Business. Whatever the reason, the diffusion of the FCPA enforcement model internationally emphasizes the importance of understanding its implications for enforcement strategy.

ENFORCEMENT STRATEGY UNDER THE FCPA MODEL

Evidence

In principle, it should be possible to draw inferences about the motivations and objectives that guide FCPA enforcement over any given period by analyzing characteristics of the cases selected for enforcement and the types of sanctions imposed. In practice, many of the relevant characteristics are unobservable. To begin, the DOJ and the SEC typically say very little about the characteristics of cases that are not selected for enforcement. This makes it difficult for external researchers to learn anything at all about why cases are selected for enforcement. There are also important gaps in published information about even the cases in which there is enforcement. For instance, the extent to which the US has an economic interest in any given firm's welfare is difficult to observe, making it difficult to determine whether an enforcement strategy is motivated by economic self-interest. The availability of evidence and perceived probability of detection are also difficult to observe, making it difficult to determine whether the pattern of enforcement is consistent with the objectives of retribution or deterrence.

Despite these constraints, a handful of studies have attempted to shed light on FCPA enforcement strategy. Some of these studies examine how FCPA sanctions vary across individual cases with a view to understanding how sanctions are determined. Other studies examine how FCPA enforcement actions vary in terms of the countries implicated in the misconduct. These studies aim to use country-level data about the incidence of corruption to draw inferences about how US agencies select cases for enforcement.

The studies that examine how FCPA sanctions vary across cases support the idea that firms incorporated outside the US pay higher penalties than firms incorporated inside the US in cases with similar observable characteristics (Garrett 2011; Choi and Davis 2014). This might be explained by self-interest. As noted, however, it is also consistent with other explanations since these studies do not take full account of the extent to which US economic interests in a firm track its jurisdiction of incorporation. Nor do they account fully for variations in access to evidence or the probability of detection.

Studies of the distribution of FCPA enforcement actions across countries suggest that enforcement is more likely when a foreign regulator with whom US agencies have a cooperative relationship is involved. This mode of analysis also suggests that FCPA enforcement is biased toward cases in which bribes are paid in relatively corrupt countries, consistent with altruism (McLean 2012; Choi and Davis, 2014).

In the absence of solid evidence, however, we are forced to resort to theorizing to understand FCPA enforcement strategies. The following sections provide conjectures on how each of the key elements of the FCPA enforcement model is likely to affect enforcement strategies.

Implications of Dominance by Prosecutors

What is the significance of the fact that the DOJ and the SEC, rather than judges, civil plaintiffs or specialized anti-corruption regulators, control FCPA enforcement strategy? One result is that their strategy for selecting cases is opaque. As noted, the US enforcement agencies are fairly transparent about how the sanctions imposed in individual cases are determined. They do not, however, provide much data on cases of misconduct in which they choose not to pursue enforcement actions. They also are not very clear about their motivations for selecting cases. It is worth noting that this lack of transparency is consistent with a legitimate effort to achieve deterrence by creating ambiguity about enforcement strategy. Whatever the reason, the result is that, to a large extent, we are forced to conjecture about this aspect of FCPA enforcement strategy based on the incentives and expertise of the DOJ and the SEC. Fortunately for researchers, the fact that all FCPA prosecutions are handled by special centralized units within the DOJ and SEC that work quite closely with one another makes it reasonable to presume that at any given point in time they will be pursuing a coherent enforcement strategy.

The US enforcement agencies have incentives to pursue easy, high-profile FCPA cases that generate substantial recoveries for the US government (Turk 2013; Lemos and Minzner 2014). Easy cases allow individual prosecutors either to earn more wins with the same amount of effort or to expend less effort. High-profile cases help individuals' careers. Winning a high-profile case may be a good way for a prosecutor to earn a promotion. It may also be a calling card for an attorney who wants to leave government and go into private practice. In the US it is common for successful prosecutors to leave the government and obtain jobs with prominent law firms where they earn, literally, millions of dollars. Meanwhile at the institutional level, enforcement agencies arguably have an interest in enforcement strategies that generate substantial recoveries because total recoveries are an easily communicable way of demonstrating effectiveness to all sorts of stakeholders, including Congressional overseers. It seems plausible that high-profile easy FCPA cases that generate large recoveries will tend to involve prominent US firms that have paid large bribes to high-level foreign public officials. This all suggests that US enforcement agencies have incentives to pursue a relatively cosmopolitan enforcement strategy that is compatible with either retribution or deterrence.

By contrast, the agencies have neither the incentives nor any obvious expertise to pursue altruistic enforcement strategies. The victims of corruption do not pay US prosecutors' salaries and those prosecutors are not accountable to anyone outside the United States. The agencies might face political pressure from US firms to pursue self-interested enforcement strategies, but the relatively high cost associated with prosecuting foreign firms might tend to counteract that incentive. It also is not obvious that the enforcement agencies have much incentive to pursue enforcement strategies designed to secure compensation for foreign victims because that would reduce the amount remitted to the US Treasury.

It is possible to imagine alternative regulatory approaches that would rely less heavily on US prosecutors to choose cases and establish sanctions. Imagine, for instance, that there was a private right of action for FCPA violations. This would give private litigants and judges a greater role in shaping enforcement strategy and would almost certainly tilt enforcement strategy toward compensation. The degree of transparency would depend on how many cases settled out of court. This would in turn depend on whether the law established bright-line standards that limit disagreement about how issues such as causation of harm would be resolved at trial. Alternatively, suppose that regulators in countries where foreign bribe-payers are based began to offer more assistance to US regulators. This would tend to reduce the costs of sanctioning foreign firms. This might make it easier for US agencies to pursue a self-interested enforcement strategy, albeit at the risk of retaliation against US firms by self-interested foreign enforcement agencies. If regulators in countries where bribes are paid began to initiate more proceedings and seek cooperation from US regulators then enforcement strategies would probably become more altruistic. The same would be true if international agencies concerned with the welfare of host countries (for example, the World Bank) began to initiate more anti-corruption cases. In this scenario US agencies would also face pressure to focus on compensation.

Implications of Organizational Liability

US law makes it exceptionally easy to attribute liability to organizational actors. This has implications for compensation, retribution and prevention. Compensation obviously is easier to secure with access to the pockets of a corporate defendant as an option, but it is less certain how broad attribution of corporate liability affects retribution and prevention.

Some scholars believe that corporate liability is an important component of a scheme of punishment committed to the objective of retribution. In an organizational context, misconduct like foreign bribery is often the result of decisions made by several individuals. These include decisions to do business in a high-risk country, to adopt a compensation scheme that provides high-powered incentives to sales people, to skimp on training on anti-corruption norms, and to avoid instituting strict financial controls. Imposing liability on the organization makes a statement that culpability lies at the organizational level.

Corporate liability is also often justified in terms of deterrence. It can be difficult to identify and sanction all of the individuals responsible for committing foreign bribery in a corporate setting, especially if you take into account all of the people who encourage or enable or turn a blind eye to the misconduct. Targeting the firm creates incentives for the firm to participate in deterring or incapacitating individuals who might be difficult to deter or incapacitate through imposition of purely individual liability. There are at least three distinct ways in which firms can do this: prevention, policing, and reporting. Prevention can range from training of employees, to adjustment of compensation policies, to financial controls. Policing involves both monitoring employees and disciplining those who have engaged in misconduct. Reporting employees to enforcement authorities and sharing evidence with those authorities can also be a potent deterrent (Arlen and Kraakman 1997).

In a deterrence-oriented framework the main concern about corporate liability is that it risks diverting attention and resources from prosecution of individuals. Prosecutors already have relatively weak incentives to pursue cases against individual bribe-payers. Establishing that an individual has committed foreign bribery can be just as costly as establishing corporate liability. In fact, a criminal FCPA case against an individual is likely to be more costly than one against an organization because criminal liability requires proof that the individual acted 'willfully'. In addition, experience has shown that FCPA cases against individual defendants are more likely to go to trial. This may be because of the difficulty of associating any particular individual with a bribe and, in a criminal case, the challenges of establishing willfulness. There is substantial room for disagreement about the outcome of a trial that turns on these kinds of factors. At the same time, individuals typically have limited assets and so for the reasons discussed above the benefits to the government of prosecuting individuals are limited.

Taking liability for individual bribe-payers off the table limits the deterrent effect of corporate liability. When individual criminal liability is a realistic threat firms can deter individuals by making credible threats to report their misconduct to enforcement agencies. Removing that threat forces firms to use other potentially more costly means to achieve any given level of corruption prevention. For instance, to compensate for the absence of individual criminal sanctions that facilitate deterrence of employees, corporations might have to invest more in prevention, for example, by reducing the scale of their activities in high-risk countries. The cost of those additional corporate efforts may be greater than the costs of criminal prosecutions.

Eliminating individual bribe-payers' liability for foreign bribery is also, of course, inconsistent with retribution, which demands that individuals be held liable for their misconduct.

Corporate liability for bribe-payers also has the potential to divert attention from seeking to punish individual foreign public officials who solicit or receive bribes. The FCPA does not create liability for foreign public officials who receive bribes (*U.S. v. Castle*). However, there are other laws, at both the federal and state level, that appear to create such liability. Most notably, if foreign public officials transfer proceeds of bribery through the US financial system they might be prosecuted under federal law for money laundering. For example, Robert Antoine, an official of the Haitian national telecommunications company was prosecuted for money laundering in connection with an FCPA case against a company and several individuals who paid him bribes (Department of Justice 2010). There is also the possibility of prosecution under state law for dealing in stolen property. Paolo Maluf, the former mayor Sao Paulo was indicted in New York on these sorts of charges (New York County District Attorney 2007). In theory foreign public officials can also be prosecuted for violating the anti-bribery laws of individual US states that criminalize receipt of bribes since some of those laws have extraterritorial effects. Violations of those laws can also provide a basis for prosecution under the US Travel Act, which makes it a federal offense to travel or use the facilities of interstate commerce to violate state anti-bribery laws. In November 2013 Maria Gonzalez, an official of the Venezuelan state development bank pleaded guilty to accepting bribes from employees of a New York investment company in violation of both anti-money laundering laws and the Travel Act. The Travel Act violations were predicated on allegations that she violated the New York Penal Law provisions on receiving a commercial bribe (Department of Justice 2013).

The threat of prosecution in the US is not an idle one for foreign public officials who have assets in the US, enjoy traveling to the US, or are US citizens. For example, Mr Antoine was apparently a resident of Florida. Even the publicity associated with the initiation of proceedings in the US might harm the reputation of the official.[1] On the other hand, the cost of prosecuting foreign public officials is likely to be even greater than the cost of prosecuting individual bribe-payers since the evidence and witnesses, including the defendant, are more likely to be located overseas.

Sanctioning foreign public officials who solicit or receive bribes is compatible with cosmopolitanism, self-interest and altruism, and can promote retribution, prevention or compensation. However, it will typically raise all of the concerns associated with any form of extraterritorial regulation. These concerns are addressed in the next section.

Implications of Broadly Defined Jurisdiction

The more expansive their jurisdiction, the greater the range of enforcement strategies the DOJ and SEC can pursue. For instance, the more foreign firms over which it can exercise jurisdiction, the easier it will be for one of these agencies to pursue an enforcement strategy designed to promote US economic self-interest. Similarly, the more bribe-payers that are subject to US jurisdiction, the more plausible it is that the FCPA can be used to sanction a meaningful portion of the foreign bribery that affects any given country deemed to be in need of US assistance.

Some of the enforcement strategies enabled by broad definitions of jurisdiction are problematic. Most of the problems stem from the fact that the broad definition of jurisdiction under the FCPA increases the likelihood that the US will be one of several countries in a position to prosecute any given bribe-payer. Unfortunately, there are few formal mechanisms for coordinating the activities of enforcement agencies across countries in order to avoid any problems that might result. For instance, many countries permit defendants to be punished a second time for the same misconduct if the previous sanction was imposed by a different sovereign.

Broadly defined jurisdiction creates the risk of enforcement strategies that undermine the retributive objective of ensuring that bribe-payers are punished fairly. The main substantive concern is that bribe-payers will be punished twice and, in the absence of coordination between the jurisdictions, may receive sanctions that are disproportionately large in relation

---

[1]   To accuse a foreign public official of corruption publicly without intending to prosecute them would be inconsistent with norms that encourage prosecutors to avoid publicly identifying wrongdoers who have not been charged. This is done in order to protect the privacy of the uncharged parties and to ensure that they have a chance to confront their accusers in court. See United States Attorneys' Manual, 9.27.760.

to their culpability. There is also a concern about procedural unfairness. Subjecting bribe-payers to the burden of being prosecuted multiple times might itself be viewed as a disproportionate sanction. Moreover, regardless of whether they are punished multiple times, broad definitions of jurisdiction make it possible for alleged bribe-payers to be forced to defend themselves in distant legal systems pursuant to unfamiliar substantive and procedural rules, which may also be considered an undue burden.

Expansive jurisdiction is not necessarily ideal in terms of prevention either. It might cause either too many or too few cases to be brought, resulting in either under-deterrence or over-deterrence. Under-deterrence is a danger because prosecutors from each jurisdiction might wait for other prosecutors to move first so that they can free-ride on their efforts. Over-deterrence is possible to the extent that countries are able to overcome these collective action problems and choose to prosecute the same defendant multiple times. One particularly troubling scenario occurs when prosecutors base sanctions on information about wrongdoing that a firm has provided to an enforcement agency in another jurisdiction in return for a promise of leniency. This prospect undermines firms' incentives to cooperate with any law enforcement agency.

Finally, defining jurisdiction broadly can thwart compensation if it allows sanctions to be imposed by countries that have limited interest in or ability to compensate victims.

The adoption of mechanisms to facilitate voluntary coordination would almost certainly improve the current system. Those mechanisms would include communication systems that allow prosecutors from different jurisdictions to make binding agreements about which cases they will and will not pursue. If the purpose is to protect the interests of countries affected by corruption then coordination mechanisms tilted in favor of those countries can be adopted. For instance, it might be desirable to adopt a version of the principle of complementarity embodied in the Rome Statute that governs the International Criminal Court. There could be a rebuttable presumption that jurisdiction over a matter will be asserted exclusively by the country whose official was corrupted. The presumption could be rebutted in cases in which that country is genuinely either unwilling or unable to investigate or prosecute.

Implications of High-powered Sanctions

There is little question that US law permits the imposition of sanctions for foreign bribery that are very high relative to sanctions imposed in other countries. What remains unresolved is whether the sanctions that have actually been imposed are too high, too low, or just right. The terms of this debate vary depending on whether the sanctions are viewed as means of achieving prevention or compensation.

As far as prevention is concerned, some critics complain that FCPA sanctions are excessive because they deter foreign bribery in ways that undermine US economic interests. There are longstanding concerns that the FCPA places US businesses at a competitive disadvantage to their foreign counterparts who face less vigorously enforced restrictions on foreign bribery (Weissmann and Smith 2010: 6).

Other critics complain that FCPA sanctions are too high because they deter investment that would, on balance, make host countries better off (Spalding 2010, 2012). The premise is that the threat of FCPA liability will induce firms to refrain from certain kinds of socially valuable investments. The assumption is that at least some firms will find this kind of response more cost-effective than other ways of preventing misconduct, such as adjusting compensation policies or increasing internal controls. If firms do in fact respond this way then countries that are perceived to be high-risk are the most likely to lose investment. Although perceptions will not always match reality, countries which are already suffering under the burden of corrupt institutions are likely to be most affected.

The other side of the deterrence debate argues that FCPA sanctions are too low to provide meaningful deterrence, taking into account the low probability that foreign bribery will be sanctioned and the large benefits to be earned from foreign bribery. The probability of detection certainly appears to be low—there have never been more than 20 FCPA enforcement actions against corporations in a single year. It is difficult, however, to make any definitive claims about the deterrent effects of these sanctions. Karpoff et al (2014) argue that sanctions are too low based on estimates of the probability that a publicly traded bribe-paying firm will face bribery charges (6.4 percent), the average value of a contract procured through bribery (2.6 percent of market capitalization), and the average cost of fines, investigation costs and reputational losses associated with being prosecuted for foreign bribery (5.1 percent of market capitalization). These estimates are, however, rather crude. The estimate of the value of contracts procured through bribery seems likely to be biased upwards because it is based on changes in firm value that occurred when contracts were publicly announced. Firms probably only choose to make announcements of this kind for relatively large contracts. The estimate of the probability that a bribe-paying firm will face bribery charges rests heavily on extrapolation based on the contestable assumption that bribe-paying firms that have not been charged resemble the ones that have been charged. Also noteworthy is the fact that the Karpoff et al. study covers few cases that could have been affected by the SEC whistleblower program. That program was created in 2010 pursuant to the Dodd-Frank Wall Street Reform and Consumer Protection Act. It allows whistleblowers who provide information about violations of the FCPA and other securities laws by publicly traded firms to recover up to 30 percent of sanctions collected from the firm. This program has the potential to significantly increase the probability of prosecution for bribe-payers.

Leaving aside deterrence, there is a largely separate debate about whether FCPA sanctions are sufficiently effective as means of compensation (see generally Turk 2013). A comprehensive recent study has shown that on a global scale only a small fraction of monetary sanctions imposed in foreign bribery cases have been returned to host countries as compensation. There have only been a handful of FCPA cases in which any form of compensation has been ordered (Oduor 2014). US law permits restitution to victims of crime and sharing of forfeited assets with jurisdictions that provide assistance in prosecution. But those provisions are not used very often. Part of the explanation may be that US prosecutors have little incentive to share money with foreign governments. A more benign explanation is that in many cases US enforcement agencies do not trust foreign governments to use repatriated funds for the benefit of the victims of corruption, or even the population as a whole. To put it bluntly, they worry about sending money back to the same people who tried to steal it.

CONCLUSION

Enforcement strategy is a critical link in the causal chain between enactment of legal prohibitions and social and economic outcomes. Unfortunately, FCPA enforcement strategy is difficult to observe directly. This chapter offers several conjectures about how the legal framework that governs FCPA enforcement is likely to influence enforcement strategies. Indications that the FCPA enforcement model is spreading to other anti-corruption regimes suggests that these conjectures merit further investigation. Further research should also consider the strategies that firms might adopt in response to the kinds of enforcement strategies outlined here.

REFERENCES

Arlen, Jennifer and Reinier Kraakman. 1997. 'Controlling Corporate Misconduct: An Analysis of Corporate Liability Regimes', *New York University Law Review* 72: 687–779.

Choi, Stephen J. and Kevin E. Davis. 2014. 'Foreign Affairs and Enforcement of the Foreign Corrupt Practices Act', *Journal of Empirical Legal Studies* 11: 409–45.

Criminal Division of the US Department of Justice and Enforcement Division of the US Securities and Exchange Commission. 2012. *FCPA: A Resource Guide to the U.S. Foreign Corrupt Practices Act* (14 November).

Cuervo-Cazurra, Alvaro. 2008. 'The Effectiveness of Laws against Bribery Abroad', *Journal of International Business Studies* 39: 634–51.

Davis, Kevin E. 2012. 'Why Does the United States Regulate Foreign Bribery: Moralism, Self-Interest or Altruism?' *New York University Annual Survey of American Law* 67: 497–511.

Department of Justice. 2010. 'Former Haitian Government Official Pleads Guilty to Conspiracy to Commit Money Laundering in Foreign Bribery Scheme'. Press release 10-260. March 12.

Department of Justice. 2013. 'High-Ranking Bank Official at Venezuelan State Development Bank Pleads Guilty in Manhattan Federal Court to Participating in Bribery Scheme'. Press release 13-358. 18 November.

Garret, Brandon L. 2011. 'Globalized Corporate Prosecutions', *Virginia Law Review* 97: 1775–876.

Hines, James R. 1995. 'Forbidden Payment: Foreign Bribery and American Business after 1977', NBER Working Paper 5266, National Bureau of Economic Research, Inc.

Karpoff, Jonathan M., D. Scott Lee and Gerald S. Martin. 2014. 'The Economics of Foreign Bribery: Evidence from FCPA Enforcement Actions' (Working Paper), available 11 May 2015 at http://papers.ssrn.com/sol3/papers.cfm?abstract_id=1573222.

Lemos, Margaret H. and Max Minzner. 2014. 'For-profit Public Enforcement', *Harvard Law Review* 127: 854–913.

Leroy, Anne-Marie and Frank Fariello. 2012. 'The World Bank Group Sanctions Process and Its Recent Reforms'. Washington DC: World Bank.

McLean, Nicholas M. 2012. 'Cross-National Patterns in FCPA Enforcement', *Yale Law Journal* 121: 1970–2012.

New York County District Attorney's Office. 2007. News release. 8 March.

Oduor, Jacinta Anyango, et al. 2014. *Left out of the Bargain: Settlements in Foreign Bribery Cases and Implications for Asset Recovery.* Washington, DC: World Bank.

Priest, George L. and Benjamin Klein. 1984. 'The Selection of Disputes for Litigation', *Journal of Legal Studies* 13: 1–55.

Spalding, Andrew Brady. 2010. 'Unwitting Sanctions: Understanding Anti-Bribery Legislation as Economic Sanctions Against Emerging Markets', *Florida Law Review* 62: 351–427.

Spalding, Andrew Brady. 2012. 'Four Uncharted Corners of Anti-Corruption Law: in Search of Remedies to the Sanctioning Effect', *Wisconsin Law Review* 2012: 661–88.

Turk, Matthew. 2013. 'A Political Economy Approach to Reforming the Foreign Corrupt Practices Act', *Northwestern Journal of International Law and Business* 33: 325–91.

United States Attorneys' Manual. Available 11 May 2015 at http://www.justice.gov/usao/eousa/foia_reading_room/usam/.

Weissman, Andrew and Alixandra Smith. 2010. *Restoring Balance: Proposed*

Amendments to the Foreign Corrupt Practices Act. Washington, D.C.: U.S. Chamber Institute for Legal Reform.

Legislation

Alternative Fines Act 18 U.S.C. § 3571.
Dodd-Frank Wall Street Reform and Consumer Protection Act. Pub. L. No. 111- 203, § 922, 124 Stat. 1376, C.F.R. § 80.7.1841-49 (2010).
Foreign Corrupt Practices Act of 1977, Pub. L. No. 95-213, § 102, 91 Stat. 1494, codified as amended at 15 U.S.C. §§78m(b), (d)(1), (g)-(h), 78dd-1, 78dd-2, 78dd- 3, 78ff; amended by Foreign Corrupt Practices Act Amendment of 1988 (part of Omnibus Trade and Competitiveness Act of 1988), Pub. L. 100-418, 102 Stat. 1107, 1415 (1988), and International Anti-Bribery and Fair Competition Act of 1998, Pub. L. 105-366, 112 Stat. 3302 (1998).
Travel Act. 18 U.S.C. § 1952.

International instruments

Agreement for Mutual Enforcement of Debarment Decisions, 9 April 2010.
MDB Harmonized Principles on Treatment of Corporate Groups (Adopted: 10 September 2012).
Organization for Economic Cooperation and Development, Convention on Combating Bribery of Foreign Public Officials in International Business Transactions, 21 November 1997, 37 I.L.M. 4 (1998).
Rome Statute of the International Criminal Court, U.N. Doc. A/CONF.183/9 (17 July 1998).
United Nations Convention against Corruption, in force 14 December 2005.
World Bank Sanctions Procedures (as adopted by the World Bank as of 1 January 2011), available 11 May 2015 at http://siteresources.worldbank.org/ EXTOFFEVASUS/Resources/WBGSanctionsProceduresJan2011.pdf.

Decisions

U.S. v. Castle, 925 F.2d 831 (5th Cir. 1991).

13. Tax avoidance, tax evasion, money laundering and the problem of 'offshore'

Peter Alldridge*

INTRODUCTION

Capital flight from developing nations to rich nations, frequently via ('offshore') secrecy jurisdictions, is said to be bad for the developing nations, because it erodes their tax base. It has a number of causes, including tax avoidance, tax evasion, corruption, fraud, plunder, money laundering, caprice and rational and irrational investment. It was facilitated by the end, in the late 1970s, of the Bretton Woods arrangements. Under the Exchange Controls Act 1947 it was a crime to take cash out of the UK whatever its provenance. There is much concern about the relationship between international capital movement and its lawfulness. In the literature on such flows the word 'illicit' is generally used. Another word frequently deployed is 'laundering'. The purpose of this chapter is to untangle some of the arguments, and to examine the relationship between the respective crimes and non-crimes. What it will suggest is that so far as possible in the formation of international policy, arguments about laundering should be kept separate from those to do with corruption, tax evasion and tax avoidance. Corruption is the logically prior issue because, of the issues under consideration, only corruption strikes directly at the rule of law. If it is possible to bribe a judge, or a police officer or a tax inspector or somebody placing government contracts, then it does not matter what the rules are, because they will not be applied. In particular the rhetorical device of branding money 'dirty' or activity as 'laundering' should be avoided.

* With thanks to Gautam Nair and all the contributors at the Castle conference.

OFFSHORE

There have been many strong attacks upon the use of 'offshore' tax havens. The Tax Justice Network argued in its widely cited report *The Price of Offshore Revisited*, that $21 to $32 trillion in 'financial' wealth in 2010 was 'hidden' in Offshore Financial Centres (OFCs) and so is 'virtually tax free' (Henry 2012, Gould 2010). Whilst OFCs have some defenders, the general idea of many of the complaints is that 'offshore' contributes to many of the world's evils (Shaxson 2012; Palan, Murphy, and Chavagneux 2013; Murphy 2013; Gould 2013). Sol Picciotto, for example, argued that, '[b]y providing a haven for routing global flows through the use of artificial persons and transactions, 'offshore' has helped to dislocate the international state system and induce its substantial reconstruction' (Picciotto 1999: 43). Recent discourse has seen rhetorical and other links being made between corruption, tax avoidance, tax evasion and money laundering.

The British Government has a reputation for being at the heart of a 'spider's web' of offshore jurisdictions which enable avoidance, evasion, corruption and laundering (Shaxson 2012: 103). Overseas territories and crown dependencies did not just appear. So far as concerns the UK, they are usually the result, of one or another eighteenth century military adventure. There are three main attractions to 'offshore'.

First, there is secrecy, in the senses both of having legal protections upon access to information, and also a culture of not asking questions. Some forms of financial secrecy have given rise to concern since the 1980s (OECD 1985), and the era of bank secrecy has now been declared to be at an end (OECD 2011; Schoueri and Barbosa 2013). The more usual mechanism for 'creating' anonymity is the shell company (Young 2012, 2013). The concerns of the NGOs and others are reflected in the establishment by the Tax Justice Network of a Financial Secrecy Index which ranks jurisdictions according to their secrecy and the scale of their activities, and it is against such anonymity that the move to instantiate mechanisms (public registers or similar) arises. Second, offshore jurisdictions tend to operate low tax rates on the relevant matters. The rate of corporation tax is the critical one. Some secrecy jurisdictions have quite high rates of consumption taxes. This matters only if the actor intends to pay any tax. Most obviously, a company might want a low tax regime because it *does* intend to publish accounts and have them audited. Third, offshore jurisdictions offer political stability (usually arising at least in part from limited local democratic accountability) (Shaxson 2012: 179–81), and financial products offering what Sharman calls 'calculated ambiguity' (Sharman 2010). A person might want to put his/her money in a politically stable and economically prosperous jurisdiction because s/he is less likely to lose it.

If a remedy is needed for 'offshore', the first two (secrecy and low taxes) of these three things would need to be challenged (Christensen 2012). Secrecy is addressed by transparency and disclosure. The US Foreign Account Tax Compliance Act 2010 (FATCA), which compels banks all over the world to disclose accounts the beneficial owners of which are US citizens is an example of compelled disclosure (Morse 2012; Grinberg 2012; Behrens 2013). The EU as part of the revision of its money launder-ing regime is putting in place regulations under which the ultimate owners of companies and trusts would have to be listed in public registers in EU countries, under updated draft anti-money laundering (AML) rules approved by the UK Economic Affairs and the Justice and Home Affairs committees. The 'remedy' for low tax rates—if it needs a remedy—is inter-national agreements to deal with 'harmful tax competition'. This is some-thing the OECD has been trying to address for some time (OECD 1998). In the wake of concerns about the use by multinational companies of the rules on jurisdiction to minimize their liability to tax, the Lough Erne dec-laration of the G8 in 2013 committed the signatory nations to 'Fair taxes, increased transparency and open trade' by the sharing of information between tax authorities, legislation against companies shifting their profits across borders to avoid taxes, and multinationals being obliged to report to tax authorities what tax they pay and where, worldwide (G8 2013). OECD has an Action Plan on BEPS (OECD 2013) and has revised the wording of article 26 of the OECD model tax convention (OECD 2003) to let tax authorities ask other countries for any financial information that is 'foreseeable relevant' about taxpayers.

The short-term remedy for the 'see no evil, hear no evil' political stability is genuine democracy and local accountability. The long term remedy is the abolition of the sorts of constitutional structures (overseas territory and crown dependency, with deniable control from elsewhere) in which they thrive.

(CORPORATE) TAX AVOIDANCE

There has been much discussion of 'aggressive' tax avoidance measures and the evils attached to them. The problem is that like that between 'harmful' and 'non-harmful' tax competition, the difference between 'aggressive' and 'non-aggressive' tax avoidance is by no means clear. It would facilitate planning if taxes—other than those imposed deliberately to achieve some change in behaviour—could be imposed so as to have no effect on the behaviour of taxpayers. It does not work like that. In order to reduce their liability to tax, people get married, make wills, have children and change their nationality. Compared to those things, there does not seem to be much that is particularly 'aggressive' about running money through a shell company in Cayman and a blind trust in Gibraltar.

The principle in the *Duke of Westminster's* (*IRC v Duke of Westminster* [1936] AC 1, 19–20) case is that: 'Every man is entitled, if he can, to order his affairs so as that the tax attaching . . . is less . . . If he succeeds in ordering them so as to secure this result, then, however unappreciative the Commissioners of Inland Revenue or his fellow taxpayers may be of his ingenuity, he cannot be compelled to pay an increased tax.' Once the *Westminster* principle is granted in unattenuated form (with no consideration for avoidance), talk of fairness makes no sense and there is no sustainable distinction between the mechanisms by which a person orders his/her affairs so as to fall outside the charge to tax. It might be that the corporation domiciled in jurisdiction A that does most of its trading in jurisdiction B pays little tax in jurisdiction B. It might be that multi-national corporations are able to shift profits to jurisdictions where the tax position is more favourable. It might be that interest on offshore bank accounts is not taxable until remitted. If these are problems the law should be changed.

So far as concerns corporations that operate globally, the legal framework for international taxation is old and messy (Picciotto 2013). The system for allocating the profits of transnational companies between the jurisdictions they touch for the purposes of taxation arose during the 1920s, primarily under the auspices of the League of Nations, and since its inception in 1961, has been controlled by the OECD (Graetz and O'Hear 1997). A range of avoidance mechanisms exist. The major one (for others see Gravelle 2014: 8), deriving from the rules on international taxation, is transfer pricing (Sikka and Willmott 2010). The idea is to ensure that profits be expressed to accrue for the purposes of the relevant legislation and double taxation treaties, in jurisdictions that attract the smallest liability to tax and losses so as to negative as much of the taxable profits as possible. This sort of behaviour is presented nowadays as being that of a parasite driven only by its own advantage. The basis of the critique is that these organisations take the benefits of national infrastructure (a comparatively wealthy customer base, roads and other infrastructure), while not making any, or only making a small contribution towards paying for them (Murphy 2013). The general claim of the 'tax justice' movement is that it is bad that corporations and/or individuals avail themselves of favourable rates of taxation, or the anonymity that can be furnished by shell companies, blind trusts, hybrid entities, attorney-client privilege, anonymous beneficial ownership and so on.

On a macro level the international cash flows generated by tax avoidance behaviour are said to be damaging because they erode the tax base for the countries from which the money moves, and conduce towards a 'race to the bottom' (OECD 1998; Reuter 2012; cf. Morriss and Moberg, 2012). The jurisdiction that regulates least, and least effectively, attracts the most business. Money migrates to offshore jurisdictions, both as semi-permanent haven and *en route*, for example, to London or New York. This is bad for the developing nations, because it erodes their tax base, and taxation is the best and most sustainable way in which to fund government.

While capital flight is frequently presented as being a problem arising from the 'illicit' nature of the money involved, it occurs for a number of reasons, legal and illegal, and insofar as the harmful economic consequences of offshore are erosion of the tax base of developing nations, they are unrelated to the lawfulness or otherwise of the provenance of the money. If capital flight is bad and it is possible to inhibit capital flight, then the inhibition ought not to be dependent upon allegations of criminality. If the use of the criminal sanction—the spread of laundering liability—had any provable effect on the rates of flight the position might be different, but as long as Anti-Money Laundering (AML) is a leap of faith it is not. In an early and highly influential piece on the economics of laundering Tanzi argued, *inter alia*, that laundering was harmful because the movements of money involved would be for reasons other than the optimal and efficient operation of markets (Tanzi 1996). The same kind of attitude underpins the later fuller account of the IMF (International Monetary Fund 2011).

On a micro level, one of the consequences of tax havens is that they skew markets to the benefit of multinationals at the expense of striving domestic entrepreneurs. How can the local independent coffee shop, which pays domestic corporation tax, contend with Starbucks, which pays little or no tax in the jurisdiction? The independent purveyor may well serve a superior *doppio* to Starbucks' but cannot compete on price. The 'Starbucks' argument from unfair competition in tax law is entirely analogous to the 'empty pizzeria' argument against money laundering. To encourage competition we may well want to do something about undesirable cross-subsidies within companies to subsidise particular activities. Whether or not the subsidy comes from a lawful source does not, on this account, affect the harm it does.

The G20 now affirms as a principle that the international community should:

(1) Address tax avoidance, particularly, base erosion and profit shifting to ensure profits are taxed in the location where the economic activity takes place.
(2) Promote international tax transparency and the global sharing of information so that taxpayers with offshore investments comply with their domestic tax obligations.

(3)   Ensure that developing countries benefit from the G20's tax agenda,
       particularly in relation to information sharing.

What the global corporations say is that they organise their affairs so as
to minimise liability to tax, that they are allowed to do it, and that if the
OECD Governments, individually or collectively, want to change the
basis upon which tax is levied, then they have it in their power to do it.
Tax planning is presented by the corporations as a rational response to tax
laws. Indeed, it is the only response possible for an individual or firm faced
with the need to comply with the conflicting provisions, definitions, and
exemptions of multiple jurisdictions' tax laws.

So for as concerns personal taxation (Gravelle 2014: 20 et seq), attention in the UK is directed against the tax status of those who are not domiciled in the UK ('non-doms'), and consequently fall outside the charge to
tax. The remedy for that might be to abolish the category. Tax avoidance,
by profit shifting or otherwise, is a natural consequence of the rules which
permit it.

AVOIDANCE—REMEDIES

Within any tax system, the remedy for avoidance is usually taken
to be specific and general anti-avoidance provisions. Attempts to
distinguish acceptable from unacceptable avoidance have been made
worldwide by reference to the form as opposed to the substance of
the transaction, to its 'commercial reality' idea, or to motive and the
idea of abuse of rights. The UK courts have at some times, especially in the period opened by *W. T. Ramsay Ltd. v. Inland Revenue
Commissioners* [1982] A.C. 300, undertaken the curious jurisprudence
of looking for the 'spirit' of a set of rules set apart from what the rules
say. As judge-made law this line was either overruled or disapproved
in *Barclays Mercantile Business Finance Ltd v. Mawson* [2004] UKHL
51 (and see Freedman 2007). Usually, and constitutionally, this is done
by legislation. In English Law, under the rules on Disclosure of Tax
Avoidance Schemes (DOTAS), there is a category of tax avoidance
scheme that has specifically to be drawn to the attention of the Revenue
before its implementation. A general anti-abuse rule was put in place
in the United Kingdom by the Finance Act 2013, ss.206 *et seq*. Many
anti-avoidance provisions involve 'deeming'—the creation of the legal
fiction that particular transactions did not happen, where they have no
commercial purpose, or are not at arm's length or have a substance different from their form, or appeal to the spirit of particular provisions. It

is much easier to make a case for such provision in tax than in criminal statutes.

So far as concerns the international system for the taxation of multinational corporations, there is much pressure for change—the 'reform agenda'—which has been brought to the political forefront by publicity given to the tax treatment of multinationals (Palan, Murphy, and Chavagneux 2013; Murphy 2013; Hodge 2013). Just as the 'aggressive vs non-aggressive' tax evasion issue is unresolved it is also contentious whether or not and to what extent tax competition between jurisdictions is a good idea or not.

So far as concerns corporate tax avoidance, the point to emphasise is that, without more, however damaging it is, it has nothing necessarily to do with crime in general or money laundering in particular. Corporate profits might end up in a bank in a jurisdiction that has low corporation tax rates. The proceeds of drug dealing might end up in the same bank because the jurisdiction offers secrecy. But that does not mean that corporate tax avoidance and money laundering are the same thing or that they require similar treatment. They are not and they do not. Anger at the losses and the damage occasioned by it should be directed at legislators, not corporations.

TAX EVASION AND OFFSHORE

The tax avoider sets out to comply with his/her legal obligations. The tax evader wants not to comply. Tax evasion *is* unlawful and usually criminal. The taxpayer has property as a result of under- or non-declaration of income or capital gains or other taxable events, or the making of untrue representations in order to gain relief from taxation. Either the property is already in, or the taxpayer sends it to, a bank account or other investment vehicle offshore. Attempts are occasionally made to quantify the amounts lost nationally or globally through tax fraud, and the proportion of that ascribable to 'offshore' (Christensen 2012). While these estimates should all be taken with a pinch of salt, there is no denying that the sums involved are large.

There are some who claim that there is no substantial difference between avoidance and evasion. The line has certainly been blurred a few times, but those who want to equate avoidance and evasion should be careful who their friends are. Russian law does not differentiate between evasion and avoidance. The original tax proceedings against Yukos were driven by a numbers of factors, (Gololobov 2008; Sixsmith 2010) including a crackdown on avoidance by using the favourable tax position of a particular area of Russia, which subsequently was held to fall foul of Article 6. In *Yukos v. Russia* the European Court of Human Rights held that although having a basis in law, the pace of enforcement measures used by the Russian tax authorities against a company which had consequently gone into liquidation, and the failure of the authorities to have sufficient regard to the economic and social implications of those measures on the company and its stakeholders, meant that the authorities had failed to strike a fair balance between the legitimate aim of enforcing a tax liability and the measures employed to achieve that aim (*Yukos v. Russia* (2012) 54 E.H.R.R. 19).

Where tax evasion stands relative to other crimes has always been contentious. Is it worse than other frauds because the victim is the State (that is, everyone) or is it not so bad because the victim is unknown? Is it less of a priority for prosecutors because the Revenue has at its disposal a range of other mechanisms for getting the money, including the imposition of administrative penalties? Or is it more of a priority because the overall sums involved are so high, because of the need to make examples, and because the victim is everyone?

TAX EVASION—REMEDIES

Whereas the remedy in the case of avoidance is to change the rule—put in place anti-avoidance provisions or similar, the standard solutions to tax evasion are, first, to structure taxes so as for them to be collected at source; second, to require entities to report payments; third, transparency requirements on banks and other financial institutions; and fourth, former enforcement. That is, with sufficient monitoring, reporting and disclosure the problems would diminish. Now, so far as concerns the use of offshore to hide money from taxation, the real problems are the mechanisms of secrecy.

MONEY LAUNDERING

So what does money laundering have to do with base erosion or tax competition or offshore? People who commit crimes and thereby make money will seek ways in which to protect, spend or invest the money. Laundering is the process by which the proceeds of crime are separated from the predicate offence and cloaked in legitimacy. The same kinds of things that make particular jurisdictions attractive to tax evaders also make them attractive to criminals wishing to protect, spend or invest the proceeds of their crimes. People wishing to hide the proceeds of crimes will want to avail themselves of secrecy provided by particular jurisdictions, just as much as will those who wish to use secrecy jurisdictions to evade tax. It is for these reasons that laundering is frequently presented as an aspect of the same problem.

In the areas of corruption, money laundering, and the international aspects of tax evasion and tax avoidance, the effect of globalisation is that more has happened since, say, 1985 than had happened in the previous millennium. The global assault upon laundering grew from concern about drugs (Vienna Convention against Illicit Traffic in Narcotic Drugs and Psychotropic Substances (1988)) and then moved into 'organised crime', typically involving other 'victimless crimes', organised crime and rackets (Convention for the Suppression of the Financing of Terrorism (1999), Palermo Convention on Transnational Organized Crime (2000)). When terrorism became an issue, rightly or wrongly (Roberge 2007; Léonard and Kaunert 2012) AML measures were adapted and the same legal structures put to work as Counter Financing of Terrorism (CFT). AML now has a particular concern with corruption and tax evasion. The mechanism—(AML)—by which in the mid-1980s the 'war on drugs' was to be prosecuted, having failed in that regard, has now been adopted as the mechanism by which terrorism is to be halted, integrity returned to our financial systems, and the flight of capital from developing countries is to be rectified.

The label 'laundering' is a difficult one, because the crime is one recognised in the popular consciousness as being serious without any single clear ideal-type of how it is committed. We have a number of vague ideas of what laundering involves. There are at least two ideal-types in popular culture—national and international laundering. One-jurisdiction laundering usually involves subsidising an apparently lawful business, usually one that deals a good deal in cash, with the proceeds of crime. The income of the business is then declared and taxed, and the remainder can be spent. These cases do not raise issues of international economic law, and they hardly call for the involvement of international agencies or financial institutions. Multi-jurisdiction laundering is the same basic structure, but tends to involve financial agencies, so as to transfer money between jurisdictions. It is more complicated and can be glamorised more easily. In terms of cases before courts, the former are far more common.

The vocabulary of laundering, especially words like 'dirty' and 'illicit', is sometimes deployed more widely than is justified. Thus, for example, when late in 2012 the bailout of the Cypriot banks was being discussed, one of the sticking points for Germany was said to be that some of the deposits in Cypriot banks that Germany was being asked to protect were the property of relatively or very rich Russians, allegedly of dubious provenance and allegedly deposited in breach or Russian tax or exchange controls, or both. There is a good deal of Russian money in Cypriot banks, and it has become commonplace to refer to it as 'dirty' (Halliday, Levi, Reuter 2014: para. 7). A more plausible explanation of the German reluctance was that the money was Russian, not that its provenance was, or might have been, dubious. How could it be justified to use German taxes to refund losses made by rich Russians in investing in banks that offered more interest than their local ones? On this account, whether the Russian money was the proceeds of crime or not was irrelevant, save for the rhetorical force of the slur of words associated with laundering. Similarly, the use of the word 'illicit' in this context to cover money movements which are part of lawful avoidance, is unhelpful.

Technically, in English law the crime of money laundering is doing 'something' in respect of 'criminal property' (Proceeds of Crime Act 2002 s.340). The list of potential 'somethings' is written very widely. It is an offence to conceal, disguise, convert, or transfer criminal property, or remove it from the jurisdiction. It is an offence to enter into or become concerned in an arrangement which the defendant knows or suspects facilitates (by whatever means) the acquisition, retention, use or control of criminal property by or on behalf of another person. It is an offence to acquire, use or have possession of criminal property. It is also an offence to be complicit in any of these things. (Proceeds of Crime Act 2002 ss. 327–329 and 340).

Since, as first introduced, laundering offences were at base a form of complicity in the offence by which the money is gained (the 'predicate offence'), laundering can always be presented as playing an integral role in whatever the crime is that is highest on the national and international criminal justice agenda of the day. Chaikin and Sharman produced a book to show that there are links between corruption and laundering (Chaikin and Sharman 2009). The OECD agrees, pronouncing that: 'corruption and money laundering are intrinsically linked' and the FATF produced data to prove it. (Financial Action Task Force, 2011; Jakobi 2010: 139). The link could be claimed equally for any offence that either yields money or (in the case of terrorism or anti-proliferation offences) requires money for its commission. If the commentators' claims are rephrased as 'corruption and complicity in corruption are intrinsically linked', then the pleonasm becomes clear. The use of the mystifying and glamorising term 'laundering' obfuscates. The idea that the property is obtained by some act or other, and that that act has a particular (limited) reprehensibility, and that there is then some additional badness involved when the criminal tries to do anything with the property is wholly artificial. Calling it 'money laundering' rather than 'participation in crime' really only adds rhetorical force, and raises the stakes by bringing the crime within the security agenda, whatever the gravity of the predicate. The problem is property crime of one sort or another.

It makes a great deal of sense for the law to attempt to recoup the profits of crime, by way of confiscation orders and other moves (civil recovery, some forfeitures, the use of tax jurisdiction and so on). It makes less sense to criminalise money laundering otherwise than as a form of complicity in the predicate, but it was necessary to make laundering a serious crime in order to justify the establishment of the AML industry.

Proceeds of crime law is strongly expansionist in three important respects: geographically, by area of the economy, and in respect of their treatment of legal and administrative impediments to the AML industry (Alldridge 2008). As the range of offences acceptable as predicates increases, the nature of the predicate becomes increasingly irrelevant. The laundering offence comes to be regarded as harmful, for reasons unconnected either to the nature of the predicate or to the mental state of the perpetrator (which in classic liberal criminal law theory, usually provides a restriction on liability for consequences). There has been a shift in the core of the offence from predicate to laundering. Money laundering as complicity in property offences is becoming property offences as a form of complicity in money laundering.

Taxation and criminal justice were amongst the last areas of domestic law to be influenced by globalisation and the instantiation of the (nascent) transnational legal order, but they are now at the forefront. Two areas of crime affected in the past few years by the expansion of laundering are corruption and tax crimes. Driven by the OECD Convention on Combating Bribery of Foreign Public Officials in International Business Transactions (1996), and the United Nations Convention against Corruption (2005), growing rigor in the enforcement of the (US) Foreign Corrupt Practises Act and (in the UK) the Bribery Act 2010, corruption has been rising quickly up the international criminal justice agenda. The OECD started a strong initiative on tax and crime in 2011, and this seems to have been the reason for the adoption of the 2012 revised recommendations of FATF (Interpretive Note to Recommendation 3, Para. 4. See definition of 'categories of offences').

The frequently incanted 'remedy' for laundering is the implementation of the FATF recommendations—a ubiquitous and (over-)homogenised legal structure. The idea is that if every jurisdiction across the world were to put in place a legal *regime* of appropriate scope and rigor then levels of crime would go down. AML mandates that firms within the regulated sector require a suite of identification documents from the customer, and then, that suspicious transactions be reported.

There is a price to all that monitoring, reporting and disclosure. There is a price in its administration (it is usually something the banks are required to do for nothing, and whose costs are passed on to their customers). We do not know the price yet. A report written for the IMF was unequivocal.

> To date there is no substantial effort by any international organization, including the IMF, to assess either the costs or benefits of an AML/CFT regime. The FATF system has proceeded as if it produces only public and private goods, not public or private 'bads' or adverse by-products against which the 'goods' have to be weighed . . .
>
> There needs to be more open acknowledgement of actual and potential financial costs of AML/CFT controls, their potential misuse by authoritarian rulers, and possible adverse effects on populations that rely on remittances and the informal economy, as well as potential negative impacts on NGOs and parts of civil society. Likewise the benefits, including a more universally compatible mutual legal assistance scheme, laundering prevention and better proceeds of crime detection and recoveries, need to be articulated more clearly. (Halliday, Levi and Reuter 2014: 9)

In spite of the mildness of the language, the message of this research is clear and striking. It is that the AML industry has been established on a hope that has not been fulfilled. The underlying article of faith of those who established AML industry is KYC—know your customer. If it is possible to operate a bank account anywhere in the world whose beneficial owner is not known to the relevant authorities, then the global AML system is defeated. What Sharman's research tends to show is that, as at the time it was conducted, it was a relatively easy to establish a company the beneficial owner of which was not known (Sharman 2011). It was slightly more difficult to operate a bank account whose beneficial owner was not known to the bank, but there were still jurisdictions in which that could be done.

In the period from around 2005, culminating in the revised FATF recommendations in 2012, pressure to bring tax evasion under the general umbrella of the FATF rose. In the same way that when the eyes of the world were upon terrorism, we were told of the links between terrorism, drug dealing and money laundering, when they fell upon tax avoidance by large corporations, or tax evasion by individuals, again this has been associated with laundering.

MONEY LAUNDERING AND TAX EVASION

It is important to the tax justice movement that evasion be amongst the predicates to laundering, and, on the face of it, it seems natural that it should. If the category of predicate offences is to be extended to make it very wide, why not include tax evasion? On the other hand, there are some considerations at play in tax cases which might militate against using the criminal law. They focus on the relationship between tax and criminal justice. On a number of issues there has been significant integration, in the UK, not so much driven by the FATF revised Recommendations but as being the product of the same forces that gave rise to the revisions of the Recommendations (FATF 2012). In an enquiry as to the relationship between evasion and laundering, issues for resolution are: first, the relationship between prosecution and other measures; second, the (technical) question whether income from crime is taxable; and third whether there can be liability for laundering the proceeds of evasion, and if there can, what follows from that.

Under the Proceeds of Crime Act 2002 as enacted, the Assets Recovery Agency (ARA) was established with the single objective of proceeding to recover proceeds of crime. It failed, not being able to recover enough to pay for itself, let alone the rest of the criminal justice system. When the ARA was abolished in 2007, the Assets Recovery Incentive Scheme was put in place, giving prosecuting and investigating agencies a share of money recovered. If tax evasion becomes a criminal matter, under the Scheme, 50 percent of the amount recovered is divided between the agencies responsible for bringing the prosecution, whereas money recovered by HMRC as tax is paid into the consolidated fund. That is, the prosecuting agency has an incentive to prosecute rather than use tax law to recover the money.

If people do evade tax, by under- or non-declaration or other means, they will have more money than otherwise they would have had, but that does not necessarily mean that so far as concerns any act that might fall within the definition of the major laundering offences. As soon as the category of predicate offences was made sufficiently broad to encompass tax evasion then the question became open—when could there be laundering of the proceeds of evasion? In English law the relevant deeming provisions (Proceeds of Crime Act 2002 s. 76(5) (confiscation) and s. 340(6) (criminal laundering)), have been construed, where the pecuniary advantage is the deferral of a debt, to impute to the defendant the value of the debt, not the value of the deferral.

The conceptual problems raised as to the quantity and identity of the criminal property have consistently been ducked in the laundering case law in England and Wales. In the case of tax fraud by under- or non-declaration, it is clear that the taxpayer will have more property, but there will not necessarily be any identifiable property arising from the evasion to which a laundering charge can be attached. Even if there is identifiable property the defendant will not necessarily hold the required mental state (knowledge that or suspicion as to whether the property in question 'represented or constituted' the proceeds of the offence) for conviction.

In English law, the criminal property is deemed to exist, and defendants have been held to launder the proceeds of the crime of evasion. In *R v. William, William & William* [2013] EWCA Crim 1262, the Court of Appeal held that where a taxpayer cheated the Revenue by falsely representing the turnover of a business, he obtained a pecuniary advantage and was taken to have obtained a benefit equal to tax due on the undeclared turnover. Moreover, the 'criminal property', was the entirety of the undeclared turnover, not merely the tax due. Once the law commits to the fiction that the tax evader actually has in his/her possession property that s/he does not have and uses that as a basis for conviction, there is no obvious point to stop. If tax evasion is a predicate offence to criminal laundering, then, since almost all income from unlawful sources is taxable, there is a danger that the chosen enforcement mechanism—against, for example, drug dealers—will be to treat their money as the proceeds of tax evasion. If the prosecution need only establish that money was undeclared income then, unless the sentences for laundering vary according to the predicate offence, there is no point in proving any other, more serious 'criminal conduct' as a predicate.

Beyond the technical detail, what does it imply that FATF requires that tax offences be now treated as predicates? Except in those jurisdictions (Germany is one—German Criminal Code § 261(9)) which do not allow liability for 'self-laundering' (laundering the proceeds of one's own crime), it is difficult to imagine any case of tax evasion that will not also necessarily amount to money laundering. What hitherto was charged (if at all) as evasion now amounts to evasion *and* money laundering. Significant shifts will follow in the reporting of laundering and capital movements. The inevitable consequence of the incorporation of tax offences as predicates has been to raise estimates of money laundered, and also both to raise the amount of laundering as a proportion of capital flight and capital flight as a proportion of laundering. The OECD identified tax crime as one of the top three sources of money laundering (OECD 2009). If it was not before it will soon, because this claim will become self-authenticating.

Before tax offences were incorporated as predicates by FATF, the empirical basis of the interrelationship between two claims:

- capital flight is bad because it involves money laundering; and
- money laundering is bad because it involves capital flight

was tenuous, since it depended upon an overlap between the two which was unsupported by the data. Not much laundering fell within the 'transnational' category, and not much capital flight was laundering. That may remain the case, but the incorporation of tax evasion as a predicate offence will raise estimates of the global sums laundered, the proportion of international capital movement that amounts to laundering, and the amount of laundering that is included in international capital movement. This will in turn add impetus to the AML industry. There will be more reports, more people employed in the industry, more suspicion and so on.

What once might have been considered tax evasion and then hiding wealth on a tropical island has now become 'tax evasion and money laundering', as though some fresh evil had been added. This has two important consequences. First, the security agenda in criminal justice follows from the idea that some crimes are so serious that their commission involves a security threat and that they can be combatted with extraordinary means. Laundering is one of the offences within the security agenda (Zedner 2010; Vlcek 2012), so the shift from 'tax evasion' *simpliciter* to 'tax evasion and money laundering' implies a move up the table of seriousness for these offences. Not all offences can be the highest priority. The AML regime is now in play, carrying with it greater investigatory powers, greater potential sentences reporting requirements, attenuated professional privileges and so on. If tax evasion is being promoted up the ladder of seriousness of crimes then this should be done as part of a conscious policy directed to evasion, rather than by the laundering connection.

The second consequence is as to sentence. Sentencing in laundering cases in England and Wales began from the assumption that laundering was a form of complicity in the predicate. Only more recently has there been a shift so that consecutive sentences may be given even for self-laundering, when it adds to the culpability of the defendant (*R. v. Greaves (Claude Clifford)* [2010] EWCA Crim 709). We need a better articulated notion of the harm in laundering so as to be able to generate rational sentences, in particular without 'double counting'.

CONCLUDING—SOME DIFFERENTIATED PRESCRIPTIONS

Capital flight is a huge problem with devastating effects. Subject to considerations about individual privacy (which do not apply to corporations) transparency and disclosure form important parts of a sensible response. The argument of this chapter is that less invocation of the rhetoric of laundering and the AML agenda, rather than more, is a better way to deal with tax, fraud and corruption. Laundering law is a scattergun. Greater precision is required. I will take the issues in turn.

Tax avoidance, whether by profit shifting or otherwise, is not criminal, and money thus retained or obtained is not 'dirty'. Elementary respect for the Rule of Law should dictate that we do not treat tax avoiders (who do set out to act lawfully) as tax evaders (who do not).

Corporations' transfer-pricing to do with money laundering. The international system for the allocation, for tax purposes, of corporate profits between jurisdictions has existed since the 1920s, and changing it will not be easy. Offshore financial centres are a direct consequence of it. We should be less concerned that corporations order their finances so as most effectively to benefit from the existing system than that legislators have failed to change the system. Legislators must act.

Tax evasion is criminal. It should be dealt with as criminal tax evasion. We should not use the artificial device of amplifying its gravity by rebranding it as 'tax evasion and money laundering'. It should be detected and prosecuted as tax evasion. Over criminalisation is dangerous. As things stand, money laundering law goes too far—the prohibitions are too extensive and the obligations on the regulated sector too onerous. The extension of the range of predicates to include tax offences does not so much increase the category of criminals. It increases, without clear justification, the number of offences those people commit and their gravity, by making every tax evasion also a laundering. There are three things that could be done to restrict the extent of the criminalisation of laundering. First, a rule against allowing liability for self-laundering could be adopted with global application. Second, FATF required that there be criminal liability for laundering when the alleged launderer *knew* that the property was of criminal provenance. English law, in important relevant areas, throws the net much wider, being satisfied by suspicion (Proceeds of Crime Act 2002 s. 340(6)). The English Law rules that suspicion is enough for liability and to trigger the reporting regime could be replaced by a 'knowledge or belief' criterion. Third, it would be an improvement to be more exacting about the rules identifying 'criminal property', and in particular not to use fictions.

Which leaves the problem of *'offshore'*. Offshore is not principally a laundering problem. It is a transparency problem, a corruption problem and a fraud problem, and it needs to be dealt with as such. A strong international system for disclosure of beneficial ownership and exchange of information needs to be established. This will reduce the extent to which offshore is used to hide the proceeds of crime, but that should not be the main objective. The AML industry ought not to be the main mechanism by which attempts are made to interdict international capital flows of which there is general disapproval, because even if they are lawful (and do not trigger AML) they should be stopped.

REFERENCES

Alldridge, Peter, 'Money Laundering and Globalization' (2008) 35 *Journal of Law and Society* 437–63.

Behrens, Frederic, 'Using a Sledgehammer to Crack a Nut: Why FATCA Will Not Stand' (2013) *Wisconsin Law Review* 205–36.

Chaikin, David and J. C. Sharman, *Corruption and Money Laundering: A Symbiotic Relationship* (Palgrave Series on Asian Governance) (London: Palgrave Macmillan, 2009).

Christensen, J. 'The Hidden Trillions: Secrecy, Corruption, and the Offshore Interface' (2012) 57 *Crime, Law and Social Change* 325–43.

Financial Action Task Force, *Laundering the Proceeds of Corruption* (2011).

Financial Action Task Force (FATF), *International Standards on Combating Money Laundering and the Financing of Terrorism & Proliferation – the FATF Recommendations* (Paris February 2012).

Freedman, Judith, 'Interpreting Tax Statutes: Tax Avoidance and the Intention of Parliament' (2007) 123 *Law Quarterly Review* 53.

G8 Lough Erne communiqué, 19 June 19 2013.

Gololobov, Dmitry, 'The Yukos Tax Case or Ramsay Adventures in Russia' (2008) 7 Bus. L. Rev. 165.

Gould, Bryan, *Myths, Politicians and Money: The Truth Behind the Free Market* (Basingstoke: Palgrave Macmillan, 2013).

Gould, James Jackson, *OECD Initiative on Tax Havens* (London: DIANE Publishing, 2010).

Graetz, Michael and Michael O'Hear, 'The "Original Intent" of U.S. International Taxation' (1997) 51 Duke L. J. 1021.

Gravelle, Jane G., *Tax Havens: International Tax Avoidance and Evasion*. Congressional Research Service 7–5700 (2014).

Grinberg, Itai, 'The Battle Over Taxing Offshore Accounts' (2012) 60 UCLA L. Rev. 304–506.

Halliday, Terence, Michael Levi, Peter Reuter, *Global Surveillance of Dirty Money* (Illinois, Centre for Law and Globalization, 2014).

Henry, James, *The Price of Offshore Revisited* (Tax Justice Network 2012).

Hodge, Margaret (Chair), Public Accounts Committee, *Tax avoidance–Google: Ninth report of session 2013–14, report, together with formal minutes, oral and written evidence* (London: Stationery Office, 2013).

International Monetary Fund, *Anti-Money Laundering and Combating the Financing of Terrorism (AML/CFT)—Report on the Review of the Effectiveness of the Program Prepared by the Legal Department* (2011).

Jakobi, Anja P. 'The OECD and Crime: The Fight Against Corruption and Money Laundering', in Kerstin Martens and Anja P. Jakobi (eds), *Mechanisms of OECD Governance: International Incentives for National Policy Making?* (Oxford: Oxford University Press, 2010), 139.

Léonard, Sarah and Christian Kaunert, '"Between a rock and a hard place?": The European Union's Financial Sanctions against Suspected Terrorists, Multilateralism and Human Rights' (2012) 47 *Cooperation and Conflict* 473–94.

Morriss, Andrew P. and Lotta Moberg, 'Cartelizing Taxes: Understanding the OECD's Campaign Against "Harmful Tax Competition"' (2012) 4 *Colum. J. Tax L.* 1.

Morse, Susan, 'Ask for Help, Uncle Sam: The Future of Global Tax Reporting' (2012) 57 *Villanova Law Review* 529–50.

Murphy, Richard, *Over Here and Undertaxed: Multinationals, Tax Avoidance and You* (London: Random House, 2013).

OECD, *Taxation and the Abuse of Bank Secrecy* (Paris: OECD, 1985).

OECD, *Harmful Tax Competition: An Emerging Global Issue* (Paris: OECD, 1998).

OECD, Articles of The Model Convention with Respect To Taxes on Income and on Capital (Paris, OECD: 2003).

OECD, *Money Laundering Awareness Handbook for Tax Examiners and Tax Auditors* (Paris: OECD, 2009).

OECD, *The Era of Bank Secrecy is Over* (Paris: OECD, 2011).

OECD, *Action Plan on Base Erosion and Profit Shifting* (Paris: OECD Publishing, 2013).

Palan, Ronen, Richard Murphy, and Christian Chavagneux, *Tax Havens: How Globalization really Works* (Ithaca, NY: Cornell University Press, 2013).

Picciotto, Sol, 'Offshore: The State as Legal Fiction', in Mark P. Hampton and Jason P. Abbott (eds), *Offshore Finance Centres and Tax Havens: The Rise of Global Capital* (London: Palgrave Macmillan, 1999) 43.

Picciotto, Sol, *Is the International Tax System Fit for Purpose, Especially for Developing Countries?* ICTD Working Paper 13 (Brighton: Institute of Development Studies, 2013).

Reuter, Peter (ed.), *Draining Development? Controlling Flows of Illicit Funds from Developing Countries* (Washington DC: World Bank 2012).

Roberge, Ian, 'Misguided Policies in the War on Terror? The Case for Disentangling Terrorist Financing from Money Laundering' (2007) 27 *Politics* 196–203.

Schoueri, Luís Eduardo and Mateus Calicchio Barbosa, 'Transparency: From Tax Secrecy to the Simplicity and Reliability of the Tax System' [2013] *British Tax Review* 666–81.

Sharman, J.C., 'Offshore and the New International Political Economy' (2010) 17 *Review of International Political Economy* 1–19.

Sharman, J.C., *The Money Laundry: Regulating Criminal Finance in the Global Economy* (Ithaca, NY: Cornell University Press, 2011).

Shaxson, Nicholas, *Treasure Islands* (London: Vintage Books 2012).

Sikka, Prem and Hugh Willmott, 'The Dark Side of Transfer Pricing: Its Role in Tax Avoidance and Wealth Retentiveness' (2010) 21 *Critical Perspectives on Accounting* 342–56.

Sixsmith, Martin, *Putin's Oil* (London: Continuum International Publishing, 2010).

Tanzi, Vito, *Money Laundering and the International Financial System*, IMF Working Paper 96/55, (Washington, DC: International Monetary Fund, 1996).

Vlcek, William, 'Power and the Practice of Security to Govern Global Finance' (2012) 19 *Review of International Political Economy* 639–62.

Young, Mary Alice, *Banking Secrecy and Offshore Financial Centres: Money Laundering and Offshore Banking* (London: Routledge, 2012).

Young, Mary Alice, 'The Exploitation of Global Offshore Financial Centres: Banking Confidentiality and Money Laundering' (2013) 16 *Journal of Money Laundering Control* 198–208.

Zedner, Lucia, 'Security, the State, and the Citizen: The Changing Architecture of Crime Control' (2010) 13 *New Criminal Law Review* 379–403.

14. Underground banking and corruption[1]

Federico Varese

INTRODUCTION

This chapter explores some theoretical and empirical features of underground banking, with a special attention to corruption. After a discussion of the nature of Informal Value Transfer Systems (IVTSs)—which I use as a synonym for underground banking—and the key theoretical questions related to IVTSs, I turn to the connection between this phenomenon and corruption. By drawing upon two case-studies, I conclude that corruption is not a key ingredient of IVTSs. Rather, pervasive corruption can fuel the demand for informal banking.

1. UNDERGROUND BANKING

Underground banking is used here as synonymous with Informal Value Transfer Systems (see Siegel and van de Bunt 2014: 252). These systems exist in several parts of the world, such as Latin America (where it is known as Black Market Peso Exchange), Burma (*Hundi*), China (*Fie Ch'ien*), Hong Kong (*Hui kuan*), Philippines (*Padala*) Thailand (*Phei kwan*), and the Arab and Muslim world (*Hawala*) (see Turnell, Vicary and Bradford 2008; Siegel and van de Bunt 2014: 252; Skarbek 2008; GF1). Simply put, it is an informal way of transferring money from one place to another through a service provider (Thompson 2008: 94). Roger Ballard describes it as a 'multi-nodal network of value transmission' (Ballard 2003: 8). The same service is provided by officially regulated banks and companies such as Western Union and Money Gram. The key difference

[1] I am grateful to Paolo Campana, Liz David-Barrett, Paul Felipe Lagunes and Susan Rose-Ackerman for their most helpful comments. A version of this paper was presented at the Yale Corruption Conference, New Haven, 2 May 2014.

is that informal banking is not regulated and operates outside government scrutiny. In most countries, the system is illegal as it breaches banking rules, as well as norms related to money laundering (van de Bunt 2008: 113; Thompson 2006; GF1 2006: 1, 10).

Today, IVTSs are used extensively by migrant workers (Siegel and van de Bunt 2014: 254–59; Skarbek 2008). According to a 2005 IMF estimate, $100 billion per year are transferred informally worldwide by migrants to their families (IMF 2005, cited in van de Bunt 2008: 113). A 2003 estimate indicates that 17 billion euros had been remitted informally from immigrants living in the European Union to Asia, the Middle East and North Africa (Margiocco 2004). Informal transfers account for around 5–20 percent of remittances to Latin America, but this estimate goes up to as much as 45–65 percent for Sub-Saharan Africa (Freund and Spatafora 2005). IVTSs are used extensively in conflict regions such as Iraq, Afghanistan and Somalia, where these providers have also facilitated the transfer of humanitarian aid (Lindley 2009; van de Bunt 2008: 113; Thompson 2008: 84; Hariharan 2012; see also Ismail 2007). In addition to servicing war-torn regions, they often offer a service that is cheaper and more effective than the official banking system. For instance, in 2005, 13 banks were operating in Kabul, but their high fees and balance requirements made them an undesirable option for the local population, 36 percent of which was illiterate. On the other hand, there were between 500 and 2,000 *hawala* shops in the country (Maimbo 2003: 8; Thompson 2006: 157, 161 and Thompson 2008: 84).

Since the terrorist attack of 9/11, IVTSs have come under intense scrutiny as a possible conduit of money financing terrorism in Central Asia, the Middle East and in the West (Passas 2003). President George W. Bush himself directly referred to IVTSs in a briefing on 7 November 2001, suggesting that underground bankers enable 'the proceeds of crime in one country to be transferred to pay for terrorist acts in another . . . all at the service of mass murderers' (Bush 2001). In the aftermath of the attack on the Twin Towers, several media reports focused on the 'Muslim' version of IVTSs, known as *hawala*. A piece in *Time Magazine* called *hawala* 'A Banking System Built for Terrorism' (Ganguly 2001. Along similar lines, see Looney 2003. For critical remarks, see Thompson 2008: 89–90). Indeed, the 9/11 Commission Report found no direct link between this system and the hijackers of 11 September. Rather, the Report showed that the hijackers had received money through the legitimate banking system. Nevertheless, the Report states that 'Al Qaeda frequently moved the money it raised by *hawala*, an informal and ancient trust-based system for transferring funds' (NCTA 2004: 171, see also 237, and 498, fn. 124).

Finally, the system is used by individuals engaged in criminal activities.

Transfers related to tax evasion, making or receiving ransom payments, and payments that facilitate human trafficking/smuggling and drugs trafficking have all been documented (Jost and Sandhu 2000; Kleemans et al. 2002; Passas 1999, 2005; Thompson 2006; van de Bunt 2008). Passas (1999) suggested that the use of IVTSs for serious criminal purposes is limited and that these networks are unable to handle large sums of money (in a later paper, he qualified this view: see Passas 2005). Thompson (2006) is a remarkable study of *hawala* bankers in Afghanistan. On the basis of interviews with 54 dealers, the author was able to show that fluctuations in the turnover of a large number of *hawaladars* corresponded to crucial phases in the cultivation and harvest of opium (see also Thompson 2011). In 2002, the Dutch Organized Crime Monitor published a report in Dutch containing an analysis of seven cases of informal banking (Kleemans et al. 2002). The study concluded that these networks were able to move substantial sums of criminal money and that the clients were of diverse ethnic backgrounds. Van de Bunt (2008) examines three of the seven cases and reaches similar conclusions regarding ethnic connections between clients, bankers and size of transfers. He also establishes that a commission is paid for each transfer that amounts to 6–8 percent of the money transferred.

How do such transactions work? Four actors are involved. The informal banker B1 receives money (or value) from customer C1 for the purpose of paying a recipient C2 in a different location. C1 hands over the money (or the value) and receives a code. The amount to be remitted is communicated by B1 to banker B2 in the destination country. C1 also communicates the code to C2, who gives the code to B2. In turn, B2 gives the recipient C2 the amount agreed upon normally in the local currency[2] from his own cash reserves (in all cases I have come across, bankers are men). At the end of the process, B1 owes money to B2. The debt will be settled in the future by offsetting transactions in the other direction, through formal bank accounts, or by delivering commodities of equal value (see Figure 14.1).

The communication normally takes place by telephone, fax, or email. The initial informal banker charges the customer a fee or a percentage of the sum transferred (van de Bunt 2008: 116). Profit for B2 comes from choosing a favourable currency exchange rate (Thompson 2006: 165; GF1 2006: 10).[3]

---

    [2] Siegel and van de Bunt (2014: 255) report that a 'euro-to-euro' system operates among the Nigerian community in the Netherlands and the African country.
    [3] I do not address here questions of pricing. I plan to return to the issues of fees, risks and profits in a separate paper.

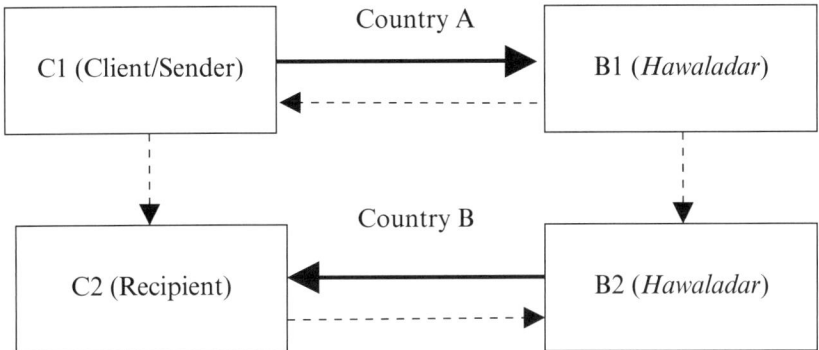

Note: The solid lines refer to the transfer of money or value. The dotted lines refer to the exchange of information on the amount to be transferred and the code.

Source: Adapted from Thompson (2006: 165). See also Bunt (2008: 122), Thompson (2008: 96) and Skarbek (2008: 6).

Figure 14.1 Stages in a typical hawala exchange

Several misunderstandings surround underground banking. First, it is often claimed that money is never physically moved, making it a distinguishing feature of the system (Jost and Sandhu 2000: 2). Although the money received by B1 is not physically transported to the location of B2, occasionally B2 delivers the cash to the place where C2 is based (although they prefer not to do so). Crucially, ordinary banks also do not move cash related to a specific transaction, so this aspect is not a distinguishing feature of IVTSs. A second source of misunderstanding is that transfers do not leave a paper trail. Quite the contrary, informal bankers take notes and carefully log each transaction (Thompson 2006: 165; Siegel and van de Bunt 2014: 253). In the case of drugs money, such notes tend to be more discreet and occasionally are absent (Thompson 2006: 165). Yet each deal is extensively discussed over the phone and by email (GF1 2006; van de Bunt 2008: 115). Hence, the best way to think about underground banking is as a network of agents who transfer clients' cash informally and between distant locations. The distinguishing feature is that such transfers are not regulated by governments and in the overwhelming majority of jurisdictions the system is illegal, although in some contexts it is tolerated (Thompson 2008: 100; van de Bunt 2008: 115; Skarbek 2008: 7).

2. THEORETICAL ISSUES

As stated by all authors, trust is critical to the functioning of the system. In the abstract, trust takes place through an agreement or a promise: a first-mover transfers resources to another actor in the *expectation* that the recipient's action will at a later point in time satisfy the terms of the agreement (Campana and Varese 2013). Such a definition begs the question of how such expectations are formed. If the transactions were legal, several mechanisms would be at the disposal of agents who want to engage in mutually beneficial actions, such as contracts and an effective court system, reputations based on easily traceable information, known inner disposition of the trustee (trustworthiness), informal sanctions for those who break their word, and prior interactions. These mechanisms increase the expectation that the recipient will fulfil her promise, making the first mover more inclined to trust her, yet they do not completely eliminate the risk of defection. None of these mechanisms is perfect: for instance, written contracts are incomplete, and resorting to courts is a costly process. Thus, to varying degrees, trusting others requires a leap of faith even among agents who engage in legal transactions.[4]

Some of the mechanisms that work in the legal sphere also operate in the illegal one, although they are less reliable. Reputations can be built among actors operating informally and illegally; however information is less easily traceable and the risk of arrest is always present. The trustee has to signal his inner disposition (trustworthiness) in ways that do not attract the attention of law enforcement. Shared ethnic and kin ties can serve as a bond among those who operate in illegal markets. Dwight C. Smith maintains that 'ethnic ties provide the strongest possibility of ensuring trust among persons who cannot rely on the law to protect their rights and obligations within cooperative but outlawed economic activity' (Smith 1980: 375). Kinship increases compliance in a variety of ways. Relatives might comply in the hope of taking over the family business in a not-so-distant future, or, at least, to share in its profits. In addition, kinship operates as a form of hostage-taking: If a member defects, relatives can punish him (Campana and Varese 2013). Several authors suggest that 'strong social ties (ethnic or family) . . . usually structure the network of *hawala* bankers' (van de Bunt 2008: 116). Thompson (2006: 164) reports that: 'In Afghanistan, intermarriages between the families of *hawaladars* are commonplace because they are seen as a way of cementing the trust between parties.' Brothers often work together in the same *hawala* busi-

---

4   I am drawing here upon Campana and Varese 2013.

ness (Thompson 2006: 164). Schramm and Taube (2003: 416) note that ties between *hawala* bankers are embedded in a common cultural and religious belief system (also Skarbek 2008). The relationship between customers and banker is also personal, and connections between the families of customer and banker can date back several generations (van de Bunt 2008: 117). Anonymity has no role in this world. Cheating and wrongdoing would lead to 'excommunication from the community and loss of honour' (van de Bunt 2008: 116. See also Razavy 2005; Schramm and Taube 2003). On the other hand, Thompson suggests that the role of ethnicity and religion should not be overplayed: Underground bankers—she maintains—are ultimately motivated by profit and are all too happy to deal with different ethnic groups (Thompson 2006: 164).

Although the totality of authors stress the importance of trust, such a mechanism is most essential only in some parts of the system. Trust between C1 and B1 is more crucial than between B2 and C2. The client who gives the money to B1 must be confident that the banker will not take the cash and run. In that scenario, C1 would lose her capital entirely. Next to reputation and repeated interaction, strong signals of immobility on the part of B1 would help increase trust. For instance, running an established and valuable business with a fixed location increases the probability that the banker will be around for a long time. As for C2 and B2, the client might travel to the location of B2 and not receive the money, hence she would have wasted her time. Yet the cash is still in the hand of B1, so the actors in this IVTS do not need to place such a high degree of trust in B2. It follows that trust between C1 and B1 is more important for an IVTS than the trust of B1 in B2. B1 can always find a new partner in the destination country to deliver the money in case B2 fails to deliver the right amount. On the contrary, B2 is most at risk from B1 asking to deliver money and failing to honour his promise to pay the debt. In sum, for the transaction to take place, we expect that:

(1) C1 has High Trust towards B1;
(2) B2 has High Trust towards B1.

B1 is the key element in the system, the person who needs to convince C1 and B2 to part with their money before both can be sure that B1 has not cheated them. This line of argument implies that actors playing the part of C1 will have more to share with actors playing the part of B1 than with those playing the part of B2 or C2. In other words, repeated interaction, a credible reputation, some form of hostage-taking mechanism and credible signals of immobility will be displayed by B1 towards both C1 and B2. B1 can substitute B2 while he cannot lose C1, otherwise he would lose the source of income for his business. Ultimately the link between B1 and C1 is the one requiring the highest level of trust. This conceptual clarification should facilitate future empirical testing.[5]

There is no evidence in the literature that physical violence is used as a form of punishment for bankers who do not keep their word. Punishment consists in expulsion from the network. Passas (2005: 19) mentions an instance in which a banker lost a fortune while gambling and went bankrupt. A meeting took place between the informal bankers involved in the network and arrangements were made to cover and support each other. No customer lost a penny. The bankrupt partner was ostracized and ended up working as a taxi driver in London. Other scholars have identified risks related to this business, but they mainly refer to the risk of theft, especially in volatile regions, such as Somalia and Afghanistan. Thompson reports that the biggest source of danger for underground bankers in Afghanistan is being robbed while their couriers transport money to a client or to a bank for deposit (Thompson 2006: 167). In 2007, a gang murdered five children of one banker, for reasons that are unclear but seem related to his job (Thompson 2006: 167). In addition, these operators claim to be routinely harassed and robbed by police officers and officials. Occasionally, firms go bankrupt, due to bad currency speculations.

In conclusion, most authors agree that trust is a crucial ingredient of informal banking, yet they fail to spell out the juncture where such mechanism is most crucial. I have argued that the key player in the *hawala* system is B1, who needs to convince both his initial client C1 to part with her money, and B2 to pay C2 before he receives the money. Repeated interaction, a credible reputation, forms of hostage-taking and signals of immobility all help to increase trust in this exchange. Above all, informal banking occurs through personal ties rather than formal channels.

3.   UNDERGROUND BANKING AND CORRUPTION

Before turning to the connection between corruption and IVTSs, we should be clear about what we mean by corruption. A corrupt exchange takes place between two actors, the *corrupter* and an official, but a third player is also relevant in this exchange: the *principal*. The official is an *agent* employed by a principal in order to implement rules set out by the

---

    [5]   I am grateful to Paul Felipe Lagunes and Paolo Campana for a discussion on this point.

principal. Bureaucrats who oversee the issuing of permits, policemen who patrol a neighbourhood, or lab scientists who check the quality of retail food products are examples of agents. The state administration is usually considered to be the principal. The corrupters are members of the public or of another organization who want to bend the rules laid out by the principal in their favor. This definition also applies to the private sector. The principal might be a private corporation that hires people to perform certain functions, such as a bank. A rival firm may wish to bribe those employees in order to obtain confidential information or to disrupt the production line of its competitor.[6]

Essentially, underground banking strives to by-pass official channels, hence for the most part it does not need corrupt agents. Precisely because certain jurisdictions are highly corrupt and/or have inefficient banking systems, an IVTS operates as an alternative channel. Those who want to transfer money obtained through serious crime might choose an IVTS because it is cheaper. Among the savings, one can count the cost of corruption. Although informal bankers tend to charge serious criminals more than ordinary clients, such criminals avoid having to pay multiple corrupt agents. The downside is that the money must be paid in cash. Hence it seems that informal banking is best suited for payments (say, drugs payments) rather than money laundering for the purpose of further investments in the legal economy.

Surely, the occasional corrupt agent can facilitate the work of the informal banker by giving him access to the official banking system when needed, for example, by turning a blind eye to fictitious commercial transactions that are used to offset debts across locations. Such services are needed when the cash flows overwhelmingly in one direction (say, from Italy to Pakistan rather than from Pakistan to Italy). Informal bankers, however, also physically transport cash between hubs. In principle, IVTSs can operate without the use of corrupt agents. Yet, pervasive corruption combined with checks on money flows can fuel the *demand* for informal banking, as I will show below. In other words, corruption is a cause for the use of IVTSs rather than a fundamental ingredient of informal banking itself.

Corruption then stands in stark contrast to the basic ingredient that is essential for an IVTS to operate, namely trust. As mentioned above, the expectation that an actor will fulfil his promise (in this case, deliver the money to the client abroad) is increased by several mechanisms, such

---

[6] I am drawing here upon Varese 2000: 101–2, and 2003. See also Rose-Ackerman 1978 and 1999, and Gambetta 2002.

as shared ethnic ties, long-term personal knowledge and repeated inter-action. In practice, some of these elements can be substituted for each other. For instance, as the network grows in size and complexity, shared ethnicity and long-term personal connections become diluted. Newcomers enter the picture and start to do business. In these instances, it is likely that (the threat of) violence becomes more relevant to ensure compliance than old ties and reputations. Contrary to what is argued by most other authors, violence has a place in IVTSs, particularly as the network grows in complexity. The threat of violence can help sustain complex *hawala* transfers, where I would also expect a higher degree of cheating. Increased complexity might also lead to the need for some corrupt services, such as a greater reliance on official banking systems. In these instances, bank employees would need to allow some transfers related to IVTSs in return for payoffs.

Below I present some anecdotal evidence supporting these statements.

Hawala Banking in Carpi, Italy

In late October 2006, the Italian police (Guardia di Finanza, henceforth GF) arrested five Pakistani brothers who lived in the small town of Carpi, just outside Modena (Emilia Romagna). The operation—dubbed Khyber Pass—was directed at disrupting a *hawala* network that reportedly was able to move up to four million euros a day out of Italy. In addition to the five brothers, seven drug traffickers were also arrested, five in Carpi and two in Turin, and seven more were notified of new charges while already serving prison sentences (TM 2006; I1). Six more people managed to avoid arrest. Some 140 kilos of cocaine and heroin were confiscated, linked to previous seizures of drugs of 200 kilos. The police had been investigating the case since 2004 and had collaborated with US, Australian, British, UAE and Turkish law enforcement (GF1 2006). On the same day, other arrests were carried out in the UK, Spain and Dubai. At the press confer-ence, Italian prosecutors maintained that this 'informal banking network managed by Pakistani nationals with international links is connected to radical Islamism' (Gazzetta di Modena 2006). The American prosecu-tors alleged that the ringleader was at the centre of a 'terror network that was taking in money for the Taliban as well as other criminal cartels' (Laville 2009).

An Indian businessman living in Dubai, Naresh Kumar Jain, known as Patel (born 1959), emerges from the record as the main organizer (GF1 2006: 14, 19). He is described by India's Directorate of Enforcement as one of the world's biggest money launderers. Allegedly, he handled $2.2 billion daily in informal banking in Holland, Italy, the US, the UK, Turkey,

India, UAE, Afghanistan and Pakistan. According to US court records, Patel was transferring money though banks and exchange houses in Dubai into some 16 bank accounts at Man Financial in Manhattan in New York. In 2009 the US government froze $4.3 million in these accounts. The Department of Homeland Security has also alleged that this man had facilitated payment to al Qaeda in Afghanistan. British and Spanish authorities claimed that he had laundered money for Latin American cartels as well (TM 2006: 23; Laville 2009; USAD 2009).

The Italian link of the network was a man running a barber shop in Carpi, Ahmed Pervaz (36 years old, born in the Punjab). He and his brothers collected vast amounts of remittances from Pakistani nationals and arranged for them to be transferred to Pakistan, where Pervaz's father was based and who ensured that funds were delivered. This side of his activity was not the focus of the Italian investigation and no substantial evidence has been collected nor have any charges been brought against Patel and his associates for this aspect of their operations. Pervaz came under scrutiny from Italian police in 2004 when the Italian investigators had started to investigate a group of Albanian drug traffickers who used Pervaz to pay for drugs originating in Turkey. As the investigation progressed, Italian authorities extended their inquiry into the entire *hawala* network, including Patel and his associates based in Holland (GF1 2006: 15).

I have obtained the original investigation files (GF1 and GF2 2006) and court documents (TM 2006) and am now in the process of coding the data. Although the Italian police files offer a limited picture of this international network, they suggest that interaction with (corrupt) officials was limited. The only instance of corruption emerging from the files reflects Pervaz's need to change euros from small to large denominations. The Italy-based informal banker Pervaz is paid in more than he pays out. In other words, Italian residents entrust their cash to him to be transferred to Pakistan, but there is next to no evidence that cash comes from Pakistan to Italy. Even drugs-related transactions are one-sided. Albanians buy drugs in Turkey and pay Pervaz in Carpi. That cash also arrives at Pervaz's place of business and accumulates in his office. A significant portion of Pervaz's job is devoted to finding ways to move the cash to other European hubs, such as Paris, Amsterdam and London. Associates of Pervaz and Patel simply drive cars across Europe to deliver the cash. In order to make these operations easier (to save on space), Pervaz developed a demand for large denominations. Officials at the local bank, the Credito Emiliano in Carpi, were willing to facilitate Pervaz's illegal activities by selling him large denominations for a fee. They charged him 100 euros for every 50,000 euros. The police intercepted a number of conversations that related to this matter, as shown below.

On 29 May 2006, an official at the Credito Emiliano—here indicated as Mr XXX—called Pervaz at 09.24:

XXX: Hello Ahmed, It is XXX calling.
PERVAZ: Yes.
XXX: I have eight 500 pieces.
PERVAZ: This is good. Thanks, I will be there in an hour.

The next day, the same bank official called Pervaz at 12.00. The conversation was very similar.

XXX: Hi Ahmed, I have got 16 pieces.
PERVAZ: Yes, I shall be with you in 10 minutes.

The next day, on 31 of May 2006, at 12.37, a second, female, official called Pervaz from the local bank.

YYY: Listen, I have nine 500 pieces, if you are interested.
PERVAZ: Do you need pieces in 20 and 50 (Euros) in exchange?
YYY: 50 is better, but I can also do 20s. When do you come by?
PERVAZ: Within 20 minutes.
YYY: Ok, I will keep them for you.

The larger denominations were delivered abroad. This is exemplified by the following conversation. The main organizer of Pervaz's network, Patel (based in Dubai) called Pervaz on 29 May 2006, at 15.09. Patel was organizing the cash transfers across Europe, and he wanted Pervaz to deliver the money to couriers in Milan. They would take care of the rest.

PERVAZ: Ok, but if you want, I can take [the money] to Lyon using my car.
PATEL: No . . . No. This is dangerous because you are a Pakistani, they always take it.
PERVAZ: Ok.

During this particular trip of Pervaz to Milan, 600,000 euros were delivered in cash to the network's couriers.

In conclusion, this network has some degree of complexity. It is spread across Europe, and some limited corruption services are used by the main actors. Yet, corruption is only a marginal ingredient of the system.

Underground Banking in China

The People's Republic of China combines two features that fuel the *demand* for underground banking: high levels of corruption and strict controls over capital flows by both corporations and individuals. Corrupt officials, as well as legitimate businesspeople wanting to bypass state regulations and hefty taxation, find ways to move money in and out of the country. IVTSs are one such system, as I discovered during a recent field trip to the border town of Zhuhai, China.

China ranks among the most corrupt countries in the world. According the 2012 World Bank Enterprise survey, 42.2 percent of enterprises in the country 'consider that firms with characteristics similar to theirs are making informal payments or giving gifts to public officials to secure contracts'.[7] According to the 2014 Transparency International Corruption Perception Index China is the 100th most corrupt country in the world (out of 175) with a score of 36 out of 100. Public officials extort large bribes and everything seems to be up for sale. For instance, a recent news report claims that Gu Junshan, a 57-year-old former Lieutenant General in the logistics department of the People's Liberation Army, accepted £63 million in bribes from the sale of military positions. Allegedly, he also gave a 20million RMB (over US$ 3million) debit card to the daughter of his superior, also accused of bribe taking (Ng 2014).

The economic, administrative and political elite of the country tries to siphon money abroad. The think-tank Global Financial Integrity has calculated that China has the highest cumulative illicit financial outflows in the world, in the region of US $1.08tn for the period between 2002 and 2011.[8] According to a 2008 report by the People's Bank of China, between 16,000 and 18,000 officials, businessmen, CEOs and others have 'disappeared, carrying about 800 billion yuan' since the mid-1990s (cited in Pomfret and Miller 2013). According to an estimate, more than 1 million officials and their families have moved assets offshore in the last five years (Wee 2014). High profile investigations by The International Consortium of Investigative Journalists and *The New York Times* have exposed the extensive use of offshore companies to hide assets by members of the political and economic elite, leading to government retaliation against the journalists (Barboza et al. 2013 and Guevara et al. 2014).

Yet moving such wealth out of the country is not easy. Strict regulations on capital movement apply to firms and citizens, while payments by

---

[7]   The answer to the same question by East Asian firms is 31 percent, while the value for all countries is 26.4 percent. See http://www.enterprisesurveys.org/data/exploreeconomies/2012/china#corruption (accessed 15 May 2015).

[8]   Russia and Mexico come respectively second and third in this list. See http://www.gfintegrity.org/report/2013-global-report-illicit-financial-flows-from-developing-countries-2002-2011/ (accessed 15 May 2015). Guevara et al. (2014) cite even higher figures.

individuals to foreigners are capped at $50,000 a year. Only a maximum of RMB 20,000 ($3,200) can be legally carried out of China, and no more than RMB 10,000 ($1,600) per day can be taken out of cash machines abroad by an individual (Pomfret and Miller 2013; Zabielskis 2013). How are the funds moved out?

Some systems are financially complex and involve the creation of offshore shell companies and false invoicing. For instance, a number of Chinese manufacturers set up subsidiaries outside the country and undersell their products to the subsidiaries. In this way, they show virtually no profit in China and avoid hefty taxes. The offshore entities then sell the products back, making a profit that is then hidden abroad, most commonly in accounts in Hong Kong and the British Virgin Islands, as documented by Guevara et al. (2014). In what follows, I will focus on a rather less complex system that revolves around the former Portuguese colony of Macau, the casino economy and IVTSs. Arguably, it is used by a substantial number of individuals and small firms, rather than large enterprises.

Modern gambling in Macau dates back to 1970, when the government granted a licence to Stanley Ho, a Chinese tycoon who opened the Lisboa Casino. After the handover to China in 1999, Beijing decided to break up Ho's monopoly and granted new licenses. The first western-operated casino opened in 2004. By 2013, the 34 casinos in the former colony were the most profitable in the world: on average gamblers spent $1,354 per visit, compared to $156 in Las Vegas, which comes second in this list (*The Economist* 2013; see also Zabielskis 2013; Varese 2011: 164). Yet, estimates suggest that 70 percent of Macau's gamblers are mainland Chinese, who are restricted in the use of their own money.

During a fieldtrip to Macau (29/X-07/XI/2014), I came across several ways to flout restrictions. One system involves minor credit card frauds: Mainland gamblers who run out of money in Macau can turn to shops which charge their credit card for a transaction that appears to have been conducted in the Mainland. The shop owner charges the card of the client and gives her the cash minus a small commission. Pawn shops are also used to generate cash: mainland gamblers enter Macau with brand new watches and jewellery and pawn them immediately obtaining quick cash in return (alternatively, they buy—and sell back immediately—some trinket). This explains the oddity that Macau's pawn shops have brand new objects (Zabielskis 2013: 23; Lages 2013: 108; Pomfret 2014).

A well-developed system to transfer money out of China involves the services of informal bankers. This system of capital flight revolves around the use of casinos in Macau. A peculiar system of VIP rooms operates in Macau's casinos (Wang and Zabielskis 2010; Wang and Eadington 2009; Godinho 2006; Veng Mei Leong 2002). These rooms are the equivalent of private clubs and are housed inside the most prestigious hotels. The first time I visited one in 2009, two heavily built bouncers dressed in tuxedos were standing in front of the door, ushering us through an additional metal detector, but there was no need to hand over eyeglass cases, bags, or keys. The decor was garish, with fake gilded columns, richly decorated sofas, and statuettes of ancient warriors. Plenty of waiters were on call to answer requests for drinks and food. We also saw a cage dispensing poker chips and, at one of the three tables, a mainland Chinese who, to my guide, looked like a wealthy official. Hovering around was a peculiar *majordomo*, who made sure that the gambler had his drink and enough room to move. At one point I thought he looked like a coach, encouraging on his athlete. He was the man we were looking for, a hulking Chinese man who we will call Mr Xin.[9]

Over several conversations, Xin told me that his business is to entice wealthy Chinese players to his VIP room to act as their lackey (by 2008, some 80 percent of the VIP players came from mainland China[10]). The room where he works is run by a contractor who rents it from the casino and puts down collateral to gain access to chips. Xin picks up Chinese high rollers in the mainland and drives them to Macau. Xin's clients are mostly from the Guangdong province, the region closest to Macau, and one of the richest in China.[11] Some of his clients, however, fly in from as far as Gansu, near Mongolia. On the way to Macau, Mr Xin pays all expenses, including transportation, accommodation and entertainment. Once in Macau, Xin suggests a visit to his VIP room. If the mainlander agrees to play, Xin is in business. If not, he has lost a lot of money and time. The high roller does not need to carry a lot of cash: Xin lends him money in the region of 500,000 Hong Kong dollars (almost $65,000). He holds the money in an account within the VIP room.[12]

Gamblers wager—and lose—fortunes in VIP rooms. At a club called Sky 33 (inside the Galaxy Hotel) players are expected to play no less than 5 million RMB ($800,000) per session, while at Sky 32, which has a colossal indoor waterfall, the minimum is 10 million RMB ($1.6m). Among the biggest losers, the former head of the propaganda department of the city of Chongqing stands out ($15 million), while the former vice-mayor of Shenyang lost more than $1.6 million in three days. Both were executed

---

[9]   I am drawing here upon Varese (2011: 164).

[10] Wang and Eadington (2008: 250).

[11] The Share of national average GDP per capita (percent) is 140. See data at http://www.tjcn.org/plus/view.php?aid=26117 (accessed 15 May 2015).

[12] In Macau, more than 200 junket operators are officially licenced (Sevastopulo 2014).

(Pontell et al. 2014: 8; O'Neill 2007). Casinos do not accept any responsibility for the destructive behaviour of players, nor are they required to follow a code by the regulator. One gambler had played six days and nights non-stop until an ambulance had to be called to carry him away. According to a study, high rollers last between one and four year before they face the consequences of their addiction and often commit suicide (Zeng and Forrest 2009). It follows that the money generated by VIP rooms is enormous: The figure for 2013 is $29.9 billion, up by 13.1 percent in year-on-year terms (GGRAsia 2014).

VIP rooms intersect with IVTSs. Agents operating in such rooms allow their accounts to be used by Chinese underground banks' customers to withdraw hard currency. A hub of IVTS operators is the underground mall in the Chinese city of Zhuhai, just a few metres across the border from Macau. With the help of a guide, I visited the mall in November 2014 (Varese 2014). Two floors below ground level, dozens of small shops purport to sell liquor, covers for IPads and cigarettes, although nothing ever seems to leave their glass cases. In fact, they operate as IVTS. Informants in Macau had suggested a particular shop to me. A middle-aged woman sat at the counter with a calculator and a cash counting machine. A client before us was changing some money. She took his Hong Kong dollars, ran them through the cash machine and then computed how many RMBs the customer could buy. After he agreed to the transaction, she took Chinese currency out of a drawer and handed it over to him. When our turn came, we said that we did not want to change money but had other questions. She agreed to take us to a room at the back of her shop (at all times, two young people were also present). There she explained how this IVTS works: she takes Chinese currency and, within a few hours, is able to deliver the equivalent in Hong Kong dollars in Macau, for a small fee. In order to collect the money in Macau, she would give us a secret number and take down the details of my passport (or whatever document I was happy to show her). The place to collect the money would be the cash dispenser of a VIP room in the former Portuguese colony. I would not be required to gamble any of the money, or do anything else. I asked her if the people I would collect the money from were known to her and how I could be sure that the money would be delivered. She replied that she works with a VIP operator in Macau who is very well known and trustworthy, although they are not related. She added that she is also well known in Zhuhai and has never cheated anyone. However, cheating does occur; she pointed to an empty shop, claiming that the banker had run away, so we should be careful with whom we deal (I-3).

An investigation by Hong (2014) on underground banks sheds further light on this type of IVTS. Mr Zhou, the banker interviewed by Hong

(2014), operates branches in both Shenzhen and Zhuhai together with his three cousins, and caters to shuttle traders and officials. '[Officials] bring us sacks of cash in Zhuhai—says the informal banker—, because they are afraid that security cameras at cash deposit terminals will record their faces . . . They ask us to give them Hong Kong Dollars in Macau. Our largest transaction with an official was ¥4,000,000 [just under $660,000].' Mr Zhou's premises have never been raided by the local police. This is possible because Zhou and his cousins 'screen their clients by requiring referrals, and relocate their branches on a regular basis, maintaining contact with clients by phone' (Hong 2014). They do no marketing or advertising, and stick to one service only, cash for cash.

Mr Zhou estimates that his business moves $500,000 a week, although this sum could increase fivefold during public holidays. According to Pomfret and Miller (2013), in Zhuhai alone, over 1 billion yuan ($163 million) is transferred daily through informal bankers. Other cities in the affluent Perl River Delta, like Guangzhou and Dongguan, appear to have many informal bankers operating out of flats, offices and shops. A 2007 report by the People's Bank of China (PBOC) stated that about one-third of underground banks are located in Guangdong province (Pomfret and Miller 2013).

This IVTS is also used to send money *to* China, making the system rather more balanced that the Pakistani *hawala* in Carpi discussed above. Pomfret and Miller (2013) write that businesspeople move money to China in order to 'to buy raw materials or cover wages during peak periods'. This system allows entrepreneurs who operate factories in Guangdong to bypass official approval which can take up to two weeks (Pomfret and Miller 2013; Hong 2014) and, one suspects, would involve paying bribes as well.

This IVTS is used to siphon corrupt payments out of China. Mr Zhou said, 'Bureaucrats here receive a good salary, but there is no way [our client] had 4 millions to toss around as betting money. It must have been from bribes' (Hong 2014). Three operators managing VIP casino rooms in Macau were arrested in 2012 in relation to an attempt to take $1.2 billion of bribes out of China by Bo Xilai and his wife, both found guilty of the murder of British businessman Neil Heywood (Stradbrooke 2012; see also Garnaut 2012). Xin confirmed to me that some of his clients—top officials and businessmen—just want to spirit money out of China, in order to pay school fees for their children in the West, buy property in London or simply to make a deal they do not want authorities to know about (I-2).

Although the evidence is limited, it appears that a well-oiled IVTS operates in the Guangdong Province of China. The purpose of the transfers is two-fold: to have cash to play in the casino as well as to siphon money abroad. China's pervasive corruption fuels a demand for informal transfers. However, corruption plays virtually no role in the actual transfer of funds. VIP room operators have control of their own accounts, although they might have to inform the VIP manager of their dealings. Strong ethnic or kinship ties play a role in one of the two banking networks discussed above. A reputation for fair dealing is the main asset of the female banker I interviewed in Zhuhai. Cheating customers and competition among underground bankers appear to be widespread, possibly more than in traditional *hawala* systems. Finally, money also flows back to China to serve entrepreneurs who need to inject capital or pay wages, by-passing hard-to-obtain official regulations.

CONCLUSIONS

Underground banking is a trust-based system used to transfer money informally between distant locations. Anonymity has made this system particularly attractive to illegal immigrants and criminals. In addition, the system is used to transfer money if the banking system is corrupt, under authoritarian governments, and in failed states such as Afghanistan and Somalia. Scholars have identified a number of mechanisms that increase trust between clients and bankers (and among bankers themselves): shared ethnicity and culture, repeated interaction, and a good reputation; punishment for bankers involves exclusion from the network rather than physical violence.

This chapter has made two crucial arguments that are not found in the existing literature. While all authors insist on the importance of trust, they do not specify at which point of the system it is most crucial. I have argued that it is most crucial for the informal banker in the source country (B1). He should convince both the client C1 to part with her money, and the banker in the destination country (B2) to anticipate the money before B1 has transferred them. He can do so by building a reputation for fair dealing, and sending out signals of immobility.

Second, I have argued that corruption is not a fundamental ingredient of IVTSs. Indeed, such systems are often used to avoid corrupt (and inefficient) banking systems. Bankers might need to pay off bank clerks to allow their accounts to be used to settle outstanding debts or obtain certain bank notes. Naturally, any businessperson operating illegally is a potential victim of police or mafia extortion (Gardiner 1970; Varese 2011), and informal bankers are no exception, some settings being more susceptible to these risks than others. Yet corruption remains a marginal ingredient of IVTSs, in contrast to trust, which is essential.

The chapter discusses two cases of IVTSs, in Italy and China respectively. In both cases, actors deal across ethnic boundaries. The Italian network involves Albanian and Turkish customers, a Pakistani banker, and an Indian as the main network organizer. In China, an extensive system of informal money transfer is active in the Guangdong Region, especially in cities near the border with Hong Kong and Macau. I documented how informal bankers located in an underground mall in Zhuhai, China, transfer RMBs to accounts inside the so-called VIP rooms of Macau's casinos. In this case bankers also trade across ethnic ties and, contrary to most authors' reports, there seems to be competition among bankers, and cheating occurs.

I found no evidence of payments to local police in the case of the Italian *hawala*, which operates in a country which is less corrupt than China. Informal bankers need only a limited range of services from state officials. For instance, in the Italian case, the only instance of corruption involved two bank employees, who were selling on the side large denomination notes to the banker, in defiance of bank regulations. In the case of the People's Republic, bankers interviewed by investigative journalists reported that they have managed to avoid extortionary payments to police officers. This is possible because they do not advertise their services. In addition, they screen their clients, request referrals, move their branches on a regular basis, and keep in touch with clients by phone. The opportunities for corrupt agents to extract cash from these bankers are lower than in other markets. For instance, there is no need to pay off quality inspectors, politicians, the military or customs officials (cf. for example, Soto 1989; Grillo 2010). While buying a permit or a passport requires a corrupt exchange, informal 'cash-for-cash' services do not. For the most part, these services can take place behind the back of the state officials.

IVTSs face several challenges the moment they grow in complexity. As the service evolves from a dyad relationship between two bankers to a complex network with multiple actors, mechanisms normally used to enforce promises, such as shared ethnicity, repeated interaction and well established reputations, are going to be less effective. Not all actors can know each other so well, and for a long time. The need to be in touch with larger client bases makes it less efficient to constantly change the address of the branch, and extortionary demands would become more likely. The moment the cash transfers extend beyond workers' remittance and involve drugs payments and larger scale money-laundering, police attention increases. The temptation to cheat will also increase. At that point, the likelihood that (the threat of) violence might be used to enforce promises increases. This dynamic is captured by a conversation between the Italian informal banker and his mother. The conversation refers to a serious mistake made by Pervaz's brother. For that reason, 'Patel's people' are extremely upset. Pervaz continues the conversation as follows:

> You do not know anything about these people [PATEL group], it is really a mafia, they have tons of money, if I do something against them *they kill me* right away, they are an *international mafia*, do you understand? (TM 2006: 178).

This IVTS risks falling apart in a vicious spiral where distrust feeds distrust. The age of innocence is short-lived.

REFERENCES

Interviews

I1. Interview with the Officer in charge of the Italian investigation Khyber Pass. Undisclosed location, December 2013.
I2. Interview with Xin, October 2009, Macau and Hong Kong.
I3. Interview with informal banker, Shoiing Mall, Zhuhai, 05/XI/2014.

Archival Evidence

GF1 (Guardia di Finanza, Comando Nucleo Regionale Polizia Tributaria Lombardia). 2006. *Comunicazione di Notizia di Reato. Capitolo I. L'Operazione Khyber Pass.*
GF2 (Guardia di Finanza, Comando Nucleo Regionale Polizia Tributaria Lombardia). 2006. *Gli episodi di consegna del denaro da parte dei trafficanti ed il trasferimento verso l'estero. Capitolo IV.*
TM (Tribunale di Milano). 2006. *Ordinanza di applicazione delle misura cautelare della custodia in carcere.*
USAD (United States Attorney Southern District of New York). 2009. *United States recovers $4.3 million from narcotics money laundering.* Department of Justice, 23 June.

Newspaper Articles

Barboza, David, Jessica Silver-Greenberg and Ben Protess. 2013. 'JPMorgan's Fruitful Ties to a Member of China's Elite', *New York Times*, 13 November. Available 15 May 2015 at http://dealbook.nytimes.com/2013/11/13/a-banks-fruitful-ties-to-a-member-of-chinas-elite/?_r=0.
Ganguly, Meenakshi. 2001. ' Banking System Built for Terrorism', *Time Magazine*, 5 October.
Gazzetta di Modena. 2006. 'Droga e arresti: legami col terrorismo?' 20 October, p.18. Available 15 May 2015 at http://ricerca.gelocal.it/gazzettadimodena/archivio/gazzettadimodena/2006/10/20/DP1PO_DP102.html.
GGRAsia. 2014. 'VIP-room Revamp Hurt Wynn Macau's Market

Share', 10 July. Available 15 May 2015 at http://www.ggrasia.com/vip-room-revamp-hurting-wynn-macaus-results-analyst/.

Guevara, Marina et al. 2014. 'Leaked Records Reveal Offshore Holdings of China's Elite', *The International Consortium of Investigative Journalists.* 21 January. Available 15 May 2015 at http://www.icij.org/offshore/leaked-records-reveal-offshore-holdings-chinas-elite.

Hong, Brendon. 2014. 'Inside China's Underground Black Market System', *The Daily Beast*, 26 February. Available 15 May 2015 at http://www.thedailybeast.com/articles/2014/02/26/inside-china-s-underground-black-market-banks.html.

Lages, Alexandra. 2013. 'Hardcore Pawn', *Macau Business*, October, p.108. Available 15 May 2015 at http://content.yudu.com/A2hgw2/MBOct2013/resources/110.htm.

Laville, Sandra. 2009. 'India Arrests *Hawala* Money Laundering Suspect Naresh Jain', *The Guardian*, 8 December.

Margiocco, M. 2004. 'Finanze occulte sulle vie degli emigrati', *Sole 24 Ore*, 29 April.

Ng, Teddy. 2014. 'PLA General Gu Junshan Faces Court Martial as Prosecutors Press Four Graft Charges', *South China Morning Post*, 31 March. Available 15 May 2015 at http://www.scmp.com/news/china/article/1461810/pla-general-gu-junshan-faces-court-martial-prosecutors-press-four-graft.

O'Neill, M. 2007. 'Macau's Perilous Lure for China's Cadres', *Asia Sentinel*, 19 November. Available 15 May 2015 at: http://www.asiasentinel.com/politics/macaus-perilous-lure-for-chinas-cadres/.

Pomfret, James and Matthew Miller. 2013. 'Despite Curbs, China's Vast Hot Money Triangle Flourishes', *Reuters News Agency*, 19 May. Available 15 May 2015 at http://www.reuters.com/article/2013/05/19/china-laundering-triangle-idUSL3N0DY0GJ20130519.

Pomfret, James. 2014. 'How China's Official Bank Card is used to Smuggle Money', *Reuters News Agency*, 11 March. Available 15 May 2015 at: http://www.reuters.com/article/2014/03/12/us-china-unionpay-special-report-idUSBREA2B00820140312.

Sevastopulo, Demetri. 2014. 'Macau's High-rolling Casinos Suffer amid China Anti-graft Storm', *Financial Times*, 26 September. Available 15 May 2015 at http://www.ft.com/cms/s/0/79e893dc-4552-11e4-9b71-00144feabdc0.html#slide0.

Stradbrooke, Steven. 2002. 'Is China's Purge of Bo Xilai behind Recent Detentions of Macau Junket Operators?' *Calvinayre Gambling News*, 4 December. Available 15 May 2015 at: http://calvinayre.com/2012/12/04/business/is-china-purge-of-bo-xilai-behind-macau-junket-detentions/.

The Economist. 2013. 'Hitting the Jackpot', 7 September. Available 15 May 2015 at http://media.economist.com/sites/default/files/media/2013InfoG/WIC-contacts/20130907.pdf.

Varese, Federico. 2014. 'How China's Corrupt Are Making Macau Rich', *Worldcrunch*, 16 December. Available 15 May 2015 at: http://www.worldcrunch.com/rss/china-2.0/how-china-039-s-corrupt-are-making-macau-rich/money-laundering-xi-jinping-venetian-hotel-gaming-room-gambling/c9s17735/#.VJFzentySrs. Originally published in *La Stampa*, 23 November 2014.

Wee, Sui Lee. 2014. 'Over 150 Chinese Economic Fugitives in the US', *Macau Business Daily*, 12 August, p.16.

Secondary Sources

Ballard, Roger. 2003. '*Hawala* Transformed: Remittance-driven Transnational Networks in the post-Imperial Economic Order.' Center for Applied South Asian Studies, University of Manchester. Available 15 May 2015 at http://www.casas.org.uk/papers/pdfpapers/transformed.pdf.

Bush, G.W. 2001. 'President Announces Crackdown on Terrorist Financial Network.' Remarks by the President in Announcement on Financial Aspects of Terrorism Financial Crime Enforcement Network Vienna, Virginia. 7 November. Available 15 May 2015 at http://georgewbush-whitehouse.archives.gov/news/releases/2001/11/20011107-4.html.

Campana, Paolo and Federico Varese. 2013. 'Cooperation in Criminal Organizations: Kinship and Violence as Credible Commitments', *Rationality and Society* 25(3): 263–89.

Freund, Caroline L. and Nicola Spatafora. 2005. 'Remittances: Transaction Costs, Determinants, and Informal Flows', World Bank Policy Research Working Paper No. 3704.

Gambetta, Diego. 2002. 'Corruption: An Analytical Map', in Stephen Kotkin & Andras Sajo (eds), *Political. Corruption in Transition: A Skeptic's Handbook* (Budapest/New York: CEU Press, 2002), pp. 33–56.

Gardiner, John A. 1970. *The Politics of Corruption: Organized Crime in an American City*. New York: Russell Sage Foundation.

Garnaut, John. 2012. *The Rise and Fall of the House of Bo*. London: Penguin Books.

Godinho, Jorge. 2006. 'Credit for Gaming in Macau', *Gaming Law Review*, 10(4): 363–8.

Grillo, Ioan. 2012. *El Narco: the Bloody Rise of Mexican Drug Cartels*. London: Bloomsbury Press.

Hariharan, Arya. 2012. '*Hawala*'s Charm: What Banks Can Learn From Informal Funds Transfer Systems', *William & Mary Business Law Review* 3(1): 273–308.

International Monerary Fund. 2005. 'World Economic Outlook. Globalization and External Imbalances.' Available 15 May 2015 at http://www.imf.org/external/pubs/ft/weo/2005/01/.

Ismail, Abdirashid A. 2007. 'Lawlessness and Economic Governance: the Case of *Hawala* System in Somalia', *International Journal of Development Issues* 6(2): 168–85.

Jost, Patrick M. and Harjit Singh Sandhu. 2000. 'The Hawala Remittance System and its Role in Money Laundering.' Financial Crimes Enforcement Network INTERPOL.

Kleemans, E.R., M.E.I. Brienen, H.G. van de Bunt, R.F. Kouwenberg, G Paulides and J. Barensen. 2002. *Organized Crime in the Netherlands; Second Report of the WODC-organized Crime Monitor*. The Hague, BJu/WODC. [In Dutch]

Leong, Angela Veng Mei. 2002. 'The Bate-Ficha Business and Triads in Macau Casinos', *Queensland U. Tech. L. & Just. J.* 2(1): 83–97.

Lindley, Anna. 2009. '"Dirty Money" and "Development Capital": Somali Money Transfer Infrastructure under Global Scrutiny', *African Affairs* 108(433): 519–39.

Looney, Robert. 2003. '*Hawala*: The Terrorist's Informal Financial Mechanism', *Middle East Policy* 10(1): 164–7.

Maimbo, Samuel Munzele. 2003. 'The Money Exchange Dealers of Kabul.' World Bank Working Paper No. 13.

NCTA (The National Commission on Terrorist Attacks). 2004. The 9/11 Commission Report. Available 15 May 2015 at: http://www.9-11commission. gov/report/911Report.pdf.

Passas, Nikos, 1999. *Informal Value Transfer Systems and Criminal Organizations: A Study into So-called Underground Banking Networks.* Den Haag: Dutch Ministry of Justice.

Passas, Nikos. 2003. '*Hawala* and Other Informal Value Transfer Systems: How to Regulate Them?' *Risk Management: An International Journal* 5(2): 49–59.

Passas, Nikos. 2005. *Informal Value Transfer Systems and Criminal Activities.* Den Haag: Ministry of Justice.

Pontell, Henry N., Quan Fang and Gilbert Geis. 2014. 'Economic Crime and Casinos: China's Wager on Macau', *Asian Criminology* 9: 1–13.

Razavy, Maryam. 2005. 'Hawala: An Underground Haven for Terrorists or Social Phenomenon?' *Crime, Law and Social Change* 44(3) 277–99.

Rose-Ackerman, Susan. 1978. *Corruption: A Study in Political Economy.* New York: Academic Press.

Rose-Ackerman, Susan. 1999. *Corruption and Government: Causes, Consequences and Reform.* Cambridge: Cambridge University Press.

Schramm, M. and M. Taube. 2003. 'Evolution and Institutional Foundation of the *Hawala* Financial System', *International Review of Financial Analysis* 12(4): 405–20.

Siegel, Dina and Henk van de Bunt. 2014. 'Underground Banking in the Netherlands', in Stefano Caneppele and Francesco Calderoni (eds), *Organized Crime, Corruption and Crime Prevention. Essays in Honor of Ernesto U. Savona.* Heidelberg, New York, Dordrecht, London: Springer, pp. 251–61.

Skarbek, Emily. 2008. 'Remittances and Reputations of *Hawala* Money Transfer Systems: Self-Enforcing Exchange on an International Scale', *Journal of Private Enterprise* 24(1): 95–117.

Smith, D C. 1980. 'Paragons, Pariahs and Pirates: A Spectrum-based Theory of Enterprise', *Crime and Delinquency* 26(3): 358–86.

Soto, Hernando de. 1989. *The Other Path: The Invisible Revolution in the Third World.* London: Tauris.

Thompson, Edwina. 2006. 'The Nexus of Drug Trafficking and *Hawala* in Afghanistan', in D. Buddenberg and W.A. Byrd (eds), *Afghanistan's Drug Industry: Structure, Functioning, Dynamics and Implications for Counter-narcotics Policy.* UNODC and World Bank, pp. 155–88.

Thompson, Edwina. 2008. 'An Introduction to the Concept and Origins of *Hawala*', *Journal of the History of International Law* 10: 83–108.

Thompson, Edwina. 2011. *Trust is the Coin of the Realm: Lessons from the Money Men in Afghanistan.* Karachi: Oxford University Press.

Turnell, Sean, Alison Vicary, and Wylie Bradford. 2008. 'Migrant-worker Remittances and Burma: An Economic Analysis of Survey Results', in M. Skidmore and T. Wilson (eds), *Dictatorship, Disorder and Decline in Myanmar*, Canberra: ANU E Press, pp. 63–86.

van de Bunt, Henk. 2008. 'The Role of *Hawala* Bankers in the Transfer of Proceeds from Organized Crime', in Dina Siegel and Hans Nelen (eds), *Organized Crime. Culture, Markets and Policies.* Heidelberg, New York, Dordrecht, London: Springer, pp. 113–26.

Varese, Federico. 2000. 'Pervasive Corruption', in A. Ledeneva and M. Kurkchiyan (eds), *Economic Crime in Russia*. London: Kluwer Law International, pp. 99–111.

Varese, Federico. 2003. 'Corruption', in I. McLean (ed.), *Oxford Dictionary of Politics*, 2nd edn. Oxford, New York: Oxford University Press. *Ad vocem*.

Varese, Federico. 2011. *Mafias on the Move. How Organized Crime Conquers New Territories*. Princeton, NJ: Princeton University Press.

Wang, Wuyi and William R. Eadington. 2008. 'The VIP-room Contractual System and Macao's Traditional Casino Industry', *China: An International Journal* 6(2): 237–60.

Wang, Wuyi and Peter Zabielskis. 2010. 'Making Friends, Making Money: Macao's Traditional VIP Casino System', in Sytze F. Kingma (ed.), *Global Gambling: Cultural Perspectives on Gambling*. London: Routledge, pp. 113–43.

Zabielskis, Peter. 2013. 'Too Big to be Bad? Crimes, Vices, and Misdeeds in the Casino Culture of Macau'. Mimeo.

Zeng, Zhonglu and David F. Forrest. 2009. 'High Rollers from Mainland China: A Profile Based on 99 Cases', *UNLV Gaming Research & Review Journal* 13(1): 29–44.

Index